The
Diligent

A Voyage Through the
Worlds of the Slave Trade

Robert Harms

The Perseus Press
A Member of the Perseus Books Group

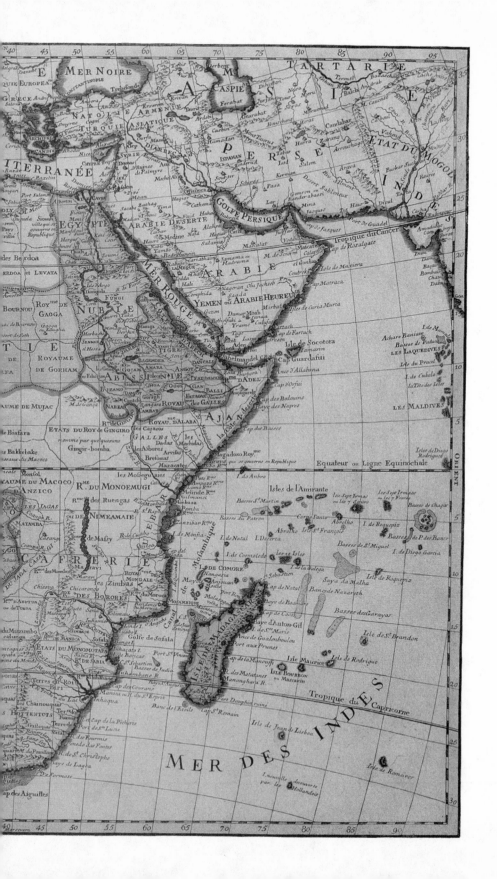

First published by Basic Books, 2002

Text design by Trish Wilkinson
Typeset in 11-point Bembo

A CIP catalogue record for this book is available from the British Library.

Printed and bound in the U.S.A.

ISBN: 1-903985-18-8

02 03 04 / 10 9 8 7 6 5 4 3 2 1

CONTENTS

List of Illustrations   VII
Preface   XI
Illustrations Credits   XXIII
Acknowledgments   XXIX

PART 1   MATTERS OF MORALITY   1

PART 2   THE FINANCIERS   29

PART 3   OUTFITTING A SLAVER   63

PART 4   SAILING SOUTH   87

PART 5   CRUISING THE
          AFRICAN COAST   119

PART 6   WHYDAH   149

PART 7   ASSOU   197

PART 8   JAKIN   225

PART 9   ATLANTIC ISLANDS   265

PART 10   THE MIDDLE PASSAGE   293

PART 11   MARTINIQUE   331

PART 12   THE RETURN   377

Afterword   409
Appendix A: Reconstructing the Balance Sheet
    of the Diligent   411
Appendix B: Abbreviations Used in Notes   415
Notes   417
Index   453

List of Illustrations

PART 1. MATTERS OF MORALITY

1.1   With three masts and a lateen mizzen, the *Diligent* looked very much like this ship painted by Claude-Joseph Vernet in 1755.

1.2   Choir habit of the nuns of Notre Dame du Calvaire.

2.1   Redrawn version of Delisle's 1730 map of Africa showing the mythical land of Nigritie.

PART 2. THE FINANCIERS

4.1   Nantes at the beginning of the eighteenth century.

5.1   Place Louis-le-Grand in Paris.

5.2   John Law.

5.3   Lorient in 1724.

5.4   Crowds of desperate sellers at the Company of the Indies stock office in Paris.

6.1   The Count of Maurepas.

PART 3. OUTFITTING A SLAVER

7.1   Durand's drawing of the *Diligent*.

7.2   Breton peasants during wheat harvest.

7.3   Port of Vannes in the early eighteenth century. Billy house is at the right corner of the port.

10.1 The harbor of Le Palais on Belle Ile.

PART 4. SAILING SOUTH

11.1   Jean Bouguer's diagram showing how to determine the angle of the sun using the cross staff.

11.2   Redrawn version of the Pieter Goos map used on the *Diligent,* showing its route from Vannes to Whydah.

14.1   Durand's drawing of the Isle of May, Cape Verde Islands.

14.2   Durand's drawing of the port of La Praya, Cape Verde Islands.

14.3   Pirate Captain Bartholomew Roberts.

PART 5. CRUISING THE AFRICAN COAST.

15.1   Durand's drawing of the African coast at Sestos.

16.1   African kingdoms of the Gold Coast as shown on this 1729 map by D'Anville.

16.2   Durand's drawing of the Dutch fort at Axim.

16.3   Durand's drawing of the fort he called "Fort Brandenburg or Fort Konny."

17.1   Durand's drawing of Elmina castle.

17.2   Durand's drawing of Cape Coast castle.

17.3   The slave dungeon was underneath the courtyard of Cape Coast castle.

18.1   Durand's drawing of the town of Keta. The Dutch trading lodge is on the right.

PART 6. WHYDAH

19.1   Coronation of the king of Whydah.

19.2   European trading compounds at Savi.

19.3   Procession of the Serpent in Whydah.

20.1   Redrawn version of Norris's 1793 map showing Whydah, Allada (Ardrah), and Dahomey.

20.2   Clothing worn by nobles and the king's wives in Whydah, 1725. Dress at the court of Dahomey was probably similar.

22.1   The king's presence chamber in St. James's Palace, London.

PART 7. ASSOU

23.1   Durand's drawing of the harbor of Whydah.

23.2   Des Marchais's 1725 map of the tents and forts on the coast of Whydah.

24.1   Portuguese sketch of Fort St. John the Baptist at Whydah, 1721.

24.2   English fort at Whydah in 1727.

24.3   French fort at Whydah in 1718.

PART 8. JAKIN

26.1   Durand's drawing of the beach at Jakin.

27.1   Durand's drawing of Joseph de Torres's Portuguese fort at Jakin.

28.1   Cross section of a slave ship showing the platforms between the main and lower decks.

28.2   Slave ship showing the barricade separating the front of the ship from the back.

PART 9. ATLANTIC ISLANDS

31.1   Durand's drawing of the harbor at Principe.

32.1   Durand's drawing of São Tomé City. Note the cathedral beside the Aqua Grande River. Sailors believed that the river was the dividing line between the hemispheres.

32.2   Durand's drawing of the fort at São Tomé.

PART 10. THE MIDDLE PASSAGE

33.1   Slave irons that bound the right leg of one captive to the left leg of another.

34.1   These drawings of the slave ship *Vigilante* from Nantes show the arrangement of the captives on the slave deck and the platforms.

34.2   Slaves on the deck during the day.

34.3   Cutaway view of a slave ship showing food and water storage.

35.1   Redrawn version of the Pieter Goos map showing the *Diligent*'s route from Whydah to Martinique.

37.1   Harbor of St. Pierre, Martinique, with Mount Pélée in the background.

PART 11. MARTINIQUE

38.1   Slave buying on the deck of a slave ship.

40.1   Slaves doing laundry in St. Pierre.

40.2   Horse-driven sugar mill.

40.3   Working in the boiling house.

40.4   Slaves preparing cassava.

PART 12. THE RETURN

47.1   Port of Vannes showing the new Billy mansion (with two figures in front).

47.2   The port of Vannes in the late eighteenth century.

47.3   The Billy mansion.

PREFACE

The Mariner's Journal

*I*N THE SPRING OF 1984 an old man approached the Beinecke Rare Book and Manuscript Library at Yale University. He had in his possession a French mariner's journal—over 250 years old—that contained 113 pages of text and drawings on fifty-eight vellum leaves, each bearing a crowned coat of arms watermark. At the top of the first page was a Latin inscription: "De Majorem Dei Glorium Virginis q: Maria" (To the greater glory of God and the Virgin Mary). Then the text switched from Latin to French. "With the help of God, we are undertaking to go from Vannes, whence we were outfitted, to the coast of Guinea in the ship *Diligent* belonging to the brothers Billy and Mr. La Croix, our outfitters, and from thence to Martinique to sell our blacks and make our return to Vannes."

The journal went on to describe the ship and the crew: "Our ship is built on a keel fifty-seven feet long, twenty-one feet wide, and of 140 tons burden, drawing twelve and a half feet of water at the rear when fully loaded. We are armed with eight four-pound cannons, fifty-five muskets, eighteen pistols, twenty swords, and two swivel guns, all in excellent condition."

"For first captain we have the *sieur* Mary, and for second captain we have *sieur* Valteau. The second lieutenant is *sieur* Thomas Laragon, the surgeon is *sieur* Devigne, and the pilot is *sieur* Sabatier. All together, we are a crew of thirty-seven men, among whom I, R. Durand, write this present journal and occupy the post of first lieutenant."

Laurence C. Witten II was a dealer in rare books and manuscripts, and he had come this morning to try to sell his discovery to the Beinecke Library. Although Witten's proffer was received with all the courtesy befitting a dealer of international repute, it was also greeted with caution. Ever since he had brought the Vinland Map to Yale in 1957, Witten had been a figure of controversy in the academic world.

Witten had discovered the Vinland Map, bound together with another manuscript, in a bookseller's shop in Geneva. After studying the document, he concluded that it came from the mid-fifteenth century. If it was genuine, then it was the earliest map ever to depict any part of North America, and it provided the only available documentary evidence that North America had been discovered and settled before Columbus. He purchased the volume for $3,500 and then offered it to the Yale Library for $300,000. Unable to afford such a princely sum, the Yale librarian turned to a benefactor, the philanthropist Paul Mellon, who agreed to purchase the map and donate it to Yale after it had been authenticated. Seven years later, after three separate authorities had pronounced the map to be authentic, Mellon donated it to the Yale Library.[1]

Despite the judgment of the three experts, the map's authenticity was questioned from the day Yale announced the acquisition. In 1974 Yale had the ink tested at an independent laboratory, and it was found to contain a compound, anatase, that was invented in 1920. The laboratory pronounced the map a fake.[2] Feeling defrauded, the Yale librarian asked Witten to refund Paul Mellon's investment. Witten refused, claiming that he no longer had the money. In 1985 a laboratory at the University of California–Davis, using proton beam analysis, disputed the earlier lab's findings and argued that the compound in question was not anatase at all.[3] Nevertheless, when Witten approached the Beineke Library with the mariner's journal in spring 1984, his reputation was still under a cloud.

One of the people whom the Beinecke Library asked to evaluate the mariner's journal was a young assistant professor of history who had recently joined the Yale faculty. I had just published a book on the slave trade in the Congo River basin, and it was for that reason, I suppose, that they sought my advice.[4] With perhaps more enthusiasm than prudence, and being totally unaware of the controversy over the Vinland Map, I urged the library to acquire the document.

The journal contained First Lieutenant Robert Durand's account of his voyage on the French slave ship *Diligent* in the years 1731–1732.[5] Durand was only twenty-six years old at the time, and this was his first voyage to Africa. His curiosity prompted him to record many of the details of the voyage that his more jaded companions might have overlooked, and his skills as a sketch artist served him in making the eighty-one drawings that accompany his text. The journal recounted a tale of greed, death, and inhumanity carried out on a transatlantic scale. Although shocking to twenty-first-century bourgeois culture, the story it tells was distressingly ordinary in its own time and place.

But was the document authentic? Given the controversy that surrounded Witten at the time, the question had to be asked. Fortunately, research that I carried out over several years abundantly confirmed the authenticity of Durand's journal. Although almost all of the shipping records for the French port of Vannes in the eighteenth century have been lost, the records of this particular voyage survived because they were moved to the admiralty court when the *Diligent* became the object of a lawsuit.[6] Tax and parish records from the seaside town of Le Croisic provided details of Robert Durand's life, and French Royal Navy draft records revealed further biographical information on Durand and many members of the crew. Details on African rulers whom Durand mentions were provided by the reports of a variety of French, Dutch, English, and Portuguese traders who operated on the Guinea coast at the time. Durand's mention of black priests on the Portuguese island of São Tomé led me to the manuscript written by the black priest Manual do Rosário Pinto in 1734. The effort to verify and elaborate on Robert Durand's journal took me to archives in Paris, Aix-en-Provence, Nantes, Vannes, Lorient, Lisbon, Rome, The Hague, London, Greenwich, and Fort-de-France, Martinique.

After I began to write this book, I tried to contact Laurence Witten to find out where Robert Durand's journal had been for the 252 years between the time it was written and the time he offered it to the Beinecke Library. But I was too late; Witten had died on April 18, 1995. Yet I doubt that he would have told me much even if he had been alive. As Witten himself once wrote, "Dealers have little motivation to reveal sources that may provide them with more books, . . . and former owners, most of them legitimate but others possibly not, may have a variety of reasons for not wanting it known that they have sold valuable things."[7] The provenance of the journal remains a mystery.

Robert Durand's journal tells the story of a great crime. It began with the departure of a converted grain ship from the French city of Vannes on May 31, 1731, and it ended with the trial of the *Diligent's* captain, Pierre Mary, in the admiralty court of Vannes in February 1733. During the course of the *Diligent's* voyage to West Africa and the Caribbean, the lives of 256 West Africans were ruined or ended, and four of the ship's crew members died. The owners of the *Diligent* viewed the deaths and ruined lives as part of the normal course of an admittedly nasty business. The real tragedy, to them, was the failure of the voyage to produce the large profits that they had anticipated. It was only later generations that would view the voyage itself as a crime.

The voyage of the *Diligent* was only one of the approximately forty thousand slaving voyages that forcibly carried off more than 11 million captives from the shores of Africa over a period of four centuries. Those individual voyages have been lumped together by historians under the label "Atlantic slave trade," or simply the "slave trade," phrases that can create the impression that it was a monolithic phenomenon with uniform characteristics. A closer look, however, reveals that the slave trade was really a kaleidoscope of diverse national and local endeavors that was constantly changing over time.

In the fifteenth century Portuguese explorers who pushed south in their caravels along the coast of West Africa sometimes raided villages to capture Africans to bring back to Portugal. They soon discovered, however, that their ships were likely to be attacked at sea by Africans who could maneuver their dugout canoes under the cannon fire. In pursuit of more peaceful relations, João Fernandes spent a full year getting to know the Africans living along the coast, and he discovered that there were markets where Europeans could exchange their merchandise for African gold and slaves. In 1468 Prince Henry the Navigator sent three caravels to negotiate treaties with African rulers, assuring them that the Portuguese would no longer steal Africans, but would purchase them like honest men.[8]

The first slaves were carried to Spain and Portugal, where they worked as the servants of noble families, on the docks, and in trades such as printing, sword making, and soap manufacture. Soon the Portuguese began to develop sugar plantations on previously uninhabited islands off the coast of West Africa that were worked mainly by African slaves. By so doing they established a prototype for sugar economies that survived by devouring African slave labor. That pattern would persist for centuries to come.

Sugar cane arrived in the New World with the second voyage of Christopher Columbus in 1493. At first, the Spanish colonists tried to coerce or enslave the indigenous populations to work in their mines and fields, but by 1510 King Ferdinand of Spain had come to believe that one African slave could do the work of four native inhabitants. He therefore gave an order for fifty African slaves ("the best and strongest available") to be sent from Spain to Hispaniola to work in the mines. The decimation of the indigenous populations of the New World further increased the demand for African slaves, and in 1518 the king authorized transporting four thousand African slaves from Africa to the new territories of the Spanish empire. Because a treaty signed in 1480 had forbidden Spain to trade in Africa, the slaves were carried on Portuguese ships.

Portuguese ships completely dominated the Atlantic slave trade during the sixteenth century, carrying slaves to the Spanish colonies and to their own colony of Brazil, where sugar production expanded rapidly after 1550. In the seventeenth century the Dutch challenged the Portuguese for control of the slave trade. They conquered and held the sugar-producing regions of Brazil from 1630 to 1640 while driving the Portuguese from their forts on the Gold Coast of West Africa. In 1662 the Dutch West India Company gained the biggest prize of all: the exclusive *assiento* contract from the Spanish Crown to provide all of the slaves to Spain's New World colonies, a trade that had been dominated by Portugal until 1640.

British involvement in the slave trade developed in the seventeenth century, driven mostly by the demand for labor in their sugar islands in the Caribbean: first Barbados, then Jamaica, which they captured from Spain in 1665. They also carried slaves to their smaller Caribbean islands and their colonies in North America. Less than 4 percent of the total slave trade went to British North America. In order to promote the slave trade, the British government chartered a succession of monopoly companies:

the Guinea Company in 1651, the Royal Adventurers into Africa in 1660, and finally the Royal African Company in 1672.

The French were relative latecomers to the slave trade. Although individual French ships were involved as early as 1525, the French slave trade did not really get wind in its sails until the seventeenth century, when French settlers began producing sugar in their Caribbean colonies, which included Martinique, Guadeloupe, and Saint Domingue (Haiti), as well as several minor islands and Cayenne (French Guyana). In 1625 the only slaves on record in France's Caribbean colonies were forty slaves on St. Christophe. Sugar production began in 1640, and half a century later there were 27,258 African slaves in France's Caribbean colonies, outnumbering free white settlers by nearly two to one. The early slaves were delivered by Dutch ships, but by the end of the century slaves were being supplied by the two French government-chartered monopoly companies: the Senegal Company, which held a monopoly on French trade in West Africa north of the Sierra Leone River, and the Guinea Company, headed by Colbert's son Jean-François, which had a monopoly of French trade from Sierra Leone south to the Cape of Good Hope. Privately organized slaving voyages, although occasionally undertaken, were strictly forbidden by law.

Unlike the Spanish and the Portuguese, the French did not import African slaves into their own country. After France's own internal system of slavery (a holdover from the Roman Empire) had gradually transformed itself into serfdom, a common law principle developed that any slave setting foot on French soil became free. So in 1538 a Greek slave who had been bought by an Italian and carried to France was declared free "according to the common law of France." Similarly, when a Norman slave merchant arrived in Bordeaux with a load of slaves in 1571, he was arrested and the slaves were set free. The handful of black slaves who arrived in France beginning in the late seventeenth century were usually residents of France's Caribbean colonies who accompanied their masters on visits to France.

The sources of the African captives who were carried to the New World varied greatly over time. In the sixteenth century the major source was the Congo/Angola region. Within West Africa, the regions of Senegambia, Gold Coast, Bight of Benin, and Bight of Biafra all provided roughly equal numbers of slaves. In the first half of the seventeenth century Congo/Angola continued to dominate the slave trade as a whole, but within West Africa the overwhelming majority of captives were coming from the Bight of Biafra. In the final quarter of the seventeenth century the focal point of the Atlantic slave trade as a whole shifted to the Bight of Benin in West Africa, a region dominated by the slaving port of Whydah. During the half century from 1675 to 1725 over 40 percent of all slaves coming out of Africa came from the Bight of Benin. In the second half of the eighteenth century, Whydah was surpassed by a huge upswing in slave departures from Congo/Angola and challenged by a rise in slave trading activities along the Gold Coast.[9] The regional shifts in the slave trade tell only part of the story, however; within any given region of Africa the rules and practices of slave trade varied greatly from one port to another, and the inland sources of slaves shifted frequently over time.

The eighteenth century was the heyday of the Atlantic slave trade. Over 85 percent of all slaves were transported to the New World after 1700. In statistical terms, the first 250 years of the slave trade were merely a prelude to the enormous expansion of the eighteenth century. The French slave trade grew rapidly, rising from 100,000 slaves in the first quarter of the century to over 400,000 during the final quarter. French ships carried over a million slaves to the New World during the eighteenth century, making France the third largest participant in the slave trade after England and Portugal. The overwhelming majority of slaves carried on French ships were taken to France's Caribbean colonies of Saint Domingue and Martinique.

During the first quarter of the eighteenth century, the city of Nantes, located in Brittany near the mouth of the Loire River, established itself as the major slaving port in France, carrying 55 percent of the entire French slave trade. For the eighteenth century as a whole, over 40 percent of the French slave trade was carried by ships sailing from Nantes.[10] If there was one place that embodied and symbolized the French slave trade, it was Nantes. Its commercial success was displayed by its opulent new mansions, its new mercantile exchange, and its opera house. The English traveler Arthur Young was astonished by the splendor of Nantes. "'Mon Dieu!' I cried to myself, do all the wastes, the deserts, the heath, ling, furz, broom, and bog that I have passed for three hundred miles lead to this spectacle? What a miracle, that all this splendor and wealth of the cities in France should be so unconnected with the country!"[11] Rival seaports in France tried to replicate the slave trading success of Nantes but never came close.

The eighteenth century also saw a major transformation in the commercial organization of the slave trade. Prior to 1700 slaving voyages were largely launched by government-chartered monopoly companies such as Britain's Royal African Company, France's Senegal Company and Guinea Company, the Dutch West India Company, and a variety of Portuguese companies holding royal charters. Their monopolies were seldom recognized by rival nations and served mainly to discourage private interlopers. By the end of the seventeenth century the demand for slaves on New World plantations had begun to outstrip the capacity of the national monopoly companies, and the slave trading nations of Europe gradually began to allow private traders to launch slaving voyages. The British parliament took the first step in 1698, when it allowed private merchants to engage in the slave trade provided that they paid a 10 percent tax to the Royal African Company. The French government briefly allowed private slave trading from 1713 to 1722 and then definitively opened up the slave trade to private traders in 1725. No group in France was more vocal in its advocacy of private enterprise capitalism than the merchants of Nantes. The Dutch followed England and France by opening up the slave trade in 1730. After that, the slave trade became largely a private enterprise affair as individual shippers and ports competed with each other for the profits of the slave trade.

Two of the people who joined the scramble to enter the slave trade in the early eighteenth century were Guillaume and François Billy, two brothers who lived in the small port of Vannes, just up the Brittany coast from Nantes. They were well aware of the commercial success of Nantes, and they hoped to use the slave trade to enrich themselves and pull their city out of a prolonged period of demographic decline and economic recession. Accordingly, they purchased the *Diligent*, hired a crew, and outfitted the ship for the first slaving voyage ever to leave from the city of Vannes.

It seems ironic that an intensely local decision rooted in the politics and social rivalries of the city of Vannes would tragically affect the lives of people as far away as Africa and the West Indies. In the interconnected worlds of the slave trade, local decisions could have international consequences. The slave trading activities of Robert Durand and his companions along the West African coast, for example, were heavily influenced by local events such as the rise of the military empire of Dahomey and the rivalry between King Agaja of Dahomey and Captain Assou of Whydah. The crew and captives of the *Diligent* could never have made it across the Atlantic had not the populations of Principe and São Tomé specialized in producing food for slave ships after the collapse of their sugar economy. When the *Diligent* arrived with its cargo of human captives in Martinique, the conditions of their sale were shaped by a crisis in the local economy resulting from the destruction of the cocoa trees.

In short, a voyage that spanned three continents was largely shaped by local events and local rivalries originating in widely scattered parts of the Atlantic world. There was no overarching "global" context to the voyage, only a series of intersecting local contexts in which the interests of the Billy brothers in Vannes encountered those of King Agaja in Dahomey, Captain Assou in Whydah, the food producers in São Tomé, the European sugar planters in Martinique, and many others. People in all of those places participated in the slave trade in very different ways and for very different reasons, but in the end it took all of them to make the voyage of the *Diligent* unfold in the way that it did. There was a kind of "logic of local interests" at work on an Atlantic-wide scale.

In any given locality, the slave trade was never an isolated sphere of activity. It was always entangled in local economics, politics, and social struggles. European investors in the slave trade also invested in other forms of commerce. A ship that carried slaves on one voyage could carry wine or grain on the next. In Africa, merchants who sold slaves might also sell gold or ivory, and King Agaja's slave trading activities cannot be separated from the military expansion of his empire. Wealthy Africans in West African slaving ports sold slaves to Europeans, but they also kept many to work on their farms and in their households. In Martinique, sugar planters traded in slaves according to the rhythms of the agricultural cycle.

At the same time, local interests in the early eighteenth-century Atlantic world were conditioned by the economic opportunities and social destructiveness of the slave trade. So seductive was the lure of profits from the slave trade that it could transform economies, reshape moral sensitivities, refocus state policies, and influence the rise and fall of kingdoms. In France, it had transformed the economy of Nantes and turned the heads of the leading citizens of Vannes. In West Africa, it undergirded the rise of new militarized states such as Asante and Dahomey. In the Caribbean, the sugar islands became totally dependent on a constant influx of new slaves. What made the Atlantic slave trade so sinister was that it could appeal to widely divergent local interests in a wide variety of places. The French owners of the *Diligent*, the king of Dahomey, the cultivators of São Tomé, and the planters of Martinique had very little in common except a belief that they could profit from participating in the slave trade. The voyage of the *Diligent* affected all of those places by linking their divergent interests together for a fleeting second in time. No place visited by the *Diligent* would ever be quite the same again.

When the *Diligent* set sail in 1731, it was traveling through an Atlantic world in transition. In Europe, the English, French, and Dutch had finally opened up the slave trade to private merchants, but company ships still competed with private ones and the monopoly companies still controlled the trading forts and castles. Along the West African coast, the open trade policies of the small African trading states that had dominated commerce on the Gold and Slave Coasts in the seventeenth century were yielding to the monopolistic practices of the rising military empires of Asante and Dahomey. The remnants of the old trading states were still fighting rearguard actions against the new militarized empires when the *Diligent* arrived. On the Portuguese-controlled island of São Tomé, black priests were struggling to eliminate the last vestiges of racism from the ecclesiastical hierarchy. In Martinique, the introduction of coffee plantations was changing the way slaves lived and worked. In each place, Robert Durand observed both the old order and the new amid the chaos of transition.

This book seeks to reconstruct the voyage of the *Diligent* in a way that reveals the various "worlds" through which it passed and the various local interests that conditioned its impact and outcome. Those interests were economic, to be sure, but also social, political, and even religious. I have tried to bring to life the slaving ports of Nantes and Vannes, the trading castles of the West African Gold Coast, the African kingdoms of Whydah and Dahomey, and the island worlds of Cape Verde, São Tomé, and Martinique. These are the contexts that shaped the voyage. During the *Diligent*'s passage through those diverse worlds, First Lieutenant Robert Durand was transformed from an innocent sailor to a hardened slave trader and the lives of 256 Africans were tragically changed. Nine of them did not survive the middle passage.

Each of the forty thousand or so slaving voyages that made up the Atlantic slave trade was in many ways unique, shaped by its time, its place, and the personalities and interests of the individuals involved. Each has its own story, but most of them can never be told for lack of surviving information. This book attempts to recover one of those stories. Because this narrative is rooted in a particular time and particular places, it makes no claim to encapsulate *the* story of the slave trade as a whole. No single voyage could. Instead, the book recounts *a* story of how the slave trade operated in certain places at a certain point in time. As such, it shines a small beam of light onto the dark underside of the Atlantic world during a crucial period of economic and political transformation.

As the 256 West Africans whose names we will never know lay in irons, packed in the stifling and stinking lower deck of the *Diligent*, a lot of questions must have gone through their minds. Who sent that ship? Why did they send it? What did they hope to gain from such activity? Why was such a trade allowed to exist? This book is a belated attempt to answer those questions.

ILLUSTRATIONS CREDITS

Cover, upper illustration. Robert Durand, "Journal de bord d'un négrier, 1731–1732," Beinecke Rare Book and Manuscript Library, Yale University, Gen Mss, vol. 7, p. 34.

Cover, lower illustration. "Case of the *Vigilante*, a ship employed in the Slave-Trade" (London, 1823), figure 4, pamphlet and illustrations in the possession of Professor Edward Tufte, emeritus professor of political science at Yale University.

Frontispiece. "Pas Caart vertoonende de West-Indische als ook de West-elyskte Custen van Europa en Africa. Eertyds in't ligt gebracht door wijlen Pieter Goos enz. Door Joannes Van Keulen en Zoonen," 1759. Gerard Hulst Van Keulen. Amsterdam, Algemeen Rijksarchief, Gravenhage, The Netherlands. 4 VEL 96. The *Diligent* used an earlier edition of this map.

1.1 Detail of Claude-Joseph Vernet's "La Madrague ou La pêche du thon. Cet aspect est pris dans le golfe de Bandol," 1755, Dépôt du Musée du Louvre, Musée de la Marine, Paris. Photo by Réunion des Musées Nationaux, Paris.

1.2 "Religieuse de Nôtre Dame du Calvaire en habit de choeur," in P. Helyot, *Histoire des Ordres Monastiques* (Paris, 1714–1719), 6:359, New York Public Library.

2.1 Map drawn by Frank Drago based on Guillaume Delisle, "Carte d'Afrique dressé pour l'usage du roy," 1730, Map Collection, Sterling Memorial Library, Yale University.

4.1 Pierre Aveline, 1656–1722, "Nantes, Ancienement Corbilo," engraving in the possession of the author.

5.1 "Veue et Perspective de la Place Louis le Grand," Bibliothèque Nationale de France, Paris, Estampes, Va 234.

5.2 "Monsieur Law," engraving by J. Langlois after a painting by Hubert, Bibliothèque Nationale de France, Paris, Estampes, N2 Law.

5.3 "Veue de Lorient et du Port Louis," 1724, Bibliothèque Nationale de France, Paris, Estampes, H 184164.

5.4 "Rue Quincampoix en l'Année 1720," Bibliothèque Nationale de France, Paris, Estampes, Qb 1 1720.

6.1 "Jean-Frédéric Phelyppeaux, compte de Maurepas, sécretaire d'état à la maison du roi," Château de Versailles et de Trianon, Versailles, France. Photo by Réunion des Musées Nationaux, Paris.

7.1 Robert Durand, "Journal de bord d'un négrier, 1731–1732," Beinecke Rare Book and Manuscript Library, Yale University, Gen Mss, vol. 7, p. 34.

7.2 "On ramasse le blé sur l'aire," in Alexander Bouet, *Galérie Bretonne*, par O. Perrin, avec texte explicatif par Alexandre Bouet (Paris, 1835–1838), vol. 2, unpaginated. Seeley Mudd Library, Yale University.

7.3 "Vue de la ville épiscopale de Vannes," lithographie vers 1750, Archives Départmentales du Morbihan, Vannes, France, 2 Fi 477.

10.1 Ozanne, "La Citadelle et l'entrée du havre du Palais à Belle Isle," 1776, Bibliothèque Nationale de France, Paris, Estampes, Va 56, Morbihan.

11.1 Jean Bouguer, *Traite complète de la navigation* (Paris, 1706), plate 4, Beinecke Rare Book and Manuscript Library, Yale University.

11.2 Map drawn by Frank Drago based on "Pas Caart vertoonende de West-Indische als ook de Westelyskte Custen van Europa en Africa. Eertyds in't ligt gebracht door wijlen Pieter Goos enz. Door Joannes Van Keulen en Zoonen," 1759. Gerard Hulst Van Keulen. Amsterdam, Algemeen Rijksarchief, Gravenhage, The Netherlands. 4 VEL 96. The *Diligent* used an earlier edition of this map.

14.1 Robert Durand, "Journal de bord d'un négrier, 1731–1732," Beinecke Rare Book and Manuscript Library, Yale University, Gen Mss, vol. 7, p. 16.

14.2   Robert Durand, "Journal de bord d'un négrier, 1731–1732," Bei-
        necke Rare Book and Manuscript Library, Yale University, Gen
        Mss, vol. 7, p. 18.

14.3   "Captain Bartholomew Roberts," in Captain Charles Johnson,
        General History of the Pyrates (London, 1726), 1:259, Beinecke
        Rare Book and Manuscript Library, Yale University.

15.1   Robert Durand, "Journal de bord d'un négrier, 1731–1732," Bei-
        necke Rare Book and Manuscript Library, Yale University, Gen
        Mss, vol. 7, p. 26.

16.1   "Carte particulière de la partie principale de la Guinée par le Sr.
        D'Anville," Avril 1729, in Jean-Baptiste Labat, *Voyage du Chevalier
        des Marchais en Guinée, Isles Voisines, et à Cayenne, fait en 1725, 1726
        & 1727* (Paris, 1730), 2:1, Seeley Mudd Library, Yale University.

16.2   Robert Durand, "Journal de bord d'un négrier, 1731–1732," Bei-
        necke Rare Book and Manuscript Library, Yale University, Gen
        Mss, vol. 7, p. 32.

16.3   Robert Durand, "Journal de bord d'un négrier, 1731–1732," Bei-
        necke Rare Book and Manuscript Library, Yale University, Gen
        Mss, vol. 7, p. 34.

17.1   Robert Durand, "Journal de bord d'un négrier, 1731–1732," Bei-
        necke Rare Book and Manuscript Library, Yale University, Gen
        Mss, vol. 7, p. 38.

17.2   Robert Durand, "Journal de bord d'un négrier, 1731–1732," Bei-
        necke Rare Book and Manuscript Library, Yale University, Gen
        Mss, vol. 7, p. 40.

17.3   William Smith, Surveyor, "The East Prospect of Cape-Coast
        Castle, 1727," in William Smith, *Thirty Different Drafts of Guinea*
        (London, c. 1727), plate 17, British Library, London, England.

18.1   Robert Durand, "Journal de bord d'un négrier, 1731–1732," Bei-
        necke Rare Book and Manuscript Library, Yale University, Gen
        Mss, vol. 7, p. 48.

19.1   "Couronnement du roy de Juda à la coste de Guinée au mois
        d'Avril, 1725," in Jean-Baptiste Labat, *Voyage du Chevalier des Mar-
        chais en Guinée, Isles Voisines, et à Cayenne, fait en 1725, 1726 & 1727*
        (Paris, 1730), 2:70, Seeley Mudd Library, Yale University.

19.2   "Comptoirs des Européens à Xavier," in Jean-Baptiste Labat,
        Voyage du Chevalier des Marchais en Guinée, Isles Voisines, et à

Cayenne, fait en 1725, 1726 & 1727 (Paris, 1730), 2:49, Seeley Mudd Library, Yale University.

19.3 "Procession au grand serpent pour le couronnement du Roy de Juda fait le 15 Avril, 1725," in Jean-Baptiste Labat, *Voyage du Chevalier des Marchais en Guinée, Isles Voisines, et à Cayenne, fait en 1725, 1726 & 1727* (Paris, 1730), 2:194, Seeley Mudd Library, Yale University.

20.1 "Dahomy and Its Environs," by R. Norris, in Archibald Dalzel, *The History of Dahomy* (London, 1793), foldout map, Beinecke Rare Book and Manuscript Library, Yale University.

20.2 "Habillement des grands, Habillement des femmes du roy," in Jean-Baptiste Labat, *Voyage du Chevalier des Marchais en Guinée, Isles Voisines, et à Cayenne, fait en 1725, 1726 & 1727* (Paris, 1730), 2:243, Seeley Mudd Library, Yale University.

22.1 "King's Presence Chamber, Court of St. James, London," in W. H. Pyne, *The History of the Royal Residences of Windsor Castle, St. James's Palace, Carlton House, Kensington Palace, Hampton Court, Buckingham House, and Frogmore* (London, 1819), 3:10, Beinecke Rare Book and Manuscript Library, Yale University.

23.1 Robert Durand, "Journal de bord d'un négrier, 1731–1732," Beinecke Rare Book and Manuscript Library, Yale University, Gen Mss, vol. 7, p. 55.

23.2 "Carte Particulière du Royaume de Juda," in Jean-Baptiste Labat, *Voyage du Chevalier des Marchais en Guinée, Isles Voisines, et à Cayenne, fait en 1725, 1726 & 1727* (Paris, 1730), 2:10, Seeley Mudd Library, Yale University.

24.1 Plan of Portuguese Fort at Whydah, November 2, 1721, Arquivo Histórico Ultramarino, Lisbon, S. Tomé, Caixa 4, Doc. 86.

24.2 William Smith, "The South West Prospect of Williams Fort at Whydah, 1727," in William Smith, *Thirty Different Drafts of Guinea* (London, c. 1727), plate 29, British Library, London, England.

24.3 "Plan du Fort St. Louis, 1717–1718," Archives d'Outre-Mer, Aix-en-Provence, France, col. C 6 27, no. 175.

26.1 Robert Durand, "Journal de bord d'un négrier, 1731–1732," Beinecke Rare Book and Manuscript Library, Yale University, Gen Mss, vol. 7, p. 66.

27.1   Robert Durand, "Journal de bord d'un négrier, 1731–1732," Beinecke Rare Book and Manuscript Library, Yale University, Gen Mss, vol. 7, p. 66.

28.1   "Case of the *Vigilante*, a ship employed in the Slave-Trade" (London, 1823), figure 5, pamphlet and illustrations in the possession of Professor Edward Tufte, emeritus professor of political science at Yale University.

28.2   Detail of "Vue du Cap Français et du navire La Marie Seraphique de Nantes, Capitain Gaugy, le jour de l'ouverture de sa vente, troisième voyage d'Angole, 1772–1773," Musée du Château des ducs de Bretagne, Nantes, France. Photo by Ville de Nantes—Musée du Château.

31.1   Robert Durand, "Journal de bord d'un négrier, 1731–1732," Beinecke Rare Book and Manuscript Library, Yale University, Gen Mss, vol. 7, p. 70.

32.1   Robert Durand, "Journal de bord d'un négrier, 1731–1732," Beinecke Rare Book and Manuscript Library, Yale University, Gen Mss, vol. 7, p. 76.

32.2   Robert Durand, "Journal de bord d'un négrier, 1731–1732," Beinecke Rare Book and Manuscript Library, Yale University, Gen Mss, vol. 7, p. 76.

33.1   "Case of the *Vigilante*, a ship employed in the Slave-Trade" (London, 1823), figure 8, pamphlet and illustrations in the possession of Professor Edward Tufte, emeritus professor of political science at Yale University.

34.1   "Case of the *Vigilante*, a ship employed in the Slave-Trade" (London, 1823), figures 3–4, pamphlet and illustrations in the possession of Professor Edward Tufte, emeritus professor of political science at Yale University.

34.2   Pretextat Oursel, "Transport des nègres dans les colonies," lithographie colorée, Saint-Malo, France, Musée d'Histoire. Photo by Michel Dupuis, Ville de Saint-Malo.

34.3   Detail of "Vue du Cap Français et du navire La Marie Seraphique de Nantes, Capitain Gaugy, le jour de l'ouverture de sa vente, troisième voyage d'Angole, 1772–1773," Musée du Château des ducs de Bretagne, Nantes, France. Photo by Ville de Nantes—Musée du Château.

35.1   Map drawn by Frank Drago based on "Pas Caart vertoonende de West-Indische als ook de Westelyskte Custen van Europa en Africa. Eertyds in't ligt gebracht door wijlen Pieter Goos enz. Door Joannes Van Keulen en Zoonen," 1759. Gerard Hulst Van Keulen. Amsterdam, Algemeen Rijksarchief, Gravenhage, The Netherlands. 4 VEL 96. The *Diligent* used an earlier edition of this map.

37.1   Ozanne. "Le Fort St. Pierre dans l'Isle de la Martinique, vu du Mouillage." Bibliothèque Nationale de France, Paris, Estampes, Ef 20 folio.

38.1   Detail of "Vue du Cap Français et du navire La Marie Seraphique de Nantes, Capitain Gaugy, le jour de l'ouverture de sa vente, troisième voyage d'Angole, 1772–1773," Musée du Château des ducs de Bretagne, Nantes, France. Photo by Ville de Nantes—Musée du Château.

40.1   Detail of Bassot, "Vue de la rivière du Fort Saint-Pierre de la Martinique." 1765, oil on canvas, Conseil Régionale, Fort-de-France, Martinique.

40.2   Jean-Baptiste Labat, *Nouveau Voyage aux Isles de l'Amérique* (The Hague, 1724), 1:258, Beinecke Rare Book and Manuscript Library, Yale University.

40.3   M. Chambon, *Le Commerce de l'Amérique par Marseille* (Avignon, 1764), 1: plate 5, Beinecke Rare Book and Manuscript Library, Yale University.

40.4   Jean-Baptiste Labat, *Nouveau Voyage aux Isles de l'Amérique* (The Hague, 1724), 1:127, Beinecke Rare Book and Manuscript Library, Yale University.

47.1   "Port de Vannes," Bibliothèque Nationale de France, Paris, Estampes, Va 56, vol. 4, H137005.

47.2   D. Bonnard du Hanlay, "Le Port de Vannes vu de la Sautière à haute mer," Collection des ports de France par Ozanne, 1776, Archives Départmentales du Morbihan, Vannes, France, 2 Fi 215.

47.3   Detail of "Port de Vannes," Bibliothèque Nationale de France, Paris, Estampes, Va 56, vol. 4, H137005.

ACKNOWLEDGMENTS

*R*ESEARCHING AND WRITING THIS book has been a long journey for me. Along the way I have received enormous amounts of help from friends, colleagues, and strangers alike.

I could not have written this book without considerable institutional support. I did the initial writing in 1995–1996, when I was a fellow at the Wissenschaftskolleg in Berlin. Conversations over meals with my colleagues played a major role in shaping the project. My own institution, Yale University, has been extremely supportive. Grants from the Yale Center for International and Area Studies, the Whitney Humanities Center, and the Yale Provost's Office made the research possible.

Throughout the process I benefited from talented and insightful research assistants who helped me navigate documents and materials in a variety of languages. I am grateful to Eric Allina, Steven Ebinger, Tim Hughes, Emmanuel Kreike, Marie-Hélène Le Ray, Mireille Hofmann-Jacquod, Teresa Köbele, Ilaria Maggiulli, Erik Myrup, Brian Peterson, Charles Riley, and Matthew Wranovix.

In trying to write a manuscript that would meet high scholarly standards and still be accessible to nonspecialists, I benefited from the comments of friends and colleagues who read all or part of the manuscript: Mary Kay Bercaw Edwards, Bonnie Collier, Katherine and Daniel Darst, John Demos and the members of his graduate seminar on historical narrative, Glenn Grasso, Joanna Hamilton, Roger Levine, Kay Mansfield, Joseph Miller, Liana Vardi, Haynie Wheeler, Sandra Wiens, and Robin Winks.

Another group of people provided hospitality, aid, and advice in a variety of important ways: Louise Bedichek, Eve Crowley, Mamadou Diawara, Frank Drago, Georges Dupré, Petra Eggers, David Eltis, Georg Elwert, Pablo Eyzaguirre, Robert Garfield, Eytan Haliban, Maija Jansson, George Miles, Mireille Mousnier, James Scott, Gerald Thomas, Martha Turner, the captain and crew of the HMS *Bounty*, and the fellows of the Wissenschaftskolleg.

In writing a book that touched on widely scattered parts of the Atlantic world, I relied on the works of many scholars to guide me through the historiography and sources on distant times and places, especially Robin Law on the Slave Coast, T. J. A. Le Goff on Vannes, Gaston Martin and Jean Meyer on Nantes, Jacques Petitjean Roget and Lucien Peytraud on Martinique, and Pablo Eyzaguirre and Robert Garfield on São Tomé. I am deeply indebted to all of them.

PART I

Matters of Morality

*A*s THE FIRST RAYS of the sun struck the Brittany coast of France on May 31, 1731, the crew of the *Diligent* was already hard at work preparing the ship for its departure. The *Diligent* was an-chored off a tiny island in the Gulf of Morbihan about six miles southwest of the walled city of Vannes. The port of Vannes was so silted up that it could not accommodate ships larger than thirty-five tons. So the *Diligent* had spent the past several months off the tip of the small arm of land jut-ting out from the western side of the Ile aux Moines getting refitted and loaded for its upcoming voyage. Now it was almost ready to sail.

The *Diligent* was sixty-nine feet long at its main deck. Four cannons ca-pable of firing six-pound balls peered out from gun ports at deck level on each side. Atop the deck was a forecastle in front housing the ship's kitchen and a quarterdeck in back containing the officers' quarters. Towering above the deck were three masts, the tallest of which was over sixty feet high. The foremast and the mainmast each carried three square sails; the mizzenmast at the back had a lateen yard to accommodate a triangular sail. The *Diligent* was twenty-one feet wide, and it drew only twelve and a half feet of water when fully loaded. It was almost one-third as wide as it was long because it had been built as a grain ship to carry the wheat and rye grown by peasants in the hinterland of Vannes to the nearby ports of Nantes and Bordeaux, or perhaps as far as Spain.

First Lieutenant Robert Durand, a tall young man with brown hair, made the first entry in his journal even before the ship left its mooring.

Figure 1.1   With three masts and a lateen mizzen, the *Diligent* looked very
much like this ship painted by Claude-Joseph Vernet in 1755.

With a flourish of his quill pen, he formed the *D* three and a half centime-
ters high with graceful curlicues at the top and bottom. He continued to
write in large Latin letters: "De Majorem Dei Glorium Virginis q: Maria"
(To the greater glory of God and the Virgin Mary). Then, switching from
Latin to French, he outlined the purpose of the trip. "With the help of

God," he wrote, "we are undertaking to go from Vannes, whence we were outfitted, to the coast of Guinea in the ship the *Diligent* belonging to the brothers Billy and Mr. La Croix, our outfitters, and from thence to Martinique to sell our blacks and make our return to Vannes."[1]

What is especially chilling about Robert Durand's words is their businesslike, matter-of-fact tone. He was writing about selling people exactly as he would have written about selling barrels of wine or loads of wheat. He gave no indication that he felt any sense of shame or moral ambivalence about his mission; otherwise he would not have dedicated the voyage with such flourish to the "greater glory of God and the Virgin Mary." Nor was Durand a hardened slave trader. He was only twenty-six years old, and this was his first trip to Africa.

How could Robert Durand outline such an evil mission in such impersonal prose? If this offhand attitude was not formed by his personal experiences, then it must have been part of a general mind-set in the seaports of early eighteenth-century Brittany. There was almost no public discussion of the morality of the slave trade in France during the first half of the eighteenth century. Most public figures were too preoccupied with problems of war, famine, inflation, taxes, religious strife, and quotidian violence to worry about the slave ships that sailed from a handful of French ports. There was far more public discussion of the grain trade in the early eighteenth century than of the trade in human beings.[2]

If slavery was discussed anywhere in France, it was in the slaving ports. Even there, however, the talk focused on issues of access, profits, tariffs, and bonuses; the humanity of the slaves themselves was conspicuously absent from public discussions. In one rare instance, however, the moral issues raised by the slave trade erupted into the open, providing us with a fleeting glimpse of thoughts and feelings that would otherwise have remained shrouded in time.

That eruption occurred in 1714 in Nantes, a city that flanked Vannes along Brittany's southern coast. Nicholas De Fer, Parisian mapmaker and "geographer of His Catholic Majesty," described Nantes as "the largest city in Brittany even though it is not the capital of anything except its own hinterland. It is situated on the Loire River a dozen leagues from where its mouth joins the sea. It is one of the most famous ports of Europe, with a very long and beautiful bridge interrupted by several very pleasant islands.

This city has a fortified castle; it is the seat of a diocese under the authority of the Archdiocese of Tours with a *présidial* court, an *élection* court, a chamber of accounts, and a university. The sea, whose tidal surge reaches its quay, makes it a great commercial city."[3]

De Fer failed to mention that Nantes was emerging as the leading slaving port in France. In 1714 three-quarters of all slave ships sailing from France left from Nantes. Despite the intense activity, the slave trade remained a veiled abstraction to ordinary citizens because they did not see slaves. The ships departed for Guinea filled with cloth, brandy, and cowry shells, and they returned over a year later with sugar, cotton, and indigo purchased in France's Caribbean colonies of Martinique, Guadeloupe, and St. Domingue (Haiti). The slaves themselves were loaded along the African coast and sold to plantation owners in France's Caribbean colonies. They never came within four thousand miles of Nantes. The only slaves who ever arrived in Nantes were the well-dressed black servants whom sugar planters from France's Caribbean colonies brought with them when they came to France for visits.

The events that brought the discussion of slavery into the open began in January 1714, when a coach wended its way along the dirt road that ran parallel with the city's western walls. Moving slowly through the puddles created by the winter rains, the coach traveled northward with its back to the Loire River for about three hundred meters before turning left onto a narrow cul-de-sac known as Calvary Alley.[4] As the road began to climb, the ruts and puddles become less deep. At the top of the hill, just beyond the small chapel, the coach came to a halt at the door of the convent of Our Lady of Calvary.[5]

A white woman and a black teenage girl entered the convent. The woman was Madame Villeneuve, a planter from the French West Indies. The black teenager was named Pauline, and she was the woman's slave. Madame Villeneuve had brought Pauline along to be her personal servant during the Atlantic crossing and her visit to Nantes, but now she was going on to Paris for a year, where she would most likely stay in a house already well staffed with servants. The girl would therefore remain in Nantes as a boarder in the convent, where she would learn piety, discipline, humility, and manners: all qualities that should be cultivated in a personal servant. After the cost of two hundred livres for a year's stay was paid in advance, the girl's name was entered into the convent's guest register as Pauline Villeneuve.[6]

A nun wearing a brown linen habit with broad sleeves and a black veil led the two visitors toward the west wing, also known as the boarding-house. Of the four wings that surrounded the central courtyard, the board-inghouse had been constructed with almost twice the width of the other wings, allowing for guest rooms that were much more spacious than the tiny cubicles that the nuns occupied. Some boarders lived in veritable apartments together with servants and family members. Pauline, however, was one of the "small boarders" with a room that was much more modest.[7] After final instructions and good-byes, Madame Villeneuve remounted the coach for the ride back to the walled city.

Although a slave from the Caribbean, Pauline was not unfamiliar with the Catholic faith. The Code Noir, the set of laws that governed slavery in France's Caribbean colonies, decreed that all slaves should be baptized and allowed to attend mass on Sundays. Whether these requirements were ac-tually honored on the rural plantations of France's Caribbean islands is doubtful. But since Pauline was Madame Villeneuve's personal servant, she was familiar with the mass and the basics of Catholic practice. In the weeks that followed, Pauline learned a great deal about life in the convent of Our Lady of Calvary. The ideal of the order of the Benedictine Sisters of Cal-vary was to attain the level of spiritual perfection embodied in the Virgin Mary at the foot of the Cross.[8] The rules and routines of the convent were designed to help the nuns reach this spiritual state through poverty, humil-iation, prayer, silence, and chastity.

Poverty and humiliation were built into the very architecture of the convent. The rooms of the nuns were small, less than ten feet on a side, and typically contained nothing more than a bed with a straw mattress, two stools, a small writing desk, and a prayer stool.[9] Nuns were not allowed to have a chest, a table, or an armoire that locked. The only heat in the room came from a charcoal foot warmer. In winter, the nuns were allowed to warm themselves twice a day in the second-floor common room fur-nished with charcoal-filled braziers. Silence was an important part of the discipline of the convent, but it was broken by recreation periods on Sun-days and Wednesdays and by assemblies on Mondays and Thursdays.

Despite the severe conditions, the convent could boast that its nuns came from the finest families in Nantes. Many of them came from the old landed aristocracy; others were daughters of members of the *parlement* of Brittany, the présidial court of Nantes, or the chamber of accounts. The bourgeoisie was represented as well: many of the nuns were daughters of merchants residing near the Loire or of men who signed their names with the title "noble man" or "honorable man," always a giveaway of bourgeois status.[10]

As the months passed, Pauline grew more comfortable with life in the convent, and the once strange routines that she watched from afar gradually became familiar. She developed respect and affection for some of the nuns, and they responded to her in kind.[11] As the time approached for her mistress to return to take her back to the West Indies, Pauline began to ponder the idea of becoming a nun and joining the convent. Whether this decision was made out of pious conviction or simply to avoid returning to the West Indies as a slave is hard to determine. Probably it was some of both.

The decision could not have been easy, for both the life of a nun and the life of a slave were dominated by poverty, humiliation, and obedience. But there was something about the shared poverty, the sense of community, and the striving for higher levels of spiritual perfection that gave the discipline of the convent a very different character from the discipline of a slave plantation. In pondering her decision, Pauline knew that she did not have a free choice in the matter because she was a slave owned by Madame Villeneuve. She had long discussions with Sister Anne of the Crucifixion, the mother prioress of the convent. In the end, both of them summoned the determination to fight for her right to become a nun.

When Madame Villeneuve was informed of this decision, she refused to allow it; Pauline was, after all, her personal property. Pauline, for her part, persisted in her desire to follow her newly chosen vocation. Realizing that the upcoming battle would be a difficult one, the mother prioress sought the support of the visitor general of the order. The Sisters of Calvary had a kind of dual-sex authority structure that permitted the female authorities to seek support and protection from powerful men when difficult issues arose. The visitor general was Etienne du Bourg, the abbot of Gimont, who held a doctorate in theology from the Sorbonne. After reviewing the case, he decided to support Pauline and the mother prioress, and he successfully obtained the backing of the director and governing council in Paris.[12]

Once solidarity had been achieved among the mother prioress in Nantes, the visitor general, and the directors in Paris, there remained the problem of how to pay for Pauline's upkeep. The convent lived on its dowries, but the meager dowries that the girls brought with them from their families covered only their own subsistence and contributed little, if anything, to the general expenses. In 1715 total revenue from investments of the dowries amounted to only 4,444 livres.[13] Given the tight financial situation, the convent could ill afford to take in the girl without adequate funding. The visitor general therefore sought a benefactor to provide a dowry of four thousand livres, plus five hundred livres for her habits and supplies, and two hundred livres to cover her board and room during her year as a novice.

The benefactor who came forward at that critical moment was René Darquistade: sea captain, merchant, and financier. He could easily afford the 4,700 livres that Pauline's dowry required, for only two months earlier he and Joachim Descaseaux, his wife's uncle, had made plans to invest a million livres to launch a new overseas trading company that would take over some of the functions of the defunct Company of the East Indies. What seems odd about his act of charity was that René Darquistade was himself a strong supporter of the slave trade. Later on, he personally financed three slaving voyages and invested in many others.[14] But for one brief moment in 1715 his charitable instincts overcame his ambition. On January 25, 1715, the community of Our Lady of Calvary assembled as a group and voted to accept Pauline as a novice.

Madame Villeneuve fought back. She filed a case in the présidial court of Nantes, arguing that Pauline was her rightful property. She noted that back in the West Indies she had once rejected an offer of five hundred gold piastres for the girl, and so Pauline's liberty would cost her a considerable financial loss. If she could not get the girl back, she at least wanted monetary compensation. To her, it was a simple case of property rights.

The court, however, saw the matter in more complex terms, since there was a customary principle in France that any slave who set foot on French soil became free. Although that principle had never been written into law, it had been upheld periodically in the recent past. In 1691, when two slaves from Martinique had stowed away on a French ship and requested asylum, the issue went all the way to King Louis XIV. The minister of the marine, Pontchartrain, summarized the king's response as follows: "He has not judged it appropriate to return them to the isles, their liberty being acquired by the laws of the kingdom concerning slaves as soon as they touch the soil."[15]

There was enormous irony in the king's statement, for it was Louis XIV himself who, only six years earlier, had promulgated the series of laws known as the Code Noir that provided the legal basis for slavery in France's Caribbean colonies. By affirming the customary freedom principle in the case of the stowaways, the king was saying that slavery was an appropriate institution for the colonies, but not for France itself. That bifurcated approach to the issue of slavery was reconfirmed in 1698 by the minister of the marine, who wrote to the governor of the West Indies that "His Majesty orders me to explain to you that all slaves who are brought from the islands to France by their masters become free, according to the laws and practices of the kingdom, and cannot be forced to return," a sentiment that the minister repeated in 1707.[16] By 1715, however, that older custom had run afoul of a newer one, which was that planters from France's Caribbean colonies who brought slaves with them to Nantes sought protection by registering them as property after landing at the port.

In deciding the case of Pauline Villeneuve, the judges of the présidial court searched in vain for any official decrees or regulations that would help them resolve the contradiction. After a considerable delay, they decided the case on a technicality. Regardless of whether the customary "freedom principle" or the new practice of registering slaves took precedence, Madame Villeneuve had failed to register Pauline when she arrived in Nantes. Therefore, she had no claims on Pauline as property. The girl would stay in the convent. In announcing their decision, the judges used the Latin phrase *in favorem libertatis*, referring to the principle in Roman law that ambiguous cases should always be resolved in favor of liberty.[17]

While the case was dragging on in the présidial court, Pauline was busy in the convent learning to read Latin and becoming initiated into the obligations of saintliness and religious life. Because she had a clear voice, she was trained for the profession of cantor, and she devoted much of her time to learning the songs and the chants. On January 27, 1716, two years after she first entered the convent as a boarder, the assembled nuns voted to accept her into the profession. She received a brown dress, a black veil, and a black hooded choir robe to mark the beginning of her six months of probation. On July 27 the sisters met to take the third and last vote on her case. She was again accepted and could now prepare to take the vows that would bind her forever to Christ.

Figure 1.2   Choir habit of the nuns of Notre
Dame du Calvaire.

At the induction ceremony, presided over by Sister Anne of the Crucifixion, Pauline made her vow: "I, Sister Theresa, formerly known as
Pauline Villeneuve, unworthy girl and very humble servant of the Virgin,
Mother of God, vow to almighty God and promise the glorious Virgin
Mary and my glorious Father St. Benedict, to observe the first and exact
rule of St. Benedict and promise the transformation of my morals and behavior, perpetual cloistering, poverty, chastity, and obedience according to
the statutes of the congregation for all the days of my life."[18] With those
words, Sister Theresa was born, and Pauline Villeneuve, the slave girl from
the West Indies, officially ceased to exist.

2

𝒯HE PRÉSIDIAL COURT'S DECISION to grant freedom to Pauline Villeneuve was greeted with dismay in many quarters in Nantes. Plantation owners visiting from the West Indies were unhappy with it because they feared that it might encourage their own slaves, whom they had brought to France as their personal servants, to seek freedom. Merchants who financed and outfitted slaving expeditions to run the triangular route from Nantes to Africa and the Caribbean were concerned because their own captains and officers sometimes brought a personal slave or two with them to Nantes. Some people were merely confused. One man wrote to the Council of the Marine, "I have not been able to decide which side is right—the masters who claim that the slaves whom they bring here to serve them on the voyage and while they are in Europe do not become free, and those slaves who, to the contrary, claim that they become free upon setting foot in France."[1]

Given that Nantes carried over 80 percent of the French slave trade in 1716, such sentiments were not unusual. What was unusual, however, was that the man who took up the cause to make sure that no more slaves would ever be freed by the présidial court was neither a planter nor a slave trader, but the treasurer of France for Brittany, Gérard Mellier. Since the matter did not come under Mellier's official jurisdiction, he apparently took it up as a private citizen. Perhaps he did it out of a civic desire to promote the commercial prosperity of Nantes, or perhaps he was already thinking of running for mayor and wished to ingratiate himself with the local shipping magnates. He was elected mayor in 1720 and held that office until his death in 1729.

There was little in Mellier's background that made him an obvious candidate to lead this cause. He was not a native of Brittany. He had come to Nantes when his mother moved there from Lyon after his father died. With his move to Nantes, he revised his family tree to portray himself as a member of the Mellier family, a family of silk and spice merchants from Lyon, even though his paternal ancestors had really been named Jacquemeton. In 1702, at the age of twenty-eight, he purchased the office of treasurer of France for Brittany with the aid of a 63,000 livre loan from his maternal uncle, Nicolas Ballet de la Chenardière, a man who had himself purchased a title of nobility only six years earlier.[2] As a seeker of office and status, Mellier did not personally dabble in business or commerce and lived in genteel poverty. In 1716, when he took up the cause of defending slavery, his debt to his uncle was far from being repaid.

As an outsider to Brittany who held an office that he had purchased with borrowed money, Gérard Mellier gradually began to work his way into the community in Nantes. His marriage in 1707 to the daughter of a lawyer at the présidial court gave him family ties to the community, and the marriage of his sister Anne into a local merchant family gradually turned his policy interests from the world of government to the world of commerce. He developed a passion for the city of Nantes and wrote two book-length manuscripts on its history while keeping up a lively correspondence with Gui Lobineau, the foremost historian of Brittany.[3] Over time, he grew to love his adopted city with an immigrant's passion, and he defended its interests with an intensity that put native sons to shame.

When Mellier took office as treasurer in 1702, Nantes had many of the attributes of a medieval port. Ships from Spain, Portugal, Holland, and Hamburg came up the Loire to Nantes and returned home with the products of the Loire Valley, such as wine, brandy, rum, prunes, and salt. Except for a few expeditions to Spain and Flanders, however, Nantes seldom sent ships to those countries in return. The balance of trade was so lopsided that the *intendant* of Brittany scolded the merchants of Nantes for failing to boost the trade of their own city.[4] The one area of commerce that the merchants of Nantes promoted was trade with France's Caribbean islands, especially Martinique, Guadeloupe, and St. Domingue. About fifty ships a year left Nantes filled with salted cod from Newfoundland and salted beef from Ireland, as well as salt, brandy, flour, slate for roofs, and various household items. They returned from the islands with sugar, indigo, cotton, ginger, and wool.

The ships did not, at the beginning of the eighteenth century, engage in the slave trade because that branch of commerce was the legal monopoly of the Senegal Company and the Guinea Company. Even so, some slave ships went out from Nantes, sometimes as interlopers and sometimes as subcontractors for the Guinea Company, which was always short of shipping capacity. When the Guinea Company went out of business in 1713, the merchants of Nantes saw an opportunity to get into the trade that had for so long been forbidden to them. Despite government restrictions on private slaving ventures, three-fourths of all slave ships that left France in 1714 were private expeditions sailing from Nantes.

At that crucial moment Gérard Mellier emerged as a major booster of the slave trade by publishing a report entitled *On the Commerce of Nantes and the Ways to Increase It*.[5] Because issues of international trade were only distantly related to his job as treasurer of Brittany, it seems likely that the report was his own private initiative. One of his major suggestions was that government policy should favor merchants who outfitted slaving vessels. In Mellier's thinking, the slave trade was one of the keys to expanding the international commerce of Nantes. Mellier must have felt tremendous satisfaction in January 1716, when the king named Nantes as one of four port cities in France that would be allowed to send out unlimited numbers of private slave trading expeditions. With the new commercial privileges, Mellier believed, Nantes was about to enjoy a major upswing in its overseas commerce. In 1716 Nantes carried 80 percent of the French slave trade.

All of that could be jeopardized, Mellier believed, by the présidial court's decision to grant freedom to Pauline Villeneuve. Mellier was well informed about the case through his father-in-law, a retired lawyer at the présidial court. He did not bear any personal ill will toward Pauline Villeneuve; in fact, he seemed to rejoice in her liberty when he quoted the line from Horace: "It is time, with unfettered feet, to beat the ground in dances."[6] But Mellier was worried. If slave owners from France's Caribbean islands feared losing their slaves when they visited Nantes, they would go to the rival slave trading ports of Bordeaux, Rouen, and La

Rochelle instead. Even though the case did not fall under Mellier's official jurisdiction, he decided to take on the project of creating a new system of registration so that Caribbean slaveholders could bring their personal slaves with them to Nantes without fear that they would be set free. He understood that for his plan to be accepted, he would first have to defend the slave trade itself. The comprehensive defense of it that he produced was the only one written by a French public official in the first half of the eighteenth century.

Mellier had never traveled to Africa to see the sorry spectacle of slaves being loaded in chains onto European ships, and he had never traveled to any of France's Caribbean islands to see slaves working in the cane fields and sugar mills. The only slaves he had ever seen were the well-dressed servants who accompanied planters from the islands on their visits to Nantes. Nevertheless, he felt that he understood the slave trade because he was in regular communication with sea captains, outfitters of slaving voyages, and Caribbean planters. In formulating his defense of the slave trade, he was not expressing his own experience as much as he was condensing the experiences of others. His views therefore represented a kind of composite viewpoint of the slave trading community in Nantes.

Like many of his contemporaries, Mellier had only a vague grasp of the geography of Africa. To him, the slaves purchased by French ships on the Guinea coast came from an interior region called Nigritie, which he described vaguely as a "large region of Africa divided into many kingdoms." The king's mapmaker, Guillaume Delisle, was equally confused about the location of Nigritie. His 1700 map of Africa pictured Nigritie as including parts of the Upper Guinea coast, but his 1730 map placed Nigritie far away from the coast so that it covered only the parts of West Africa that no European had ever visited.[7] Nigritie was, in short, an imaginary construction of European mapmakers. Mellier was better informed about the coastal regions of West Africa, and he noted that the best place to purchase slaves at that time was the kingdom of Allada, situated along the Guinea coast between the Benin River and the kingdom of Benin.

Based on his shaky grasp of African geography, Mellier claimed that Nigritie was so overpopulated that its people would starve unless they sold their surplus population into the Atlantic slave trade. In making this claim, he was confusing the interior with the coast. Coastal kingdoms such as

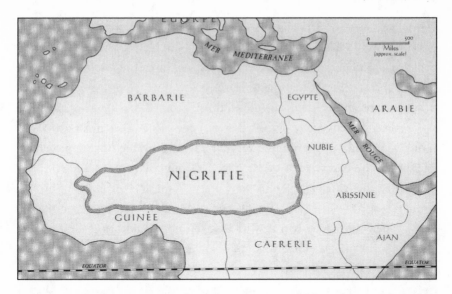

Figure 2.1   Redrawn version of Delisle's 1730 map of Africa showing the mythical land of Nigritie.

Allada were heavily populated, in part because they served as the terminal point for slave trade routes coming from the far interior. Since wealthy Africans in the coastal kingdoms often purchased slaves to work in their fields and serve as their personal servants and concubines, population densities actually increased in the coastal areas, whereas the demographic damage of the slave trade was felt mostly in the interior regions that no Europeans ever visited.

If Mellier's grasp of geography was vague, so were his notions of race. Although he was well aware that Africans had black skin, he did not necessarily link that observation with a set of negative judgments, unlike racist thought of the second half of the eighteenth century.[8] French dictionaries in Mellier's time defined the word *nègre*, a term the French applied to black slaves, more in geographical terms than in racial ones. Savary des Bruslons's *Dictionnaire Universel de Commerce*, published in 1723, defined *nègre* as "peoples of Africa whose country extends along the two sides of the Niger River," and the 1728 edition Trévoux's *Dictionnaire Universel François et Latin* defined the term as "the proper name of the people who inhabit Nigritie." By those definitions, only some black Africans were included in the category of *nègre*. Thirty-five years would pass before dictionaries began to define *nègre* exclusively in terms of skin color.[9]

Mellier's view of Africans was influenced less by notions of race than by his concepts of social ranking. The hierarchy of nobles, government officials, merchants, and peasants in early eighteenth-century Brittany had produced a social system that allowed the upper classes to treat the peasants very badly while still regarding them as fully human.[10] Since Mellier had spent his whole life maneuvering within that system, it is not surprising that he would view the African nobility very differently from the African peasantry. He showed his bias in favor of the African nobility when he noted with approval that the African king of Albany, on the Guinea coast, had sent his son to be educated in France under the care of Mr. Pradine, a financier of slave ships. Mellier also proposed that each slave ship should bring back one or two free Africans, presumably from noble families, to learn French and join the crews of sailing ships in order to facilitate trade with Africa.

On the other hand, when speaking of the ordinary African slaves drawn from the African peasantry whom planters from the islands brought with them to Nantes, Mellier's tone and vocabulary changed to reflect the street talk of a slaving port. "Fundamentally," he wrote, "the *nègres* are naturally inclined toward theft, larceny, lust, laziness, and treason. . . . In general, they are suited only to live in servitude and cultivate the fields of our colonies in America." The stereotype that he invoked revealed extreme prejudice, differing more in degree than in kind from the descriptions that urban sophisticates in Nantes applied to Breton peasants.[11]

Even though he defended the slave trade, Mellier had few illusions about its nature. He readily admitted that it was "driven by greed and afflicted with inhumanity" and caused people to be treated "like cattle." He also expressed sympathy with African captives, torn from their country of birth never to see it again. He noted they sometimes became so depressed that they became vulnerable to disease and death. One cause of their depression, he concluded, was their fear that they would be eaten by white cannibals.

Mellier's acknowledgment of those cruel realities did not, however, dissuade him from launching a defense of the slave trade. Sitting in his office at the chamber of accounts, a four-story building with its back wall running along the left bank of the River Erdre, he prepared his arguments carefully. After fourteen years of working in that building, he no longer noticed that under one of the vaults in its facade was a plaster bas-relief sculpture of King Henry II on a horse.[12] Henry, he might have remembered, was the king who abolished some of the remaining forms of servitude in France in 1552.[13]

Mellier's first argument in defense of slavery drew on mercantilist economic theory, which saw France locked into a zero-sum competition with the other nations of Europe for national wealth and power. In order for France to triumph over its commercial competitors, Mellier argued, the slave trade was "absolutely necessary for the cultivation of sugar, tobacco, cotton, indigo, and other products" that were exported from the Caribbean colonies to France. Mellier further noted that the authority to carry on the slave trade came from the king himself, and that the slave trade "would not have been authorized except for the indispensable need that we have for their services in our colonies."

In proclaiming the slave trade "necessary" and "indispensable" for the economic well-being of France, Mellier indicated that he had already decided the matter. He could have ended his discussion right there, except that he was apparently uncomfortable with the idea of treating people like cattle, even under conditions of "necessity." He therefore went on to outline three supplementary arguments to salve the conscience and make his fellow citizens feel better about this deadly and sordid commerce.

Mellier's first supplementary argument was that the slave traders were rescuing slaves from "error and idolatry" by taking them to a place where they could be baptized and instructed in the Catholic religion. Mellier was undoubtedly referring to the Code Noir, the law governing slavery in France's Caribbean colonies, which required all slaves to be baptized and buried in holy ground.[14] His assumption that African slaves were non-Christians, however, was not entirely correct. One of the slave ships that sailed from Nantes in 1716, the *Marie Anne*, was bound for Kabinda, where it purchased 183 slaves who had been captured in the civil war that raged in Kongo in 1714 and 1715. The kingdom of Kongo was at the time was recognized by the pope as a Catholic kingdom, and the Kongolese people, the vast majority of whom had been baptized, considered themselves Catholics.[15] The *Marie Anne* was carrying enslaved African Catholics to the New World.

Mellier's second argument was that in the land of Nigritie, "the people are so numerous that it would be difficult for them to maintain a subsistence were it not for the fact that each year the slave trade carries away a portion of the inhabitants." Here Mellier was confusing the population densities of the coastal regions, where many slaves ended up, with those of the interior regions, where the slaves originated. The region shown on French maps as Nigritie, explorers would later discover, was in fact underpopulated. Mellier's third argument was that the slaves actually owed their lives to the slave traders. "These peoples, being accustomed to make war with each other, would kill their prisoners of war were it not for the fact that they must spare their lives order to sell them or exchange them for the merchandise that we bring in our ships." What Mellier ignored was that Africans had a variety of ways of dealing with prisoners of war, including exchanging them, holding them for ransom, enslaving them for their own uses, or selling them in the internal African slave trade.

All three of Mellier's supplementary arguments were actually variations on a single theme: that masters and slaves had implicitly entered into a kind of reverse Faustian bargain, the slaves giving up their freedom in exchange for their temporal or eternal lives.[16] Mellier was picturing slavery as a path to salvation. Despite the fantasies and logical contradictions of Mellier's arguments, they nevertheless had a powerful appeal in early eighteenth-century Brittany because they tapped into a strain of thought that allowed slave traders to see the suffering and degradation of their African captives as the price they were paying for their lives and their souls.

Mellier's arguments in defense of the slave trade were echoed in Paris eight years later when Savery des Bruslons published his *Dictionnaire Universel de Commerce*. Under the heading *nègre*, Savary wrote a brief defense of the slave trade. "It is difficult," Savary wrote, "to fully justify the trade in slaves." He followed that extraordinary admission with two arguments in defense of the slave trade: (1) in losing their liberty, the slaves gained eternal salvation as a result of the Christian teaching that they received and (2) slave labor was "indispensable" for the cultivation of sugar, tobacco, and indigo in France's Caribbean colonies. These arguments, claimed Savary, "soften what seems inhuman in a trade where men are merchants of other men and buy them just like cattle to cultivate their land."[17] Justifications for slavery had become so well disseminated in early eighteenth-century France that the Parisian author of the dictionary was echoing, almost point by point, the arguments of Gérard Mellier in Nantes.

3

$\mathcal{J}$F GÉRARD MELLIER HAD stopped with his defense of the slave
trade to France's Caribbean colonies, the matter might have
ended right there. Most people in France, and even those in Nantes, the
major French slaving port, cared little about what happened in Africa and
the Caribbean. Because Mellier was defending a trade that was not under
attack, his arguments were not seen as controversial. They merely summarized and articulated the consensus opinion of the planters, merchants, and
slaving captains in Nantes.

Mellier inadvertently ignited a controversy, however, when he went on
to propose that Caribbean slavery should be legally recognized in France
itself. As he saw it, the only existing statute law on slavery was the Code
Noir—the set of laws regulating slavery in France's Caribbean colonies—
which had declared slaves to be "movable property" (in contrast to serfs,
who were tied to a particular piece of land). Accordingly, a slave in the
colonies ought to remain a slave if he or she was brought to France. The
problem, reasoned Mellier, was that the Code Noir applied only to
France's Caribbean colonies. He accordingly devised a system for registering slaves from the colonies that were brought to France by their owners,
thereby extending the "movable property" provisions of the Code Noir
into France. Slaves who were properly registered would remain the movable property of their owner.

Mellier's plan differed sharply from the official French position toward
slavery. Up until that moment, the French government had lived with a

bifurcated system in which slavery was encouraged in France's Caribbean colonies but was forbidden in France itself. Mellier saw clearly that the official position was contradictory, and the extension of the Code Noir into France would be a first step toward resolving it in favor of slavery.

By advocating official recognition of slavery, Mellier inadvertently invoked the long history of forced servitude in France, which went back to Roman times. As one of the great agricultural regions of the Roman Empire, the fields of Gaul were tilled by unfree cultivators who were designated by the Latin term *servus*, meaning "slave." Slavery continued after the fall of Rome. During the sixth to eighth centuries, slaves were treated in legal codes as the equivalent of livestock, and masters had the right to kill or mutilate them at will. By the end of the tenth century, however, slavery had largely disappeared, and agricultural labor was done mostly by smallholders and tenants working on seigneurial estates. In the eleventh century the lords violently enserfed the mass of the peasants. Serfs in the early Middle Ages nevertheless remained bound to their masters by a variety of personal ties. Under certain conditions, they could be bestowed as gifts, sold, or moved to new lands. It was only in the twelfth and thirteenth centuries that the personal ties between master and serf weakened as the lords coalesced into a hereditary nobility and the serfs coalesced as a servile class. The serf's legal position of being bound to a certain piece of land became more important over time as his or her personal ties to the lord diminished.[1]

Although the condition of French serfs in the Middle Ages differed in many ways from that of slaves in Roman Gaul, they were far from free. They made annual payments to the lord, they could not marry outside the manor, and they risked confiscation of all their earthly goods if their children were not living in the same house with them when they died. Serfs were bound to work a certain number of days each week in the lord's fields using their own plows and oxen, work in the harvest, and do carting when required. Various fees were levied on special occasions at the pleasure of the lord. If a serf wanted to grind grain or press grapes, he had to use the lord's facilities and pay the charges. If a serf got into trouble, the lord was the judge. Manors often possessed their own prisons and gallows.[2]

During the thirteenth to sixteenth centuries, serfdom went into decline throughout France as various types of rent payments replaced labor duties. One reason for the lords' willingness to manumit their serfs and renegotiate the conditions of servitude was their need for cash. Everywhere serfs had to purchase their own freedom. Even when King Louis IX (who was later canonized as St. Louis) freed the serfs on some of his royal domains in 1246–1263, the serfs paid for their liberty with cash. King Philippe le Bel went so far as to send out commissioners armed with royal seals to negotiate the price of freedom for serfs on royal lands during a period when his treasury was nearly empty. In spite of such occasional manumissions, the last vestiges of serfdom on the royal domains were not removed until 1779. Like the king, the Church owned vast domains that were worked by slave labor up until the tenth century and by serfs after that.[3]

By 1716, when Gérard Mellier was advocating the extension of Caribbean slavery to French soil, the serfdom of the Middle Ages had largely been replaced by a peasantry of rent-paying tenants and small proprietors who lived on the old manorial lands. Many of the lords had left their rural manors for the cities, living off the rents that came in from the countryside. The conditions of rent tenure could nevertheless be oppressive, and the British traveler Arthur Young was struck by the abject poverty he saw in rural Brittany.[4]

Many of the vestiges of feudalism still hung on in the French countryside, however. On the lands of the Viscount of Léon in Brittany, serfs were obliged to reside near the lord for a year and a day to serve him at his pleasure. There was another category of subjects called *mottiers*, who could not leave the land or even marry without the permission of the duke.[5] If they died without male heirs, the duke himself inherited their assets. As late as the second half of the eighteenth century, the philosophe Voltaire used the word "slaves" to describe French serfs, and he insisted that, contrary to popular belief, slavery had not yet been abolished in France. On the eve of the French Revolution, estimates of the number of serfs in France ranged from 300,000 to over a million. Many of the serfs were owned by the Church.[6] It was not until the revolution that the last vestiges of serfdom were eliminated.

It was against this backdrop of slavery and serfdom in the French countryside that Gérard Mellier proposed his extension of Caribbean slavery into France. Despite the uncomfortable echoes embedded in Mellier's proposal, the king and the regent proclaimed the "King's Edict Concerning Negro Slaves from the Colonies" in October 1716, only a few months after

Mellier had sent them his memorandum. The edict contained fifteen articles that closely followed Gérard Mellier's suggestions. Slave owners from
France's Caribbean colonies could bring their slaves to France as domestic
servants, for instruction in religion, or to learn a trade without fear of losing them as long as the slaves were properly registered. Further articles
held that slaves could not marry in France without permission of their
masters, that runaway slaves from the colonies could not gain freedom by
coming to France, and that masters could not sell their slaves while in
France.[7]

The King's Edict Concerning Negro Slaves from the Colonies could
not take effect until it was registered by the regional *parlements*, bodies
that served as high courts and also had legislative functions. The *parlement*
of Rennes, which had jurisdiction over Brittany, registered the edict on
December 24, 1716. Things went very differently, however, in the *parlement* of Paris. Given that the *parlement* of Paris had little direct interest in
the fate of West Indian slaves living in France's coastal ports, the edict
might have been approved with minimal debate had it not landed in the
middle of a fight between two antagonistic religious groups: the Jansenists
and the Jesuits.[8]

The Jansenists, in contrast to the Jesuits, were not a religious order. They
represented a set of theological tendencies rather than an organized movement. Jansenists used a rigid reading of St. Augustine to stress the depravity
of man and the grace of God to elect and save sinners. Jansenism was, in
short, a kind of Catholic version of Calvinism. Politically, Jansenists embraced a Gallican nationalism that was wary of the authority of the pope
and the pope's messengers—the Jesuits. The disagreements between the
two groups had turned deadly serious in 1711, when King Louis XIV, with
the blessing of his Jesuit confessor, ordered his troops to raze the Abbey of
Port Royal des Champs in Paris, a center of Jansenist theological influence.
So complete was the destruction that the bones in the cemetery were dug
up and hurled into a common grave.[9] Shortly the king forced the *parlement*
of Paris, the center of Jansenist political influence, to register a papal bull
attacking Jansenist teachings that he had solicited from the pope with the
support of the Jesuits.[10] The fight did not end until 1764, when the
Jansenists succeeded in getting the Jesuits expelled from France and its
overseas possessions.

What caught the attention of the Jansenists in the *parlement* of Paris when the King's Edict of Concerning Negro Slaves from the Colonies was presented to them in 1716 was not the issue of slavery as much as the opportunity to seize the high moral ground in a battle with the Jesuits.[11] The Jansenists interpreted the king's edict as an extension of the Code Noir and therefore a project of the Jesuits. They were correct on both issues. The preamble to the edict stated explicitly that it was being issued in order to uphold the Code Noir, which "maintains the discipline of the Catholic, Apostolic, and Roman Church." The writing of the Code Noir itself had been heavily influenced by the Jesuits.

The Jesuits were the first missionary order to settle in the French West Indies, coming to Martinique in 1640.[12] It was Jesuits who started the first sugar plantation on Martinique, and by 1650 they had become the second largest slaveholder on the island.[13] Given that the Church in France had long supported itself with the labor of slaves and serfs, it is not surprising that religious orders in France's Caribbean colonies used slave labor to support their activities. Father Labat, a Dominican priest who directed a slave plantation in Martinique, did not seem at all embarrassed at being a slave owner, but he became extremely upset when people accused him of dabbling in commerce.[14] After King Louis XIV took over direct royal control of the islands from the French West Indies Company in 1674, he became a champion of the Jesuits, writing to the new governor that his top priorities should be the advancement of religion and the protection of the Jesuits.[15] Being in favor with the king and the local officials, the Jesuits were in a good position to exert influence on the drafting of the Code Noir.

The earliest draft of the Code Noir, submitted by the governor of France's Caribbean colonies on May 20, 1682, dealt with issues of slave subsistence, policing, judgments, and punishment, but did not mention religion at all. Later that year the Jesuits of Martinique submitted a memorandum to King Louis XIV warning him about the harmful religious influences that Jews and Protestants were exerting on slaves in the islands.[16] The Jews, the Jesuits charged, "have in their homes a great number of slaves whom they introduce to Judaism, or at least divert from Christianity." As for the Protestants, the Jesuits urged, "they should not be allowed to practice their religion in any way."

When the Code Noir was issued by Louis XIV in March 1685, its religious emphasis was obvious. The preamble specified that its primary purpose was "to maintain the discipline of the Catholic, Apostolic, and Roman Church." Article 1 called for the expulsion of all Jews from the islands within three months. Article 2 required that all slaves should be baptized and given instruction in the Catholic religion. Article 3 attacked the Protestants by forbidding the public exercise of any religion other than Catholic. Article 4 made it illegal for any commander who did not profess the Catholic religion to supervise slaves. Article 5 forbade Protestant slaveholders from exerting any religious influence over their slaves, and Article 6 ordered all subjects to observe all Catholic holidays.[17]

The Jesuits saw the Code Noir as a humanitarian document that curbed some of the worst abuses of slaveholders. It set minimum food and clothing rations for slaves, forbade masters from murdering their slaves, and made provision for manumission. At the same time, however, it provided legal standing for slavery in the islands, and it protected the rights of slaveholders by declaring slaves to be movable property and stating that any personal property possessed by a slave ultimately belonged to his or her master. It also gave masters permission to enchain or whip their slaves at will, and it prescribed the death penalty to any slave who struck his or her master.[18]

The Code Noir caused little discussion in France as long as it applied only to France's Caribbean colonies. Its extension to France by the Edict of October 1, 1716, however, aroused the opposition of the Jansenists in the *parlement* of Paris who felt that they were on solid ground for doing battle with the Jesuits. By this circuitous route, issues of slavery and freedom came to be debated in the *parlement* of Paris at a time when the French slave trade was beginning an unprecedented period of expansion.

To prepare for the debate, the advocate general of the *parlement* asked Pierre Lemerre the Younger, a Jansenist sympathizer and expert on canon law, to write an opinion on the edict.[19] The legal brief that Lemerre produced was largely a compilation of references to the Bible, canon law, French law, previous legal judgments, and opinions of lawyers.[20] Its arguments were sometimes confusing because Lemerre, like most of his contemporaries, used the words "slave" and "serf" interchangeably, thus revealing how issues of slavery in the Caribbean could not be disentangled from the history of slavery and serfdom in France. Yet it is clear that Lemerre was attempting to go beyond the narrow issues raised by the king's edict and build a case against slavery itself.

In the opening section of his brief, Lemerre searched in vain through the Old Testament, the New Testament, canon law, and Roman civil law for material to bolster his case against slavery. Old Testament law was concerned mostly with the distinction between Hebrew slaves and non-Hebrew slaves, and the New Testament recommended obedience of slaves to their masters. The Roman code was no help at all, as slaves had no rights under Roman civil law. A number of councils of the Catholic Church had issued decrees and canons advocating obedience of Christian slaves to their masters, and prior to the ninth century the councils did not regard slavery as against the religion of Jesus Christ.

Against the backdrop of the long history of servitude in the Roman Empire and France, Lemerre tried to argue that the French had broken free of their past and had developed a concept of liberty that was founded on two pillars. The first was natural law, which "holds that all men are equal and has made us reject the odious forms of servitude that place people almost at the level of animals." Lemerre argued that Roman laws upholding slavery were against the law of nature, which held that all men are equal. The second pillar was Christianity. As soon as Christianity was introduced into France, claimed Lemerre, it recognized that "slavery and servitude were contrary to the purity of the new law," and that it was "incompatible that man, who was made in the image of god, would be delivered like an animal into the domination of another man." In his flights of rhetorical fancy, Lemerre conveniently ignored the glacial pace and opportunistic nature of the royal emancipations and the fact that a great many French slaves and serfs had worked on the lands of the Church and religious orders.

Moving toward the climax of his argument, he quoted extensively from the writings of Antoine Le Maistre, a seventeenth-century Jansenist lawyer who had argued against slavery on the basis of Christian principles and natural law. "God," Le Maistre had argued, "is the God of Liberty. In taking on the form of a servant, he pulled us out of servitude; he broke the chains, he made us walk with our heads held high." Le Maistre had also argued on the basis on natural law, noting that "servitude is an offense to natural liberty." According to natural law, men should only command animals and not other men. Servitude was therefore a "monster that deforms human nature." Lemerre was arguing, in short, that the Edict Concerning Negro Slaves from the Colonies should not be registered by the *parlement* of Paris because it was in conflict with the fundamental laws of the realm.

For all its factual and interpretive flaws, Lemerre's brief nevertheless carried the day. The *parlement* of Paris defied the king and refused to register the edict.[21] It was a victory for antislavery sentiment, but it was a victory narrowly cast. The legal case had been argued in terms of French national history, and Lemerre did not extend his arguments to cover the slave trade or slavery in the France's colonies overseas. Although the *parlement* of Paris had successfully challenged the extension of the Code Noir to France, it did not challenge the Code Noir itself. Faced with an opportunity to attack slavery in France's Caribbean colonies, Pierre Lemerre the Younger had blinked. Caribbean slavery would not again be the subject of serious public debate in France until the 1770s.[22]

Perhaps it was in response to Lemerre's timidity that the philosophe Montesquieu wrote a passage in his *Persane lettres*, published in 1721, pointing out the hypocrisy of Christian rulers who freed the slaves in their own countries and then introduced slavery into the foreign lands that they conquered.[23] Gérard Mellier had recognized that contradiction in 1716 and had sought to resolve it by extending Caribbean slavery into France, albeit with stringent limits. The other way of resolving the contradiction would have been to extend Pierre LeMerre the Younger's claims about liberty to France's Caribbean colonies. Lemerre had won a limited victory in the *parlement* of Paris, but Gérard Mellier had carried the day in the slaving ports of France.

Justifications of the slave trade such as those articulated in Mellier's memorandum and later repeated in Savary's *Dictionnaire Universel de Commerce* were spread by word of mouth along the quays of Nantes and through the lesser slaving ports of Brittany. During the ensuing years they were repeated over and over in shipboard and dockside conversations. Such arguments provided First Lieutenant Robert Durand, a young officer preparing for his first voyage to Africa, with the mental defenses he needed to dedicate the slaving voyage of the *Diligent* "to the greater glory of God and the Virgin Mary."

PART 2

The
Financiers

4

*A*MID THE FLURRY OF activity in preparation for the *Diligent's* imminent departure from Vannes, two men wearing flowing wigs and brocaded silk coats stood calmly on the quarterdeck.[1] The Billy brothers, Guillaume and François, looked too young to be the owners and outfitters of a slave ship. Guillaume was only thirty-six and François was ten years younger. Between them, they owned 60 percent of the ship and had financed two-thirds of the cost of outfitting it with supplies, trade goods, and a crew. In order to make the departure a festive and ceremonial occasion, they planned to accompany the ship as far as Belle Ile, some twenty-two miles away. They had ample justification for doing this ceremonial sail with the *Diligent*: this was the first slave ship they had ever outfitted and the first slaving vessel ever to sail from the city of Vannes.

As the outfitters of the voyage, the Billy brothers would never actually see any of the slaves that their money would purchase nor would they smell the stench of death on the lower deck of their ship. The only slave they had ever seen in their lives was a well-dressed young black man named La Fleur, who was brought from Martinique in 1729 on the ship *St. Pierre* to be instructed in religion and learn a trade in Vannes.[2] Yet it was the Billy brothers and the many other slaving outfitters like them, rather than the captains and crews of the slave ships, who were the driving force behind the rapid expansion of the French slave trade in the eighteenth century.

The Billy brothers were entering the slave trade at a time when its nature was changing. The previous three decades had witnessed a series of battles between the state-chartered monopoly companies and the private enterprise traders based in Nantes. The battles had ended in a kind of draw: private traders were permitted to compete with the monopoly companies, though not on equal footing. The transformation of the French slave trade paralleled a larger shift from mercantilism to private enterprise capitalism in the Atlantic slave trade as a whole. The British Royal African Company, which had monopolized the British slave trade in the late seventeenth century, was forced by an act of Parliament in 1698 to tolerate competition from private slave traders. The Dutch West India Company, which had held a monopoly on the Dutch slave trade, was opened to private traders in 1730. Among the major European slave trading nations, only the Portuguese maintained their complex system of government-chartered monopoly companies and government-issued slave duty contracts into the second half of the eighteenth century.[3]

When the *Diligent* set sail on May 31, 1731, the old charter companies and the new private enterprise traders were in open competition with one another. The companies still controlled the European forts and castles on the West African coast, but those possessions were a burden as much as an asset. Although company ships sailed fixed routes from company ports in Europe to company forts in Africa, private merchant ships could go wherever they chose. Standing on the deck of the *Diligent* in the Gulf of Morbihan, the Billy brothers could almost see that conflict inscribed into the geography of Brittany. Sixty-two miles to the southeast was Nantes, which had long been the hotbed of agitation for private enterprise. Thirty-one miles to the northwest was Lorient, the home port of the Company of the Indies. Lorient was the ultimate company town, having no independent existence outside of the company. Together, Nantes and Lorient accounted for three-quarters of the entire French slave trade in 1731. Situated literally between the two contrasting commercial systems, the Billy brothers were trying to emulate the slave traders in Nantes without antagonizing the Company of the Indies. In the end, this would prove more difficult than they imagined.

The monopoly system had been established in the seventeenth century, when the French government chartered fourteen separate companies between 1626 and 1698 to colonize overseas territories and carry out overseas trade. Each had a monopoly over French trade in a certain part of the

Figure 4.1   Nantes at the beginning of the eighteenth century.

world.[4] In the late seventeenth century the slave trade was in the hands of two chartered companies: the Senegal Company, which had a monopoly on French trade in West Africa north of the Sierra Leone River, and the Guinea Company, headed by Colbert's son Jean-François, which had a monopoly on French trade from Sierra Leone southward to the Cape of Good Hope. Privately organized slaving voyages, although occasionally undertaken, were strictly forbidden by law.

That was a situation that Joachim Descasaux hoped to change when he was elected representative from Nantes to the newly formed French Council of Commerce in 1700. The major wholesale merchants of Nantes, who referred to themselves as *négociants* in order to distinguish themselves from retail merchants, could not have found anyone better to represent their interests.[5] As the son of one of the most important *négociants* of Nantes, Descasaux had considerable experience in trade, fishing, and privateering. In 1694 he had begun outfitting long-distance voyages and soon became a specialist in trade with the French islands in the Caribbean. His marriage to an Irish woman, Françoise Sarsfield, gave him an international outlook that was useful in formulating commercial policies.

At the Council of Commerce in Paris, Descaseaux was a forceful advocate for the rights of the private traders of Nantes to participate in the slave trade. He complained bitterly that the Guinea Company, by monopolizing the slave trade along most of the African coast, had "deprived us of a chance to make great progress in trade and navigation in relation to the American islands." He accused the company of stifling the economic growth of the French colonies in the Caribbean, claiming, "They have so limited the supply of slaves to the islands that they do not even bring a tenth of what is necessary to clear the land that needs to be cultivated."[6]

Having castigated the monopoly companies, Descasaux then made his pitch for opening up the slave trade to private traders, boasting, "We can be certain that private trade in slaves will provide more slaves to the American islands in a few years than have been delivered up to now by the company." He understood that the advocates of monopoly companies feared that large numbers of private traders descending on the African coast would deplete the region of slaves and drive up prices, but he found that argument groundless. "The breeding ground," he argued, "will not be soon depleted. Because Africans are permitted to have as many wives as they please, they propagate abundantly. The slave traders reduce that growth due to the unfortunate nature of their business, but they do not negate it." As long as there was one slave left on the African coast whose labor was needed in the Caribbean, he wrote, there would be private traders coming to meet the need.

At the time Joachim Descasaux wrote those words, the Guinea Company was almost moribund, and Descasaux hoped to convince the Council of Commerce to open up the slave trade to private traders. Living in Paris on the Rue d'Orléans in the quarter where most royal ministers resided, he was well placed to lobby such people as Chamillart, the controller-general of finances, Desmaretz, the director of finances, Pontchartrain, the minister of the marine, and, most importantly, his close friend Samuel Bernard, a banker and the principal creditor of King Louis XIV.[7] Descasaux later named one of his ships the *Samuel Bernard*.

The Guinea Company was saved when France received the *assiento* contract from the Spanish crown to supply slaves to the Spanish colonies in the Americas. Because Spain was barred by a 1480 treaty with Portugal from trading along the African coast, the *assiento* contract for supplying slaves to the Spanish colonies in the New World had been in the hands of other countries. Up until 1640 the Portuguese had held it; in 1662 it went to the Dutch, who had driven the Portuguese from their forts on the West African coast. In 1701, however, the French government managed to win the coveted *assiento*, which saved the Guinea Company from ruin.

In July 1701, Descasaux's close friend Samuel Bernard was appointed to the board of directors that would reorganize the Guinea Company for the task of transporting slaves to Spanish America. As a part of the reorganization, Bernard got the Guinea Company to agree to license two private ships per year to carry slaves to France's Caribbean colonies.[8] In 1703 Joachim Descasaux took advantage of this arrangement to invest in the first authorized private slaving ship ever to sail from Nantes. Because the Guinea Company lacked the shipping capacity to supply slaves to both the Spanish colonies and the French islands, it began to subcontract more and more of its slaving voyages to private traders from Nantes. Despite this loophole in the company system, the *négociants* of Nantes still lacked government permission to go out on their own.

The monopoly system that dominated the French slave trade reflected a general philosophy of international trade, sometimes called "mercantilism," that had governed the overseas commerce of the major maritime nations of Europe in the seventeenth century. Mercantilists viewed international trade as a form of war in which the trading nations of Europe competed for shares of a relatively fixed supply of gold and silver. Each nation sought to maintain a favorable balance of trade in order to gain gold and silver from its rivals. Colbert, the minister of Louis XIV from 1661 to 1683, never tired of repeating that *le grand commerce* was the best way to increase the power of France and decrease the power of its enemies and rivals. Like his predecessor, Cardinal Richelieu, he believed that overseas trade was too important to be entrusted to private traders, who did not necessarily have the interests of the French government at heart.

Although monopoly–company mercantilism was under attack in France by private enterprise capitalists such as Descasaux in the early eighteenth century, it still had its defenders. A memorandum written in the early eighteenth century by a French admiralty officer named Jean Le Pottier outlined the case for government regulation of trade.[9] Le Pottier made a distinction between individual merchants, who "seek only their own profits," and the state, which seeks "the general good." Trade, he argued, should have no other object than to enrich the state in gold and silver. To this end, international maritime trade was the key to national prosperity, and so it needed to be carefully controlled, regulated, and promoted by the government. Le Pottier greatly admired the trading success of the Dutch, English, and Genoese, noting, "Among those nations the first purpose of the state is trade."

The mercantilist emphasis on international trade reflected ideology more than economic reality. The French economy in the early eighteenth century was overwhelmingly agricultural, and most economic activity was related to the production, marketing, and consumption of grain.[10] The administrative apparatus of the French government served primarily to control and tax the agricultural economy, and the most important group of French economists in the eighteenth century, the Physiocrats, devoted their talents to studying grain supplies and prices.

In stark contrast to the dominant agricultural economy of eighteenth-century France stood the maritime commercial cities such as Nantes and Bordeaux. Whereas agricultural market towns lived off the produce of their own hinterlands, the trade of commercial cities was largely conducted with other commercial cities that might be located thousands of miles away. The English traveler Arthur Young clearly understood that point when he wrote that the splendor and wealth of Nantes was "so unconnected with the country."[11] Society and government in the commercial cities were often at odds with the rest of France. French society as a whole was dominated by a hierarchy of fixed estates and orders, while the commercial cities were hotbeds of upward mobility. A cumbersome government bureaucracy exercised administrative authority over the French countryside, whereas the commercial cities exploited vast trading empires with minimal bureaucratic apparatus. In some ways, the *négociants* of Nantes were citizens of the Atlantic world as much as citizens of France, and they saw the French state as an unwelcome intrusion into their activities. When the state attempted to control the expanding overseas trade of the commercial cities much as it had traditionally controlled the grain trade of the market towns, it provoked fierce opposition from the local merchants and officials.[12]

The slave trade was an integral part of the larger debate between the mercantilists and the private enterprise capitalists. Even though the slave trade made up only a tiny part of France's overseas commerce, it nevertheless played a key role in creating the favorable trade balances that the mercantilists sought. The profits did not come from the slave trade itself as much as from the products produced by slaves in France's Caribbean colonies. Most of the sugar, cocoa, cotton, and indigo that the slaves produced was shipped to France and then reexported to other nations of Europe, where it earned France foreign exchange crucial to a favorable trade balance.[13] That is why the government subsidized the slave trading companies with bonuses and tariff reductions.

The mercantilist view of the slave trade was articulated in the late seventeenth century by De Gaullitzer, who argued that a "multitude of slaves is necessary to compete successfully with the English, Dutch, and Portuguese in the production of plantation staples and in navigation." Reflecting the mercantilist view of trade as a zero-sum game, he added, "We must try to trade as many slaves as possible so that those nations will find that many fewer slaves for themselves."

In a similar vein, Jean Le Pottier's mercantilist memorandum in the early eighteenth century recommended an increase in the French slave trade. "The companies that we have established and given exclusive rights do not have enough posts in Africa, do not have enough funds, and do not send out enough ships," he complained. The problem, according to him, was that the existing monopoly companies were undercapitalized and the strategy of dividing world trade among different companies had fragmented the market. The solution was to unify the French chartered companies into a single company with a worldwide reach. A unified trading company, Le Pottier argued, "will carry greater numbers of slaves to populate our colonies, something that today's companies cannot do because they are so weak."

After years of debate between the mercantilists and the capitalists, the French slave trade was finally opened to private traders because France lost the *assiento* contract to Britain on March 29, 1713, a blow that forced the financially strapped Guinea Company to begin a long process of liquidation.[14] As soon as the loss of the *assiento* became known, the *négociant*s of Nantes clamored for the slave trade to be opened. The Guinea Company, they claimed, had failed to supply enough slaves to the French islands, creating a labor shortage that had forced planters to abandon sugar production in favor of indigo, which was less labor-intensive. If trade were opened up to "all subjects of the king," they argued, private traders were prepared to carry four thousand slaves a year to the islands. That development would reinvigorate sugar production, drive the English, Dutch, and Danish slave traders out of the French Antilles, and provide the *négociants* of France a "means to augment their fortunes."[15] The argument was cleverly conceived. Rather than force a philosophical choice between mercantilism and capitalism, they argued that capitalist means could accomplish mercantilist ends.

The Council of Commerce was receptive to those arguments, and it drew up a series of recommendations that were presented to the controller-general, Desmaretz. After reflecting on the matter, he decided to open the slave trade to private traders as an experiment. There was no risk to the experiment, he argued in a letter to the minister of the marine, because if the increased trade promised by the private outfitters did not materialize, the government could always form a new monopoly company.[16]

As for the practical arrangements, the French government would take over the Guinea Company's fort at Whydah, on the West African coast, and pay for its upkeep by taxing the private traders fifteen livres for each slave they delivered to Martinique or Guadaloupe, and thirty livres for each slave they delivered to Saint Domingue. Private traders would enjoy the same tariff reductions that the Guinea Company had enjoyed, but they would not get the thirteen livres per head subsidy that the company had received for each slave it delivered to the islands. The controller-general recommended limiting the number of ships that sailed for Guinea to twelve to fifteen per year because he feared that too much competition would drive up slave prices on the West African coast while at the same time driving down slave prices in the Caribbean. Such a development, he warned, would squeeze profits, drive out the private slave traders, and bring about a collapse of the trade in slaves. The minister of the marine, Pontchartrain, accepted the recommendation and set the number of annual sailings at twelve.[17] The first authorization was delivered in November 1713, just as the *assiento* contract officially expired.[18]

The *négociants* of Nantes were greatly upset by the limit on the number of annual permits. In 1714 they wrote a memorandum of protest in which they argued that France's Caribbean colonies required many more slaves than twelve ships per year could possibly deliver because so many of the slaves died during transit and in the islands.[19] The traders estimated that a sixth of the slaves died during the middle passage, and that another quarter of them died in the islands before they had adjusted to the new climate. Moreover, the *négociants* claimed, the majority of the slaves in France's Caribbean colonies had died from disease or other causes during the recent War of the Spanish Succession, and their labor needed to be replaced. There was enormous irony in the argument that high death rates among slaves justified an increase in the slave trade.

In February 1715 the *négociants* of Nantes wrote a second memorandum rebutting the arguments of the controller general and the minister of the marine that too many slaving ships descending on the coast of Africa would drive up slave prices and cause the trade to collapse. In making their arguments, the traders of Nantes revealed clear differences in the ways that government officials and *négociants* understood basic economic concepts such as supply, demand, and competition. They also revealed the difference between mercantilist thought, which saw economic activity as a zero-sum game, and a capitalistic approach, which viewed international trade as a dynamic and expanding enterprise.[20]

The *négociants* pointed out that the restrictions on the number of annual sailings effectively limited the trade to very large ships that went exclusively to the major slave markets of West Africa. If there were unlimited access, small and medium-sized ships would seek out infrequently visited African ports where they could buy slaves cheaply. Their voyages would be shorter and more cost-efficient because they would fill their holds quickly, and fewer slaves would die during the middle passage. Unlimited private access would thus lower slave prices instead of raising them.

The government's fear that the *négociants* of Nantes would drop out of the slave trade if they began losing money, they argued, was based on a misunderstanding of the nature of private trade. "One must not fear that a few losses that traders suffer, or might suffer, will frighten off all the others. Traders never act in concert, and they do not communicate anything about their business. They hide their losses rather than broadcast them. The trader is always mysterious, whether he loses or wins; what one abandons, another takes up. We will therefore continue to trade in slaves whether the conditions are favorable or unfavorable. We can even assure you that there are fewer dangers to fear in the slave trade than in other types of trade because any slave ship that sells its entire cargo cannot fail to make a profit." Their expectations of profits were well founded. A sample budget of a private slave trading expedition prepared by Gérard Mellier projected that an initial investment of 100,000 livres would bring a return of 158,000 livres, generating a profit of 58 percent.[21]

Having made the economic case for freedom of trade, the *négociants* of Nantes advanced a bold proposal: they would take over the operation and maintenance of the forts and trading lodges on the African coast that had formerly belonged to the Guinea Company. In return, they wanted the right to tax slave traders ten livres for each slave they carried to the West Indies in times of peace, and fifteen livres in times of war. In effect, they wanted to form a merchants' cooperative to replace the Guinea Company. To show that they could manage the trade more cost-effectively than either the Guinea Company or the government, they pointed out that their proposed tax was much lower than the fifteen to thirty livres per slave the government was demanding, and they were not asking the government for the thirteen livres per slave subsidy that the Guinea Company had received.

The private traders of Nantes did not have long to wait for their answer. Less than a year later, in January 1716, the French government issued royal "*Lettres patentes* for Freedom of the Commerce of the Guinea Coast," which opened up the slave trade in the Guinea Company's old territory (the Atlantic coast of Africa from the Sierra Leone River to the Cape of Good Hope) to all private traders from four port cities: Nantes, Rouen, La Rochelle, and Bordeaux. Any outfitter operating in one of these cities could receive royal permission to undertake a slave trading voyage provided that he agreed to pay the government a tax of twenty livres for each adult captive delivered alive to the islands; boys under twelve years of age were taxed at two-thirds the adult rate, and girls under twelve were taxed at half.[22] The tax was supposed to pay for the upkeep of the former Guinea Company fort at Whydah.

In return, the *négociants* received the right to export French manufactured goods destined for the Africa trade duty-free. In addition, international trade goods such as cloth from India or pipes from Holland that were brought into these five French ports for reexport to Africa were totally exempt from customs duties. Ships returning from a slaving voyage would receive an exemption from half the customs duties on sugar, cotton, and other goods from the West Indies that they had obtained in return for slaves. These exemptions were retroactive to all ships that had left France since November 1713, when the *assiento* contract had expired.[23] Even though the government was no longer paying a commission of thirteen livres for every slave delivered alive to the islands, as it had done for the Guinea Company, slave trading remained a state-subsidized business.

The significance of these subsidies for slave traders became apparent the following year, when the government issued new rules governing direct trade to the islands. Articles produced in France could be exported directly to the islands duty-free, and no duties would be levied on goods imported into France for direct reexport to the islands. On these issues, the direct traders enjoyed the same privileges as slave traders. However, upon returning from the islands with sugar, cotton, and indigo, the direct traders had to pay full tariffs, whereas the slave traders paid only half tariffs.[24] In terms of tariff regulations, the slave trade was clearly a privileged form of commerce. The *négociants* of Nantes believed that the era of company trade was over and that a new era of private enterprise was beginning. Little did they know that at that very moment an exiled Scot in Paris was plotting to bring back the monopoly trading companies.

5

THE SOUNDS OF STONEMASONS' hammers echoed across Place Louis-le-Grand, the newest royal square in Paris. Many of the houses that enclosed the square in 1715 were still under construction, and others were nothing but empty facades with bare lots behind them. At the center of the square was a huge statue of King Louis XIV on a horse. Place Louis-le-Grand had become *the* popular address for the high financiers of Paris. Antoine Crozat, the receiver general of finances for Bordeaux and treasurer of the Guinea Company, owned numbers 17–19. Poisson de Bourvalais, the secretary of the Council of Finances, lived at numbers 11–13, and Claude-François Paparel, the treasurer-general for war, lived at number 14.[1] For all their wealth, the financiers were despised by the nobility as "men of nothing" who lacked refined tastes, much like the ridiculous Monsieur Jourdain, the main character in Molière's popular play *Le bourgeois gentilhomme*. By living on a royal square that bore the king's name and was dominated by his equestrian statue, the financiers gained a kind of prestige and proximity to royal power that other locations could not offer.[2]

The newest resident of Place Louis-le-Grand was a Scot named John Law, who had rented one of the houses in May 1714.[3] A sumptuously furnished house at this address was useful, Law calculated, for entertaining guests and receiving visitors. Law's arrival in Paris did not go unnoticed by the superintendent of police, who wrote to the foreign minister: "A Scot named Law, a gambler by profession and suspected of evil intentions

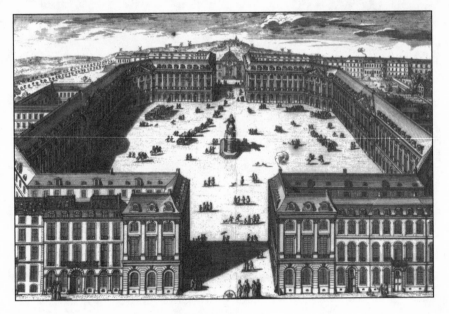

Figure 5.1   Place Louis-le-Grand in Paris.

toward the king, appears at Paris in high style, and has even bought an impressive home in the Place Louis-le-Grand, although no one knows of any
resource except his fortune in gambling, which is his whole profession."[4]

Given that Law's purpose in moving to Paris was to cultivate influence
with people such as the Duke of Orleans, Controller-General Desmaretz,
and the financiers of Place Louis-le-Grand, the house fit well into his plans
for attracting the right people and making the right friends. Law was soon
a regular player at the high-stakes gambling parties indulged in by the
moneyed elites of Paris. He typically arrived with two large bags containing at least a hundred thousand livres worth of gold coins. When the large
sums of money he was betting became too cumbersome to handle, he used
special gold five hundred–livre tokens that he had designed for just that
purpose.

John Law lived well for a man who was a fugitive from a murder conviction. When he was a young man living in London, he had been sen-
tenced to death for killing a certain Edward Wilson in a sword duel at
Bloomsberry Square. Wilson had apparently insulted Law's mistress, Mrs.
Lawrence. Had the sentence been carried out, Law's life would have
ended at the age of twenty-three. With the help of friends in high places,

Figure 5.2   John Law.

however, he escaped from the King's Bench Prison after two underkeep-
ers, who had been bribed, drugged the guards and a used a file to remove
his fetters. Friends waiting on the outside carried him to Sussex and put
him on a boat to France.[5]

For the next two decades he roamed the capitals and gambling resorts of
Europe, making his living as a gambler and periodically getting himself
banned from certain cities for being too successful. His personal secretary,
Mr. Gray, described him as "handsome, tall, with a good address, and had a
particular talent of pleasing the ladies." He always dressed well, Gray noted,
"making a good figure in all public places." If Gray was correct, then Law's
appearance must have improved considerably since the time of his escape

from prison, when the notice in the *London Gazette* described the fugitive as "a very tall, black, lean man, well shaped, above six feet high, large pock-holes in his face, speaks broad and loud."[6]

John Law was no ordinary gambler. Having spent considerable time in Europe's great banking centers, including Venice, Genoa, and Amsterdam, he had become an avid student of banking, currencies, and finance. In Venice, he went regularly to the Banco di Rialto at money-changing time, where he observed, according to this secretary, "the course of exchange all the world over, the manner of discounting bills at the bank, the vast useful-ness of paper credit, how gladly people parted with their money for paper, and the profits accrued to the proprietors from this paper." All the while, he was developing his own ideas about trade, finance, credit, and the role of paper money in national economies.

With his obvious intelligence, exquisite manners, and intimate knowl-edge of banking and finance, this fugitive from the gallows cultivated friendships with people in high places all over Europe. The British ambas-sador to France, the Earl of Stair, was so impressed by Law that he wrote to the English secretary of state, "He is a man of very good sense, and who has a head fit for calculations of all kinds to an extent beyond anybody. In the matters that he takes himself up with, he is certainly the cleverest man that is." Even the Duke de Saint-Simon, an early opponent of Law's proj-ects, praised the range of his mind, his genius, his penetrating intelligence, and the wisdom of his policy. What distinguished Law from other gamblers and financiers, noted the philosophe Montesquieu, was that "he loved ideas more than money."[7]

In late 1713 John Law arrived in Paris, bringing with him a fortune of 1.6 million livres. He intended to gamble, to be sure, but in his mind was nothing less than a plan for reorganizing the economy of France. Some of his ideas were radically new, such as his plan for a central bank that would issue a new kind of paper money. Other ideas harked back to the seven-teenth-century mercantilism of Colbert, especially his belief that overseas trade should be carried out through government-chartered monopoly companies. His arrival in Paris did not receive a particularly warm wel-come from the French authorities, and considerable time went by before he finally[8] received an audience with the controller general, Desmaretz.[8]

The death of Louis XIV on September 1, 1715, created a new opportu-nity for Law. Because the great-grandson and legitimate successor to the deceased king was only five years old, France would be governed by the Duke of Orleans, who would rule as regent with the power of an absolute monarch.[9] Law had known the Duke since 1707, and the two had frequently matched wits and strategies in high-stakes games of backgammon. The duke's main problem was that the wars and extravagances of King Louis XIV had left the French government bankrupt. The national debt was 3.5 billion livres, and it was growing by 150–200 million livres each year.[10]

The conjuncture of political and economic crises presented Law with an extraordinary opportunity to try out some of his ideas. He had already presented his plan for establishing a central bank of France to Controller General Desmaretz in May 1715. In December he informed the regent that "the bank is not the only nor the greatest of my ideas. I will produce a work that will surprise Europe by the changes that it will bring in favor of France, changes greater than those that were produced by the discovery of the Indies or the introduction of credit."[11] He was referring to his intention to establish the greatest monopoly trading company that France had ever seen.

John Law's ideas began to be realized on May 1, 1716, when the Council of Finances approved his plan to open the Banque Générale. Unlike the national central bank that he had originally envisioned, this one was a private bank, but it was like no other private bank France had ever seen. One distinguishing feature was that investors in the Banque Générale needed to make only one-fourth of their investment in hard currency; the other three quarters could be made in the new government bonds that had been issued by a bankrupt French government in late 1715. In their first few months in circulation, the bonds had already lost more than half of their value. Law was, in effect, financing his bank by buying up government debt.[12]

The second feature of Law's Banque Générale was that it issued its own paper banknotes, but it did so in a new way that guaranteed the value of the paper currency. The problem of retaining value arose from the fact that in eighteenth-century France prices and accounts were reckoned in livres, but there was in fact no physical currency called a livre. Currency was instead coined in *Louis* of gold or *écus* of silver, and the king and the Council of Finances determined how many livres a *Louis* of gold or an *écu* of silver was worth at any given time. The value of a *Louis* of gold, for example, dropped from twenty livres in 1713 to fourteen livres in 1715 as a result of eleven successive reevaluations. Unlike previous banknotes, which had been issued in livres, and whose value in gold or silver was thus vulnerable to wild fluctuations, Law's paper money was issued in terms of silver *écus*, and it could thus be redeemed for the same weight in silver as the original deposit, regardless of its value in livres.[13]

When his bank opened at the end of June 1716, Law acquired the credit and monetary instruments he needed to create a monopoly company that would control the overseas trade of France. His first opportunity came when the government, eager to exploit its newly acquired Louisiana Territory in North America, created a company for that purpose which absorbed the moribund Guinea Company. The government wanted to put the entire operation in the hands of John Law's bank. They envisaged 2 million livres of initial capital, but Law insisted on issuing 100 million livres' worth of shares that could be paid for at face value with government bonds, even though they were now trading at less than 30 percent of face value. He was financing the company, as he had financed his bank, with a kind of "junk bond" built on government debt.[14]

The new company, first called the Mississippi Company and later the Occident Company, came into existence on January 1, 1718. In September Law's Occident Company acquired the monopoly over the sale of New World tobacco in France, and in December it acquired the Senegal Company. To make the reach of his company truly global, Law also acquired the debt-ridden French East India Company and the China Company.[15] All of these entities were united into a single company called the Company of the Indies on May 23, 1719. The king granted the company a monopoly on trade "from Guinea to the Japanese archipelago, of colonizing especially the Cape of Good Hope, the east coast of Africa, that which is washed by the Red Sea, all the known islands of the Pacific, Persia, the Mogul empire, the kingdom of Siam, China, Japan, and South America."[16] Unlike its bankrupt predecessors, the Company of the Indies had a worldwide reach. It also enjoyed a variety of government subsidies and customs exemptions, and it was authorized to man its ships with conscripted sailors recruited by the Royal Navy's draft board.

Once the new company had been formed, it had to find a location for its home port and warehouses. Lorient, on the Brittany coast some thirty miles northwest of Vannes, was one of the options being considered. It had

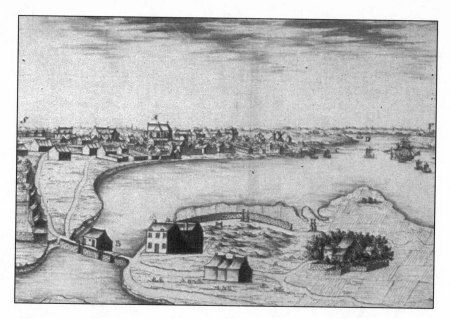

Figure 5.3   Lorient in 1724.

been the home port of the defunct French East Indies Company. Lorient was an object of scorn in 1719 because of its inconvenient location and its rudimentary facilities. One observer wrote scornfully of "L'Orient . . . which is, so to speak, at the end of the earth, and where there is not even enough room to lodge a dozen merchants."[17] In 1719 the town could still be described, as it had been over a decade earlier, as a collection "of mean earthen huts not surrounded by fences, covered with straw, made of sticks covered with earth."[18]

After the demise of the East Indies Company in 1706, privateering during the War of Spanish Succession kept the port alive. Privateers from Saint-Malo set up their headquarters in Lorient in order to avoid the British warships that patrolled the English Channel. At first, the war was a boon for the shipyards of Lorient,[19] but the failure of the privateers to pay wages on time made life difficult for the workers. A royal official remarked in 1709 that "the workers suffer such great misery that the majority of them have been forced to abandon Lorient." Two years later he warned, "If there are no new ship constructions or outfittings here soon, Lorient will become deserted, as it was before." After the War of the Spanish Succession ended in 1713, the privateers went back to Saint-Malo, and the port of Lorient limped along on minimal activity.[20]

In 1719, as the day of decision on a home port for the new Company of the Indies approached, those who opposed locating the company in Lorient spoke scornfully of its inconvenient location and the rudimentary nature of the town itself. The argument in favor of Lorient, on the other hand, was that the old company compound had shipbuilding and warehouse facilities which had proven valuable to the nation in time of war. Installing the company there was a way of keeping those facilities in operating condition in case they might be needed in the future. This argument won the day,[21] and the new company installed itself in Lorient at the end of 1719, taking over the shipping fleets of the companies it had absorbed.

On January 5, 1720, following his blatantly opportunistic conversion to Catholicism, John Law was named controller general of the finances of France. Less than two months later the royal bank was incorporated with the Company of the Indies, though the king remained the guarantor of its banknotes. John Law now held the post once occupied with great effect by Jean Baptiste Colbert, but he had more instruments of power at his disposal, controlling the bank, the finances of the kingdom, and its external commerce.[22] The former roving gambler and fugitive from a murder conviction had become the most powerful man in France.

As the value of Company of the Indies shares soared to sixty times their original value, a frenzy of speculation gripped the country. At the Place Louis-le-Grand, where Law lived, the square became covered with the shanties and tents of people who had come in from all the provinces of France and traded their jewels, goods, or even their horses for company shares or banknotes, while others traded shares for banknotes or vice versa according to the movements of the market. Seeing the elegant square turn into a boisterous encampment, John Law moved out to find some solitude in the Soissons mansion.[23]

Even though the new Company of the Indies had a worldwide reach, Law and the directors of the company were unsatisfied because it lacked a monopoly over the slave trade. By absorbing the Senegal Company, the Company of the Indies had gained a monopoly on the slave trade with Senegal, but the Atlantic coast of Africa from the Sierra Leone River to the Cape of Good Hope (the former monopoly territory of the Guinea Company) had been opened up to individual private traders by the royal *lettres patentes* of January 1716. It was the *négociants* of Nantes, above all, who had taken over the slave trade. In the years from 1716 to 1720 Nantes sent out sixty-seven slaving vessels, whereas the other authorized private slaving ports combined sent out only twenty-two and the Company of the Indies only three. In 1720 Law and the directors of the Company of the Indies began an intense lobbying effort to regain control of the Guinea trade.

Law knew that the major opposition to his ambitions to take over the slave trade would come from the *négociants* of Nantes. On that front, he had an unexpected ally. The representative of Nantes to the Council of Commerce, Jean Piou, had been a supporter of Law's various projects since 1715, when he had been one of only four people to argue in favor of Law's national central bank before the Council of Finances. When the Company of the Occident was formed two years later, Piou was named to the board of directors. In 1719, with the support of Law, Piou received a letter of nobility from the king. The creation of Law's Company of the Indies in 1719 created an obvious conflict of interest for Piou, so he resigned as the representative of Nantes and was immediately reappointed to the Council of Commerce as the representative of the Company of the Indies.[24] In the ongoing battle between the mercantilists and the capitalists, Piou had switched sides.

With the help of Jean Piou, the company's lobbying efforts met with success on September 27, 1720, when an order from the Royal Council of State revoked the rights of private traders along the Guinea coast and awarded the Company of the Indies exclusive and perpetual rights to the commerce of the Guinea coast from the Sierra Leone River to the Cape of Good Hope. The council justified its decision in terms that had long been used by partisans of monopoly companies. "Instead of the advantages that one hoped for from that freedom of trade," the council wrote, "it has created great problems. The competition among private traders who go to trade on that coast and their haste to acquire cargoes in order to reduce their daily operating expenses have caused the natives of those countries to drastically lower the prices that they pay for the merchandise that we bring them. And the private traders so overpurchase slaves, gold dust, and other products that we go there to buy, that trade has become ruined and impractical."[25]

The order from the Council of State forbade all private subjects of France from trading along the Guinea coast or from carrying any slaves, regardless of their origin, to the French islands in the Caribbean. The company was obligated to deliver three thousand slaves per year to the islands. In return, it received substantial customs exemptions and exemption from the tax of twenty livres per slave that private traders had been paying. Most importantly, the government would pay the company a bonus of thirteen livres for each slave delivered to the islands, and the navy would draft sailors for company slave ships. Slave trading was once again a directly subsidized business.

The company sent out thirteen slaving voyages to Africa during its first two years, but it did not have the shipping capacity to take full advantage of its monopoly over the slave trade. Rather than risk failure to meet its quota, the company gave permission to private traders, mostly from Nantes, to outfit slaving expeditions. In return, the traders paid the company twenty livres for each slave they delivered alive to the islands, an amount that was reduced to ten livres in 1720.[26] The private outfitters of Nantes responded energetically, launching seventeen slave ships in 1720, twenty-four ships in 1721, and twelve in 1722.[27]

By late 1722, however, the company had built up its shipping capacity to the point at which it could at last claim its legal monopoly. After January 1, 1723, it refused permission to all private traders and relied instead on its own ships sailing from Lorient. During the next three years the company sent out some sixty slave trading voyages.[28] The result of this decision was felt keenly by the private traders in Nantes. In 1723 only two slaving expeditions left Nantes, and during the subsequent two years none left at all. The mayor of Nantes, Gérard Mellier, complained bitterly that *négociants* were going bankrupt. Without the profits of the slave trade to subsidize it, the West Indies trade from Nantes was being conducted at a loss.[29] But the protests made by the mayor and private traders of Nantes were to no avail. The Company of the Indies was now king, and its domination of the slave trade was both "exclusive" and "perpetual."

The company that successfully reclaimed its monopoly over the slave trade in 1722 was very different in both its operations and its financial structure from the one that John Law had created only three years earlier. The major reason for the change was that Law had left France and was living in exile. The transformation in 1719 of John Law's Banque Générale into the Royal Bank of France, which issued paper money valued in livres

Figure 5.4   Crowds of desperate sellers at the Company of the Indies stock office in Paris.

of account instead of *écus* of silver, had unleashed a wave of speculation and reevaluation that came crashing down in the second half of 1720. As people flocked to the bank to convert their paper money into coins, bank openings became brief and sporadic. On days when the bank was open, people would begin lining up as early as two A.M., and even those who were lucky enough to get in were allowed to exchange only one ten-livre note per day. At the same time, shares in the Company of the Indies, which had reached an official high of ten thousand livres in the autumn of 1719 (with forward contracts selling for as much as fifteen thousand livres per share), had fallen to four thousand livres by the end of May 1720. Fortunes that had sprung up overnight disappeared just as quickly. Fortunes that had been built up over centuries disappeared in days or weeks.

There were riots in Paris. On July 10 some young men started throwing rocks at the bank, and one of them was shot dead by a guard. On July 17 a large crowd—one report says as many as fifteen thousand—gathered in front of the bank in the early morning darkness because they had heard that for the first time in over a week the bank would be open to convert ten-livre notes into coins. When the gates to the courtyard were opened at eight or nine in the morning, a dozen people were crushed or trampled in the stampede. At least one of them died. As the crowd dispersed, a large mob marched on the Palais Royal to take their grievances to the regent. When someone in the crowd spotted John Law's carriage leaving the Palais Royal, a mob followed it to Law's house at Place Louis-le-Grand. Discovering that Law was not in it, they beat the driver and broke his leg. Unable to force the gates of Law's house, the mob hurled cobblestones through his windows.[30]

Throughout late summer and fall, crowds of ruined stockholders regularly besieged the mansions of financiers at Place Louis-le-Grand. In the middle of the square, ruined investors formed a squatter settlement known as Camp Condé, where they lived in miserable tents around the statue of Louis XIV. During the night of December 21, 1720, John Law slipped across the border into Flanders in a closed carriage to begin the roving life that he had led prior to his move to Paris. The only wealth he managed to carry with him was a single diamond of mediocre quality.[31]

Only a few days after Law's flight, the assembly of the shareholders of the Company of the Indies met to elect a new board of directors to reorganize the company and put it back on a sound financial footing. One of the eight men chosen to oversee the reorganized company that would exercise its monopoly over the slave trade was a *négociant* from Nantes who had only recently moved to Paris and purchased the Morstin mansion overlooking the Quai Malaquais. That man was Joachim Descasaux.[32]

6

$\mathcal{T}$HE COUNT OF MAUREPAS was frustrated. As minister of the
marine and the holder of a seat on the Council of Commerce, he
was continually bombarded with requests from the *négociants* of Nantes
and the other former slaving ports to reopen the slave trade to private
traders. "Two major bankruptcies have just been declared in Nantes,"
wrote mayor Gérard Mellier angrily, "and we greatly fear that there will be
more. The reports from the colonies show losses ever since the gentlemen
of the Company of the Indies invoked the exclusive privilege that was
given to them to go to Guinea and buy slaves that they transport to the
colonies. It is in vain that we have protested to the council on behalf of the
private traders of Nantes, La Rochelle, and Bordeaux that the colonies will
fall along with the commerce of those cities."[1]

The Count of Maurepas was only twenty-three years old, and he had
taken over the Ministry of the Marine only two years before. Being so
young and coming to the post with no background in maritime affairs, he
did not feel bound by decisions and policies of his predecessors, but he had
no clear alternative to offer. He was described by one of his colleagues as
"superficial and incapable of serious and profound thinking, but gifted
with astute perception and intelligence that quickly unties the knot."[2] But
this knot was especially tangled. Although Maurepas strongly sympathized
with the advocates of private slave trading, he felt helpless to do anything,
given the company's legal monopoly over the slave trade. John Law had removed the Company of the Indies from the authority of the minister of

Figure 6.1   The Count of Maurepas.

the marine and placed it under the authority of the controller general, who, at the time, was Law himself.

Now, however, Maurepas had received information from the West Indies that gave him new leverage against the company. In the fall of 1724 he wrote two reports to the controller general attacking the performance of the company and arguing for reopening the slave trade to private traders. He began his first report by observing that the wealth of France's Caribbean colonies lay in the sugar, indigo, cocoa, and cotton that they produced. They could not produce these products, he noted, "but by means of slaves. It is by their work and their sweat . . . that the colonies produce these goods." The problem, Maurepas noted, was that the loss of slaves through mortality, disability, and flight had been much greater than their natural increase. As a result, the islands needed "an annual infusion of blacks." Without that, he wrote, "production will fall and cause a consider- able decrease in the fortunes of the planters, in the commerce of the king- dom, and in the customs revenues of the king. The planters even fear that if the production of their lands diminishes, the foodstuffs and merchandise that they need daily will no longer be brought from France, leaving them in a state of famine." Maurepas calculated that Martinique, Guadeloupe, Granada, and Marie-Galante together needed ninety-three hundred new slaves annually for maintaining and expanding production, more than three times the number that the Company of the Indies was obligated by its charter to furnish.

Because of the unmet demand for slaves, a huge clandestine slave trade, mainly carried on by the Dutch, had arisen. The *intendant* of Martinique reported that the illegal commerce was being carried out in all regions of the island with the full complicity of its inhabitants, who had become very adept at smuggling and hiding slaves. The Company of the Indies, the *in- tendant* complained, did not bring even a quarter of the number of slaves needed for the plantations.[3]

The company replied that it would be difficult to increase its delivery of slaves to the islands because it had been losing money on its slaving opera- tions and was heavily in debt. That admission gave Maurepas an opening for a new attack the company's monopoly. In his second memorandum he outlined his true agenda: "to reestablish the freedom of trade in blacks."[4] Using his calculation that the islands needed ninety-three hundred new slaves per year, he argued that such an expansion of the slave trade would not be profitable to the company.

His calculations went as follows: to deliver ninety-three hundred slaves alive to the islands each year, the company would have to purchase eleven thousand slaves to allow for deaths in transit. They would need to send out twenty-eight to thirty ships per year, which would force them to invest in new ships and make a considerable investment in trade goods to purchase the slaves in Africa. After adding up the costs and income on a sample balance sheet, he calculated that at best the company would make a profit of 14 percent. But if in the cost of credit and losses from accidents were factored in, "far from being profitable for the company, there will instead be a loss."

Maurepas then proposed that the company did not need to abandon its participation in the slave trade but should instead open it up to all private traders who agreed to pay the company a fee of twenty livres for each slave they carried. This system, he argued, would generate a profit of over 120,000 livres per year for the Company of the Indies.

Maurepas had some unexpected allies; many of the company's shareholders had come to believe that the slave trade would bring about the total ruin of the company.[5] Contrary to popular belief, they claimed, there were no large profits to be made in the trade in slaves. The directors of the company responded by asking the obvious question: If the slave trade were so unprofitable, then why were the private traders so eager to enter it? The cost advantages were actually on the side of the company, they claimed. The conscripted crews of company ships cost a third less than the privately engaged crews of the independent slave traders, and the power of buying in bulk made it possible for the company to outfit ships with trade goods more cheaply than could private traders.

The major argument raised by the shareholders was that private traders created a kind of synergy between the direct trade that France carried on with its Caribbean colonies and the slave trade. The amount of sugar received for a shipload of slaves was about twice as much as the ship could carry. Private traders, the shareholders argued, retrieved the surplus sugar by sending out ships loaded with merchandise from France that traveled directly to the West Indies. Since the average amount of sugar received in return for a shipload of French goods filled only one-third of the ship, the direct trading ships had empty cargo space for carrying back the excess sugar from slaving expeditions.[6]

The company could not match this synergy, argued the shareholders, because its ships sailed the triangular route exclusively. Even though the company had occasionally taken the drastic and inefficient measure of sending out empty ships to the West Indies to pick up excess sugar, it had gotten hopelessly behind in collecting its debts. Company of the Indies slave ships sometimes deposited their loads of slaves in Martinique and returned home empty if the purchasers had no sugar on hand.[7] The shareholders claimed that the company was already owed 5 million livres in undelivered sugar, and that soon the uncollected debt would reach 8 million livres. In any given year, the company recovered only about a third of the 4–5 million livres it invested in the slave trade.

Having made their arguments against the Company of the Indies monopoly on the slave trade, the shareholders proposed their solution. The company, they suggested, should abandon the slave trade and subcontract out all of the Guinea trade to private traders in return for a fee of thirty livres per slave. The shareholders did not favor free competition because they believed that it had caused problems after trade was opened up in 1716. Free competition, they argued, had driven up prices and had increased the death rates of sailors along the coast of Africa because of the long waits to complete their cargoes. The solution, they said, was to give a quota to each city that had been permitted to trade in slaves in 1716 (Nantes, Bordeaux, La Rochelle, Rouen) and to coordinate monthly schedules of ship departures so as to avoid congestion in the slaving ports of Guinea. At Whydah, where the Company of the Indies maintained a fort, all slaves should be purchased by the company and resold to private slaving ships for an average profit of sixty livres per slave. The company would receive as much as 600,000 livres per year by furnishing slaves to private traders.

The directors of the company angrily rejected the proposal on the grounds that such an arrangement would reduce the company to the role of a subcontractor for private slave traders. Moreover, they claimed that there were considerable profits to be made in the slave trade. The best proof of its profitability, they argued, was the clamor of the traders of Nantes seeking permission to participate.

There was another problem with the company's slave trade that was perhaps more decisive than the issues raised by the shareholders. Although the company vessels, averaging some three hundred tons, were over twice as large as the average independent slave ship, they carried only 40 percent more slaves. In terms of carrying efficiency, the company was loading only one slave per ton of capacity as opposed to its optimal goal of two. This situation had arisen because the company ships purchased slaves only at the company forts in Senegal and Whydah. If there were no more slaves to be purchased and the captain was getting impatient, he simply sailed for the Caribbean instead of seeking slaves elsewhere along the African coast. Similarly, the failure to collect full loads of sugar in Martinique and Saint Domingue resulted from the eagerness of captains and their conscripted crews to go back to France rather than wait for the next harvest. The company's incentive system gave captains a bonus for each slave that they delivered to the islands, not for each barrel of sugar delivered to France. The company's directors admitted that they had morale problems, blaming the situation on bad management and poorly motivated crews.[8]

In August 1725, after monopolizing the French slave trade for less than three years, the directors of the Company of the Indies reversed themselves and reinstated the system of giving permission to private slave traders. In making this decision, they tacitly admitted that Maurepas and the dissident shareholders were right. The large ships and limited routes favored by the company were not profitable, and the directors apparently found no easy way to make them so. Conscripted company crews were not willing to wait for months in distant ports for full cargoes of slaves or full loads of sugar. Thus the philosophical debate between the mercantilist monopolists and the private-enterprise capitalists ultimately came down to mundane issues of ship size, trade routes, company organization, and debt collection.

The Company of the Indies opened up the slave trade to private traders in the areas south of the Sierra Leone River, but it retained its monopoly over trade with Senegal and maintained its fort at Whydah. The number of slaving voyages outfitted by the company dropped from eighteen in 1725 to four in 1726. During the five years after abandoning its monopoly, the company sent out twenty-two slaving ships that carried over seven thousand slaves. About two-thirds of those ships went to its monopoly area of Senegal, and the remaining third went to the company fort in Whydah. As before, the company ships were much larger than most private slave trading ships of the time, averaging around 275 tons.[9] In financial terms, the decision to open up the slave trade to private traders was a profitable one: in 1727 the company earned 350,000 livres from the commissions paid by private slave traders, whereas it lost 260,000 livres on its monopoly possession of Senegal.[10]

With the decision of the Company of the Indies to open up the slave trade to private traders, the French slave trade shifted definitively from a company affair to a private enterprise affair. The *négociants* of Nantes sent eight permission requests to the company headquarters before the end of the year, and Nantes quickly reestablished itself as the leading slave trading port in France. Between 1726, when it reentered the slave trade, and 1731, when the *Diligent* began its voyage from Vannes, Nantes sent out eighty-three ships that carried more than twenty-four thousand captive Africans to the French islands of the New World. This represented 55 percent of the total French slave trade for those years.[11] In contrast to the company ships, which loaded slaves only at the company forts in Senegal and Whydah, the private traders bought slaves in a variety of places in West and Central Africa. This added flexibility was the key to their success.

The company's decision to abandon its monopoly turned out to be profitable for all parties concerned. Nantes experienced an unprecedented spurt of construction and economic growth, and Lorient, with the Company of the Indies freed from the losses it had incurred in the slave trade, was on the brink of unparalleled expansion. Lying almost obscured between those two cities was the city of Vannes, where the Billy brothers and other prominent *négociants* and local officials enviously watched events unfold and began to calculate how they could share in the profits.

PART 3

*Outfitting
a Slaver*

7

S THE CLOCKS OF Vannes struck 6:00 A.M. on May 31, 1731, the sailors on the *Diligent* were up on the yards unfurling the fore and main topsails to catch the slight breeze that had arisen from the east-northeast. Edging away from the masts with their bare feet on the footropes and their bodies leaning on the yards, they untied the gaskets that held the sails tightly furled. As the sails dropped down from the yards, other sailors secured the ropes that held their lower corners in place.[1]

A group of sailors took hold of the line that raised the main topsail yard to its sailing position. To help them pull in rhythm, they sang a sea shanty. The leader called out, and then the others joined in as they hauled on the line. When the yard reached its proper position, the hauling and the singing stopped instantly, even if the verse was not finished. The song was a work tool, not an amusement.

The wind blew from the port city of Vannes, at the northeastern edge of the Gulf of Morbihan, toward the narrow opening on the southwestern edge of the gulf that gave ships access to the Atlantic Ocean. The distance across the gulf from Vannes to the open sea was eleven miles, but the route traveled by ships was considerably longer. The waters of the gulf were so shallow that ships traversed it by following a serpentine underwater channel known as the "river" of Morbihan. Ships that strayed from the channel risked running aground on shallow shoals and sand banks or striking a submerged rock. Even English pirates avoided the Gulf of Morbihan for fear of running aground, but the *Diligent* had a local pilot on board to safely navigate the "river" and break free to the open sea.[2]

Figure 7.1   Durand's drawing of the *Diligent*.

At 7:30 A.M. Captain Pierre Mary ordered the crew to weigh anchor. "Silence sailors!" he called out to prepare them to receive their orders. "Pilot, right the helm," he ordered. Then he called out, "Place the bars into the capstan." Working almost as one, eight sailors inserted wooden bars into pigeonholes in the capstan and began to walk in a tight circle, singing lustily to maintain their rhythm. Two other sailors worked to keep the "tail" of the anchor line, which had been wrapped two times around the capstan, taut, while another wound the retrieved line into large coils.[3] The 550-pound anchor broke free of the sandy bottom, and the ship began to move. The crew members who were aloft scrambled to finish setting the sails before the ship got swept backward by the incoming tide. Suddenly everything was happening at once.

The tide began rising just as the ship left its mooring, sending a hundred million cubic meters of seawater per hour through the thousand-yard-wide opening from the Atlantic. The "river" of Vannes began flowing backward! With the wind and the current moving in exactly opposite directions, the progress of the *Diligent* depended on whichever was stronger.

For two and a half hours the ship advanced ever so slowly as the wispy breeze fought against the currents created by the incoming tide. Shortly after 10:00 A.M., the breeze died down to a dead calm. They had traveled less than two miles. To keep from being swept aground by the current, they dropped anchor into the sandy seabed thirty feet below.[4]

Standing on the quarterdeck, Guillaume and François Billy, the owners of the *Diligent*, were increasingly frustrated. If all had gone according to schedule, they would be out of the Gulf of Morbihan and approaching Belle Ile, where they planned to disembark after seeing the ship off on its maiden voyage to Africa. This was not quite the triumphant departure they had envisioned.

Vannes was an unlikely port for a slave ship to sail from. Unlike the neighboring ports of Nantes and Lorient, whose economies were "so unconnected with the country," Vannes was a quintessential French market town with an economy that was deeply embedded in the social hierarchy of eighteenth-century France. As the second largest exporter of grain in Brittany, Vannes lived off the wheat and rye produced by the peasants in its hinterland.

Despite the surplus of the countryside, many of the peasants lived in dire poverty. Ninety percent of them were landless sharecroppers who were lucky to keep half the grain they produced after paying rent, taxes, and tithes, and a third of the peasants lived just above the hunger line in situations whereby even minor drops in production or prices could reduce them to famine. Arthur Young described some peasant cottages in Brittany as "miserable heaps of dirt with no glass and scarcely any light." He noted that the women were "furrowed without age by labor to the utter extinction of all softness of their sex" because they worked "harder than the horses."[5]

After each harvest, the peasants brought the wheat and rye that they owed their landlords to designated collection points. Then it was taken to Vannes in wagons for sale to grain dealers who shipped it out by sea. By the beginning of the eighteenth century many of the nobles had abandoned their rural chateaux and manor houses to live inside the walled city in Vannes. The grain trade turned the rents-in-kind that they received from the peasants into the cash that supported their noble lifestyles. The *intendant* of Brittany summed up the situation succinctly when he noted that peasants lived off the local markets, whereas the nobility lived off exports.[6] The peasants, nobles, and grain merchants all played vital roles in keeping the system going.

Figure 7.2   Breton peasants during wheat harvest.

The system was on daily display at the large flourmill at the Place des Lyces in the center of Vannes near the city hall. The square was crowded with oxcarts and men who had business at the mill. Some of them were well-dressed merchants, but most wore the flat-brimmed hats, baggy knee breeches, and wooden shoes of Breton peasants. In the cacophony of voices and shouts, French words were frequently drowned out by peasants speaking Breton and Gallo, two languages with origins in the British Isles that dominated the surrounding countryside. Grain or flour for export was taken down St. Vincent Street and through St. Vincent's Gate to the port.

Guillaume and François Billy were grain merchants, as their father had been before them. They lived together in the Billy family house located just outside the city walls by the port. By the standards of Vannes, it was a grand house with a great room adorned by six chandeliers, a large landscape painting, and a large tapestry. To facilitate loading the grain, their father, Robert Billy, had personally built an eighty-foot stone quay behind his house, even though the port was too silted up to receive anything except

Figure 7.3   Port of Vannes in the early eighteenth century. Billy house is at the right corner of the port.

small, flat-bottomed barges called *chalans* that ferried grain to ships an-chored in the Gulf of Morbihan. When the elder Billy died in 1722, his granaries contained over fifty tons of wheat and ninety tons of rye, and his desk contained banknotes worth over thirty thousand livres. Robert Billy had tempered his trading activities with charity. When his sons Guillaume and François were baptized, he chose illiterate indigents from the charity hospital to be their godparents, thus establishing lifelong bonds with the poor.[7]

In some ways, Guillaume Billy had followed in his father's footsteps. He invested in the grain trade in Vannes and had garnered an appointment as a judge at the consulate court following his father's death. But he also had ambitions in the wider world, and he married the daughter of a bourgeois landowner living in Nantes. One difference between Guillaume Billy and his father was evident at the baptism of Guillaume's daughter on September

26, 1727. Instead of naming an indigent person from the charity hospital to be her godfather, he chose Jean Baptiste Fournier, sieur of Guillardays and the king's prosecutor for the fortified town of Guerande.[8] The choice signaled a kind of ambition and social climbing that his father had disdained.

Judging from the amount of capitation tax they paid, the Billy brothers were among the wealthiest men in Vannes. Only fifteen people in the entire city paid higher tax bills than Guillaume. If his tax bill and François's had been combined, then only two people in the city paid higher taxes than the Billy brothers.[9] Still, merchants such as Guillaume Billy were despised and shunned by the nobles living in the walled city. The traveler La Vallée described high society in Vannes as divided into two separate castes that did not interact socially—the society of the nobility and the "society of the port," as the nobles referred to the bourgeoisie. Any nobleman who ate or danced with a member of the bourgeoisie, claimed La Vallée with some exaggeration and caricature, would be rejected from noble society.[10]

What kept the noblemen from engaging in trade was not only disdain for commerce but also fear of losing their privileges (or at least having them suspended) if they engaged in trade. Even though the king's edict of December 1701 had permitted noblemen to engage in wholesale commerce by land or sea without losing their noble titles and privileges, it ran afoul of the laws and customs of Brittany.[11] Article 561 of the Coutume de Bretagne explicitly stated that if a nobleman engaged in trade, his noble privileges would be suspended.[12]

Successful merchants, however, could gain inheritable noble status without giving up trade by getting a letter of nobility from the king. Joachim Descasaux of Nantes had received such a letter from King Louis XIV in 1703 after arguing before the Council of Commerce: "If nobility resides in virtue, in integrity, and in good faith, then it belongs to the *négociants*; one cannot honor or esteem them too much."[13] It did not go unnoticed that Descasaux's best friend in Paris, the banker Samuel Bernard, was also the major creditor of the king.

Wealthy traders could also gain inheritable nobility by purchasing a position as "counselor secretary of the king at the Chancellerie of Brittany." Between 1700 and 1788 over fifty of these offices were purchased by slave traders from Nantes and Saint-Malo. One of them was René Montaudoin from Nantes, the biggest slave trader in France, who used his profits to purchase his nobility and buy up the lands and manors of impoverished nobles. By offering substantial dowries, he married off three of his daughters into the nobility. During the eighteenth century nearly a hundred outfitters of slave ships in Nantes carried noble titles, but only two of them came from the old landed nobility. The business methods of the *négociants* may have been capitalist, but their social goals often remained feudal.[14]

Although Guillaume Billy was well off by the standards of Vannes, he had neither the wealth nor the connections necessary to move into the ranks of the nobility. Instead, he contented himself with using of the title "noble man" in legal documents and parish records, an act of pretension that revealed his bourgeois status. In 1711 the *parlement* of Brittany officially defined the term "noble man": "It is not a mark of nobility; it is commonly used by the bourgeoisie."[15]

The major barrier that stood in the way of Guillaume Billy's ambitions was the city of Vannes itself. While the neighboring city of Nantes, with its freewheeling merchant capitalism, and Lorient, the home of the largest monopoly company in the history of France, were both exploding with population growth and economic activity, Vannes was a city in decline. The population dropped from twelve thousand at the beginning of the century to nine thousand in 1733, while at the same time the number of professionals fell by over 40 percent and the number of merchants dropped by over a third. Inside the walled city, revenue from the capitation tax, which was a tax on total wealth, declined by nearly half, and the revenue from the merchant quarter dropped 44 percent.[16]

The economic decline of Vannes was largely the result of a crisis in the grain trade. When Guillaume Billy was born in 1695, ships from Vannes carried grain to Spain and Portugal, and they returned with oranges, lemons, iron, and the balance in letters of exchange drawn on Paris banks. But in the wake of the famines of 1698 and 1709 the French government outlawed the export of grain to foreign countries, and the merchants of Vannes had to content themselves with shipping grain to Bordeaux, Bayonne, and Normandy. When the *intendant* of Brittany discovered in 1724 that merchants who claimed to be sailing for other ports in France were really smuggling grain to foreign ports, he prohibited all shipments of grain from Brittany to other provinces, effectively shutting down grain exports from Vannes.[17]

The town council, which included members of the judiciary, the church, the nobility, and the bourgeoisie, met at city hall on November 10, 1728, to protest the decision. The grain trade, they contended, "is the only substantial economic activity in the region, and without it people will cry out from famine." They argued that the ban was hurting all the inhabitants of Vannes, not just the wealthy ones. If the judges, clergy, nobility, and bourgeoisie were deprived of their income from the grain trade, they reasoned, then they would not be able to hire artisans to work for them or give charity to the poor. Knowing that they had very few options, they appointed a committee to draft a letter to the lieutenant general of Brittany even though they had no illusions about its success.[18]

8

HE GRAIN MERCHANTS OF Vannes watched the economic expansion in nearby Nantes and Lorient while the population of their own city dwindled. They could not avoid thinking that Vannes might also enjoy economic growth if only they had permission to participate in the trade to the French West Indies. The royal decree of April 1717, which regulated commerce between France and its Caribbean colonies, had limited direct trade with the islands to merchants from thirteen ports, including Nantes but not Vannes. Since then, Marseille and Dunkerque had received authorization as well. *Négociants* from authorized ports had the right to export necessary food and ammunition for the islands, including Irish salted beef, free of export duties.[1] We don't know if the idea of turning Vannes into a port that sent out slave ships was already on the minds of the merchants in 1728 or whether that idea came up later, but applying for authorization to participate in the island trade was a logical first step for any group that ultimately hoped to enter the slave trade.

The committee set up by the town council on November 10 duly filed its letter of protest against the restrictions on the grain trade, but it also made an end run around the *intendant* of Brittany and the lieutenant general by applying directly to the Council of Commerce in Versailles for permission to conduct trade with the French islands of the West Indies. The petition claimed that Vannes had a harbor only one league from the city that could shelter more than fifty ships in bad weather. This was a rather large exaggeration. Though the Gulf of Morbihan had the appearance of an inland sea, most of its waters were too shallow for large ships, and the deeper waters were concentrated in the serpentine channel. The petitioners also wrote that the ship *St. Pierre* was already sitting in the Gulf of Morbihan loaded with salted beef, flour, wine, brandy, cloth, and other goods, just waiting for permission to sail to the West Indies.[2]

When the Council of Commerce met in Versailles on November 25, 1728, to discuss the request, the royal customs officials opposed it. Fifteen port cities in France already had permission to trade with the West Indies, and the customs officials saw no need to increase the number. In any case, they argued, Vannes was an unworthy candidate because there was no proof that it could significantly develop its overseas trade. Finally, they noted that giving the requested customs exemptions would result in loss of revenue to the customs bureau.[3]

A memorandum read earlier at that same meeting noted with alarm that British settlers from New England were carrying out a brisk trade in timber, boards, horses, mules, and fresh meat with the French West Indies. The French needed to take aggressive action to increase their trade with the West Indies, and the Council of Commerce decided that approving the Vannes petition was a step in that direction. On December 21 the King's Council of State issued an order permitting the merchants of Vannes to "conduct trade with the French islands and colonies." The council noted the zeal of the merchants of Vannes and repeated the bogus claim that Vannes had a harbor that could hold fifty ships. They wrote that they were permitting the *St. Pierre* to sail to the West Indies in hope that other outfitters would follow its example.[4] The order was followed fifteen months later by a handwritten order signed by King Louis XV himself.[5]

If the claim that the Gulf of Morbihan could shelter fifty ships was exaggerated, so too was the claim that the *St. Pierre* was loaded and ready to sail. Though Guillaume Billy and his neighbor Michel Buat de la Croix worked feverishly on behalf of the other six partners to organize and outfit the voyage, nearly two months passed before the *St. Pierre* set out for Martinique. This was a simple trading voyage that carried goods from France to Martinique and returned with sugar and cotton produced on the island, but it was not unrelated to the slave trade. The *St. Pierre* returned to Vannes fourteen months later carrying an eighteen-year-old African named La Fleur who had been born in Timbo, in the Fuuta Jalon region of West Africa, and taken to Martinique as a slave. Under the provisions of the edict of October 1716, he was now being sent to Vannes to receive instruction in the Catholic religion and learn a trade. He was the first black slave that the people of Vannes had ever seen.[6]

The voyage of the *St. Pierre* was also related to the slave trade in another way. A load of African slaves arriving in the islands could be traded for nearly twice as much sugar as the ship could carry back to France. Conversely, ships arriving in the direct trade generally carried low-value cargoes that only bought enough sugar to fill one-third of their holds. It took the unused cargo space of approximately two direct trading voyages to carry back the excess sugar from a single slave trading voyage. The slave trade thus subsidized the direct trade, and in return the direct trade solved the problem of how to transport the excess sugar received by the slave traders.[7]

The money that direct trading vessels earned by carrying back sugar belonging to slave traders could make the crucial difference between profit and loss. The judge and consuls of Nantes complained that the direct trade had become "ruinous" because of high duties and unfavorable exchange rates for their trade goods. In a report, they gave several hypothetical examples of how it had become unprofitable. One example concerned a ship carrying ordinary French cloth that was exchanged in the islands for low-grade "head" sugar that, after duties and expenses, resulted in a loss for the voyage of 25 percent. A ship that traded the same cloth for high-grade clayed sugar would lose five livres per thousand, or 0.5 percent.[8] If their calculations were even roughly accurate, then carrying sugar for slave traders was what kept the direct trade profitable.

Even before the *St. Pierre* had returned from its maiden voyage to Martinique, a second departure from Vannes was already in preparation. On July 20, 1729, a group of partners headed by Alexander Corbun, a merchant, broker, and erstwhile sea captain who lived in nearby Redon, purchased the three-masted ship *Marie-Joseph*. It had been constructed in Pennerf, just down the coast from Vannes, by the master carpenter Rollando. Corbun brought with him Hubert de la Massuë, another investor from Redon. The other investors were all from Vannes: Joseph-Ange Dubodan, a grain merchant and judge on the consular court who carried a purchased title of nobility; Jean-Baptiste Lucas, prosecutor for the présidial court and administrator of the general hospital; Charles Delourme, the son of a well-known architect; Charles Grané, a large bourgeois landowner; the widow Brunet, whose husband had been a wealthy wine merchant; and Guillaume Billy. The buyers changed the name of the vessel to the *Diligent*.[9]

Refitting the ship, hiring a crew, and loading the merchandise for its first trip to Martinique took nearly nine months. Since Vannes had no tradition of launching long-distance voyages, the owners had to look elsewhere for a captain. The small fishing village of Le Croisic, near the mouth of the Loire, had a formidable reputation for producing captains, ships' officers, and seamen. The owners hired Pierre Mary, forty-three years old and from Le Croisic, to be the captain and young Robert Durand, also from Le Croisic, to be the second captain. The ship's pilot was hired from Redon, and the mate and gunner were hired from Le Croisic. Ten of the crew members came from the islands and towns of the Gulf of Morbihan, and the three cabin boys came from Vannes. The rest of the crew of twenty-seven came from various places along the Brittany coast.[10] The *Diligent* left for Martinique on March 6, 1730. Unlike the accident-plagued *St. Pierre*, which took fourteen months to complete its voyage, the *Diligent* made the round trip in only five months.

With their success in the West Indies trade, many of the investors who had purchased the *St. Pierre* and the *Diligent* began to negotiate to purchase the *Concorde*, a ninety-eight-ton ship armed with ten cannons built in Redon by the master carpenter Priou. But this time Guillaume Billy was joined by his younger brother François. The *Concorde* left for Martinique on June 17, 1730.[11]

Sometime during the fall of 1730, when the *St. Pierre* and the *Diligent* had both returned from their initial voyages to Martinique, the Billy brothers began to think seriously about entering the slave trade. Perhaps they felt that their success in launching two voyages toward Martinique had prepared them for the longer and more complex project of launching a slaving vessel. Perhaps they were disappointed at the profits made by the *St. Pierre* and the *Diligent* on their direct voyages to Martinique.

The Billy brothers had been minor investors in the transatlantic ships that sailed from Vannes. But late in 1730 they made their first move toward becoming major investors and outfitters of a slaving voyage when they purchased the *Diligent* from the other partners for 18,500 livres. The *Diligent* was a used ship, but it was seaworthy and a bargain compared with the

Concorde, which had cost over 28,000 livres. Following the common practice of spreading the risk, the Billy brothers put up 30 percent apiece and
went in with two other partners to make up the balance. Michel Buat de
la Croix, their next-door neighbor and partner in the *Concorde* and *St.
Pierre*, put up 30 percent, and Hubert de la Massuë from Redon, one of the
original investors in the *Diligent*, put up the remaining 10 percent. Guillaume Billy agreed to serve as the outfitter and secure a crew and cargo.
For his efforts he received a commission of five hundred livres. They sealed
the deal on January 8, 1731, and immediately began to plan for sending out
the first slave ship ever outfitted in Vannes.[12]

9

$\mathcal{T}$HE ROYAL DECREE OF January 1716, which had given the cities of Nantes, Bordeaux, Rouen, and La Rochelle permission to send out slaving voyages, was totally separate from the decree of April 1717, which had authorized thirteen French cities to trade directly with the French colonies in the West Indies. The authorization that Vannes had received from the King's Council and King Louis XV applied only to the West Indies trade and made no mention of the Guinea trade. Guillaume Billy used a backdoor: by obtaining a subcontracting agreement from the Company of the Indies in Lorient, he could send out a slaving voyage under the legal authority of the company. Although he was in legally murky territory, no royal officials tried to stop the voyage.[1]

The Company of the Indies now allowed private slave traders to sail to Africa under subcontracts, but it still had a royal monopoly on the Africa trade and could seize any ship that lacked proper papers. The owners of the *Diligent* had to sign two forms.[2] The first form stipulated that they were free to trade for slaves, gold, or other merchandise between the Sierra Leone River and the Cape of Good Hope, but they could not land anywhere along the African coast between Cape Blanc and the Sierra Leone River, as this region was still the monopoly of the company. If a storm or other troubles forced them to land in the forbidden region, officers of the company had permission to search the vessel to make sure it had not engaged in trade. If they traded for slaves in Whydah (where the company maintained a post but which was outside the company's monopoly territory), they were to present their permission papers to the director before beginning trade. After trading in Africa, the *Diligent* was to take the slaves directly to the French colonies in the Caribbean.

In the second form, the Billy brothers promised to pay the company ten livres for each slave, regardless of sex or age, that they delivered alive to the islands. In return, the ship would receive all the customs exemptions enjoyed by the company, except that the company would receive the thirteen-livre bonus from the government for each slave that the *Diligent* delivered. In effect, the company got twenty-three livres for each slave: ten livres from the outfitters of the ship and thirteen livres from the government.[3]

Guillaume Billy also hired a slaving crew. He asked Captain Pierre Mary, who had experience in the slave trade, to stay on as captain and recruit a crew that was more experienced in slave trading. Instead of asking Robert Durand to serve as second captain, as he had done on the *Diligent's* voyage to Martinique, Captain Mary recruited his brother-in-law from Le Croisic, Pierre Valteau, as second captain and demoted Robert Durand to first lieutenant, making him third in the chain of command. With the exception of the two ship's doctors, all of the officers came from Le Croisic, as did most of the members of the crew. Only a cooper, the accordion player, and the two cabin boys were from Vannes.[4]

The shift in the composition of the crew may well indicate that the local sailors were reluctant to go on a slaving mission. The voyage would last fifteen months, and the increased dangers from pirates, tropical diseases, and shipboard slave revolts made it risky. Nearly one crew member in four died on French slaving voyages in 1731, and even the Company of the Indies complained that the high mortality of crews on its slave ships had led to a shortage of sailors.[5] As compensation for the risk, crew members on slaving voyages got higher salaries: Captain Mary received a pay raise from one hundred livres per month to 120, the second captain went from fifty to eighty livres, and ordinary sailors went from twenty-five livres to thirty.

Guillaume Billy most likely traveled to Nantes to pick out merchandise for the *Diligent* and find out what the slave traders of Nantes were carrying. African consumers in the slaving ports of West Africa were extremely sophisticated, and fashions in cloth and other consumer goods changed rapidly. Slave traders who went to Africa with the wrong goods had a hard time finding customers. Billy was no stranger to Nantes; his wife's family lived there, as did some of his maternal relatives.

One of the places that Guillaume Billy visited in Nantes was the new Company of the Indies warehouse on the Quai de Chézine, where he purchased Indian cloth and cowry shells to fill the hold of the *Diligent*. The company conducted its sales in Nantes even though its ships sailed from Lorient. The Indian cottons had a bewildering variety of names: salempouri, guinée, baffeta, limancas, allibani, coupi, guigan, chalbasis, and others. Some were white, some were solid colors, and others were decorated with multicolored stripes and designs. The problem was to pick just the styles and colors that were in demand along the Guinea coast of Africa that year. After much consultation, he purchased limancas (a fine striped cloth from the Coromandel coast), salempouri blue (cotton cloth of varying quality), and "Indian cloth" (a general term for printed cottons, calicoes, and chintzes).

The warehouse also contained wooden barrels filled with cowry shells. Many tons of cowry shells were brought each year from the Maldive Islands (near India) on Company of the Indies ships. They were shoveled loosely into the holds of the ships to serve as ballast and as packing material between the barrels of porcelain. When the ships arrived in France, the cowries were packed into barrels to be sent to the Slave Coast of West Africa.[6] Over 40 percent of the value of the trade goods carried by the *Diligent* was made up by cloth and cowries from India. So crucial had Indian products become that in 1718 a group of *négociants* in Nantes petitioned the Council of Commerce for permission to send out two ships to India each year for the sole purpose of bringing back cowry shells and Indian cloth to use in the slave trade.[7]

Of the 37,782 livres in trade goods that Guillaume Billy purchased for the slaving voyage of the *Diligent*, cloth accounted for almost a third of the total value. Nearly two-thirds of the cloth was platilles, a very white linen cloth that French traders imported from Hamburg.[8] The rest was Indian cloth from the warehouse of the Company of the Indies. Close to another third of the value of the cargo consisted of 7,050 pounds of cowry shells packed into thirty barrels.[9] The cowry shells served as a currency along the Slave Coast of West Africa. In addition to being a necessary trade good for purchasing slaves, they were very useful for purchasing small items along certain sections of the African coast. At Jakin, for example, an egg cost twenty cowries in 1731 and a banana cost thirty.

Nearly a quarter of the total value of the cargo was made up of nine hundred kegs of brandy, which came mostly from the Loire valley near

Nantes, though some of them may have come from Bordeaux. French brandy was eighty-five proof and could be watered down before sale to make it more like the fifty proof brandy from Holland.[10] Guns and ammunition accounted for nearly 14 percent. There were eight cases containing twenty-five flintlock muskets apiece, a barrel of flints for muskets, and forty barrels of gunpowder. These arms had almost certainly come from Holland via Nantes, as the French did not begin to manufacture trade rifles until 1739. Rounding out the list of trade goods were sixteen cases of long smoking pipes from Holland and ninety-nine bars of Swedish iron.

Though the voyage of the *Diligent* gave a boost to the wine growers and brandy makers of Nantes and Bordeaux, slave trading voyages did little to support French industry. Instead, the *Diligent* was supporting the cloth industries of India and Hamburg, cowry diving in the Maldive Islands, the firearms and pipe industries of Holland, and the iron industry in Sweden. French slave traders were middlemen in a vast system of international exchange that stretched from India to the Caribbean. Only about a quarter of the total value of the *Diligent's* merchandise came from France itself.

The merchandise was taken in small sailing vessels to the Gulf of Morbihan, where the *Diligent* was sitting at anchor just off the western arm of the Ile aux Moines, some six miles from the port of Vannes. It was one of the few places in the Gulf of Morbihan that had water deep enough to accommodate a ship that drew twelve and a half feet of water when fully loaded. The small boats pulled alongside the *Diligent,* and the trade goods were hoisted up by means of ropes and pulleys fastened to the *Diligent's* yards and then lowered through the hatch on the *Diligent's* main deck. It could take months to load a ship.

In addition to loading the trade goods, they also had to load enough supplies to feed the crew. The *Diligent* took fifteen tons of firewood, three-quarters of which would be used for baking bread on the voyage, and the other quarter for cooking. It carried twenty-two barrels of flour, which would allow the crew to have fresh bread one day out of three. On the other days they would eat hard biscuits, and they brought along eleven thousand of them. The staple food for both crew members and slaves would be a souplike gruel made from fava beans, and the *Diligent* carried fifteen tons of beans. They carried thirty-four barrels of salted beef from Ireland, twelve smoked hams, and twelve cheeses. For drink they had thirty-four barrels of white wine and twelve barrels of red wine. Fresh water was a major problem. Robert Durand did not record how many barrels of water were put on board, but if they followed the rule of thumb used by the Company of the Indies, they loaded three quarts of water per person per day for as many days as they would be at sea before replenishing their supplies.[11]

A variety of other supplies for the *Diligent* were being loaded as well. There were staves and hoops for barrels, compasses and clocks for navigation, a doctor's chest, mattresses and blankets for the sick, supplies for the kitchen, and extra ropes. Other supplies were more sinister. There were 150 slave irons with locks and keys manufactured in Nantes by the Taquet brothers. Each slave iron was designed to lock two slaves together, and so 150 irons could hold three hundred slaves. There was also a special stove and oven for preparing food for slaves during the middle passage. For quelling shipboard slave revolts and fighting off pirates they loaded fifty-five muskets, eighteen pistols, twenty swords, two short-barreled swivel guns that fired grapeshot, sixty cannonballs, and a supply of fuses for the ship's eight cannons.[12]

Guillaume Billy recorded the value of each item that was loaded onto the ship in an accounting document called the *mise-hors*, or outlay list.[13] The cost of the merchandise that he would trade for slaves came to 37,782 livres. However, the total cost of outfitting a slave ship—including food, supplies, loading costs, advances of two months' salary to the crew—came to 80,000 livres, over four times the cost of the ship itself.[14] The salaries of the crew, minus their advances, would have to be paid at the end of the voyage, which would cost another 15,000 livres, and there were also insurance costs and interest on loans.

With expenditures for outfitting the ship mounting throughout the winter months, the Billy brothers and their partner, La Croix, were running short of money. On April 17, 1731, about six weeks before the *Diligent* sailed, the three partners took out two loans totaling three thousand livres from a merchant in Nantes who charged them 30 percent interest, and they returned three days later to borrow another 2,500 livres at the same rate. The loans were negotiated with the help of Guillaume Billy's maternal relative, François Gauvin, who lived in Nantes.[15] The fact that they were willing to borrow money at 30 percent interest gives us a hint of the kind of profits that they were expecting to make.

The Billys' substantial investment in the *Diligent* and its cargo had to be insured.[16] The legal framework for marine insurance policies had been set out in the Ordonnance de la Marine of August 1681, which specified that the ship and the cargo could be insured against "all losses and damages that happen at sea," but the lives of the crew members could not be insured, nor could the anticipated profits. Slaving voyages presented special problems for insurers. Unlike crew members, whose lives could not be insured, slaves were considered part of the cargo. Article 11 of the Ordonnance stated that slaves could be insured for their purchase value against death by killing, drowning, or other unnatural means. As interpreted by insurers, this meant that if a slave died of disease, the death was considered natural and was not covered by insurance. Similarly, if a slave died of despair and depression, the death was attributed to the harsh realities of life or the negligence of the owner, and it was not covered. In practice, slave deaths were only covered if they were drowned during a storm or killed during a naval battle. If the ship and the cargo were lost during a slave revolt, they were not covered. Slaving captains argued that a slave revolt was the equivalent of a war and should thus be covered. Insurers argued that slave revolts were the result of negligence by the captain.

Though the insurers managed to avoid paying for most of the special losses associated with the slave trade, they charged high rates of between 6 and 8 percent on slaving voyages, whereas the rate for direct voyages ranged from 2.25 to 3.25 percent.[17] The Billy brothers most likely obtained their insurance from wealthy brokers in Nantes. This was the common practice until 1739, when a group of Nantes businessmen and outfitters, including many major slave traders, went together to form the Maritime Insurance Society.[18]

When preparations for sailing were almost complete, the Diligent picked up two last-minute passengers: Pierre Verger, who was to be director of the Company of the Indies trading lodge at Jakin, and his assistant, Dubourdieu. Normally, the company did not send out its officials on private slave ships, but in this case the last company ship going to Jakin had left on March 8, and the next one would not leave until November 27. The two men had been scheduled to travel on the private slaver Superbe, which sailed out of Nantes on April 10, but they had missed the ship. The next ship from the region ready to depart for the Slave Coast was the Diligent, and so they went to Vannes and boarded the ship as paying passengers. They brought with them twenty-one small cannons as a gift for the African ruler of Jakin.[19]

AT 3:30 A.M. ON June 1, 1731, a stiff breeze from the north-east swept over the Gulf of Morbihan. The *Diligent*, which had been sitting becalmed since ten o'clock the previous morning, began to move. A little more than an hour later, it traversed the narrow passage that separated the Gulf of Morbihan from the Atlantic and broke free into the open sea. At 5:30 A.M. it passed a low-lying schist and quartz rock, not more than three hundred yards in length, known as the Isle of Méban. Robert Durand noted the time of passage precisely because it was at this point on the voyage that the crew began to get full seafaring wages instead of the half wages they had received during the loading process.

By 8:00 A.M. they had passed the tiny lighthouse rock known as La Teigneuse, and they would soon come into sight of Belle Ile, with its gray and somber cliffs rising forty-five meters above the sea. Soon Durand could identify the port city of Le Palais nestled at the base of the cliffs and the stone walls of the citadel on the heights. When they had come within two miles of the port of Le Palais, the sailors lowered the yards to "spill the wind" from the sails and hauled on the clew lines to bring up the corners of the sails. Then they scrambled up the masts and edged out on the yards to furl the courses and haul down the topsails. As the ship slowed, they fired a cannon to signal for a longboat.[1]

At ten o'clock the longboat arrived to pick up the local pilot and the Billy brothers. An hour later, after the Billy brothers had bid farewell to the officers and crew, the longboat departed for Le Palais. After passing

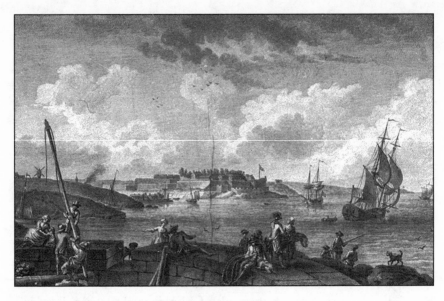

Figure 10.1   The harbor of Le Palais on Belle Ile.

through the bustling port, with its sardine boats docked so close together that they resembled their prey,[2] the Billy brothers disembarked and went to the top of the cliff to watch the *Diligent* make its way toward the northern tip of the island. It rounded the Point des Poulins and then turned sharply southwest and disappeared into the open Atlantic.

PART 4

Sailing South

S THE SUN APPROACHED its zenith on June 3, 1731, First Lieutenant Robert Durand headed for the spot behind the mainmast where the officers of the *Diligent* gathered for the daily ritual of fixing the ship's position.[1] Captain Pierre Mary was already there, as were Second Captain Pierre Valteau and Second Lieutenant Thomas Laragon. Even though officers on merchant ships were not required to wear uniforms, their dress generally echoed that of officers in the French Royal Navy: a blue, hip-length, sleeveless jacket over a shirt with lace ruffles on the sleeves; black breeches over crimson silk stockings; buckled shoes with red heels; a white satin scarf; and a black felt hat decorated with plumage. The captain's outfit set itself apart from the others by its gold braid decorations and red cuffs.[2]

The sea was calm and pretty, and the wind was light but variable.[3] Soon the pilot, François Sabatier, arrived, and the ritual could begin. As the other officers watched, Robert Durand picked up the wooden cross staff to measure the north-south angle of the sun. It was a simple instrument composed of a square ebony staff three feet long with two pearwood crosspieces that had square holes in them so that they could slide along the staff. The longer of the two crosspieces, about twenty-four inches long, was set at the end of the staff and tightened in place with a thumbscrew. Using the method taught him by his mentor, Jean Bouguer, Durand faced north with his back to the sun and placed the small metal eyepiece mounted at the lower end of the crosspiece against his eye. He moved the other end of the staff up and

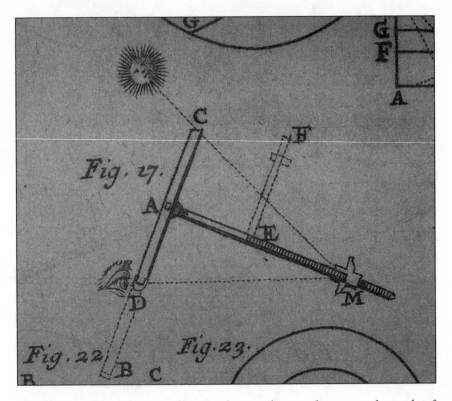

Figure 11.1   Jean Bouguer's diagram showing how to determine the angle of the sun using the cross staff.

down until it appeared to touch the horizon.[4] Then he slid the smaller crosspiece, which was only four inches long, along the staff until the shadow cast by the long crosspiece struck it exactly in the middle. Tightening the thumbscrew on the smaller crosspiece to mark the spot, he examined the degree marks carved into the staff to determine the angle of the sun above the southern horizon. Over the next twenty minutes he took a series of these observations until the sun's angle stopped rising and began to drop. The greatest angle marked the point of the sun at high noon.

Then it was time to do some calculations. Knowing the angle of the sun above the southern horizon at high noon, he subtracted that number from ninety degrees to get the zenith angle, which was the angle between the sun and a point directly over his head.[5] Then he looked in his mariners' almanac, *Connoissance des temps pour l'année 1731*, to find the sun's declination, which was its angle from the equator on June 3. In early June, the sun was just south of the tropic of cancer. Strictly speaking, the declinations listed in the almanac were only good for the meridian of Paris, which was two degrees east of the prime meridian, which ran through Greenwich. Given that the perceived path inscribed by the sun around the earth was not precisely parallel to the equator, any deviation east or west from the meridian of Paris would affect the declination number, but the *Diligent* was sailing close enough to the Paris meridian to make the difference almost negligible. By adding the declination angle from the almanac to the zenith angle that he had just calculated from his cross staff observation, Durand calculated the ship's latitude to be forty-six degrees, eighteen minutes. At the beginning of the voyage he had calculated his point of departure at Belle Ile to be forty-seven degrees and twenty-four minutes of latitude. In the two days that had passed since then, the ship had moved southward more than a full degree.

Calculating latitude was relatively easy, even with the crude wooden instrument that Durand was using. Longitude, on the other hand, was not so easily determined. Because the earth's rotation made the sun seem constantly on the move from east to west, the best way to calculate longitude was with the aid of two clocks. Every hour of difference between the times when the sun reaches high noon at different spots on the globe was equal to one twenty-fourth of the earth's circumference, or fifteen degrees. Four minutes of difference in time, therefore, equaled one degree of longitude. Ideally, the way to calculate longitude would have been to mark high noon at the position of the ship and compare it to the time at the starting point of the voyage in order to calculate gains or losses. But there is no way to keep track of the time at the starting point because pendulum-driven clocks were thrown off by the pitching and rolling of the ship, and even the best spring-driven pocket watches gained or lost five minutes between morning and noon.[6] Timekeeping aboard ship was still done with sandglasses that were reset every day at noon if the sun was visible. So important had it become to find an accurate way to calculate longitude that in 1714 the British Parliament established a prize of £20,000 (a major fortune in the eighteenth century) for anyone who could develop an accurate technique or instrument. The prize was not awarded until 1765—and then only partially.[7]

In the absence of a definitive solution, Robert Durand tried to estimate his longitude based on the direction and speed of the ship. For direction, he used a mariner's compass and corrected for the variation between the magnetic north and true north. To calculate speed, he used a log line, which was a line about three-sixteenths of an inch thick with knots tied every forty-one feet and eight inches. At the end of the rope, attached by a kitelike harness, was a heart-shaped piece of wood known as a log chip that was weighted at one end so that it would keep upright in the water. The pilot threw the log chip off the stern of the ship while a second seaman payed out the rope from its spool and a third watched the sand drain from the thirty-second sandglass. Then they hauled in the rope and counted how many knots had gone out during the thirty seconds. The number of knots, in theory, was equal to the ship's speed in nautical miles per hour, although a French sea captain had already demonstrated in 1727 that the knots on the rope should really be forty-seven feet and six inches apart, nearly six feet more than the existing practice.[8] Ideally, if Robert Durand knew the ship's starting point, its speed, the time traveled, and the direction of travel, he could estimate the new longitude. The problem was that with speed and direction both varying throughout the day, the results of the calculations were very imprecise, and one day's error became compounded as new errors were added on successive days. The daily estimates of longitude were little more than rough guesses.

Once the latitude, direction, and speed of the ship had been determined, the officers retired to the table in the officers' quarters in the quarterdeck. Unrolling a Dutch map of the Atlantic world that was thirty-nine and a half inches wide by thirty-five and a half inches tall, drawn by the seventeenth-century Dutch mapmaker Pieter Goos, they located the *Diligent*'s position to see where they were in relation to their destination: Whydah, on the Guinea coast of West Africa.[9] Whydah had been chosen in part because it was, in the early eighteenth century, the single largest slaving port in all of Africa. More than 40 percent of all slaves carried across the Atlantic in the first quarter of the eighteenth century came from Whydah.[10] Another reason for choosing Whydah was that the French Company of the Indies maintained a fort there that could perhaps facilitate their trade. They planned to reach Whydah as much with the aid of currents as winds. Once they were west of the Iberian Peninsula, they would pick up the Canary Island current, which would carry them south at speeds varying from twelve to twenty miles per day past the Isle of Madeira, the Canary Islands, and the Cape Verde Islands. They would then

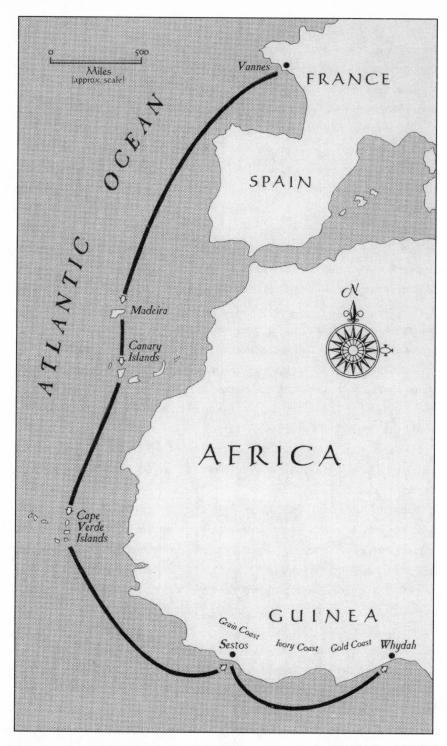

Figure 11.2 Redrawn version of the Pieter Goos map used on the *Diligent*, showing its route from Vannes to Whydah.

leave the Canary Island current and head toward landfall on the West African coast just south of the Sierra Leone River, where they would enter the Guinea current that would carry them along the West African shoreline all the way to Whydah.

Sitting at the table in the officers' quarters, Durand recorded the day's latitude and longitude in his journal and estimated that during the previous twenty-four hours the *Diligent* had traveled forty-two miles to the west-southwest. French maritime law required all ship's officers to keep a journal, which remained in their possession after the voyage. Many officers, jaded by numerous voyages, made rather perfunctory entries, but Robert Durand's entries were detailed and carefully considered. He noted not only the latitude and longitude but also the winds, the weather, which sails they set, the distance and direction traveled, and any extraordinary events. His very meticulousness marked him, perhaps, as a person traveling to Africa for the first time, but there was more to it than that. He wanted to master the technical details of the voyage so that in the future he would be able to command a ship bound for West Africa. After sailing on the *Diligent* as second captain on the voyage to Martinique in 1730, he found it disappointing to be demoted to first lieutenant for this trip. Yet he understood that he lacked experience in the Africa route, and he was eager to learn the complex techniques and routines of sailing south through the Atlantic. The name of the ship, *Diligent*, seemed to characterize his approach to the voyage.

Robert Durand was ambitious. Even as a boy growing up surrounded by boats and ships in Le Croisic, a seaside fishing town near the mouth of the Loire, he had striven to do more with his life than simply follow the career of a common sailor. His father, Pierre Durand, had spent his life sailing as an ordinary seaman on small ships carrying salt from Le Croisic to Spain, and occasionally on larger ships sailing out of Nantes, until he died a seaman's death and was buried at sea during the 1720s, leaving almost nothing for his family to live on. By becoming a ship's officer, Robert Durand had significantly risen above his father's professional and economic level; in 1731 he paid over eight times as much in taxes as his father had paid before his untimely death.[11]

The key to Robert Durand's success had been his education from the Capuchin priests in Le Croisic, perhaps made possible by his brother Guillaume's earnings as a carpenter. In a province where less than one adult male in ten could sign his name, and in a town where the dominant language was Breton, not French, Robert Durand had learned to read and write in both Latin and French.[12] The spelling, capitalization, and punctuation in his journal entries were irregular, as was much of the writing of his time, but the fact that he could write at all set him apart from most of his boyhood friends. In addition to studying with the priests, he had also studied navigation at the school on Quai Lenigo in Le Croisic founded by Jean Bouguer, one of the leading hydrographers in France. Bouguer's book *Traite complet de la navigation* was the authoritative text on the subject.

It was Durand's scholastic skills as much as his seafaring experience that had helped him garner an appointment as an apprentice officer. Le Croisic had a reputation for supplying officers for large ships sailing out of Nantes, and certain families such as Sabatier, Laragon, and Valteau had produced famous sea captains during the seventeenth century.[13] The Durand family had no history of producing captains or even maritime officers, and so Durand's appointment in 1727 as an apprentice officer on the merchant ship *Judith*, which carried salt from the saltpans of Le Croisic to Spain, was a major victory in his struggle to rise above his family's station. His second ocean voyage was identical to the first. His third voyage took him to Ireland and Hamburg, where the *Judith* was sold, leaving Durand stranded until he landed a job on the *Emmanuel* and returned to Le Croisic more than eight months after his departure.[14]

A major advancement in his career came only two years after his first voyage, when he was hired as lieutenant on the *Espérence* for a trip from Nantes to the sugar island of St. Domingue in the Caribbean. The ship had a crew of nineteen and Durand, as the lieutenant, was second in command. It was in the harbor of Cape Français in St. Domingue that he had first encountered ships loaded with slaves and had seen enslaved Africans being sold and transported to the sugar plantations.[15] Although ships leaving from Nantes on slaving voyages to Africa had regularly passed within a few miles of Durand's home town of Le Croisic ever since his childhood, they were not carrying slaves at that point on their voyage. When they passed Le Croisic on their return trip, they had already deposited their slaves on Caribbean islands. Like the slave ships, the *Espérance* returned to Nantes with 220 barrels of sugar and three barrels of indigo after a five-month voyage. One of the nineteen crew members had died on the return trip. After proving himself on that transatlantic voyage, Durand was hired by

Captain Pierre Mary to serve as second captain of the *Diligent* on its maiden voyage from Vannes to Martinique in 1730. He had risen from apprentice to second captain in only three years.

Prior to departing for St. Domingue in 1729, Robert Durand realized another of his goals. On January 22 he married Marie Janne Hoscouet, the daughter of a wealthy shipbuilder. Rather than bring his new bride into the humble Durand family house, he moved into the large Hoscouet house on Quai Lenigo, just down the street from Jean Bouguer's navigation school. Less than two months after his wedding, he left for St. Domingue on the *Espérence*. And it was only two weeks after the *Diligent* returned to Vannes from Martinique on August 26, 1730, that his wife gave birth to twin girls: Marie Janne and Françoise.[16] The parish priest acknowledged Robert Durand's new professional status when he noted in the parish register that the father of the twins was a "ship's officer." Now, with his twin girls only nine months old, Durand was again at sea.

AY AFTER DAY THE *Diligent* headed southwest, its latitude dropping about one degree each day. By Wednesday noon, June 6, it had arrived at 44.9 degrees north latitude. A brisk wind from the west-northwest filled its sails. The masts and yards creaked as the ship picked up speed and plowed through the large waves. Running before the wind was a good way to make time, but the *Diligent* was now moving too fast for the choppy sea! At one o'clock in the afternoon Captain Mary sent sailors aloft in the stiff winds to make the main topsail smaller by two reef bands. At seven o'clock, the ship was again moving too rapidly, and the masts were bending in the wind. In response, the seamen furled the main topsail and the main course, leaving only the sails on the foremast to propel the ship. Then they diminished the size of the foretopsail by reefing it one reef band. The ship, as Durand described it, was "fleeing before the wind."

At three o'clock the next morning the ship was rolling so violently that the main yard became loosened and began to swing. Fighting the heavy wind, the crewmen lowered it until it rested on the main rails. As the ship pitched and rolled, Robert Durand's anxiety turned to cold fear. He made a vow to Saint Anne that if he survived, he would attend two masses for her and make a pilgrimage to the shrine of Saint Anne of Auray, a shrine located near Vannes that was frequently visited by sailors.[1] By noon the next day the seas had calmed somewhat, and Durand calculated that during the past twenty-four hours the ship had traveled 306 miles, which was about twice its daily progress in previous days.

Even with calmer seas, the *Diligent* was still running before the wind using only the foretopsail. At four o'clock in the afternoon the winds calmed down and the men set the main topsail. Suddenly, at eleven o'clock at night, the wind stopped and the air became still. Fearing the approach of a storm, they lowered the topsail yards to "spill the wind" from the topsails, and they clewed up the fore and main courses to make the sails billow. Although the wind was calm, the waves were large, and the heavy-laden ship was riding low in the water. At four o'clock in the morning, the entire crew was awakened when a series of huge waves crashed over the aft part of the ship and water entered the officers' quarters through the stern windows. It was becoming clear that the ship was too heavily loaded in the aft section.

Captain Pierre Mary ordered the weight redistributed on the *Diligent*. With the entire crew awake, he took command and ordered all hands on deck. The crew could be mustered rapidly because the sailors were required to sleep with their clothes on, and they did not need to put on their shoes because they normally worked barefooted. Working by lantern light (which was unusual because they normally worked only with the light of the moon and the stars), they moved their personal chests from the quarterdeck, which was in the rear, to the forecastle, in the front. Going down to the lower deck, they moved the chests of smoking pipes and kegs of brandy forward to better trim the ship. The space thus freed up was filled with bread that had been stored in the officers' quarters and had become soaked with seawater that had come in through the windows.

The next morning, with the winds still calm, Captain Pierre Mary inspected the ship to check for damage and was relieved to find that there was none. Sailors had been manning the ship's two pumps since 4:00 A.M., and the hold was now almost free of water. The redistribution of the weight would reduce the danger of similar problems during the rest of the voyage, he thought, but he knew that he was responsible for overloading the rear part of the ship in the first place. Such mistakes could be costly because the captain was legally responsible for the loading and trimming of the ship. He had been lucky this time.

Pierre Mary was forty-eight years old and was beginning his second career at sea. He had retired in 1727 from his long career as a ship's officer, and for three years he had lived quietly in Le Croisic, drawing on his savings. His retirement had been bittersweet because even though Mary had spent many years as a ship's officer and had risen to the level of second captain, he had never been promoted to captain. He was listed in the tax rolls in Le Croisic simply as a "maritime officer." He had come out of retirement in 1730 when the owners of the *Diligent*, needing a captain to take their ship to Martinique, offered him the job. After that Pierre Mary was listed in the local tax rolls as a "sea captain," and his name was entered in the Register of Captains kept by the Royal Navy draft board.[2]

Despite the official recognition, the title of "captain" rested awkwardly on Pierre Mary. The normal process of becoming a captain required examination and certification by the admiralty court in Nantes, but Pierre Mary had never been certified. The clerk of the Royal Navy draft board left a blank on the line in the register where he was supposed to note the date and place of Pierre Mary's certification. Even though it was illegal for an uncertified person to serve as captain of an oceangoing ship, his new job as captain of a ship sailing out of a minor port had given Pierre Mary a chance to salvage his undistinguished career and gain the respect and social status that his first career had denied him.

Born in Nantes in 1683, Pierre Mary had grown up at ease in the world of seafaring commerce. As a young adult he settled in the town of Chateaurenault, up the Loire River near Tours, and from there he sailed on a variety of ships out of Nantes to a variety of destinations. Sometime around 1718 he moved to Le Croisic, and from then on his voyages were either direct voyages to the West Indies or slave trading trips to the Guinea coast of Africa. He prospered greatly while sailing on transatlantic voyages. During the decade of the 1720s his capitation tax bill tripled, and he could afford to hire a live-in servant girl for his household.[3]

After two successive trips to the West Indies in 1718 and 1719, Pierre Mary made his first slaving trip to the Guinea coast in 1720, when he sailed as second captain on the *Marie*, owned by René Montaudoin from Nantes. The destination was Whydah, on the Slave Coast, which was the favorite destination of slave traders from Nantes, in part because the French fort there was maintained by the Ministry of the Marine. At Whydah they purchased 241 slaves, thirty-one of whom died during the loading of the ship and the middle passage. Five crew members also died during the fourteen-month voyage. When the ship arrived back in Nantes on July 23, 1721, Captain Jean Denis was too sick to make the required report on the voyage at the Admiralty Office. So Pierre Mary, as second captain, made the report in his place and signed his name at the bottom.[4] That was the closest he would come in many years to performing the duties of a captain.

Pierre Mary's second slaving voyage—this one as second captain on the *Marie Heureuse* to Whydah in 1726—was even more of a disaster. Of the 295 slaves that they packed into the ship at Whydah, 104 of them died either during the middle passage or during the sale in Martinique. In addition, six crew members died and four deserted in Martinique. While he was in Martinique, Pierre Mary learned that the West African kingdom of Whydah, which he had visited only a few months earlier, had been conquered by the king of Dahomey, and Savi, its capital city, had been burned. The voyage lasted over nineteen months, five months longer than the previous one.[5]

Perhaps the trauma of all those deaths prompted Pierre Mary to retire from the sea. Perhaps it was the nineteen months at sea under conditions that had caused four of his fellow crew members to desert the ship. Perhaps it was simply because seafaring was a young man's occupation, and by the standards of his profession a forty-five-year-old officer was an old man. Or perhaps it was because he had made enough money from trading in slaves for his own personal account on that voyage—thirty-five of the slaves on the *Marie Heureuse* belonged to the officers—that he felt he had enough money to retire. At any rate, he did not sail again for three years, until the owners of the *Diligent* enticed him out of retirement with an offer to captain their ship from Vannes to Martinique.

His first voyage as captain did not start smoothly. Only four days after leaving Vannes for Martinique on March 6, 1730, he encountered a terrible storm. The winds were so fierce that it was impossible to maneuver the ship, and so the *Diligent* ran straight ahead using only the sails on the foremast. Huge waves crashed over the deck, breaking three windowpanes in the captain's cabin and soaking the six hundred loaves of bread that he had stored there. During the night Mary discovered that his pilot, Augustin Gautier, was missing. Apparently he had been washed overboard by a wave. Fearing disaster, they sought shelter at the northern Spanish port of Estaca de Bares, where they spent eleven days repairing the ship and waiting for the weather to clear before continuing on.[6]

When the Billy brothers and La Croix bought the *Diligent* from their other partners and decided to send it on a slaving voyage, they chose Pierre Mary as their captain, in part because of his experience in the

Guinea trade. Mary, for his part, knew that he needed an experienced and loyal second captain, and so he chose his brother-in-law from Le Croisic, Pierre Valteau. Mary was the godfather of Valteau's son, Pierre, and he knew that he could count on absolute loyalty from his second in command.[7] Mary's authority on board was also enhanced by the fact that he was the oldest and most experienced seaman on the *Diligent*.

As captain of the *Diligent*, Pierre Mary operated in a kind of legal no-man's-land of conflicting interests. French maritime law made it clear that as captain, he represented the interests of the owners and outfitters of the ship. His job was not only to complete the voyage successfully but also to protect the merchandise and profits of the outfitters. Once at sea, however, he was something of a feudal lord, dispensing punishments like a judge, dealing with foreign officials like a diplomat, and leading his crew in battle. On a day-to-day basis, his job was more mundane, and he busied himself with plotting his position, punishing sailors who had fallen asleep during the night watch, and, above all, rationing the food, wine, and water aboard the ship. Sailors caught taking unauthorized food or drink could be punished with the loss of a month's pay, and if they seemed to be endangering the voyage by destroying food and beverages, they could even be put to death.[8] On the open sea or in distant ports, the line between discipline and despotism often became blurred, but in this case the relations between captain and crew were especially complex: Captain Mary and fifteen of his crew members all came from the neighboring small towns of Le Croisic and Batz. Quarrels and resentments that began at sea had a way of continuing once everybody was back on land.

On June 26, nearly a month after their departure from Vannes, the sea was pretty and they were sailing into a light breeze from the west-southwest. They were among the Canary Islands to the west of Tenerife and heading toward the island of Gomera. At four o'clock in the afternoon they spotted another ship on their leeward side that seemed at first to be running parallel with them. When it spotted the *Diligent*, it tacked and changed course, moving in their direction. Captain Mary's first thought was that this was a ship of the Barbary pirates, who often hunted in the waters off of Tenerife in the month of June.[9] Many of these pirates were based in the Moroccan city of Salé, near Rabat. The local pirates at Salé had been joined by an odd assortment of foreigners, and in 1728 a Frenchman named Piller and a Spaniard named Moreno had begun sending out armed ships, the largest of which had twenty-two cannons and a crew of 120 men.[10] Fearing that the *Diligent* was about to be attacked, Captain Mary ordered the decks cleared, the muskets readied, and the cannons primed. Within minutes the *Diligent* was transformed from a merchant ship to a warship. Because the French navy's draft system made each sailor eligible to be called up for navy service one year out of every four, many of the crew members had experience on French men-of-war. With the crew on full alert, Captain Mary watched the other ship carefully until five o'clock in the afternoon, when he saw it trim its sails to run perpendicular with the wind and away from the *Diligent*. False alarm!

13

AT FIVE O'CLOCK IN the morning on June 29 the stillness of the early light was broken by a shouted command of "fire!" followed by the boom of a cannon. Another cannon shot followed, then another: seven in all. The gunner, Charles Auger, and his cannon crew were firing a seven-gun salute to Captain Pierre Mary and Second Captain Pierre Valteau. June 29 was the feast of St. Peter, a day that celebrated authority and hierarchy. St. Peter was, after all, the first pope. The sailors' eagerness to observe the religious holiday did not indicate that they were particularly devout or even religious. The seaside towns of Brittany had a long-standing reputation for being irreligious, and the repeated failure of evangelization missions to coastal Brittany led certain priests to develop a theory that proximity to water and salty air had a dampening effect on religious life. Among themselves, the sailors referred to the feast of St. Peter simply as "Captain's Day."[1]

The high point of the celebration came at noon, when the cook, François Gauguin, brought out the feast he had been preparing all morning. He had slaughtered the last of the sheep that they had brought along so that the crew could enjoy fresh meat, as opposed to the salted beef that they normally ate three times a week at most. He even baked some fresh loaves of bread to replace the shriveled and hardened loaves that had been soaked by seawater during the storm, and he set out a modest amount of cheese to eat with the bread. To celebrate the feast, he served the wine straight instead of following his usual practice of watering it down with an equal portion of water in order to make the foul-tasting water in the barrels palatable. The crew members lined up outside the galley (located in the forecastle) with their wooden bowls and their wooden spoons in hand. After the cook filled their bowls, they looked for places to sit and eat. Some simply sat on the deck; others found a coiled rope or other object to sit on.

Their clothes made it obvious that this was a feast day. Normally the sailors worked barefooted, wearing shorts that came down to their knees and shirts like jerseys with a slit below the neck that could be laced up. Their shoulder-length hair—the pride of Breton sailors—was normally topped by a wool stocking cap. On this day, however, many of them were wearing shirts with buttons, vests, hats, and shoes that they brought along to wear during shore visits. The most colorful people in the whole crowd were the six crew members who came from Batz, a suburb of Le Croisic where men typically wore wide, pleated shorts, shirts with lace-edged collars that had been stiffened to stand up at the back, and several vests of different colors, arranged so that all of the colors would show.[2] Although the crewmen from Batz were unable to outfit themselves in their full regalia due to the limited space in their sea trunks, they were unmistakable as they stood in line waiting for their food.

The *Diligent*'s four officers—Mary, Valteau, Durand, and Laragon—were also dressed in their finery. As the guests of honor at the feast, they did not stand in line for food nor did they sit on the deck to eat. Instead, they sat at the large table in the great room of the officers' quarters in the quarterdeck and waited for their food to be served. The eating area was lighted by four glass windows at the back. Although they were served the same menu as the regular crew, they got the choicest cuts of meat, the freshest loaves of bread, and the best wine. Compared with ordinary crew members, the officers lived in luxury. On the starboard side of the officers' quarters was the captain's cabin, decorated with paneled walls and a finished ceiling. It had a bunk with a curtain to darken it during the day, a desk that closed with a lock, and a window with glass. Behind it was a smaller cabin for First Lieutenant Durand, which was darkened with a curtain. The larboard side was similar, with the front cabin for Second Captain Valteau and the smaller back cabin for Second Lieutenant Laragon. Jutting out sideways from the officers' quarters were two quarter galleries. The one on the larboard side housed the officers' toilet with a lead pipe that dropped waste into the sea.[3]

Before sitting down to eat, the officers conducted the daily ritual of determining the angle of the sun at noon. Durand calculated his latitude at twenty-two degrees, nineteen minutes, more than a full degree south of the Tropic of Cancer; they must have passed it during the previous night. Crossing the Tropic of Cancer normally triggered the Baptism of the Tropics ceremony, but they could not hold it immediately because they were already celebrating the feast of St. Peter. The Baptism of the Tropics would take place the next day.

When Saturday dawned, the atmosphere aboard the *Diligent* had changed to something lighter and more playful. The ceremony of the Baptism of the Tropics—a carnivalesque inversion of the religious order and the social hierarchy—was in many ways the opposite of the feast of St. Peter. Instead of celebrating hierarchy, it was designed to create solidarity among ordinary crew members and relieve the pressures created by the rigid shipboard command system. The immediate purpose of the ceremony, however, was to baptize the six crew members who had never before crossed the Tropic of Cancer—people who had never been to the Guinea coast of Africa or the French islands of the West Indies. The group of initiates included the two cabin boys—Guillaume Allançon and François Lefur—and the two officers in training, Pierre Mathieu Letheris and René Bonet.

Unlike the previous day's ceremonies, when the captains held the places of honor, this ceremony was presided over by the pilot, Sabatier, and by the painted and masked figure representing the Good Man Tropic. The thirty-one crew members who had already crossed the tropic painted their faces and arms red, black, white, and yellow, and they fashioned bandoleers out of ropes and blocks. Each one carried a pot or a pan that he beat with a piece of iron. Making a frightful racket, they sought out the novices who were to be baptized. Once the novices were assembled, Sabatier gave a short speech. To the beating of the pots and pans, four masked men led the novices to the main deck at the foot of the forecastle where there was a large tub filled with seawater. The initiate was asked to sit on an iron bar that had been placed across the tub. There he made the customary vows, the main one being that he would never try to seduce the wife of another sailor. Experience had shown that sexual competition was a serious threat to crew solidarity.

If the young man had prepared for this ceremony by giving or promising gifts of brandy, wine, figs, or nuts to the other crew members according to his means, his baptism went smoothly. The Good Man Tropic sprinkled three or four drops of water on his head and presented him with a covered basket containing a small piece of gold. The Good Man Tropic then asked, "Who will be the godfather of this young man?" When the godfather, who had been chosen in advance, identified himself, he was asked to give the novice a new name. The name was ribald and grotesque, designed to amuse the crowd and embarrass the novice. Once the name had been announced to the cheers and jeers of the assembled sailors, the initiate could then climb out of the tub.

If the initiate had been stingy with his gifts, however, the experience could be rough. He was asked to sit on the iron bar that straddled the tub of seawater. As soon as his baptismal name was called out, two sailors pulled out the bar so that he plunged into the water. The nearby sailors rushed up to dunk him, and other sailors, armed with buckets of seawater, doused him so that no matter which way he turned, he got a face full of seawater. When up to fifty buckets of water had been thrown on him, the initiate was allowed out of the tub after promising enough gifts to satisfy the crew. The officers in training probably got harsher treatment than the ordinary crewmembers and cabin boys. This was the day when the crew got its revenge.

When all six novices had been baptized, they presented the crewmembers with the presents they had promised them. Then Noël Magré, the ship's accordion player, brought out his instrument, and the rest of the day was spent, in the words of Robert Durand, in "entertainment and pleasure." By the end of the day, the novices felt as if they had become hardened veterans of the tropics.[4]

When Sunday, July 1, dawned, a wispy breeze was blowing from the north-northeast and the crew scrambled up the ratlines to outfit the *Diligent* in full sail. They set all three topgallant sails and added studdingsails to the courses and topsails to catch every bit of wind. As the crew members washed down the decks and put the ship in order, all signs of the previous day's festivities were obliterated. The crew members went about their tasks with a seriousness that masked their hangovers, and the normal hierarchy of command and control was gradually reestablished.

At the top of the *Diligent*'s hierarchy of command were its four officers: Captain Pierre Mary, Second Captain Pierre Valteau, First Lieutenant Robert Durand, and Second Lieutenant Thomas Laragon. An officer's place in the hierarchy was defined by salary as well as title, and there were huge disparities in pay within the officer corps: Captain Mary made 120 livres per month, Second Captain Pierre Valteau made eighty, First Lieutenant Robert Durand made fifty, and Second Lieutenant Laragon made only forty. The first doctor, Devigne, who was sometimes considered an officer even though he had no command functions, was paid fifty livres a month, the same as Robert Durand.

At the next level of the hierarchy came the "marine officers," who were not really officers, but rather specialists whose tasks distinguished them from ordinary crewmembers. They included the pilot, the first mate, the second mate, the gunner, the boatswain's mate, the two carpenters, the three coopers, the second doctor, the longboat operator, and the skiff operator. Their salaries ranged from twenty-four to fifty livres a month. Then came the six helmsmen, who earned about thirty livres per month, and the nine ordinary sailors, whose salaries ranged from twelve livres a month to thirty-six. There was also a cook, who made thirty-six livres per month, and two cabin boys who each made twelve livres per month. The two officers in training received trainee wages of only twelve and eighteen livres per month respectively. The *Diligent* carried no priest—ships with fewer than forty crew members were not required to carry one—but it did carry a professional accordion player, who was paid thirteen livres per month for his music, only one livre more than the cabin boy.[5] Crew members had no special quarters. They slept in hammocks strung in the forward part of the lower deck, and they kept their seamen's trunks in the forecastle.

Cutting across the hierarchy of rank, task, and salary was the division of the crew into two teams, referred to as the "starboard watch" and the "larboard watch." Each team included officers, helmsmen, and sailors (but not specialists such as carpenters and coopers), and the two teams replaced each other in successive periods of duty. On the morning of the *Diligent's* departure from Vannes, Captain Mary had assembled the crew at first light and called the roll. As each crewmember answered the call, he was assigned his counterpart on the other team. The French word for sailor, *matelot*, came from the Dutch term *mattenoot*, which meant "companion of the same bed." *Matelots* were quite literally people who took turns using a single bed, as one would sleep while the other was on duty.[6] The *Diligent's* crew was well balanced for division into two watch teams, having a first and second captain, a first and second lieutenant, and a first and second mate. The watch-team system meant in practice that even though the *Diligent* had thirty-seven crew members, there were only about a dozen men available to sail the ship at any given time.

In contrast to Saturday's festivities, Sunday passed uneventfully. Breakfast, which consisted of a hard biscuit that the sailors ate by hand, was served around 8:00 A.M. in two shifts so that the crew members belonging to the starboard watch team could eat before going on watch and the members of the larboard watch team could eat after their watch ended at eight. Sailors who had completed their watch could sleep until almost noon, when they ate a kind of gruel made from grain and beans and then went back on watch from noon to 6:00 P.M. The evening meal of gruel was served at six o'clock, a time that coincided with the end of the afternoon watch and the beginning of the great watch, which lasted from 6:00 P.M. to midnight.

Throughout every watch, the watchman kept time using thirty-minute sandglasses. As the last grain of sand drained from the glass, he rang the bell and called out, "All's well! Keep a good lookout!" Then he turned over the sandglass. A four-hour watch ended at eight bells; a six-hour watch finished at twelve bells. As twelve bells sounded at midnight, the starboard watch team, which had kept the great watch, could go to sleep, and the larboard watch team would keep the night watch. This was the most difficult of the watches, and French maritime law imposed severe penalties for falling asleep on duty. During the night, watches were only four hours long, and the night watch ended at 4:00 A.M., followed by the daybreak watch, which ran from 4:00 A.M. to 8:00 A.M. Because each twenty-four-hour day was divided into five watches—two six-hour watches and three four-hour watches—the two teams worked different watches on alternating days.[7]

During the night between July 2 and 3, Robert Durand was on the night watch. He placed himself on the quarterdeck and observed the almost silent workings of the ship. At night people didn't light candles or lanterns because that would prevent their eyes from adjusting to the darkness. It was a clear night with the moon and stars providing sufficient light for running the ship. The winds were steady and the sail settings had not been changed since the previous day. With little to do, the crew members stood or sat silently in the darkness; conversation at night was not allowed. When eight bells sounded to mark the end of the watch, Robert Durand felt very satisfied that the voyage was going well. "Good watch," he wrote in his journal.

14

*A*FTER CROSSING THE TROPIC of Cancer on June 30, the *Diligent* continued south-southwest following the Canary Island current. At eleven o'clock on the morning of July 4, the lookout spotted the Isle of May, one of the Portuguese-controlled Cape Verde Islands. The Isle of May was largely barren and had only 375 inhabitants, concentrated in three towns, who lived in houses made of fig wood that an English visitor had once described as "low and mean." With the exception of two Portuguese men, the inhabitants of the Isle of May were all descendants of African slaves who had run away or been manumitted from Portuguese farms on the nearby islands of Santiago and Fogo. The governor of the Isle of May, who derived his authority from the Portuguese governor on Santiago, was also black.

The inhabitants of the Isle of May eked out a living growing corn, yams, potatoes, and some plantains in the arid climate and barren soil, but their most productive economic activity was the annual harvest of salt from the island's salt pond during the dry season from September to May, when all of the islanders were employed in digging and transporting salt. So poor were the islanders that most of them did not demand to be paid in money but accepted food and old clothes instead. Up to a hundred English ships came annually in search of this salt, but July was beyond the end of the salting season and there were no ships at anchor. The *Diligent* continued on to the island of Santiago, the political and ecclesiastical capital of the Cape Verde Islands.[1]

Figure 14.1   Durand's drawing of the Isle of May, Cape Verde Islands.

At 6:30 A.M. on July 5 the *Diligent* entered the bay at the port of La Praya on the island of Santiago and began the elaborate greeting ritual expected of a ship entering a foreign port. Before dropping its anchor, the *Diligent* raised its French flag. In response the fort on shore raised its Portuguese flag, and the lone ship in the bay raised a British flag. Then Captain Mary ordered the longboat lowered and sent Robert Durand with five sailors to the English ship to introduce themselves and show their peaceful intentions. At eight o'clock, with the courtesy call completed, the sailors on the *Diligent* scrambled up the ratlines to furl the sails, and the gunner saluted the Portuguese fort with five blank cannon shots. The fort, which was armed with fourteen cannons capable of firing twelve- and eighteen-pound cannonballs, fired three shots in return. Only after all the formalities had been completed did the *Diligent* drop three anchors into the mixture of sand and pebbles that made up the seabed.

The *Diligent* stopped at the island of Santiago to refill its water barrels and purchase food, having been at sea for over a month.[2] Most French slave ships stopped in Madeira, the Canary Islands, or the Cape Verde Islands to replenish their supplies before heading for the West African coast. Going ashore amid the run-down buildings and dilapidated houses of La Praya, Robert Durand and his companions spent the next five days buying cattle, pigs, goats, sheep, turkeys, and chickens, as well as onions and other vegetables. In the marketplace they observed people of all colors and shades. The majority of them were black, but there were many shades of brown and even a few people who looked white. Food was so cheap that instead of purchasing it with money or using their trade goods, they simply traded old clothing and used hardware.

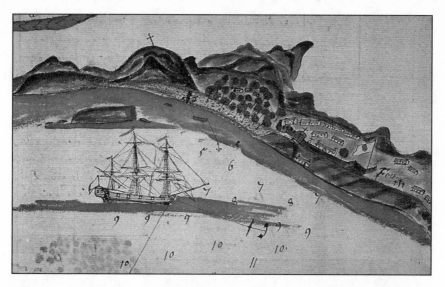

Figure 14.2   Durand's drawing of the port of La Praya, Cape Verde Islands.

The island of Santiago, like all of the Cape Verde Islands, was experiencing an economic depression. Money was so scarce that exchange was done by barter, written IOUs, cotton cloth that served as a currency, or even counterfeit coins made by slaves from bits of copper. The municipal council of Ribeira Grande, Santiago's capital city, blamed it on the Portuguese policy forbidding them to trade with any country other than Portugal. At the beginning of the century one ship from Lisbon had come out each year to purchase a hundred tons of sugar, and one or two Portuguese ships had come to purchase the locally produced cotton cloth and take it to Brazil. Now, according to the Municipal Council, "Trade comes to this island from the Royal Government in no more than one or two ships from one year to the next, and these buy a few cloths, and not with money, but in exchange for such things as handkerchiefs, coarse hats, bad baize, and other things that are bought very cheap in Lisbon but that our necessities force us to buy very dear." The sugar industry, which had always been limited by the aridity of the islands, had declined since the beginning of the century, and it was said to produce "some sugar, but mostly molasses." So poor had the island become that Santiago's capital city was described by its own municipal council in disparaging terms. "The greater part of this whole city," wrote the council, "only consists of hovels, and the few houses that remain standing are completely dilapi-dated." One result of the poverty was that some inhabitants had taken up banditry and had even launched attacks on marketplaces, thus disrupting what little commerce still existed. The Portuguese governor complained bitterly about the lawlessness, but he was powerless to stop it as he had only volunteer soldiers at his disposal.[3]

The Cape Verde Islands had not always been so poor. In the sixteenth and seventeenth centuries the Portuguese settlers on Santiago had oper-ated a slave-based economy in which slaves brought in from the nearby West African coast were either put to work growing sugar and cotton on the island or were transshipped to Spain, Portugal, and the New World. Missionaries on Santiago made a business out of transforming *bocales* (slaves who were not Christian and could not speak Portuguese) into *ladinas* by converting them to Christianity and teaching them the rudiments of the Portuguese language so that they would fetch higher prices.[4] Slave exports in the sixteenth century had averaged between 650 and 800 per year, but by the end of the seventeenth century they had fallen to under two hundred per year. When the Company of the Islands of Cape Verde and Guinea, which had a contract to supply slaves to the Spanish Indies, went out of business in 1703, the slave transshipment business declined.[5]

The slaves who worked the land on Santiago grew some sugar cane, which they made into sugar in several small mills on the island. But mainly they produced cotton and wove it into cloth using African-type looms and weaving techniques. By interweaving threads of different colors, they made geometric designs of great intricacy and beauty, and by using locally made indigo dyes, they made varieties of light blue, dark blue, and striped cloth. Cape Verdian cloth found a welcome market on the West African coast, where it was traded for slaves, but it also found markets as far away as Brazil, Spain, and Flanders. Cloth production had already lost some of its markets with the decline of the slave reexport trade, but the real blow came in 1721, when Portugal prohibited the sale of Cape Verdian cloth to for-eigners on penalty of death.[6]

The rigid lines of caste and color that had once separated white Por-tuguese settlers from their black African slaves had become blurred over time as more and more slaves gained their freedom through manumission or by running away to the interior of the island and creating free black communities. Slave weavers often purchased their freedom with money they earned by weaving on their own account during Sundays and saints' holidays. By the time the *Diligent* arrived in 1731, free blacks on Santiago outnumbered slaves by nearly four to one, and the importation of new slaves from the Guinea coast was a mere trickle. In May 1731, just before the *Diligent* departed from Vannes, the Portuguese bishop of the Cape Verde Islands, José de Santa Maria de Jesus, wrote to the king of Portugal questioning whether, as a matter of conscience, the importation of slaves from Guinea should continue at all.[7]

The free black population on Santiago grew, and racial distinctions became blurred as Portuguese men continued to father children with their slave wives and concubines. A *mestiço* community on Santiago had been recognized as early as 1582, and by 1731, Santiago counted 394 whites and 2,461 *mestiços*. The Portuguese governor, who seemed obsessed with issues of race, griped that most of the people who were classified as whites were actually *brancos da terra* of mixed descent. Although most of the land on Santiago was still owned by "whites," free blacks and *mestiços* were moving into positions of authority. Most of the priests were black—the bishop valued them far above the mostly illiterate priests sent from Portugal—and the local officials were mostly blacks or *mestiços*. Even the governor's militia had black captains and lieutenants. It would only be a short time, groused the Portuguese governor, before *all* of the island's military officers would be black.[8]

For Robert Durand and his fellow crew members, the Cape Verde Islands represented a kind of cultural "halfway house" between the society they had left behind in France and the ones they would encounter in Africa. Not only did the skin tones they observed on the island cover the full spectrum from white to black, but the cultural mixture also defied existing stereotypes. Santiago had literate black priests and illiterate white priests, and the only dynamic sector of its economy was dominated by enslaved weavers using African technology. Culturally, as well as geographically, the crew of the *Diligent* was halfway between Europe and its designated landfall in West Africa.

Upon leaving the Cape Verde Islands on July 9, the *Diligent* changed its course. Until now it had been sailing generally southwest, first to get around the Iberian Peninsula and then to get around the westward protrusion of

West Africa. At the Cape Verde Islands it was opposite the westernmost point in Africa—Cape Verde—and from there on the African coast began to curve back toward the southeast. Having signed an agreement with the French Company of the Indies, they were well aware that the company claimed a monopoly on French trade along the African coast from the mouth of the Senegal River to the mouth of the Sierra Leone River. This territorial delineation was based on the ocean currents. Ships that came from Europe to Senegal could turn around and return directly to Europe, thus allowing for a direct trade in goods such as hides and gum arabic. South of the Sierra Leone River, however, ships encountered the Guinea current, which carried them along the coast of West Africa all the way to Gabon. Since the Company of the Indies carried on a substantial direct trade with Senegal, it had retained its monopoly on the area north of the Sierra Leone River. The *Diligent* was forbidden even to stop at a company post for food and water unless blown there by a storm.

Carefully avoiding the forbidden territory, the *Diligent* was headed for a landfall along the Guinea coast of West Africa. "Guinea" was one of those imaginary geographical constructions of European cartographers that kept showing up in different places on different maps. The 1730 French map by the chief royal geographer, Guillaume Delìsle, had Guinea running all the way from the Senegal River to the Gabon River, whereas the 1729 map by D'Anville, who was also a French royal geographer, showed the Guinea coast as starting at the Sierra Leone River and ending at the Cameroon River. If there was little agreement about where Guinea began and ended, there seemed to be a general agreement among European mapmakers that south of Sierra Leone it was subdivided into the Grain Coast, the Ivory Coast, and the Gold Coast, so named because of the major products that the Europeans sought in each region.[9]

Now moving in a generally southeasterly direction, the *Diligent* sailed for two weeks seeing nothing but the sea and the sky. At 2:00 P.M. on July 25, as they tacked into a southwest wind, they spotted a ship ahead of them. It tacked to approach them, and as it came near, it tacked again to put itself on a parallel course. As the two ships sailed within hailing distance of each other, the mysterious ship ran up an English flag. The *Diligent* responded by running up its French flag. Seeing the English flag, Captain Mary ordered all hands to their battle stations. On the main deck, the

Figure 14.3   Pirate captain Bartholomew Roberts.

gunner, Charles Auger, directed the men in charging the cannons with powder and fuses. On the quarterdeck and forecastle, they manned the swivel guns. Since England and France were not at war, Captain Mary did not fear that it was an English warship or privateer, but a pirate ship that was flying the English flag as a ruse to get close enough to attack.

Captain Mary had reason to be worried because the *Diligent* was off the coast of Sierra Leone, an area frequented by pirates. Many stories of pirates had been told and retold during long watches at sea. Perhaps he knew the story of William Snelgrave stumbling onto three English pirate ships when his slave ship, *Bird Galley,* entered the mouth of the Sierra Leone River in April 1719. This was also the place where the notorious pirate Bartholomew Roberts had based himself in July 1721 and prepared his three ships to maraud the coast all the way to Old Calabar, taking every ship he encountered, including the French slave ships *Saint René* and *Hermoine.* When news of the approaching pirates reached Whydah, it inspired such fear that four French ships departed immediately. One of them, the *Union,* left in such a hurry that it abandoned twenty crew members on shore.[10]

When Bartholomew Roberts came back up the coast in January 1722, he came across eleven ships lying in the Whydah road with their captains and most of their crews ashore buying slaves. The ships surrendered immediately and paid a ransom of eight pounds of gold dust apiece, except for the *Porcupine*, whose captain on shore refused to pay. Roberts then sent a longboat to the *Porcupine* to free the captives and set the ship on fire. Having trouble unshackling the slaves and being in a hurry to make his escape from Whydah, he set the *Porcupine* on fire with eighty captives chained together two by two on board. Then he fled Whydah. By this time the British man-of-war *Swallow* was in pursuit of Roberts's ships, having arrived in Whydah only twenty-four hours after Roberts had departed east. Over three weeks later the *Swallow* caught up with Roberts's three ships at Cape Lopez. Roberts was killed in the ensuing battle, and the man-of-war captured two hundred Englishmen and seventy freed African slaves. The prisoners were taken to Cape Coast Castle, the African headquarters of the British Royal African Company, where they were tried and then hanged, imprisoned, or acquitted according to the outcome of the trial.[11]

But the end of Bartholomew Roberts and his crew did not signal the end of piracy in the region. Later that same year another pirate ship, with a crew of thirty white and twenty-two black pirates, captured the French ship *Duc de la Force*. In March 1731—just two months before the *Diligent* left Vannes—the governor general of the Dutch West India Company sent out a general warning along the Guinea coast that a pirate ship with thirty-six guns and two hundred men was in the neighborhood of the Upper Guinea coast and "is expected to come down any moment from now." All forts and ships were warned to prepare for battle. The rumor turned out to be an "invented lie of some sailor," but the fact that the Dutch West India Company took it so seriously hints at the fear that pirates inspired among slave traders along the Guinea coast.[12]

Pirate ships represented a kind of maritime counterculture that reversed the strict regulation and hierarchy found on authorized merchant vessels. Captain Roberts and his motley band had drawn up a set of articles that each member of the company swore to uphold. The articles said that "every man has a vote in the affairs of the moment" and "equal title to the fresh provisions or strong liquors" unless scarcity made it necessary for them to vote for rationing. Even the sharing of the loot was more democratic. In the crews under Roberts's command, the captain and quartermaster received double shares, the master, boatswain, and gunner received one and a half shares, the other officers one and a quarter shares, and the ordinary seamen received one share each. The captain of a pirate ship thus received twice the remuneration of an ordinary sailor, whereas the captain of the *Diligent* received ten times the salary of the lowest-paid seaman. This democracy of thieves had arisen in part because there was no state or maritime legal system to back up the prerogatives of pirate captains and officers.

Many sailors found the limited democracy of pirate vessels a welcome relief from the legal despotism of merchant ships. When Roberts's vessels were taken, his crew was found to include sixty-nine sailors who had joined him from other ships that he had captured. When those men protested to the court that they had been forced into a life of piracy, their cases were considered individually. Twenty-seven of them were found guilty of voluntarily joining the pirate band.

Such stories had to be on Pierre Mary's mind as he eyed the approaching ship. He watched closely for the wisps of smoke that foreshadowed the boom of cannons. Instead of firing its cannons, however, the mysterious ship hauled down its main course in a peaceful gesture. It was now close enough to the *Diligent* that shouts across the water could be understood. An officer aboard the mysterious ship communicated that it was an English trading vessel that had left the Gambia River three weeks earlier and was headed for Cape Mont. Relieved to learn that they were not about to be attacked by pirates, Captain Mary ordered the crew of the *Diligent* to lower the yards of the topsails and furl the course sails. With the two ships nearly at a standstill, the English ship lowered its longboat and sent an officer to the *Diligent* to purchase some supplies. At 4:00 P.M. the officer left the *Diligent* without buying anything. The crew of the *Diligent* set its topsails and courses, and they continued on their way. At six degrees, forty-two minutes north latitude, they were now well south of the Sierra Leone River and heading toward landfall on the West African coast.

PART 5

Cruising the African Coast

$\mathcal{T}$HREE WEEKS AFTER LEAVING the Cape Verde Islands and two months after leaving Vannes, the lookout spotted the West African coast on July 31 at 6:00 A.M. Judging from their latitude, Robert Durand calculated that they were probably near the mouth of the Sestos River. Tall, oddly shaped trees and white houses indicated the village of Sanguinee and confirmed their position. The *Diligent* dropped its anchors into the sandy bottom twenty-three fathoms below.[1]

The Sestos River was a popular stopping point for ships on their way to Whydah because they could get timber and fresh water free of charge, if they gave a small gift to the local ruler, and could purchase rice cheaply. In the seventeenth century French merchants from Normandy had established two trading posts here, which they called Little Dieppe and Little Paris, where they purchased ivory and malaguetta peppers. But they were now long gone. The *Diligent* was apparently well enough stocked with provisions from the Cape Verde Islands that it left the next day for the nearby coastal town of Bassa.[2]

They were on a part of the West African coast identified as the Grain Coast on maps because of the malaguetta peppers that Europeans purchased. Most ships did not attempt to purchase slaves here because few were available. No major slave trade routes from the inland regions led to this stretch of the Guinea coast, and the few slaves that were sold were often the victims of local African kidnappers who seized them when they were traveling or visiting neighboring towns. This practice, known as "panyarring,"

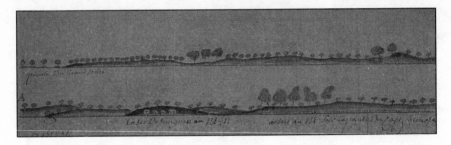

Figure 15.1   Durand's drawing of the African coast at Sestos.

made people afraid to travel more than a couple of miles from home without carrying firearms.[3] Because there were no regular slave markets in this region, African chiefs and merchants with slaves for sale sent up smoke signals when they saw a European ship. This occasional slave trade exported fewer than two hundred slaves per year in the first quarter of the eighteenth century. For every slave taken from the Grain Coast, one hundred were taken from Whydah.[4]

Relations between Europeans and Africans were tense along this coast because European captains sometimes kidnapped and enslaved Africans who came to their ships to sell food and supplies. British private traders from Bristol and Liverpool were notorious for doing this, and French ships did it as well. When the British surveyor William Smith visited in 1727, he noted that the people "live in peace with all their neighbors and account Europeans their only enemies." Similarly, the British naval surgeon John Atkins observed that canoe men coming out to sell goods to his ship hesitated as they approached. "The boldest," observed Atkins, "would sometimes come aboard bringing rice, malaguetta peppers, and ivory, but staying under fear and suspicion."[5]

Africans got revenge for the kidnapping of their countrymen by "panyarring" Europeans who came ashore or even going out to ships on pretense of wanting to trade and then pulling out weapons hidden among their trade goods.[6] Only a few months after the *Diligent* passed Bassa, the British slave ship *Dove* anchored there to trade. When the first mate Theodore Coote went ashore, he was taken hostage. A group of Africans captured the *Dove*, killing all aboard and running the vessel aground. Coot remained in captivity for sixteen days until he was ransomed by a passing

English ship. Given the ongoing cycle of European kidnapping and African retaliation, it is no wonder that John Atkins described European–African relations in this area as characterized by "mutual distrust."[7]

Before arriving at Bassa, Robert Durand checked the pilot's guide for advice on landing. It was a large book in two volumes, called *La Tourbe Ardent*, which can be roughly translated as "The Burning Fen." The author was the Dutch mapmaker Arent Roggeveen. The Dutch version had first appeared in 1675 and the French version had followed a year later.[8] So accurate were its descriptions of the moorings and landings on the West African coast that it was still in wide use over fifty years later. According to the guidebook, the ship should anchor at a spot with the forest to the north and the mountain to the east-northeast to find sandy bottom at a depth of twenty-two or twenty-three fathoms.

After leaving Bassa, they continued to follow the West African coast. Watching the shore, Robert Durand saw a few clear stretches of coastline between long stretches of low-lying mangrove swamps. Occasionally he spotted African villages. To locate their position they now depended less on calculations of latitude and longitude and more on spotting certain hills, villages, or clusters of trees along the shore. Durand sketched the shore formations in his journal so that he would recognize them if he ever returned. They were moving rapidly in the Guinea current, which would carry them all the way to Whydah and beyond.

16

ON AUGUST 9 AT 10:30 A.M. the lookout spotted the Dutch fort at Axim rising from a rocky ledge on the shore. The *Diligent* had arrived at the Gold Coast. The landscape changed dramatically as the mangrove swamps gave way to rocky outcroppings framed by steep hills. The hinterland of the Gold Coast contained gold mines and gold-bearing streams where African miners and prospectors extracted gold that African merchants brought to the coast for sale.

The Portuguese had first visited the area in 1471, finding people wearing heavy gold ornaments and much gold for sale at cheap prices. They mistakenly thought the mines were very near the coast, which they named *Mina de Ouro*, the gold mine. Eleven years later a small army of Portuguese soldiers and craftsmen began building São Jorge da Mina castle, using stone quarried from the rocky shoreline and red burned brick carried from Portugal. The fort served as an outpost for buying gold, which was carried back to Portugal by the fleets of caravels that arrived about once a year. The Portuguese built a second fort in 1515 and a third around 1550. Unlike their practice in other parts of the world, the Portuguese did not try to conquer the land or take possession of it. They remained tenants of local African chiefs to whom they paid rent, even though they claimed sovereignty inside the walls of their forts. Similar arrangements were later adopted by all the other European nations that settled along the Gold Coast.[1]

In the early seventeenth century the Dutch challenged the Portuguese monopoly, sending out a ship loaded with bricks, timbers, carpenters, and masons to construct a fort quickly before the Portuguese could interfere. From that base they launched attacks on the Portuguese, capturing all three forts between 1637 and 1642. No sooner had the Dutch completed their conquest of the Gold Coast than the British-chartered Company of Adventurers of London began constructing a fort, and the Swedish Africa Company began building Fort Carolusburg. To counter the Swedes, the Dutch built a new fort at Butri. By the time the Dutch drove the Swedes out of Fort Carolusburg, the Danes had begun construction of Christians-borg Castle at Accra. The main purpose of the forts was to purchase gold and have it ready so that arriving company ships could load their cargoes quickly and return home.

During the 1660s many forts changed hands as the British and Dutch fought a series wars to oust each other from the Gold Coast. In the after-math, both sides began to expand and strengthen their fortresses. The Dutch built a new fort and greatly expanded four existing ones, while the English built Cape Coast castle on the ruins of the old Swedish Fort Caro-lusburg. After the 1672–1674 naval war between Holland and England, the English built a number of forts and lodges near those of the Dutch, who responded by building new forts at Sekondi and Takoradi. The later seven-teenth century saw the entry of the Prussian-based Brandenburg Africa Company into the trade, building three forts in the 1680s. The French too tried to get into the gold trade. They established a trading post in 1687, but the Dutch burned it down. In 1701 they returned to build a wooden fort but changed their plans after France received the *assiento* contract to supply slaves to the Spanish colonies of the New World. Deciding to concentrate on the slave trade rather than gold, they abandoned the Gold Coast and built a fort at Whydah, on the Slave Coast. Since the Spanish often paid for their slaves with gold and silver, the French used the slave trade as an indi-rect means of gaining precious metals.

When the *Diligent* arrived in 1731, the Dutch controlled fifteen forts, the English controlled nine, and the Danes controlled one.[2] The Swedes, Brandenburgers, Portuguese, and French were all gone. Twenty-five major forts and castles—some of them within cannon shot of one another—were situated along a three-hundred-mile stretch of coastline, producing a greater concentration of fortresses here than in any other place on earth. They were all built right up against the rocky shore so that their cannons

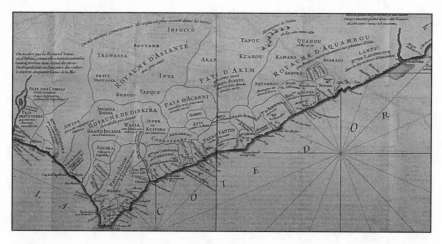

Figure 16.1 African kingdoms of the Gold Coast as shown on this 1729 map by D'Anville.

could command their harbors and enforce their national or company monopolies. Above each fort flew an enormous national flag so that ships at sea would identify it correctly.

Because so many of the forts had been built for strategic reasons growing out of European rivalries, their size and number did not in any way correspond to the value of the trade they conducted. The gold trade, which had provided the original justification for the forts, was in decline, and the European trading companies were trying to make up the shortfall by increasing their trade in slaves. During the first quarter of the eighteenth century, 20 percent of all slaves shipped across the Atlantic came from the Gold Coast.[3]

Behind the thin line of forts was a series of small independent African states. D'Anville's 1729 map identified thirty-three separate states stretched out along the coastline and stacked several tiers deep.[4] African traders from the far interior had to pass through a series of states on their way to the coast, paying customs duties and brokerage fees to each one. Political tension and warfare often flared when states closer to the coast sought to control the trade routes, as interior states sought free access to the coast.

The major political development in the early eighteenth century was the rise of the inland African state of Asante, which by the 1720s had gained enough control of the trade routes that it could send merchant caravans and

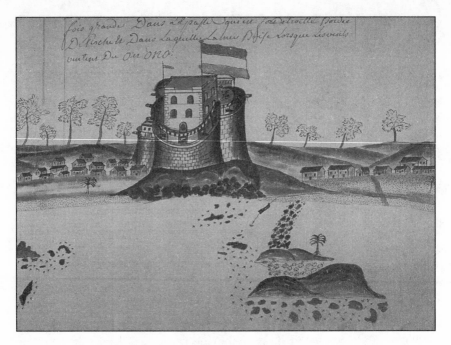

Figure 16.2   Durand's drawing of the Dutch fort at Axim.

armies to the coast almost at will. In February 1731, just six months before
the arrival of the *Diligent*, an Asante army ten thousand strong had encamped within range of the guns of the Fort at Axim looking for refugees
from their recent war with the African state of Wassa. The Dutch, since the
well-being of the company's trade depended on maintaining good relations
with Asante, did not interfere.[5]

Fort Axim was the first Gold Coast fort encountered by the *Diligent*. It
had three bastions and was armed with twenty-four cannons. It exported
more gold than all the other Dutch forts on that coast put together, in part
because it drew on the western trade routes from the gold fields of Asante
and Aowin.[6] It also had a reputation as an excellent place to get water and
wood. After the *Diligent* dropped its anchors in ten fathoms of water, the
gunner saluted the fort with five cannon shots. The fort responded with
three, and selected crew members headed for land with both the longboat
and the skiff. Second Captain Valteau asked the Dutch director of the fort
for permission to cut ten cords of wood at a price of eight akies (one-half
ounce) of gold per cord and paid for the wood with brandy. The *Diligent*'s

two carpenters cut firewood and sawed boards that they would later use for refitting the *Diligent* into a slave ship. African employees of the fort loaded the wood on the longboat. The crew also refilled the water barrels at a well, which required three trips in the longboat.

It was at Axim that they first encountered the slave trade. The Dutch director of the fort tried to sell Captain Mary a captive African boy, but they could not agree on the price. Another chance came at night, when local African slave merchants smuggled African captives out to the ships. Since the Dutch fort had declared a monopoly on trade in the port, both the African merchants and the European captains risked severe reprisals for such activities. Captain Mary declined several invitations to purchase slaves surreptitiously, in part because he knew that he would have many more opportunities in the coming weeks and months.

With the wood and water loaded, the *Diligent* headed east from Axim and anchored for the night. Since they were hugging the shoreline, it was dangerous to sail at night, when they couldn't see the rocks. Robert Durand noted in his journal that the ship was anchored only fifteen miles from the fort, which he referred to as "Fort Brandenburg, or Fort Konny." Durand had the name wrong. The actual name of the fort had been Gross Friedrichsburg until 1724, when the Dutch had taken it over and renamed it Fort Hollandia. However, both of the names Durand gave—Fort Brandenburg and Fort Konny—referred to particular aspects of the fort's history.

Fort Gross Friederichsburg had been built nearly fifty years earlier, in 1683, when the Prussian-based Brandenburg African Company wanted to get a foothold in the gold trade. By the second decade of the eighteenth century it had met with some success, in large measure because a local African broker and merchant named John Konny used his contacts with the inland regions to tap the gold trade from the states of Asante and Aowin. Konny also encouraged the Brandenburg Company to welcome interlopers: vessels sailing without authorization from their national government or trading company. By bringing together European interlopers and inland African merchants, he could provide European goods at cheaper prices than could the British and Dutch, and he built up a large clientele among Asante traders.

In 1715 John Konny took command of the fort away from the company-appointed director, Nicholas Dubois. The English commented that

Figure 16.3   Durand's drawing of the fort he called "Fort Brandenburg or Fort Konny."

little had actually changed, since before the coup, the European director could not act without Konny's consent. Konny then sent Dubois to Europe to consult with the company directors and was left in sole command of the fort. He dismissed all white employees who could not maintain themselves and left only a commandant and a sergeant to administer the fort. In November 1717 the Brandenburg Company sold the fort to the Dutch without Konny's knowledge. Konny rejected the deal, saying that the king of Prussia was merely his tenant and had no right to sell property on his land without his permission. The Dutch sent three shiploads of armed men to attack the fort. When their advance was met with a charge led by John Konny himself, they retreated, leaving thirty-six dead Dutchmen behind.[7]

When the Englishman John Atkins visited the fort in 1721, Konny was waiting on shore to receive him and conduct him to the house that he had built with stones from the fort. As a man who had worked with the Prussians for years, Konny spoke fluent German, and he also spoke English well enough to swear in it. "He is a strong-made man," observed Atkins, "about fifty, of a sullen look." Konny's house, said Atkins, "ascends with a double-stone staircase without, of twelve steps; on that floor are three good rooms; one his armory, another his chamber with a standing bed in it, and the third for entertainment of guests, furnished with tables, chairs, etc." That evening John Konny served his guest a dinner of "canky bread, salt butter, cheese, palm wine, and beer served with clean plates with knives, napkins, etc." Although disappointed by the meal, Atkins observed that Konny conducted himself with great ceremony and "knew how to put on a significant countenance."[8]

The Dutch West India Company continued to press its dubious claim to the fort, in part because Konny had made it a haven for European interlopers. Konny wanted his place to be a "free port where all nations could trade, but none could settle," a philosophy that was anathema to the national trading companies that wanted to keep monopoly control. In November 1724 a Dutch force successfully stormed the castle using hand grenades and mortars. John Konny went into exile in the coastal state of Ankober, just across the Ankober River from the Dutch fort at Axim. Using an English ship from Cape Coast castle to trade from Ankober, Konny created serious competition to the Dutch at Axim, who complained that "John Konny obstructs everything and lets no traders pass." They also complained that the English were negotiating with Konny to purchase the two smaller Brandenburg African Company forts—Fort Dorothea and Fort Louise—that were still under Konny's control.[9]

The *Diligent* sat at anchor only five leagues away from Fort Gross Friedrichsburg, now renamed Fort Hollandia by the Dutch. A canoe carrying two Africans approached, bringing a letter from the director of the fort inviting the *Diligent* to anchor in front of the fort and offering them his services. This was an astonishing offer because the Dutch West India Company still maintained a monopoly over the slave trade from its forts. The director of the fort was apparently conducting clandestine trade with foreign ships. The *Diligent* moved closer to the fort, in part because it offered better anchorage, but declined any services. The next morning another letter arrived asking Captain Mary to come ashore and look over African captives. Mary refused. Perhaps he figured that the prices were too high.

Over the next four days the *Diligent* sailed past the English Fort Dixcove, the Dutch Fort Batensteyn, the English and Dutch forts at Commendo, and the Dutch Fort Hampeny. Durand sketched each of them in his journal so that he could identify them the next time he came. At Commendo they encountered a Dutch coast guard ship armed with fifty cannons that served mainly to make sure that the Portuguese ships that came to the Guinea coast from Brazil paid a 10 percent tax to the Dutch. At nine o'clock on the morning of Tuesday, August 21, Second Captain Pierre Valteau left the *Diligent* in the longboat in order to go ahead of the ship to Elmina castle and find a canoe that would take him to Whydah to alert the French fort of the *Diligent's* imminent arrival. Carried by the Guinea current and not depending on the wind, human-powered boats could make better time than a large sailing ship. The unfavorable August wind was slowing the *Diligent's* progress.[10]

17

*O*N TUESDAY, AUGUST 21, the *Diligent* came to the fabled castle of Elmina, which Robert Durand referred to simply as "the mine." The oldest and largest of the European forts along the Gold Coast, Elmina had been built by the Portuguese, beginning in 1482, as São Jorge da Mina, and Christopher Columbus had visited it sometime before his voyage to the New World.[1] The Portuguese had used it as the center for purchasing gold brought by African traders from the inland gold fields.

The Dutch, who had built their first fort on the Gold Coast in 1612, tried to oust the Portuguese from Elmina in 1625 but were soundly defeated. They returned in 1637 and installed heavy artillery on Santiago Hill and bombarded the fort on its weakest side. During the next five years they ousted the Portuguese from their forts at Shama and Axim as well. In 1661 Holland and Portugal reached a permanent settlement that deprived the Portuguese of all rights to trade along the Guinea coast. Although ships sailing from Portugal apparently honored the agreement, ships sailing out of Brazil did not, and so in the 1690s the Dutch agreed to let Portuguese ships trade along the Guinea coast if they first received permission from the Dutch governor-general at Elmina and paid a 10 percent tax.[2] This agreement was still in force when the *Diligent* sailed. In 1730 thirty-one Portuguese ships had paid the tax and one had been captured and confiscated for nonpayment.[3]

Even though Robert Durand had by now seen many Gold Coast forts, he found Elmina to be truly impressive. "Elmina," he wrote, "belongs to

Figure 17.1   Durand's drawing of Elmina castle.

the Dutch, and all the other forts of this coast belonging to that nation are
subordinate to it because the governor-general resides here. It is undoubtedly the most handsome and the strongest fort of the coast. It is situated on
the seashore, and farther up on a mountain is another fort that dominates
the one below. They are separated from each other by a small stream that is
crossed by means of a drawbridge. Its port is on the northeast side, where
there is a quay that receives longboats and small ships, which can only enter and leave at high tide. The village at the foot of the two forts resembles
a small city. The streets are well laid out, and there are workers of all professions. The houses are very pretty." Durand then focused on the fort itself. "This place is considered impregnable," he wrote. "It is armed with
over two hundred cannons, most of them of cast iron. The Portuguese
who come to trade at the coast pay tribute of a tenth of their cargoes to
the Dutch, and they don't dare trade a single slave without first stopping at
Elmina to pay what they owe. For that reason there are always Dutch coast
guard ships that stop the Portuguese vessels and make them show their letter of permission from the governor-general at Elmina."

During the first two decades of the eighteenth century, Dutch trade
along the Gold Coast had undergone a major transition, shifting from a

predominant trade in gold to a predominant trade in slaves. The gold and slave trades had been intertwined from the very beginning of European activity along the Gold Coast, but in a very curious way. When the Portuguese first started buying gold from African merchants at Elmina, they paid for it with cloth, metal goods, wine, and also with slaves that they imported from the Bight of Benin and the island of São Tomé. The slaves were purchased by wealthy Africans to serve as porters on merchant caravans, workers in the gold fields, and agricultural laborers. Between 1475 and 1540 more than twelve thousand slaves were *imported* into the Gold Coast by the Portuguese. After that slave imports declined, but forts such as Elmina and Axim continued to be major slave markets for slaves brought into the Gold Coast. During the seventeenth century between forty thousand and eighty thousand slaves *entered* the region via the coastal ports.[4]

When the Dutch drove out the Portuguese, they tried to maintain the distinction between the Gold Coast, which concentrated on the gold trade, and the Slave Coast, where they bought slaves. Elmina castle did not even have slaveholding facilities until 1687—more than two hundred years after its original construction—and even then they were supposed to be used for temporary storage of slaves for ships coming from the Slave Coast.[5] Nevertheless, small numbers of slaves—averaging less than two hundred per year—were exported from the Gold Coast on Dutch ships between 1675 and 1720. After 1720, however, there was a dramatic rise in Dutch slave exports from the Gold Coast: a thousand per year between 1721 and 1725 and two thousand per year between 1725 and 1730.[6] The forts became sites where slaves were purchased and held until a company ship arrived to carry them away.

A Dutch memorandum written in 1730 outlined the reasons for the change very clearly: "That part of Africa which as of old is known as the Gold Coast because of the great quantity of gold that was at one time purchased there by the company as well as by Dutch private ships, has now virtually changed into a pure Slave Coast. The great quantity of guns and powder that the Europeans have brought here from time to time has caused terrible wars among the kings, princes, and caboceers of those lands, who made slaves of their prisoners of war; these slaves were increasingly bought up by the Europeans at steadily increasing prices. Consequently, there is now very little trade among the coast Negroes except in slaves, and those coast Negroes constantly keep the trade routes closed, preventing nations situated more in the interior from bringing their gold, ivory, and so on, to the coast."[7]

The writer of the Dutch memorandum had correctly identified the role of guns in revolutionizing warfare among the small African states of the Gold Coast. There had been a significant rise in African demand for guns after flintlocks replaced the unreliable matchlocks in the 1690s, and African armies always seemed in need of fresh gunpowder, which didn't store well in the humid climate. In 1700 the Dutch alone sold twenty thousand tons of gunpowder annually along the Gold Coast, and by 1730 about 180,000 guns per year were coming into the Gold and Slave Coasts combined.[8] The rise in the gun trade was driven as much by demand as by supply. In August 1718, when Asante was preparing for war against the states of Wassa and Aowin, it purchased three tons of gunpowder from the Dutch in a single transaction. In preparing to defend themselves, Wassa and Aowin also stocked up on guns and gunpowder at Fort Axim. Elmina castle suffered a minor crisis on April 2, 1732, when a caravan from Asante arrived with slaves and demanded flintlocks in return. The governor-general sent a desperate circular to all the other forts ordering that all flintlocks be sent to Elmina at once.[9]

The warfare that was carried out with those guns was not as random or haphazard as the writer of the Dutch memorandum seemed to imply; rather, it involved a complex struggle for control of the trade routes and especially the rise of the Asante empire in the hinterland of the forts. At the beginning of the eighteenth century, Asante had been a loose military alliance of several small states in the interior that began a process of consolidation and expansion under the reign of Osai Tutu. Asante's trade with the coast had been blocked by the state of Denkyira, and so in 1701 the Asante army invaded Denkyira and forced it to acknowledge Asante authority. This victory gave the Asante traders freer access to the forts along the coast, but they were still forced to pass through the territory of small states such as Aowin, Wassa, and Twifo, which exacted charges for tolls and brokerage services and could block the trade routes at will. By 1727 many of the middleman states had been reduced to tributaries of Asante.[10]

In the 1720s at least one major trading expedition from Asante arrived at Elmina or one of its satellite forts every year. They brought little gold, in part because gold was in demand within Asante itself, but mostly they came with ivory and slaves.[11] Prior to the 1720s Asante had been capturing slaves in its wars, but it had used them internally for agriculture and gold mining. By the 1720s Asante had built up such a large slave population that there were reports of massive slave desertions.[12] Having first supplied their own labor needs, the Asante rulers felt free in the 1720s to begin exporting their surplus slaves. In return for their slaves, they wanted mainly guns and gunpowder to support the further expansion of their growing empire. Just five months before the *Diligent* arrived, a "great multitude" of Asante slave traders arrived at Elmina, causing a problem for the Dutch West India Company because the castle and its satellite forts were out of trade goods. In panic, the company diverted a private Zeeland slave ship from going to Jakin so that its trade goods could be used to buy slaves from the Asante traders.[13] Expeditions such as that one account for much of the rise in Dutch slave exports in the 1720s.

The Dutch West India Company's shift toward slave trading was one of the factors that led to the loss of its monopoly. A gold monopoly was easy to justify, but monopoly control over the Dutch slave trade was becoming an anachronism. The English and French, who now relied heavily on private traders, had greatly increased their slave trade since the beginning of the century to the disadvantage of the Dutch West India Company, which was sending out only five or six ships a year. The company hadn't paid any dividends from profits in fifty-five years. The only way to compete with the British and French, the Dutch capitalists argued, was to follow their lead in allowing private traders, who would pay fifteen hundred florins per ship (the value of about twenty slaves) for the privilege of using company facilities. Left out of that argument was the fact that private interlopers were becoming very bold; between 1713 and 1724 the company had confiscated twenty-six private ships from the Dutch province of Zeeland alone.[14] Those who opposed privatization argued that in order to police the proposed permission system, the company would need to outfit two new cruisers at a cost of 200,000 florins per year, which is more than it would take in from the fees. Moreover, they argued, the private merchants would trade at the beaches directly with the Africans and bypass the forts entirely.[15]

When the States General in Holland renewed the Dutch West India Company's charter in 1730, it compromised on the issue: the company

Figure 17.2   Durand's drawing of Cape Coast castle.

would retain its monopoly on trade along the Gold Coast, but private Dutch ships would be allowed to trade along other parts of the African coast provided that they purchased a permit from the company and followed company rules. The Gold Coast was later opened to private traders by an amendment to the company's charter in 1734.[16] The system of national chartered monopoly companies that had dominated Atlantic trade in the seventeenth century was, for all practical purposes, dead.

After picking up Second Captain Valteau, who had failed to find canoe passage to Whydah, the *Diligent* continued along the coast to spend the night at a spot about halfway in between Elmina castle and Cape Coast castle, the administrative center of the British Royal African Company's eight other forts along the Gold Coast. When the *Diligent* dropped its anchor, both castles were in view, being only three leagues apart. Comparing the Dutch and British castles, Robert Durand wrote, "The fort at Cape Coast is the most handsome that the English have along this coast, and although it doesn't exactly have the appearance of Elmina, it cannot fail to be more vast on the inside, and its power is hardly any less. It is situated on a low-lying point about three leagues from Elmina." In a single sweep of his eyes, Robert Durand had the major centers of European power along the Gold Coast in view. Together, the two nations owned twenty-four of the twenty-five European forts and castles.

Just as the changes at Elmina were not apparent to the eye of a casual passerby, the towering ramparts of Cape Coast castle hid a company in transition. Even the castle itself was not what it appeared to be. The walls were high but thin, and the entire structure was vulnerable because it had been built using mud instead of mortar. Residents complained that "there is never a dry room to lie in," and they feared that the castle was "likely to be washed down by the rains."[17] So serious were the maintenance problems that at the time Robert Durand arrived, Cape Coast castle employed fifty armorers, smiths, and carpenters, but only forty soldiers.[18]

The problems facing the Royal African Company were quite different from those facing the Dutch. The British had never adhered to Portuguese and Dutch notions about the geographical separation of the gold trade from the slave trade. They had always traded gold, slaves, and ivory indiscriminately. When the Company of Adventurers of London built the first English fort along the Gold Coast in the 1640s, it contained a slave prison, and when the Royal African Company, formed in 1672, started building Cape Coast castle in 1674 by enlarging and expanding the old Swedish Fort Carolusburg, they built an underground slave prison with large, vaulted cellars cut into the rock below the parade ground. Divided into several large rooms, the dungeon could easily hold a thousand slaves.[19]

Although the underground dungeon was effective in preventing African captives from escaping until a Royal African Company ship came along to take them away, the captives died in such numbers that company officials in London became concerned. In 1718 the surgeon at Cape Coast castle suggested that deaths could be reduced by building special quarters for sick slaves, lining the bottom and sides of the dungeon with boards half an inch thick to mitigate the effects of the damp stone walls, and constructing platforms eighteen inches above the ground for the captives to sleep on. To improve hygiene, he recommended tubs "for the slaves to ease themselves at night." The underground prison, he recommended, should be cleaned every morning with lemon or lime juice to reduce the stench and smoked once a week to "refresh and sweeten it."[20]

Despite the surgeon's suggestions, nothing was done, and in 1721 the company's court of assistants complained that "notwithstanding all our care to accept none but choice slaves from any of your factories, yet we

Figure 17.3   The slave dungeon was underneath the courtyard of Cape Coast
castle.

have lately had a great mortality besides a number of them very much reduced and in a bad state of health." The mortality was blamed squarely on
"the great detriment the slaves' hole is for their health." To remedy this
problem, the company made plans for building a new slave prison above
ground and outside the castle walls. Such a move, the company believed,
would not only provide healthier conditions for the captives, but it would
free up the underground vaults for "the keeping of liquors and other
goods which may properly be kept underground." As with the earlier
schemes, nothing was done.[21] By 1731 the captives were still being held
underground. Only eight months before the *Diligent* arrived, a group of
slaves in that dungeon had managed to remove an iron bar from an opening, and they were working on a second bar when their escape plan was
discovered. They were immediately moved to another holding pen. After a
day of brutal interrogation, their leader was identified and given a hundred
lashes with the whip.[22]

Despite the vast capacity of their grisly slaveholding facilities, British
slave shipments from the Gold Coast had averaged less that two thousand
slaves per year throughout the second half of the seventeenth century.
Then, around the end of the seventeenth century, their slave exports
tripled to about six thousand per year and were still at that level when the
Diligent arrived.[23] One reason for this upsurge was that the British Parliament had passed an act in 1698 opening up the Guinea trade to private
traders long before the French and Dutch followed suit. That act gave all

private traders the right to trade anywhere in Africa as long as they paid the company a 10 percent duty on all goods they exported from England. English private traders thus became known as "ten percenters." When the act expired in 1712, the Royal African Company made some pretenses of reclaiming its former monopoly rights, but by then British private trade in Africa had become so firmly established that it was no longer realistic to try to suppress it. The main effect of the expiration of the act was that the Royal African Company lost its right to collect the 10 percent duty from the private traders.

The major financial issue for the Royal African Company was how to maintain its forts after losing the 10 percent duty from private traders. During the 1720s the forts stood as white dinosaurs decorating the rocky coastline of the Gold Coast. In 1726 the slaving captain William Snelgrave gave the commissioners of trade and plantations in London a rundown on the state of the English forts. Fort Dixcove, he said, had only five English-men and the trade was so insubstantial that it was not worth keeping; the same was true for the fort at Sekondi. Komenda had only five Englishmen to guard it. Cape Coast castle had twenty Englishmen and over forty can-nons, but the guns were not effective. Ships had to anchor too far out to enjoy any protection from the castle's guns because the area close to the castle was rocky and dangerous. The castle, Snelgrave reported, was in a bad state of disrepair, and the trade there was not considerable. Anamabu, about five leagues east of Cape Coast castle, was a neutral port that was drawing quite a bit of trade away from Cape Coast castle, but the Royal African Company's fort there had fallen down and Snelgrave doubted whether the local Africans would ever permit them to repair it. The forts at Tatumkwery, Winneba, and Accra had between two and five Englishmen apiece and were not capable of commanding the trade. Snelgrave also re-ported that the Dutch governor-general at Elmina had told him, some-what disingenuously, that even if the English tried to *give* him their forts, he would not take them.[24]

Such reports prompted the Royal African Company to send out the surveyor William Smith to "take exact plans, draughts, and prospects" of all the company's forts and settlements in West Africa.[25] When Smith re-turned to London in September 1727 with the results of his surveys, it be-came apparent that the Royal African Company could not maintain its own facilities. In 1730 the British Parliament voted an annual subsidy of £10,000 to the Royal African Company for upkeep and maintenance of the forts.[26] Given that the company's total expenses for personnel and maintenance of the forts in 1731 was £13,500, the British government had, in effect, assumed financial responsibility for the company's establishments along the Gold Coast.[27]

The forts were repaired, but the Royal African Company—the last and largest of the British chartered slave trading companies—never again stood on its own financial feet. Like the French, the British understood that the real profits lay not in the slave trade itself, but in the products produced by slaves in the New World colonies. Britain was willing to subsidize the Royal African Company in order to maintain its strategic position along the Gold Coast and keep up the supply of slaves to the New World.

After sailing past Cape Coast castle, Robert Durand noted and sketched eight forts over the next four days. Four of them belonged to the English, three to the Dutch, and one to the Danes. Realizing that the *Diligent* would soon be leaving the Gold Coast, Captain Mary took a renewed interest in buying slaves. Despite the fact that slave trading officially took place in the forts, independent African slave traders, operating in the spaces between the forts, often set fires at night to signal to passing ships that they had slaves for sale. Small French slave ships frequently took advantage of such clandestine sales in hopes of filling their holds before they reached Whydah, where they had to pay high customs duties.[28] On the night of August 23, when the *Diligent* was anchored between the Dutch Fort Amsterdam at Kormantin and the English fort at Tatumkwery, Captain Mary thought he saw smoke on shore and ordered the gunner to fire a cannon shot signaling his desire to trade. Although the ship normally spent the night in total darkness to allow the seamen's eyes to adjust to the night, they kept a lantern burning on the stern of the ship to guide canoes, but none came.

Two days later they arrived at Accra, where there were three forts built close together: one Dutch, one English, and one Danish. A canoe approached the *Diligent* carrying a letter from the director of the English fort informing them that he had slaves for sale. This was unexpected news to Captain Mary for two reasons. First, English forts usually sold slaves only to English ships. Second, slaves were scarce at Accra because several of the coastal African states had blockaded the trade routes to keep Asante merchants from selling slaves for guns and powder from the European forts. The Danes complained that the blockade had totally ruined the slave trade from Akyem, an inland state situated between Accra and the Asante heartland. If there were slaves for sale in August 1731, they most likely came from the region near the Volta River.[29]

Knowing that the forts at Accra were the last substantial forts along the Gold Coast, Captain Mary sent Second Captain Valteau to shore to conduct the negotiations. It turned out that the English director wanted to exchange the slaves for salted beef and other European food supplies that the *Diligent* was carrying, a transaction that would have depleted their supplies. Also, the director had no canoes for transporting slaves. If they wanted to buy slaves, they would have to wait four days while the director sent for canoes. Not wishing to delay their voyage any longer, they bade farewell to the Gold Coast and moved on.

18

T ONE O'CLOCK IN the afternoon of August 27 a lookout
spied the mouth of the Volta River, which marked the end of
the Gold Coast and the beginning of what some people at the time called
the Slave Coast. The French did not use that term; French ships simply
listed their destination as Whydah, which was the dominant port on that
part of the coast. The Pieter Goos map that the *Diligent* used did not use
the term "Slave Coast," and neither did the 1729 French map of Guinea
made by the royal geographer D'Anville.[1] The term had gained popularity
in the early eighteenth century with the publication of a book by Willem
Bosman, who had been the Dutch factor at Elmina. Bosman entitled his
book *A New and Accurate Description of the Coast of Guinea, Divided into the
Gold, Slave, and Ivory Coasts*, thus identifying each part of the Guinea coast
with the trade items most sought by European traders. The map accompanying the book, drawn by the geographer H. Moll, was called "A New and
Exact Map of Guinea, Divided into ye Gold, Slave, and Ivory Coasts." The
dividing line between the Gold and Slave Coasts, according to the map,
was the Volta River. Although the book was originally published in Dutch
in 1704, English, French, and German translations appeared during the
next four years, making the book into a kind of international best-seller.
When William Smith, the surveyor for the Royal African Company, produced his "New Map of Guinea from Cape Mount to Jacquin" in 1727, he
also used the Volta River as the dividing line between the Gold Coast and
the Slave Coast.[2]

Figure 18.1   Durand's drawing of the town of Keta. The Dutch trading lodge is on the right.

Robert Durand did not use the term "Slave Coast," but he recognized that the coastline changed noticeably once they had passed the Volta River. The rocky coastline now gave way to a low-lying flat coastline with an almost complete absence of rocks. No longer did European forts dominate the landscape.

The *Diligent* dropped anchor in eleven fathoms of water into a bottom of sand mixed with shells in order to pass the night near the African town of Keta. They fired a blank cannon shot to alert the people of Keta to their presence. At six o'clock the next morning they set some sails to move closer to Keta. They were barely under way when an African canoe approached with news that there were slaves for sale in Keta at a cheap price because no ship had stopped there in over a month. At seven o'clock they anchored in front of Keta and fired three cannon shots to salute the local king.

There was no European fort in Keta, but there was a Dutch trading lodge. Since the decline of the slave trade at Accra, the English, Dutch, and Danes had taken a new interest in buying slaves at Keta. This sudden upsurge in European activity provoked local resistance. Only three weeks before the arrival of the *Diligent*, the two Royal African Company representatives stationed in Keta had been forced to leave after their trade goods had been plundered. Two months after the passage of the *Diligent*, the trading lodge of the Dutch West India Company was ransacked and burned.[3]

At eight o'clock Second Captain Valteau, who had rejoined the *Diligent* at Elmina after failing to find canoe passage to Whydah, and the pilot, Sabatier, set out in the longboat to make contact with the king of Keta.

This was the first time on this voyage that the *Diligent* entered fully into the rituals of slave trading. The longboat stayed ashore all day. In the evening it returned with an African merchant who wanted to inspect the merchandise aboard the *Diligent*. The pilot, Sabatier, was not on the boat; he had been left on shore to serve as a hostage.

The *Diligent* had to leave a hostage on shore before any African officials would come out to the ship because six months earlier a French slave ship from Bordeaux had abducted several Africans who had come out to inspect its cargo. Robert Durand noted in his journal that the actions of the Bordeaux slave trader had made trade difficult for "honest men" like himself.[4] The African king at Keta had since carried out a selective boycott of the French. He had agreed to trade with the *Diligent* only because no ship of any flag had arrived for over a month.

The ship from Bordeaux was not the only French slave ship that regularly engaged in kidnapping. The director of the French Fort in Whydah, Dupetitval, had noted in 1738 that the practice was common, and he blamed it on the private traders. Company ships would not kidnap people because they relied on the goodwill of the local ruler to maintain their forts and conduct ongoing trade. But private traders often tried to make a fortune in one voyage. If they did return, they had great freedom to trade at different places on different voyages. "Before arriving in Whydah," wrote Dupetitval, "they conduct trade along the coast. Ordinarily several canoes from the country go aboard to conduct trade. When they board, the captain retains them as captives and carries them away. This results in angry incidents. The Negro nations who see that we kidnap their compatriots take vengeance on the ships that send their longboats ashore and massacre all those whom they capture. There is no longer confidence and good faith, and these actions have caused irreparable harm to our commerce."[5]

Dupetitval cited the recent case of a ship from Martinique whose crew had been attacked when they stopped along the coast. The local chief had lured them to shore with a promise that he had many captives for sale. As soon as they landed, his forces attacked them in reprisal for some kidnappings done by a ship from Nantes. And the distrust was mutual. After news of a kidnapping spread along the coast, Africans who came out in their canoes to trade with slave ships were afraid to come aboard to see the merchandise, and they often insisted on conducting the trade without leaving their canoes. Those who came aboard were known to flee to their canoes at any sign of sudden movement by the crews of the slave ships. Sometimes, as with the *Diligent* at Keta, they would send a single person to inspect the merchandise while the others waited nearby in a canoe.

After the African inspector had examined the merchandise aboard the *Diligent* and pronounced it suitable, the crew prepared to purchase slaves. By six o'clock the next morning they had loaded both the longboat and the skiff with brandy, muskets, gunpowder, and bales of different kinds of cloth. Second Captain Pierre Valteau had gone ahead to rent a building for storing the merchandise. Robert Durand commanded the longboat, and he would ferry merchandise and slaves between the *Diligent* and Keta. Prices for slaves were normally fixed in ounces of gold and then converted into the merchandise at hand. The African merchants at Keta wanted six and a half ounces of gold per slave, whereas Captain Mary had authorized them to pay only five ounces for ordinary slaves, including beautiful women, and six ounces for the beardless adolescent males who were known as "Portuguese slaves" because they were preferred by the Portuguese. With no agreement on price, Durand returned to the *Diligent* in the evening with his longboat full of merchandise. He noticed that a Dutch ship and a ship from Hamburg had arrived during the day and anchored nearby.

At six o'clock the next morning Durand again went ashore in his longboat filled with merchandise in hopes that a second day of bargaining would lead to slave purchases. He found that the arrival of the Dutch and Hamburg ships had caused the king of Keta to lose interest in any further dealings with the French. The king was, after all, boycotting the French, and he had only agreed to deal with them in the first place for lack of alternatives. Seeing that their opportunity for trading had been lost, Durand returned to the *Diligent* and began reloading the merchandise. Pierre Valteau, who had spent the previous night on shore in his rented building, caught a ride back in the canoe belonging to the Dutch lodge. Their first serious attempt at slave trading had failed. In giving the orders to set sail, Captain Mary decided to head directly for their final destination. At Whydah, he hoped, they would be better received.

PART 6

Whydah

𝓘T WAS NEARLY NOON when the Diligent departed from Keta on August 30, 1731, borne by a brisk breeze from the west-northwest. Exactly twenty-four hours later Robert Durand and his companions found themselves at Popo, a village with houses that stretched out along the shoreline for over a mile. There they anchored alongside a French ship from Saint-Malo named the Hirondelle, whose captain gave them discouraging news about obtaining slaves.1 After spending a full five months along the Slave Coast, the Hirondelle had purchased only two hundred slaves because the wars that were wracking the countryside had disrupted the trade routes and very few slaves from the interior were arriving at the coast. Even though a substantial portion of the Hirondelle's trade goods were still unspent, its captain, Duponcel, had decided to depart immediately because the slaves chained below the deck were beginning to die from the "sickness of the country." He wanted to get his ship to Martinique as quickly as possible before his human cargo died and his profits vanished.

Robert Durand must have felt discouraged when Captain Duponcel warned them not to stop at Whydah (which was their destination) but to continue on to Jakin instead. Whydah was not safe because armed forces commanded by Chief Assou were attacking the tents of slave traders who were camped on the beach. Although there were three European forts at Whydah, they were located three miles inland just beyond the lagoon, and they could not protect the slave traders' tents on the beach.

The captain of the *Hirondelle* then filled them in on current prices. Slaves were valued at seven ounces of gold apiece, each ounce being the equivalent of one keg of brandy or one fifty-pound barrel of gunpowder or sixteen thousand cowry shells. Because of the wars in the countryside, muskets were fetching high prices, but the *Diligent* could not take advantage of this situation because it was carrying only 150 trade muskets.

Aware that the *Hirondelle* would get back to Brittany long before the *Diligent*, Robert Durand and his colleagues wrote letters home and gave them to Captain Duponcel. Captain Mary's sailing instructions required him to send back reports to the *Diligent*'s owners at every opportunity.[2] Then an African canoe from Popo arrived to take Captain Mary ashore to discuss trading. When the captain inquired about the customs fees that the chief of Popo required before trading could begin, he was told that merchandise equivalent to the value of eight slaves would have to be paid before the terms of trade could even be discussed. Not knowing if the investment would bring satisfactory returns, Captain Mary decided to forgo trading at Popo and go to Whydah despite Duponcel's warning.

The war-torn conditions at Whydah came as no surprise to the crew of the *Diligent*. One member of the *Diligent*'s crew, first mate Jean Leglan, had been in Whydah on March 9, 1727, when the army of Dahomey, a kingdom located fifty miles inland, launched the attack that destroyed Whydah's capital city, Savi, and drove King Huffon and Chief Assou into exile. At the time, first mate Leglan had come to Whydah aboard the slave ship *More*.[3] The merchandise from the *More* had been stored in a warehouse in Savi, about six miles inland from the coast, where it was being traded for slaves. Three hundred slaves had already been loaded when the crew members in Savi heard that the army of Dahomey was encamped less than a mile away and was burning the countryside around the city. The captain of the *More,* Jean Guesneau, returned to his ship so hurriedly that he didn't even have time to take an inventory of the trade goods that he was leaving behind. When the soldiers of Dahomey entered Savi, they burned and pillaged the city, carrying off all the merchandise belonging to the ship and making prisoners of the crew members who were guarding the warehouse. In all the confusion, a sailor named Pierre Le Roy slipped away and stayed behind when the *More* set sail with its cargo of three hundred captives. Pierre Le Roy was a free black.

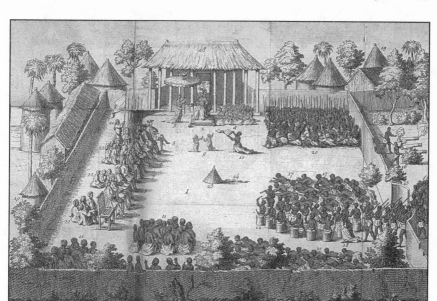

Figure 19.1   Coronation of the king of Whydah.

Other slave ships that were anchored in the harbor of Whydah at the time of the Dahomian attack had similar experiences. The *Jolie*, a ship from Nantes, lost a crew member who was killed while guarding its merchandise in Savi. On the *Cézar*, another ship from Nantes, the 334 captives chained below deck took advantage of the situation to stage an unsuccessful revolt. Thirty Africans were killed during the uprising and its aftermath.[4]

The attack by Dahomey in March 1727 signaled a major change in the political and economic organization of the Slave Coast. The tiny kingdom of Whydah had functioned mainly as a terminus for the trade routes that came from the interior. Thus the slaves who were sold in Whydah did not come from Whydah itself. The rise of the inland kingdom of Dahomey had transformed the commercial geography of the region with far-reaching consequences for the structure and practice of the slave trade.

In April 1725, when African and European dignitaries had gathered for the coronation of King Huffon, the kingdom of Whydah had been prosperous and at peace. At five o'clock in the afternoon, King Huffon stepped out into the great courtyard of his palace in Savi, accompanied by forty of his favorite wives.[5] Each wore a series of overlapping skirts of the finest silks; the inner skirt was draped down to the ankles and the successive outer skirts were shorter and open in front in a manner reminiscent of the "open robe" style that was fashionable in Europe. At least one European at the time speculated that the fashions of Paris were copied from the palace of Whydah.[6] Nude above the waist, the bodies of the king's wives were adorned with necklaces, earrings, bracelets, and ankle chains of gold, silver, and precious jewels.

Not to be outshone by his wives, King Huffon also wore several pieces of fine silk cloth wrapped around his waist. His bare torso was adorned with gold chains and necklaces, and his fingers displayed jeweled rings. On his head he wore a gilded helmet covered with red and white plumes. A European visitor once described King Huffon as an exceedingly handsome man with a gentle manner, while another noted that the king was "the largest and fattest man I ever saw."[7]

Accompanied by the royal guards and his feminine entourage, the king walked slowly across the courtyard and seated himself on a gilded wooden throne, the back of which bore the coat of arms of France, revealing that it had been a gift from the French. The king sat on a cushion decorated with gold braid, and a similar cushion was placed beneath his feet. At his side, one of the dignitaries of the kingdom held up a great umbrella made of gold-embroidered cloth and ringed with gold fringes and tassels. It was ten feet across, with a rooster of gilded wood crowning its peak.

The forty wives sat on the ground to the king's left. To his right, sitting on stuffed chairs, were the representatives of the great trading nations of Europe. Closest to the throne sat the representatives of the French Company of the Indies, followed by the representatives of the British Royal African Company, the Dutch West India Company, and, last, the Portuguese. All of the Europeans were slave traders.

The coronation ceremony was taking place many years too late, as King Huffon had been in power since 1708. At first it had been put off because Huffon was only thirteen years old when he took the throne. When he reached the age of majority, it was further delayed because of rocky relations with the neighboring kingdom of Allada, whose representative was required by custom to preside over the ceremony. Given all the delays, there is some controversy as to exactly when the ceremony took place. Chevalier des Marchais, the French slaving captain who sketched the ceremony and wrote a detailed description of it, clearly dated his sketch April 1725, but modern historians have been skeptical of that date, and one has suggested that the ceremony may have taken place in 1717–1718 instead.[8] For our purposes, the exact date matters less than the rich description that Des Marchais has left us of the court of Whydah during the reign of its last king.

Nobody in Whydah was surprised to see European slave traders playing such a prominent role in their king's coronation ceremony. The Europeans had been in league with Huffon ever since he had come to power under questionable circumstances in 1708. When Huffon's father died suddenly after a reign of only three years, none of his children had yet reached the age of majority. Since the customary practices of the kingdom made no provision for a regent, some officials believed that the Gogon of Savi should accede to the throne. Supporters of the deceased king, however, brought his three young sons in from the provinces to select one of them as the successor, thus thwarting the ambitions of the Gogon. Political tension mounted in the kingdom. The French, fearing that a civil war was brewing, rounded up 160 armed men from among the crews of slave ships in the harbor and brought them to their fort on the shore. The British brought in soldiers as well.

Whether or not those armed Europeans actually played a role in the succession struggle, or whether they were there to protect European traders and goods in case war broke out, is still a matter of dispute among historians. But there is no question that the representatives of the European trading companies were present at the meeting at which Huffon was chosen king.[9] After Huffon was installed as king of Whydah, the European trading firms began to compete for his favor. The English presented him with a crown, and the French countered by giving him the entire cargoes of two ships.[10] The ornate Louis XIV–style throne came later.

The tight relationship between the European trading companies and King Huffon was inscribed into the very architecture of the royal palace in Savi. The company compounds of the Dutch West India Company, the British Royal African Company, and the French Company of the Indies abutted the walls of the palace, and the Portuguese compound was only a few feet away. The British surveyor William Smith described the houses in the European company compounds as "built in the European fashion, being lofty, spacious, and airy, containing many neat and commodious apartments;

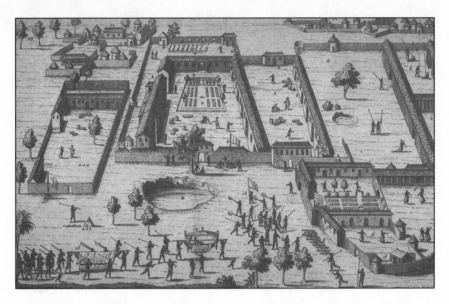

Figure 19.2   European trading compounds at Savi.

also, to each a fine large open hall with cool balconies, etc., all these upon the first floor. Underneath upon the ground floor were the warehouses."[11]

The city of Savi itself was about four miles in circumference. It was so populous that the throngs of people made it difficult to pass along the streets even though some of them were very broad. The daily markets featured all sorts of European and African commodities. Near the European compounds was a square shaded by tall trees where the English, French, Dutch, and Portuguese directors, merchants, and sea captains sat and transacted daily business, much like a European mercantile exchange.

If the company compounds in Savi served as the diplomatic and commercial outposts of the European trading companies, the bases of European operations in Whydah were still the forts belonging to the French Company of the Indies, the British Royal African Company, and the Portuguese Crown, which stood almost side by side near the coast by the town of Glewe. Located about three miles from the coast, on solid ground just beyond the beach and the lagoon, the forts served as a point roughly halfway between the seashore and Savi for storing merchandise that came in from slave ships and for holding slaves who were ready to be shipped out. When the French built their fort in 1704, the site at Glewe was chosen because they found it difficult to unload goods from a ship and transport them all the way to Savi in a single day. With the forts located so far inland, it was impossible for their cannons to dominate the harbor of Whydah or even to protect ships sitting at anchor.[12] Because ships of all European nations could anchor in the harbor, Whydah was, in the terminology of the time, a "free port."

The walls of the forts were made of mud because, it was said, there was not a stone larger than a walnut to be found in the entire kingdom. Each fort was surrounded by a moat that had been dug to provide the soil for constructing the earthen walls.[13] The French fort, ironically named Fort St. Louis (after the French king who had freed the many serfs in France), had earthen walls that were approximately a hundred yards long on each side. It had about thirty cannons mounted on three bastions, over half of them pointing directly at the English fort, a rifle shot away. It contained warehouses for merchandise, holding cells for slaves, and lodging for company employees. After the Company of the Indies took over the fort from the French government in 1722, it reduced the French personnel from thirty to eleven in order to save money and replaced the dozen or so French troops with locally recruited African soldiers.[14] The English fort, named William's Fort, was of similar design and construction as that of the French. It was a square construction about a hundred yards on each side with bastions on each of the four corners.[15]

The Portuguese fort, named Fort St. John the Baptist, was still unfinished, having been begun in 1721. Its builder, Joseph de Torres, described it as having a single round bastion with eight cannons surrounded by a rectangular wall. But the reality was much less impressive, and by 1724 less than half of the buildings had been completed.[16] The Dutch, who had driven the Portuguese from the West African coast in the seventeenth century, were furious that King Huffon had permitted the construction of a Portuguese fort in a place where they were allowed only an unarmed trading lodge. They soon abandoned their lodge in Savi and relocated their operations to the rival port of Jakin, twenty miles down the coast, demanding that King Huffon tear down the Portuguese fort or they would not return. On March 30, 1726, the Dutch launched a sneak attack on the Portuguese fort, throwing two flaming spears over the walls in a failed attempt to set the thatched roofs on fire.[17]

Like the forts along the Gold Coast, these fortresses served mainly as warehouses for merchandise and barracoons for slaves. The agents of the European companies would purchase slaves at their compounds in Savi and then send them down to the forts to be imprisoned until a company ship came along to carry them away. The purpose of the system was to provide a fast turnaround time for company ships, since the longer they sat in the harbor, the greater the chance of crew members getting sick or dying from tropical diseases. If a company ship arrived when there was a waiting supply of captives in the fort, it could depart as soon as it had unloaded its merchandise and loaded the captives. Private slave traders, on the other hand, stayed much longer, usually several months, because they purchased slaves in small lots until the ship was full.

The Europeans were well aware that their continuing presence in Whydah depended on the goodwill of the king. Although the forts were strong enough to protect the Europeans and their merchandise from bandits or local riots, they knew that the mud-walled structures could not withstand a determined effort to expel or exterminate them. Being located three miles inland, they could not expect help from ships in the harbor, and they were totally dependent on local Africans for supplies of water, food, and firewood. Together, the French, English, Portuguese, and Dutch could barely muster a hundred European fighters, who were vulnerable to being starved out even if they managed to defend their bastions from a direct attack.[18]

The seaside kingdom over which Huffon was crowned king in April 1725 was tiny. Its coastline extended for about forty miles, and it reached inland only twenty-five miles. The British surveyor William Smith, who visited Whydah in 1727, reported that "all who have been here allow this to be one of the most beautiful countries in the world. The great number and variety of tall and beautiful shady trees, which seem to be planted in fine groves for ornament, being without any underwood or weeds, as in any other parts of Guinea; also the verdant fields are everywhere cultivated, and no otherwise divided than by those groves and in some places a small footpath; together with a great number of pretty little villages, encompassed by a low mud wall, and regularly placed over the face of the whole country. All these contribute to afford the most delightful prospect that imagination can form." Smith described the inhabitants of Whydah as gentlemanly people who abounded in good manners and ceremony to one another. All of them, he said, were naturally industrious and found constant employment: the men in agriculture and the women in spinning and weaving cotton to make cloth.[19]

What surprised visitors who had observed the sparse populations elsewhere in West Africa was the incredible density of the population. Chevalier Des Marchais, who mapped the kingdom of Whydah in 1725, noted that the population was so dense that the kingdom could almost be said to comprise a single village, and William Smith wrote that "this place is so well inhabited that a man here cannot fail of being in sight of ten or twenty Negro towns anywhere within twenty miles of the seaside."[20]

The population was fed by a thriving agriculture that was based on the production of millet but also included New World crops such as maize and sweet potatoes. European visitors wrote of agriculture in Whydah in rapturous terms. William Smith noted that "the natives were so industrious that no place that was thought fertile could escape being planted, though even within the hedges that enclose their villages and dwelling places, and they were so very anxious in this particular, that the next day after they had reaped they always sowed again without allowing the land any time to rest." In this way they managed to get three or even four harvests in a single year. Although they did not let the land lie fallow, they preserved the fertility of the soil by a system of crop rotation: peas, rice, millet, maize, potatoes, and yams were planted in strict succession. The areas near hedges and walls were used for planting melons and vegetables. One visitor observed that not an inch of land was wasted.[21]

Although Whydah was a tiny kingdom with a total population that could not have exceeded 100,000, it was said to export sixteen to twenty thousand slaves a year in the early eighteenth century. It was reported that Whydah exported more slaves annually than all the other West African slaving ports combined. Modern research confirms that in the first quarter of the eighteenth century over 400,000 slaves—60 percent of the slaves carried from West Africa and over 40 percent of all African slaves carried across the Atlantic during that period—came from Whydah alone.[22] If there was one spot in Africa that embodied the Atlantic slave trade in the early eighteenth century, it was Whydah.

Whydah was able to export so many slaves without any visible signs of depopulation because slaves who were shipped out did not come from the kingdom itself, except for a few criminals and rebels against the king. Instead, the slaves arrived via the trade routes from the inland regions, brought down by African slave merchants. The captives represented as many as thirty different ethnic groups.[23]

The slaves whom the Europeans purchased usually bore scarification, or "country marks," that had been incised into their flesh when they went through initiation as youths. The European slave traders used them to identify the geographical and ethnic origins of the slaves. Over time a series of ethnic stereotypes developed by which slave traders distinguished among different characteristics that they imputed to different ethnic groups. The most sought after category of slaves, according to Chevalier Des Marchais, who described the system in 1725, were people known as "Mallais."[24] The name did not refer to the slaves themselves, but to the Muslim merchants, dressed in long robes typical of the Sahel region of West Africa, who brought the slaves to Whydah from the north. Some of the captives, it was said, had spent three months en route before arriving in Whydah. Marchais described the Mallais captives as "strong, accustomed to work, and capable of withstanding fatigue."

The "Ayois," from the inland kingdom of Oyo, were identifiable by scarification in the form of rays running from their eyes toward their ears. They had a reputation for being great warriors, brave, hardy, and enterprising. They were said to be strong people who could work harder than the people of any other nation. What worried slave traders, however, was that they frequently organized revolts on slave ships. They were fearless, the Europeans believed, and even a single one of them on a slave ship could incite the rest of the captives to revolt. Des Marchais reported that slaving vessels of all the European nations had experienced revolts of Ayois captives in which crew members and captains had been killed.

Several other ethnic groups were also considered desirable by European slave traders. The Aqueras, recognizable by the tattoos of lizards and serpents on their backs and chests, were considered cooperative and loyal to their masters. The Aradas,[25] marked by incisions on their cheeks, were considered the best all-around slaves because they were said to be docile, faithful, and hardworking. Similar characteristics were imputed to the Nago, a Yoruba-speaking group, who were marked by long rays on their foreheads.

The stereotypes created by the Europeans also identified ethnic groups that slave traders wished to avoid. The Foin (undoubtedly the Fon of Dahomey), who were identified by the scarification on their temples, were thought likely to become depressed in captivity and commit suicide. Europeans also considered them lazy workers who ate too much. The Tebou, with sacrification on their cheeks, chest, and stomach, were considered to be even less desirable than the Foin. Des Marchais recommended that any slaves purchased from among that group should be younger than ten or twelve so that they could be retrained into new habits. The Guiamba were considered similar to the previous two groups, with the exception that they were more prone to depression. Des Marchais suggested that slave traders should purchase as few Guiamba as possible because he believed that they could spread depression through a whole cargo of slaves. The Minas, from the Gold Coast or Popo, were said to be unsuitable for field labor because they were not used to it in their home country, but they were thought to make excellent household servants and craftsmen. They were said to be persons of honor with great powers of reason and good sense. They were also believed to be faithful to their masters and brave in the face of danger.

One reason why King Huffon allowed his kingdom to be a major terminus of the slave trade routes was the revenue he received from the trade: a thousand cowry shells for each slave that was sold in his kingdom and customs payments from European slave ships. In 1725 the customs payment was 1,080 cowries plus the value of three slaves. Other customs payments were made to the three "great captains" of the kingdom—Captain Assou, Captain Agou, and Captain Carter—before any trading could begin. More payments to the king followed, and one European estimated that the king received the value of at least twenty slaves from each European vessel that landed at the port of Whydah.[26]

In April 1725 the slave trade in Whydah had come to a momentary halt because the entire kingdom was focused on the task of ceremonially installing King Huffon to the throne that he had occupied since 1708. On April 16, 1725, his coronation was finalized by the procession of the serpent.[27] This procession was extremely important because the national deity of Whydah was a sacred python called Dangbe, which was housed in a temple a mile and a half west of Savi. The high priests of the serpent cult

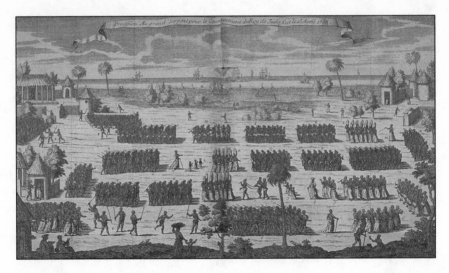

Figure 19.3   Procession of the Serpent in Whydah.

had great political power in the kingdom, and their support was essential if the king was to rule effectively.

The procession was led by forty musketeers with their guns on their shoulders, marching in rows of four. Then came twenty trumpeters, twenty drummers, and twenty flutists. The musicians were followed by twelve wives of the king carrying presents of cowry shells, brandy, cotton cloth, and silk to present to the sacred serpent. After the king's personal valet had passed, there were more musketeers, drummers, and flutists, marching three abreast. Then came twelve more of the king's wives carrying great baskets on their heads filled with food to present to the serpent, followed by three of the king's dwarves. Then came more musketeers, trumpeters, drummers, flutists, and wives bearing gifts. Toward the end of the procession came the king's mother, carried on a stuffed chair, who presided over the entire procession. King Huffon himself was not present. After arriving at the Temple of the Serpent and presenting the gifts to the serpent priests, the procession returned to Savi.

Three months later the ceremony was repeated, but this time it was presided over by King Huffon himself, who was carried in a covered hammock surrounded by his closest aides. After that, the king would never again need to leave his palace in a ceremonial procession.[28] He planned to spend the remainder of his days in his palace in Savi, a bamboo structure a mile or two around. It was as richly furnished with magnificent beds, stuffed chairs, sofas, and mirrors as any royal palace in Europe. The royal kitchens were stocked with imported coffee, tea, chocolate, and jellies, and the royal cooks knew how to prepare the traditional dishes of Whydah as well as the finest delicacies of Europe. The royal wine cellar contained wines from France, Spain, Madeira, and the Canary Islands, as well as French liquors and brandy.[29] Above all, the palace was the home of the king's wives, who numbered over a thousand. Everything that King Huffon could desire was at his bidding.

As the coronation ceremonies came to a close, King Huffon would have found it difficult to imagine that less than two years later he would leave his palace again, and this time he would be fleeing for his life. He could not have known, at that moment, that the trouble that would engulf his kingdom was already brewing some sixty miles to the north in Abomey, the capital of the small kingdom of Dahomey.[30]

20

I N THE HEAT OF the dry season in January 1726, three men sat in one of the smaller courtyards of the great and principal palace of the kingdom of Dahomey. King Agaja was seated in an elaborate chair and shaded from the sun by three large umbrellas. His face was pitted from smallpox, but it was nevertheless attractive and even somewhat majestic. The king was in his forties, of average height, and stoutly built. A French-man once described him as slightly taller and slightly portlier than the French playwright Molière.[1] Sitting at a respectful distance and speaking in words that alternated between English and Gbe was a young African man whom the Europeans called "Captain Tom." He was the interpreter for the meeting. At a nearby table a white man was writing hurriedly with a quill pen as if he were the king's scribe.

The scribe's name was Bulfinch Lambe, an Englishman who had for-merly been a trading agent for the Royal African Company. Through a strange twist of fortune, he had become King Agaja's slave. Although a captive, he was probably one of the best-treated slaves on earth. He had been given his own house with half a dozen servants, all the food he could eat, and all the French brandy he could drink. He once noted that if he were fonder of brandy, he could easily drink himself to death because it was provided in such abundance. It was his preference for Irish whiskey that had saved him from this fate. To create the comforts of home, some of the king's female relatives lived with him as his wives. The poor condition of his clothes reflected his insistence on wearing his English outfits while refusing all gifts of Dahomey-style cloth that he could wrap around his waist in the fashion of his interpreter. Bulfinch Lambe's only regular duties were to fire the king's cannons to announce the opening of trading at the market held every fourth day and to sit alongside the king's Portuguese mulatto slave as a kind of royal trophy when the king held audiences. Otherwise, he was generally free to do as he pleased. Lambe was even provided with a horse that he rode when accompanying King Agaja on his outings into the Dahomian countryside. While Lambe rode bareback on his horse, the king was carried in the royal hammock decorated with gilded awnings and curtains.

Nevertheless, Bullfinch Lambe was bitterly unhappy. "I am banished," he wrote to the Royal African Company in 1724, "from all the pleasures of this life, not only from my wife and other friends, but all conversation in general, so that I am like one buried alive from the world, and think nothing can come near my unhappy fate, to lose my time and spend my youth, as it were, for nothing in such a cursed place as this, and not see a likelihood of getting out of it."[2] In the midst of his self-pity, he experienced an important insight: that slaves—even those who were well treated—suffered terribly from their captivity.

During his four years of captivity under two different masters, Bulfinch Lambe had ample time to ponder the irony of being a slave trader who became a slave. In 1722 he had been sent by the Royal African Company to arrange some business with King Sozo of Allada, a kingdom situated between Whydah and Dahomey. At the time, King Sozo was trying to collect a debt that the company owed him for a hundred slaves that he had delivered to them. Failing to receive satisfaction from the company, the king detained Bulfinch Lambe and threatened to make him a permanent slave unless the debt was paid. The company was apparently in no hurry to get its agent back, and so matters remained stalemated for two long years.

In March 1724 rumors reached King Sozo that his brother Hussar, a bitter political rival, had secured military assistance from King Agaja of Dahomey by promising to pay him a large sum of money. Soon the army of Dahomey was marching south toward the capital, Allada, to drive King Sozo from his throne. In response, Sozo raised an army of about fifty thousand men to defend his capital city against the forces of Dahomey. Fearing that Bulfinch Lambe might try to escape in the fog of battle, the king had him locked up in a house near the palace.

The army of Dahomey laid siege to Allada. For two days its attacks were repelled by spirited resistance, but on the third day the defense collapsed and the attackers entered the city. They dragged King Sozo out of his palace, which he had never left during his reign, and beheaded him in front of the palace gates. As the news of the king's death spread through the city, any remaining resistance collapsed, and the victorious army of Dahomey began an orgy of killing, looting, and taking prisoners. They set fire to the thatched roofs of the mud-walled buildings, including the house in which Bulfinch Lambe was imprisoned. In the middle of the dry season the thatch was brittle and perfect for burning. The heat of the fire seared Lambe's skin, and the smoke choked his lungs.

Just when he felt that all was lost, someone—he didn't know who—reached in over the top of the earthen wall and pulled him out. Emerging from the house, he saw that the entire city was in flames. His rescuers immediately took him prisoner and led him to the palace, where he was presented to the victorious general of the army of Dahomey. At first Lambe believed that he was meeting King Sozo's brother, who was rumored to be behind the attack. But when he saw the lines of scarification etched into the general's temples, he recognized the country marks of Dahomey. Still shaky from escaping the fire, he was greatly relieved when the general handed him a dram of brandy to calm his nerves.

With the flames starting to consume the palace itself, the African general and Bulfinch Lambe retreated. Outside, the streets were littered with bodies. "If it had rained blood," noted Lambe, "it could not have lain thicker on the ground." With night falling, they walked through the smoke and fires to the military camp outside the city. Lambe was given three more drams of brandy and placed in the care of a junior officer of the Dahomian army. Two days later the general, who certainly knew that Lambe was a slave trader, called him to watch the counting of the prisoners taken in the battle. As each prisoner filed past, a cowry shell was thrown into a basket. Then the cowries were divided into piles and counted: forty cowries made a *toque*, five *toques* made a *galina*, twenty *galina* made a *cabesse* (four thousand cowries). The total surpassed two *cabesse*, representing over eight thousand captives. Many of those captives were designated for sale to European slave traders. The director of the Portuguese fort reported that in the wake of the battle there were six thousand slaves for sale but no ships in the Whydah harbor to buy them and carry them away.[3]

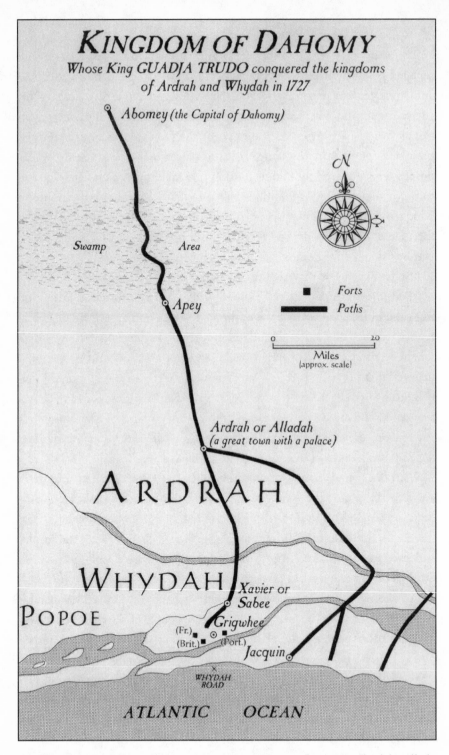

Figure 20.1   Redrawn version of Norris's 1793 map showing Whydah, Allada (Ardrah), and Dahomey.

Over the next few days, the remaining prisoners were marched inland toward the capital of Dahomey, about forty miles to the north. The procession stretched out for miles along the road, which passed through the forested areas of northern Allada and then entered the Ko swamp, passable only during the dry season. Leaving the swamp, the road climbed steadily upward to the nearly treeless plain of the Abomey plateau, over a thousand feet above sea level. Many of the prisoners, unable to keep up the pace as a result of old age, wounds, and burns, were treated harshly by the soldiers. Lambe, however, was lucky. As a white man, he was considered a special prize and was carried in a hammock like an African dignitary. After several days on the road, he arrived in Dahomey's capital city, Abomey. There he would be presented to King Agaja.

Thus King Agaja finally met one of the white strangers about whom he had been hearing all his life. Although he had regularly received shipments of goods made in Europe, India, and China that had come up from the coast along the trade routes, he had never seen the ocean or met a European because his country had been blocked from the sea by the two small kingdoms of Whydah and Allada. His father and his brother, who had reigned before him, had sent out invitations for European traders to visit Dahomey, but none had ever come until now, and even this one had not come of his own choice.

Communication problems between the king and his prisoner were solved when King Agaja discovered the young African man called Captain Tom, a former interpreter for the Royal African Company. Like Lambe, he had been captured in the conquest of Allada. Over the next two years the king took advantage of Captain Tom's linguistic skills to hold many long conversations with Lambe. On the rare occasions when Lambe received letters from the Royal African Company fort in Whydah, the king would ask Lambe to read them aloud and write his answers in his presence. King Agaja was fascinated by the whole idea of literacy and written communication; he often scrutinized the book of Latin masses that he had confiscated from his Portuguese mulatto slave, and he even experimented at inventing his own script. When the king wrote letters to Lambe in his experimental scripts, he always took care to send along an interpreter to decipher the message.

As the first white person ever to visit Abomey, Lambe had a rare opportunity to observe life in King Agaja's capital firsthand. He noted that the

Figure 20.2 Clothing worn by nobles and the king's wives in Whydah, 1725. Dress at the court of Dahomey was probably similar.

king had eleven palaces (he would later say seven) spread throughout the country. The great and principal palace he described as "big as a small town," and even the second one was "larger than St. James Park, about a mile and a half around." The palaces served mainly to house the king's many wives, more than two thousand of them. The internal affairs of each palace were governed entirely by the king's chief wives, and robust women served as palace guards and doorkeepers. No man other than the king was allowed in the palaces after sunset.

Lambe liked to watch the king's wives going daily to the stream in groups of as many as two hundred to fetch water. The junior wives wore multilayered silk skirts, and their bare chests were adorned by multiple necklaces of coral beads imported from the Mediterranean. The senior wives wore velvet clothes in crimson, green, and blue, varying the colors from day to day. They carried "silver-gilt staffs in their hands like golden canes." What is noteworthy about those outfits is that all of the items were imported and could be obtained only through trade. The splendor of the royal court was paid for with slaves.

King Agaja recounted to Lambe that he was only the fourth king to reign in the relatively young kingdom of Dahomey. Agaja's grandfather, who was a peaceful man, had fought only one battle during his entire reign, Agaja's father had fought only nine, and his older brother Wegbala had fought seventy-nine battles. But Agaja, who had succeeded his brother, had fought over two hundred battles and was already planning for future campaigns.[4] Agaja had served as commander of the army during the short reign of his brother and had come to power in a kind of military coup after his brother's death. From Agaja's repeated emphasis on his place in the military history of Dahomey, it was clear that he saw himself as a conqueror who had turned a small, peaceful kingdom into a powerful militarized state. Several years later he embellished that image by obtaining a French suit of armor that made him look "like Don Quixote."[5]

Agaja had built up the best-trained and best-equipped army in the region. Its recruitment, organization, and armament differed completely from those found in the neighboring kingdoms of Whydah and Allada. In Whydah, all able-bodied men were mobilized for military service in times of war, creating mass armies of fifty thousand or more. The hurriedly mobilized conscripts had to supply their own weapons. Having little or no military training, they fought in "large platoons without straight lines or order." The primary military strategy was to overwhelm the enemy by sheer numbers. If the army of Whydah was victorious in battle, the soldiers looted the weapons of the dead and tried to capture the fleeing enemies. Ten percent of the prisoners of war were claimed by the king; the rest could be sold into slavery by the soldiers who had captured them.[6]

As conscripts who had been pressed into battle, the Whydah soldiers were quick to retreat when the battle turned against them. If they saw themselves confronted by a larger army, they sometimes retreated before the battle began. The reason for their flight was probably related to the slave trade. Labat reported that the Whydah soldiers feared capture and enslavement more than they feared death. King Huffon of Whydah made a similar point when he told the English slave trader William Snelgrave that if he ever captured King Agaja, he would not take his head but would "keep him for a slave to do the vilest offices." In Whydah there seemed to be a consensus that slavery was a fate worse than death.[7]

King Agaja's Dahomey, in contrast to Whydah, relied on a professional standing army numbering only about ten thousand. He recruited boys as young as seven or eight years old to serve as shield carriers for the regular soldiers. During their years of apprenticeship, the boys were indoctrinated in the glories of war and trained to endure the hardships of military life. Later they were allowed to join the army as regular soldiers. The resulting army was described by a European as consisting of "elite troops, brave and well-disciplined, led by a prince full of valor and prudence, supported by a staff of experienced officers."[8] If the years of training were not enough to turn the men into loyal soldiers who were ready to kill, and perhaps die, for their king, they received bonuses paid in cowry shells (the currency of the kingdom) for each enemy that they killed or captured in battle. The cowry shells, which came from the Maldive Islands near India, were obtained by selling slaves to Europeans.

King Agaja had modernized his army by equipping it with flintlock muskets to replace the traditional longbows. Even though the muskets supplied by European slave traders were often of inferior quality, the king's blacksmiths repaired them by soldering the barrels and realigning the flints. For close combat, the soldiers used steel swords and cutlasses imported from Europe, and they protected themselves with locally made shields that were almost as tall as they were. King Agaja had also acquired twenty-five cannons, some of which were described by Lambe as weighing "upwards of a thousand weight, so that a man would think the devil helped to bring them here." The king lamented to Lambe that he did not possess the formula for making his own gunpowder. He was well aware that in modernizing his military, he had made himself dependent on European traders for regular supplies of guns, powder, musket balls, and cannonballs. Like the silks and velvets of palace life, the arms and ammunition were paid for by selling slaves.

While King Agaja was investing heavily in his military buildup, he was also establishing a royal monopoly on the spoils of war. One European reported that the Dahomian soldiers were so well disciplined that "there is not an officer or a soldier who dares take even the smallest item of booty and the spoils of the enemy for fear of losing his head on the battlefield. They are obliged to bring everything to a common collection point where the king divides it up as he judges proper."[9] All prisoners taken by the army of Dahomey belonged to the king. Once the captives came into King Agaja's possession, he could dispose of them in a variety of ways: some would be sacrificed to his "guardian angel" to give thanks for the victory and ensure future success; other prisoners would be put to work as laborers on the king's farms or as servants in his palaces; others would be distributed as patronage to army officers and royal officials; and the rest would be sold to European slave traders to meet King Agaja's continuing need for guns, powder, swords, silks, velvets, and cowry shells.[10]

So complete was the royal monopoly that even the skulls of slain enemies belonged to the king. Bulfinch Lambe observed that King Agaja "has already set his two chief palaces round with men's skulls as thick as they can lie one by the other, and are such as he has killed in war." The walls of the royal palaces, like the public sacrifices of war captives, served as instruments of military propaganda that gave courage to Dahomian soldiers and spread terror among the king's enemies. Psychological warfare was as much a part of King Agaja's overall military strategy as the professionally trained army and the flintlock muskets.[11]

The martial image that King Agaja worked so hard to project was later enshrined in a Dahomian oral tradition. According to the tradition, King Huffon of Whydah sent King Agaja a gift of forty lengths of cloth, forty barrels of gunpowder, forty muskets, forty bottles of rum, and forty *cabesse* of cowry shells (one *cabesse* equaled four thousand cowries). He taunted Agaja, asking if he was wealthy enough to give such an expensive gift without demanding anything in return. In response, King Agaja ordered his prime minister to prepare a path lined with two parallel rows of skulls of defeated enemies. He marched the emissaries of the king of Whydah along that grisly path and then gave each one a mere forty cowry shells. The point of the demonstration, he declared, was that his wealth consisted of the spoils of war, and he would not hesitate to teach that lesson to the king of Whydah. The contrast between the merchant kingdom and the military kingdom could not have been set out more clearly.[12]

Relations between the two states were tense because King Agaja had long been frustrated by his dependence on Whydah for the guns, powder, cowries, cloth, and other imported goods that he needed to sustain his military and maintain the courtly lifestyle of his palaces. Agaja complained that the Whydah merchants profited unduly from their middleman position between the European slave traders on the coast and his landlocked kingdom, and he charged King Huffon with "many villainies" against him in matters of trade. Agaja's conquest of Allada in 1724 gave him nominal control over the port city of Jakin, but he still lacked direct access to the European trading forts along the Whydah coast. In 1725 he sent an ambassador to King Huffon "requesting open traffic to the seaside and offering to pay him his usual customs on Negroes exported." The request was denied. Mindful of his successful conquest of Allada, the idea of conquering Whydah was beginning to form in King Agaja's mind.[13]

As a slave trader who had himself become a slave, Bulfinch Lambe knew that the best way to gain release from his gilded captivity was for his employer, the Royal African Company, to buy him back. The problem was how to set the price. When he asked King Agaja to make a specific ransom demand to the company, the king made a jesting request for goods equal to the value of seven hundred slaves, which translated to about ten thousand pounds sterling at the time. In despair, Lambe wrote to the company in 1724, "I don't find that there is any other way of redeeming me, than by the Company's sending him a present of a crown and a scepter, which must be paid for out of what remains due to the late king of Allada. I know of nothing else but what he will think mean, being stocked with great quantities of plate, wrought gold, and other rich things. He likewise all sorts of common goods beyond measure, and gives away cowry shells like dirt and brandy like water; for he is prodigious vain and proud, but he is withall, I believe, the richest king and the greatest warrior in this part of the world."

In truth, there was nothing in the storehouses in the English fort at Whydah that would impress King Agaja or even capture his attention. In desperation, Bulfinch Lambe wrote to the Royal African Company, "If there is any cast-off whore, either white or mulatto, that can be persuaded to come to this country, either to be his wife or else to practice her trade, I should gain his majesty's heart entirely by it." With little hope of finding any volunteers, Lambe requested English saddles and bridles for himself and the king, some paper and ink, and some fuse twine and matches for firing the king's cannons. Finally, he requested a little English dog and a pair of shoe buckles for the king. All the items were to be charged to his account at the fort.

In the course of his many conversations with Bulfinch Lambe, King Agaja had queried the Englishman about the Europeans' seemingly insatiable appetite for slaves. The king was too worldly to believe the local folklore that the Europeans purchased African slaves in order to eat them as food, but the continuous arrival of slave ships year after year had piqued his curiosity. When Lambe described how the slaves produced sugar on Caribbean plantations to be sold in Europe for substantial profits, the king got an idea. Agaja was familiar with refined sugar, for he kept a supply of it at his palace. If he could produce the sugar himself, he reasoned, then he could make some of the profits that now went to Europeans. Why should he be a mere supplier of labor to the plantations of the New World when he himself could put slaves to work growing sugar or other export commodities on the Guinea coast?

That idea provided the opening that Bulfinch Lambe needed to scheme his way out of captivity. He wrote out a "Scheme of Trade" that called for King George I to work cooperatively with King Agaja to set up plantations in Dahomey that would use slave labor to produce export commodities such as sugar, cotton, and indigo. As an employee of the Royal African Company, Lambe was aware that the English had discussed and abandoned plans to establish indigo and cotton plantations in Whydah, and he may have known that repeated Dutch attempts to establish sugar, cotton, and indigo plantations along the Gold Coast had not succeeded.[14] But none of that was relevant because Bulfinch Lambe had no intention of following through on the scheme.

In January 1726 King Agaja finally agreed to release Bulfinch Lambe to return to England to negotiate the agreement with King George I. King Agaja, who was fascinated by written communication and later told another Englishman that he had sent Mr. Lambe and Captain Tom to England "to give an account of his grandeur and conquests,"[15] dictated a personal letter to King George through the African interpreter Captain Tom. It was the preparation of that letter that had brought King Agaja, Captain

Tom, and Bulfinch Lambe together in the courtyard of the palace on that January afternoon.

Sitting at his table under the shade of the huge umbrella, Lambe wrote down King Agaja's descriptions of the history and customs of the kingdom of Dahomey and described his restructured military system.[16] The letter made several references to Agaja's interest in establishing direct trading relations with the nations of Europe, asking King George to "promote trade to these parts, and they shall find much better usage and treatment than they did in the reign of the arbitrary king or emperor of Allada." It also stated King Agaja's intention to continue his warfare "till I had subdued other petty kingdoms and made myself sole monarch down to the sea; and then in land I have enough work for many years, so that there will nor shall [not] be any want of slaves." It added, "This white man will inform your merchant traders what I desire and is fit for me, for there is nothing so costly, rich, and fine but what I'll purchase, even to a thousand slaves for any single thing."

The letter also contained hints about King Agaja's own motives for participating in the slave trade. He noted that by converting his army from bows and arrows to guns, he needed a steady supply of gunpowder from the Europeans. He also described the fine clothing of his wives and the opulence of his royal court, implying that he needed a reliable supply of imported cloth and other luxury goods in order to maintain the court lifestyle. Finally, he noted that, as king of Dahomey, he had an obligation to distribute cowry shells and other common goods periodically among the common people. The cowry shells for the common people, like the silk cloth for the royal wives and the gunpowder for the army, could be obtained only through the slave trade.

A similar point was made by a Dahomian oral tradition which held that when the king of Dahomey wanted cowry shells, his assistants would tie a rope around the neck of a slave, break his arms and legs, and throw him into the ocean to drown. Cowry shells on the ocean floor would attach themselves to the slave's body like barnacles. The king's assistants would then pull up the body and retrieve the cowries. Although cowry shells in fact came from the Maldive Islands near India and arrived in West Africa on slave ships, the vivid imagery of the oral tradition makes the point that wealth in cowry shells was paid for with the lives of slaves.[17]

The parts of the letter that later became controversial dealt with the future of Captain Tom and Bulfinch Lambe. Of Captain Tom, the letter said,

"I send him [to England] that on his return, unless death prevents, he may give me a large account of your majesty's countries and dominions; and that he may better qualify himself for the great post . . . which I design to give him on his return." As for Bulfinch Lambe, whom the king referred to as "my son," the letter stated, "I hope you or at least your trading subjects will send me back this white man as governor or chief over other white men and women, and they shall have as many subjects as they desire to assist them in building a castle, fort, house, or houses, as they shall think fit and convenient for trade."

When the letter was finished, Bulfinch Lambe read it aloud in English, and Captain Tom translated Lambe's words into the Gbe language for King Agaja's approval. A few days later, after another round of feasts and good-byes, the king was ready to send them on their way. As he had promised, he gave them a gift of eighty slaves—forty for Lambe and forty for King George. Agaja later told the British slave trader William Snelgrave that he had also given Lambe 320 ounces of gold, though no trace of that gold was ever found. He then sent them on their way to the coastal port of Jakin. As the procession of Bulfinch Lambe, Captain Tom, the eighty slaves, and the numerous guards and retainers slowly made its way to the coast, King Agaja sent messengers ahead ordering all the villages to show Lambe respect and to entertain him nobly.

Embedded in the flowery language of the letter that Bulfinch Lambe carried was an ominous warning to the kingdom of Whydah. King Agaja wrote, "But now I find I have no way to bring the Whydahs under but by force. It must be done, and when I send my generals and captain of war on an errand, they must not come back without success." Later in the letter he assured King George, "When I send my forces against Whydah, as I fully propose to do, I shall give orders to my generals to take care not to hurt any of the white man's goods or persons if they keep in their fort or factory. But if they come in a warlike manner to assist the kings and people, and happen to be killed and wounded, you must not blame me or [my] people." Those warnings would come to fruition long before Bulfinch Lambe and Captain Tom got back to England with the letter.

21

$\mathcal{T}$HE BOOM OF A cannon broke the stillness of the evening on
March 4, 1727, and raised a cry of alarm. Word spread quickly
through Whydah's capital city that the army of Dahomey had attacked
Paon, a dependency of Whydah located only fourteen miles from Savi, and
had left it in flames. A messenger from the governor of Paon had arrived in
Savi to ask why King Huffon had slept while his neighbors were being
burned.

The city of Savi was awake all night as trumpets and drums signaled the
alarm for war and called for soldiers to assemble from all over the kingdom.[1] The next morning the army of the king was joined by the armies
coming in from the provinces to muster at least forty thousand men. The
combined army marched toward Paon to engage the much smaller army
of Dahomey. At noon, a runner arrived in Savi with the message that the
army of Dahomey had fled. The soldiers of Whydah, claimed the messenger, had managed to slip some of their forces behind the enemy lines and
had trapped the enemy in their crossfire. The Europeans in Savi began to
anticipate that a large number of captives would soon be arriving to fill the
holds of their slave ships.

When the army returned to Savi that evening, the soldiers trudged in silence and refused to answer any questions. They had no captives, and it was
apparent that they had been defeated. Captain Assou reported that the soldiers of Whydah were so afraid of the army of Dahomey that they had lost
their will to fight. Only the forces commanded by himself and two other

captains had thrown themselves into the battle; the rest of the army of Whydah had held back and then fled. The mighty army of Whydah, Assou reported angrily, had been defeated by an army that numbered only about fifteen hundred troops and another fifteen hundred women camp follow-ers and boys who served as shield carriers. Whydah outnumbered their en-emy by better than twenty to one and were better armed. "But," asked As-sou rhetorically, "what good were superior numbers and superior arms when courage was lacking and terror and panic reigned?"

The next day rumors of the magical powers of the Dahomian army be-gan to circulate in Savi. Some of the soldiers claimed that as soon as the army of Dahomey fixed its gaze on them, they sank to the ground like dead men, lacking the strength to carry their weapons. Clearly, King Agaja's psychological warfare was having its intended effect by striking ter-ror into the hastily mobilized soldiers of Whydah.

The next day the army of Whydah reassembled, larger than it had been the day before, and again it set out to engage the army of Dahomey. Again the soldiers returned in defeat. The triumphant Dahomians burned the provinces of Miltere and Aploya, and by nightfall they had arrived within five miles of Savi. On the evening of March 6, they reached the river that separated them from Savi and made their camp. Captain Assou, disgusted with the performance of the troops, complained that the country was lost because the soldiers lacked the will to defend it.

The military situation caused the Europeans in Savi to panic. Over the previous two days they had been emptying their warehouses and sending the merchandise toward the coast to be stored in the forts. If they had been able to recruit enough porters, they remarked, there would have been no trade goods left in Savi. On March 7 many of the European traders left Savi to seek refuge in the English, French, and Portuguese forts near the coast. This move put the directors of the European trading companies in a dilemma. King Agaja of Dahomey had sent word to the Europeans that if they remained neutral and did not take up arms in defense of Savi, no harm would come to their persons or goods. Moreover, King Agaja had promised that if he won the war, he would facilitate their trade and remove the various taxes and duties imposed by the king of Whydah; but if they opposed him, they could expect retaliation. The Europeans did not want to take an active role in opposing the army of Dahomey, but if they retreated to their forts at the coast, the move would be interpreted by King Huffon of Whydah as an act of disloyalty. Many officials of the European companies, therefore, remained in Savi as the army of Dahomey laid siege to the city.[2]

On the afternoon of March 9 a group of two hundred Dahomian soldiers forded the river without opposition and marched on Savi, sounding their musical instruments to announce their coming. At about three o'clock in the afternoon the town sentinels heard the sounds and spread the word that the army of Dahomey had crossed the river. As soon as King Huffon heard the news, he and his entourage fled the city. By five o'clock in the afternoon the countryside south of Savi was filled with people fleeing toward the coast carrying whatever belongings they could. King Huffon and his chief officials made it to Popo and entered waiting canoes to reach an island in the middle of the Glewe River. The common people, however, were not as fortunate, and many drowned while attempting to swim to the island. Others fled into the bush and perished afterward by sword and famine.

The Dahomian soldiers who entered Savi went straight to the king's palace. Finding it abandoned, they set it on fire. The advance party then sent word back to their general on the other side of the river that the town had been taken, and the whole army soon descended on the city. Entering into the houses of the royal officials and priests, they occasionally came upon pythons, which were the sacred serpents of Whydah. Killing a python was punishable by death, but the soldiers of Dahomey had such disdain for the serpent cult of Whydah that they held up the snakes and said, "If you are gods, save yourselves." Then they cut off the heads of the serpents, broiled them over coals, and ate them.

Entering the compound of the Royal African Company, the soldiers encountered its director, Mr. Duport, and seemed unnerved at seeing a white man for the first time in their lives. At first they kept their distance, but after he held out his hand to them, they approached and touched him. Deciding that he was a person like themselves, they took him prisoner and confiscated everything he had in his pockets. About forty Europeans from the English, French, Dutch, and Portuguese trading companies were captured in a similar fashion. All together, five thousand inhabitants of Savi were killed in the attack and eleven thousand were taken prisoner.[3]

The fall of Savi brought recriminations because many people had a hard time believing that a kingdom as powerful as Whydah could be toppled so easily. The Dutch trading representative in Jakin, Hertogh, blamed the defeat on treachery by the African officials responsible for overseeing Dutch trading activities and by Assou, the local official responsible for French traders. Hertogh charged that those officials were in league with two members of the Whydah aristocracy who had been cheated of their inheritance by King Huffon and were now taking their revenge.[4]

A Dahomian oral tradition gives a very different view of internal treachery. It states that one of King Huffon's wives was Na Geze, the daughter of King Agaja, who served as a spy for Dahomey. On the eve of the Dahomian attack, Na Geze entertained King Huffon and many of his officials. Having received large quantities of food and palm wine from her father, she got the king and his chiefs drunk and then sent her servants to wet the king's supplies of gunpowder, leaving the army helpless when the attack came. Although this account, which was probably created long after the events themselves, is best read as an interpretation of the fall of Savi rather than a narrative of the actual events, it nevertheless expresses the local view that guile and treachery led to the destruction of Whydah.[5] It also makes a telling point about the power of women in the rise and fall of kingdoms.

On May 10, 1727, the day after the Dahomian attack, the forty white prisoners were taken north to Allada, about sixteen miles away. Even though they were prisoners of war, the directors of the European trading companies were carried in hammocks, as befits men of high standing. Arriving in Allada, they were separated according to nationality and put in the care of separate overseers. Several days passed before Mr. Duport, the director of the Royal African Company, got an audience with King Agaja, and he used the occasion to complain about his detention and his treatment. King Agaja replied that he was very sorry for the bad treatment. He had given orders to his captains to treat Europeans well, but such details had gotten overlooked in the confusion of war. King Agaja confessed that he had been very surprised to learn that so many white people had been captured in the battle. A few days later, he set the Europeans free and sent them down to the English and French forts with an armed escort to ensure their safety. Before releasing them, he presented the major European officials with prisoners of war that they could sell as slaves, and he assured them that as soon as the warfare was finished he would make the slave trade flourish.

Only a few days after Duport and the other company officials were returned to the English fort, the English slave trader William Snelgrave anchored in front of the fort in the ship *Katharine Galley*. The sight of bones whitening in the fields gave Snelgrave a sense of the devastation caused by the recent wars. With no possibility of trading slaves at Whydah, he continued twenty miles down the coast to Jakin, a port city that had once been under the control of the king of Allada and now was under the authority of King Agaja. Several days later, Snelgrave received an invitation to visit King Agaja at his military camp outside the former capital city of Allada. The messenger was a young African who had learned to speak excellent English at the English fort and had worked at one time for Bulfinch Lambe. He had been captured along with Bulfinch Lambe when the army of Dahomey had conquered Allada, and he now worked as an interpreter for the king of Dahomey.

On the morning of April 8, William Snelgrave set off in the company of the duke of Jakin and the secretary of the Dutch trading lodge to meet the king of Dahomey.[6] As was the custom of the country, Snelgrave was carried in a hammock by a team of two bearers who worked in rotation with two similar teams. Snelgrave was also given a small horse to ride when he wearied of lying in the hammock. By this means, the entourage moved slowly through the countryside, which, like the countryside around Whydah, had been devastated by war. After camping for the night, the group arrived the next morning at a spot about half a mile from King Agaja's military camp.

The next day Snelgrave and his companions were received by King Agaja himself. After the usual ceremonies and greetings, the king invited the visitors to observe the ceremony in which he paid his soldiers for their victory in a recent war. Following his victory over the king of Whydah, King Agaja had sent an army to the north about six days' journey to battle a country called Tofo, which had attacked some of his wives while he had been preoccupied with the attack on Savi. After conquering Savi, he exacted his revenge on Tofo.

About eighteen hundred captives taken in the attack on Tofo were brought into the courtyard. Military officers received the captives from common soldiers and paid them in cowry shells. Translating the cowries into shillings, Snelgrave estimated that the soldiers were paid twenty shillings for every adult male prisoner they captured, and ten shillings for every woman, boy, or girl. Then the soldiers were paid the equivalent of five shillings for the head of each enemy that they had killed. King Agaja's incentive system heavily favored capturing rather than killing the enemy: a soldier who captured an adult male prisoner was rewarded with four times the payment he received for a dead enemy.

The following afternoon Snelgrave met with King Agaja to discuss the purchase of war prisoners. The king agreed to supply him with a shipload of captives and to accept a customs payment amounting to half of what had been paid to the king of Whydah. He also agreed that Snelgrave's load of slaves would have a ratio of three males to one female, a ratio that Snelgrave believed was ideal. Finally, he agreed that Snelgrave would get first pick from the caravan of captives that he would send down to Jakin. King Agaja explained his ready agreement to Snelgrave's terms by saying that since Snelgrave was the first English slaving captain with whom he had traded directly, he was treating him like a young bride to whom nothing must be denied at first.[7]

As an experienced slave trader, Snelgrave recognized that the nature of the slave trade along the Slave Coast had changed dramatically. Whereas Whydah and Allada had been middleman states whose kings had profited by taxing the flow of slaves and imported trade goods that passed through their countries, King Agaja's Dahomey was a militarized state that had no interest in being the middleman for other people's commerce. Now Europeans purchased their slaves directly from the king and his agents, and the slaves were people who had been captured in Agaja's wars of conquest instead of purchased from countries farther inland. Snelgrave observed that King Agaja "drives no regular trade in slaves, but only sells such as he takes in his wars."[8]

King Agaja made a handsome profit from the sale of his prisoners of war. He paid his soldiers one pound sterling (twenty shillings) for each adult male captive and sold them to Snelgrave for about twenty pounds each. From those profits he had to subtract the cost of maintaining his army. Muskets cost one pound each, and then there was the cost of musket balls, powder, and steel swords. Food for the army was obtained by looting

the granaries of conquered villages or was produced by slaves who belonged to the king and the great officers. Even by a rough calculation, the
king's income from the sale of a slave was five to ten times the cost of capturing the slave.[9]

The slave trading arrangements completed, the king turned to the subject of Bulfinch Lambe. He told Snelgrave that over a year had passed since
he had given Bulfinch Lambe 320 ounces of gold and eighty slaves. Despite Lambe's solemn promise to return within a reasonable time, the king
had heard nothing from him. Snelgrave replied that he did not know
Lambe personally, but he had heard rumors that Lambe had gone to the
Caribbean after leaving Whydah in 1726. The king replied that although
Lambe had not proven to be as good as his word, he would be patient. If
Lambe returned quickly, even with a very large ship, it would be instantly
filled with slaves.

Before leaving King Agaja's camp, Snelgrave had a chance to observe the
arrival of the last remaining troops who had fought at Tofo. The army consisted of about three thousand regular troops divided into several companies, each with its own officers and colors. The troops marched in regular
order with each soldier carrying a musket, a steel sword, and a shield. Behind the troops were about ten thousand porters, shield carriers, and camp
followers. Arriving at the main square of King Agaja's camp, the troops
performed military exercises for two hours in front of the king and a large
number of spectators, firing about twenty volleys of musket shots in the
process. Snelgrave judged the exercises to be "well worth seeing." At nine
o'clock the next morning, he and his companions departed for the coast.

Three days after Snelgrave's return to Jakin, a large number of slaves arrived, sent down by King Agaja. Although Snelgrave had been promised
that he would get his pick of the slaves, he had a hard time filling his ship.
The reason, he learned, was that two Portuguese ships had arrived in the
harbor of Whydah, and King Agaja preferred to sell the strongest and
healthiest captives to the Portuguese, who were carrying gold from Brazil.
After a long delay in filling his ship, Snelgrave found himself needing only
eighty more slaves for a full load. When he sent a message requesting King
Agaja to send down eighty slaves, he was told that the king had no more
slaves for sale. All of the captives who had not been sold to European slave
traders had been given to military officers as a reward for their services or

had been put to work tilling the king's fields or serving in his palaces. Once a slave was enrolled in the service of the king, Snelgrave was told, that slave could never again be sold. After further delay, eighty slaves arrived, and on July 1, 1727, Snelgrave sailed from Jakin with six hundred slaves, fifty of whom died during the seventeen-week passage to Antigua. Once there, Snelgrave spread the word that King Agaja was awaiting the return of Bulfinch Lambe.

T MIDMORNING ON MAY 7, 1731, Bulfinch Lambe and his African companion, Captain Tom, stepped out of the coach in the great courtyard of St. James's Palace in London. Lambe wore a three-cornered hat and a curly wig that fell over his shoulders. His coat, which descended to just above his knee, was flared below the waist. Velvet knee breeches and a silk cravat completed the outfit. Captain Tom was similarly dressed in a new outfit made for him by the London tailor John Lucas and new buckled shoes made by the shoemaker Theodore Jackson.[1] Lambe's fortunes had certainly improved since the time five years earlier when he and his African interpreter had been captives of King Agaja in Dahomey.[2]

After being released from captivity in spring of 1726 and sent down to the port of Jakin with King Agaja's gift of eighty slaves, Lambe and Captain Tom had found passage to Whydah on a ship commanded by Captain Richard Baugh. Arriving at the English fort after four years in captivity, Lambe discovered that the Royal African Company had discharged him as a company employee once they learned that he had been detained by the king of Allada, and therefore they did not owe him any back pay.

Lambe, for his part, did not tell the company that forty of the slaves he had brought with him were intended as a gift to King George I. Instead, he sold as many of the eighty slaves as he could to Portuguese slave traders for five ounces of gold (equal to twenty British pounds) apiece, and the rest he exchanged for muskets, gunpowder, brandy, and cloth. He asked the fort's director, Jeremiah Tinker, to find him and Captain Tom passage to

England on a company ship, but the request was refused on the grounds that they were no longer company employees. Finally they secured passage on a private slave ship belonging to Humphrey Morice that was bound for Barbados. Lambe left £285 worth of goods at the fort with the agreement that Tinker should sell them and deliver the money to him in England. After three months at the fort, Lambe left the coast of Africa carrying over a £1,000 worth of Brazilian gold and a promissory note from Tinker worth £285.[3]

Although Lambe had originally intended to stay in Barbados only long enough to catch a ship to England, fear of his creditors caused him to change his mind. He owed the Royal African Company over £400 for supplies that they had sent him during his captivity and money they had advanced to his wife in England, and he was in no mood to pay it back. Instead, he settled in New England. With his newfound wealth from the sale of the slaves, he invested in a variety of trading ventures, at one time going to Madeira to finance a shipload of wine and later returning to Madeira to keep a tavern for a while. Lambe's fortunes as a merchant-investor, however, were not much better than his fortunes had been as a slave trader for the Royal African Company. With his money gone from bad investments and debts piling up to English creditors, he sold Captain Tom to a ship owner in Annapolis, Maryland, named Robert Alexander.[4]

Things began to turn around after November 1727, when William Snelgrave arrived in Antigua and spread the word that King Agaja had promised Bulfinch Lambe a shipload of slaves if he and Captain Tom would return to Dahomey. The word somehow reached Lambe in New England. Although he had left Dahomey with no intention of ever returning, the proposition now seemed attractive in the light of his straitened conditions. After thinking it over, he decided to return to London and try to arrange a slaving voyage to Dahomey. The problem was that he could not return without Captain Tom. With some difficulty, he managed to buy Captain Tom back from Robert Alexander for twenty-six pounds and smooth over his former interpreter's feelings of betrayal by promising him great wealth to be gained in their new venture.[5] Although Lambe was in debt to the Royal African Company and assorted English creditors, the Act for the Relief of Insolvent Debtors passed by the British Parliament in 1728 kept him out of debtors' prison, at least for a while. In February 1731 Bulfinch

Figure 22.1   The king's presence chamber in St. James's Palace, London.

Lambe and Captain Tom arrived in England, where Lambe had not set foot in over a decade.

Soon after his arrival, Lambe paid a visit to the house of William Snelgrave to ask if it was really true that King Agaja had promised him a shipload of slaves. When Snelgrave confirmed the story, Lambe showed Snelgrave the letter from King Agaja to King George and asked him about the feasibility of returning to Dahomey. Snelgrave warned him not to go, saying that by letting several years pass he had missed his opportunity, and he risked becoming the object of King Agaja's resentment.[6] Undeterred, Lambe approached the Royal African Company in hopes of getting support for his voyage. He showed them King Agaja's letter, pointing out the passage in which the king of Dahomey asked King George to make Lambe chief of the Europeans in Whydah. He offered to suppress the letter if the company would give him command of a ship or appoint him director of the fort at Whydah. The company responded that "they had no reason to be

satisfied with his services, and that they would give him no encourage-
ment."[7] Rebuffed, Lambe then contacted some private traders in Bristol,
and it was they, in all likelihood, who helped arrange the audience with
the king.

Bulfinch Lambe and Captain Tom were ushered into the palace and led
through the first hall, decorated with tapestries from the looms at Mort-
lake, then the second hall, decorated with tapestries and a canopy, and into
the king's presence chamber. At the far end of the chamber, King George
II sat on the chair of state under a large canopy. The wall behind the chair
was covered with a large tapestry that was partly obscured by a banner
bearing the royal coat of arms.[8]

Captain Tom was introduced as Adomo Oroonoko Tomo, who had
been sent to England by the king of Dahomey.[9] Captain Tom had clearly
embellished his name for greater effect: "Tomo" was derived from Tom,
"Adomo" from Adam, and "Oroonoko" came from Aphra Behn's novel of
the same name about an African prince who had been wrongfully enslaved.[10] That very evening, in fact, Thomas Southerne's drama *Oroonoko*,
based on Behn's novel, was playing in the Theatre Royal in Drury Lane.[11]
The play had been very popular ever since it first opened there in 1695,
and Captain Tom, undoubtedly aided by Bulfinch Lambe, had made a
clever choice in borrowing its hero's name.

After the introductions, Lambe recounted the story of how he had been
taken captive at the conquest of Allada and carried before King Agaja, who
had never before seen a white man. He explained that he was treated with
great kindness and respect and sent back to England with instructions to
present King Agaja's greetings to King George I. In the intervening years,
however, King George I died, and so the tale was now being told to
King George II. The climax of the meeting came when Lambe presented
King George with the letter from King Agaja that described the history
and customs of Dahomey and called for King George to appoint Lambe as
his representative to King Agaja's court. Such an appointment was bound
to be controversial because it would give Lambe a special status and, more
seriously, would bypass the bureaucracy of the Royal African Company.

The original version of King Agaja's letter had been written in Lambe's
own hand in January 1726. Since that time Lambe must have recopied it at
least once, as he had a habit of making corrected versions of his original

drafts.[12] There is no way of knowing what changes he may have introduced during the recopying, but it seems likely that any alterations would
have been in the parts of the letter that bore on Lambe's future appoint-
ments. The parts of the letter that described the history and customs of
Dahomey were regarded in England as mere curiosities, and there was
little to be gained by altering them. The controversy that was about to
erupt would focus on the question of what official positions, if any, should
be found for Bulfinch Lambe and Captain Tom.

That issue came before the commissioners for trade and plantations just
twelve days later, on May 19, 1731, when the commissioners read a petition
and a memorandum from Bulfinch Lambe "relating to some transactions
he had had with the King of Dahomey."[13] They asked Lambe to appear
before the board on Friday, two days later. Lambe read them the letter and
told the commissioners that he desired an immediate answer so that he
could carry it back to King Agaja, who had released him from his captivity
on condition that he would return to Dahomey. The commissioners requested that Lambe appear again the next Thursday, when representatives
of the Royal African Company as well as several private traders would give
testimony.

The hearing on Thursday, May 27, had a long list of witnesses.[14]
Bulfinch Lambe arrived together with Captain Tom. Two directors of the
Royal African Company were there, as were Jeremiah Tinker and Thomas
Wilson, former directors of the company fort at Whydah. At least five pri-
vate traders who had traded in Whydah and Jakin were present, including
William Snelgrave. After everybody was seated, the secretary read the letter
from King Agaja and then asked the attending witnesses whether they
thought the letter was "genuine."

It was a curious way of framing the issue. Everybody in the room knew
that the letter had been written by Bulfinch Lambe's hand, and everybody
knew that Lambe had been a captive of King Agaja for nearly two years.
The issue of genuineness was not susceptible to determination one way or
the other by the commission. The real issue was whether Bulfinch Lambe
should be sent back to Dahomey as the king's representative as the letter
requested, a move that would effectively bypass the administrative hierarchy of the Royal African Company. By framing the question in terms of
"the genuineness of the letter," the commissioners were giving themselves

cover for their decision on the real question, which was what to do with Bulfinch Lambe.

There was also a second issue at stake. Along with the letter, Lambe had presented a memorandum containing the proposal for the British to aid King Agaja in setting up plantations in Dahomey that would produce export commodities such as sugar or cotton. The proposal had originally been a ploy by Lambe to gain his freedom, but now he realized that he could not return to Dahomey without an answer. The Royal African Company would never agree to the proposal because it would create competition for the British sugar planters in the Caribbean. Moreover, the employment of slaves in plantations in Dahomey would reduce the number available for toil in the New World colonies. By discrediting the letter, the commissioners could render the entire plantation proposal irrelevant.

William Snelgrave was the first witness. This was his first time before the commissioners since he had reported on the condition of the Royal African Company's forts in 1726. Snelgrave testified that King Agaja had told him that he had given Lambe eighty slaves and 320 ounces of gold, and had sent Lambe and Captain Tom to England to "give an account of his grandeur and conquests." When asked if King Agaja had specifically mentioned a letter, Snelgrave replied that he had not, but that he, Snelgrave, believed the letter to be genuine. Jeremiah Tinker, who had been the director of the English fort at Whydah at the time of Bulfinch Lambe's captivity, said that he was aware of the eighty slaves that King Agaja had given to Lambe but he had never heard of any gold dust, nor of the letter. Mr. Hays of the Royal African Company got to the heart of the matter when he volunteered that if the company made Lambe its director at Whydah, he would be satisfied and give the commissioners no more trouble. Mr. Harris, one of the private traders, testified that he believed it would be in the interest of trade that Mr. Lambe and Captain Tom should be sent to Whydah.

The key testimony came from Bulfinch Lambe and Captain Tom. Lambe recounted his travels since leaving Whydah in an effort to explain why he had let nearly five years pass before returning to England with the letter. He acknowledged receiving the eighty slaves—forty for himself and forty as a present to King George—but he denied ever receiving any gold. The crucial testimony on the issue of the genuineness of the letter came from Captain Tom, who said that he had been the interpreter when the letter was written. He assured the commission that the letter from King Agaja to King George "did contain all that the emperor did him write." He added that after the letter was written he had translated it back to King Agaja for his approval.

The commissioners of trade and plantations were not happy with the day's testimony, which had clearly gone in favor of Lambe and Captain Tom. Instead of making an immediate decision, they decided to gain some time by sending out a questionnaire to the Royal African Company and some private traders asking three questions: Was the letter genuine? Should Lambe and Captain Tom be sent back to Dahomey? If so, in what manner and with what credentials?

The Royal African Company replied on June 10 with a long memorandum that disputed the genuineness of the letter from King Agaja. The company's main argument was that Bulfinch Lambe had spent three months at the company fort in Whydah after his release from Dahomey, and during that time he had not mentioned the letter nor shown it to anybody. Since the letter proposed that Lambe should be made King George's representative to Dahomey, however, it would have been foolish and perhaps even dangerous for Lambe to show it to the company officials at the fort. The company also advised against sending Lambe back to Dahomey. "We are therefore humbly of the opinion," wrote the company's representative, "that a person who has behaved so ill, and who has not only broke his promises to the king of Dahomey in so notorious a manner, but likewise spent and misapplied much of the greatest part of the produce of the eighty Negroes which he was entrusted with, is not a person to be sent back with any character or entrusted any further with the conduct and management of such an affair." The report concluded, "If the said Lambe deserves anything, it would be some exemplary punishment."[15] The company's report apparently gave the commissioners the cover they needed to deny all of Lambe's claims.

On July 6 the Commission on Trade and Plantations informed King George II that "the African Company and the separate traders believe the letter not to be genuine." Therefore it did not require a response. Instead the company proposed to send "the black man who is called Adomo Oroonoko Tomo" to King Agaja along with gifts, which would be paid for from the sale of the slaves that Agaja had sent to King George. The report concluded, "We further think that to promote the commerce of this nation in Africa, it may be convenient that a letter should be written to the said emperor . . . by one of your principal secretaries of state, or by this board, in which he should be made acquainted with your Majesty's good will towards him; and that your Majesty has received his present of slaves, and accepts his offers of friendship and good correspondence made on his part by your subject Mr. Lambe; and that your majesty returns his servant Adomo Oroonoco Tomo to his safe hands."[16]

The commissioners had decided, in effect, to respond to King Agaja's letter in a way that cut Bulfinch Lambe out of the picture and totally ignored the plantation proposal. To further isolate Lambe, the commission concluded that Captain Tom should no longer be entrusted to his care, but that he should be "left at liberty to return to Africa, or otherwise dispose himself as he shall think proper." This suggestion was made into policy on September 2, when the Royal African Company voted money to pay the living expenses of Captain Tom and also to pay for a tutor to teach him to read and write English.[17] Tom, who had been living for the past several months in an alehouse in Old Bailey, moved to an apartment in Africa House, the headquarters of the Royal African Company. Lambe, outraged at being cut out of the picture, filed a petition to the Royal African Company demanding reimbursement for the £152 that he had spent supporting Captain Tom since leaving Dahomey.[18] Like Lambe's other petitions, this one was also rejected.

Now free of Bulfinch Lambe's tutelage, Adomo Oroonoko Tomo (a.k.a. Captain Tom) became the toast of London. Many people thought that he was the official representative of the king of Dahomey; others believed him to be an African prince. As such, Captain Tom had joined the small but elite group of Africans living in London as royalty in exile. The English, it seems, made a clear class distinction between Africans whom they thought to be of royal blood and ordinary chattel slaves whom they carried to the New World in ever increasing numbers. When a certain Robert Whydah, who was said to be a great officer of King Agaja, married an Englishwoman named Mrs. Johnson in December 1731, Captain Tom may well have been the black "best man" who was reported at the wedding.[19] William Snelgrave reported that Captain Tom was even the guest of honor at certain theater productions, though he did not identify which ones. It nevertheless seems a good bet that he was at the November 22 production of *Oroonoko* at the Theatre Royal in Drury Lane. This was the theater's first performance of *Oroonoko* since May 7, the day that Captain Tom had been received by King George.[20]

Captain Tom probably sat in a box seat on the stage level on the right side of the Drury Lane Theatre's stage. The "side boxes," as they were called, were more suitable for being seen by the audience than for really seeing the play, but that was precisely the point. His box was not far from the royal box, which was identifiable by the royal crest displayed above it even though it was unoccupied that evening. Although he had a sideways view of the stage, he had a good view of the actors, who were illuminated by the candles on the huge chandeliers that hung over the stage.[21]

Mr. Marshall played the title role of Oroonoko, just as he had done in the Drury Lane Theatre's previous performance of the play on May 7. Made up in blackface,[22] Marshall played an African prince from Angola who had been treacherously kidnapped by a slaving captain of his acquaintance and taken to Surinam. From his side box, Captain Tom fixed his eyes on the stage as a group of black slaves consisting of men, women, and children passed by two by two. Some of the walk-on players were actually Africans; others were whites in blackface. They were followed by the hero, Oroonoko, in chains. Oroonoko's new master, Blandford, suggested that class and rank were almost as important as race in the social hierarchy when he said of the slaves, "Most of 'em know no better! They were born so, and only change their masters. But a prince born only to command, betrayed and sold! My heart drops blood for him."[23] A few minutes later Oroonoko showed his noble character when he said, "Hard fare, and whips, and chains may overpower the frailer flesh, and bow my body down. But there's another, nobler part of me, out of your reach, which you can never tame." Like the character Blandford, the English audience could sympathize with the noble Oroonoko without in any way condemning the slave trade as a whole.

When Oroonoko was the prince of Angola, the play revealed, he had sold slaves to the treacherous captain. The captain explained, "I have formerly had dealings with him for slaves which he took prisoners, and have got pretty roundly by him. But the war being at an end, and nothing more to be got by the trade of that country, I made bold to bring the prince along with me." When Blandford recoiled in horror at the very idea of stealing an African prince from his own country, the captain recounted, "This Oroonoko . . . is naturally inquisitive about the men and manners of the white nations. Because I could give him some account of the other parts of the world, I grew very much into his favor. In return of so great an honor, you know I could do no less upon my coming away than invite him on board me." Once Oroonoko was on board, the captain got Oroonoko's henchmen drunk and then seized him.

Once enslaved, Oroonoko railed righteously against his personal betrayal by the white captain, but he did not attack the slave trade itself. Of his new masters in Surinam, he said, "If we are slaves, they did not make us slaves; but bought us in a honest way of trade: As we have done before 'em, bought and sold many a wretch, and never thought it wrong." Those words could have applied equally to Captain Tom. As a former interpreter for the Royal African Company, he had helped negotiate many slave sales before being captured by King Agaja, and he had later sailed as a paying passenger on a slave ship bound for Barbados. But he had also been a slave in both Dahomey and Maryland. Now he was the guest of honor at a playhouse in London while he prepared his return to Dahomey to negotiate good trading relations between King Agaja and the slave traders of the Royal African Company.

As the play continued, it began to display the erotic transgressing of racial and gender boundaries that had made it so popular.[24] Oronooko, the black slave, discovered that the white slave Imoinda was his long-lost wife. At the same time, the white widow Lackit tried to buy Oroonoko for sexual purposes. Then Mr. Welldon, who wooed and married the widow Lackit, turned out to be a woman in disguise. When the play first opened in 1695, its success helped to pull the Drury Lane Theatre out of an economic decline,[25] and nearly four decades later it was still drawing crowds. As the play came to an end, Oroonoko led an unsuccessful slave rebellion and then heroically committed suicide in order to gain the happiness in the next world that was denied to him in this one. As the curtain went down, the audience erupted in thunderous applause.

PART 7

Assou

*A*T SEVEN IN THE morning on September 1, 1731, the *Diligent* entered the harbor of Whydah. As it approached the shore, Robert Durand could hear the roar of the triple surf interspersed by the rhythmic sounds of crashing waves. In the background he could barely make out the outlines of the English, French, and Portuguese forts as they emerged from the morning haze. Four months after leaving Vannes, the *Diligent* had finally arrived at its destination, but a stop at Whydah could put them in danger. In order to assess the situation, he needed to get in contact with other ships and catch up on the latest developments.[1]

In the harbor were an English ship that they had earlier seen at Cape Coast castle, two Portuguese ships, and one French ship belonging to the Company of the Indies. As the *Diligent* drifted slowly just outside the waves of the triple surf, its longboat was lowered so that Durand and a crew of oarsmen could row to the company ship. Soon the rhythmic splashes of the oars melded with the noises of the surf. The company ship was called the *Pontchartrain*, named after the former French minister of the marine. As a 220-ton ship armed with fourteen cannons, it was almost twice as big as the *Diligent*. It was manned by a crew of forty-seven, nearly a third of whom would die before the end of the voyage.

As Durand's longboat pulled alongside the *Pontchartrain*, a rope ladder was lowered so that he could climb aboard. Arriving at the deck, he was met by the captain, Noël du Rocher Sorin. Durand greeted him politely, but formally, because relations between company ships and private trading

Figure 23.1   Durand's drawing of the harbor at Whydah.

vessels were still somewhat tense. The officers on company ships regarded the private traders as little better than interlopers, even though the Company of the Indies had agreed in 1725 to open up the slave trade to private traders. The director of the company fort at Whydah complained that the private traders caused a lot of trouble and had driven up the price of slaves by 50 percent in the past eighteen months. Moreover, in their hurry to complete their cargoes, the private slavers sometimes kidnapped Africans, inviting retaliation on their compatriots. Private slave ships, the director concluded, were against the interest of the French nation.[2]

After Durand had identified himself and explained his mission, the captain of the Pontchartrain asked if the *Diligent* was carrying a passenger named Pierre Verger who had been left behind when the *Superbe* departed from Nantes on April 10.[3] Durand responded that Verger, who had been sent out by the Company of the Indies to manage the company trading lodge in Jakin, had missed the sailing of the *Superbe* and had subsequently come to Vannes along with his assistant, Dubordieu, to seek passage to Whydah on the *Diligent*. Upon hearing the news, Captain Sorin showed Durand a letter signed by the director of the French fort at Glewe containing orders to arrest Verger on sight. If the captain of the *Diligent* failed to obey, he would be punished as a rebel against the Crown. Robert Durand did not record the specific offense with which Pierre Verger was charged, but it probably had something to do with the Ordonnance de la Marine, book 2, title 6, article 3, which stated that if a crew member left his captain before the beginning of a voyage, he could be arrested in any spot on earth and imprisoned for as long as was appropriate.[4]

Distressed by the news, Durand wanted to return immediately to the *Diligent* and seek the advice of Captain Mary, but the captain of the *Pontchartrain* refused to allow him to leave. Instead, the captain wanted to send Durand's longboat back to the *Diligent* under the command of a company officer. Finding himself a temporary prisoner, Durand scribbled a quick note to Captain Mary explaining why he had been detained on board the *Pontchartrain*. The first lieutenant of the Pontchartrain, Barthelemy Le Blanc, commandeered Durand's longboat and set out to arrest Pierre Verger.

As a detainee who could do nothing but wait for the return of his longboat, Robert Durand had a chance to look over the ship and gain a sense of what it was like to work for a large international trading company. Worldwide, the Company of the Indies employed 1,925 shipboard personnel, of whom 1,526 were engaged in the Asia trade and 399 in the "second navigation," as trade to Africa and the Caribbean Islands was called. Of the employees engaged in the second navigation, 43 were officers and the remaining 356 were sailors.[5]

The *Pontchartrain* carried six officers, including a doctor, a scribe, and a priest. Captain Sorin's salary of 150 livres a month was only moderately higher than that of Captain Pierre Mary, who made 120 livres, but the first lieutenant on the Pontchartrain, who in practice served as the second captain, made the same salary as Pierre Mary and over twice as much as Robert Durand. In addition to their salaries, the officers received a bonus for each slave they delivered to the islands. The officers had been recruited from among the sons of officers of merchant ships and Company of the Indies vessels. Recruits started out as volunteers who received only their food and expenses, but after completing four or five voyages and passing courses on navigation, they entered the officer corps. Each captain had the right to recruit his own volunteers from among his family and friends, a practice that kept the officer corps of the company a closed and clannish social group.[6]

Ordinary sailors on the *Pontchartrain* made between fourteen and eighteen livres per month, about half the salary of the sailors on the *Diligent*. Most of them were on the *Pontchartrain* only because they had been drafted by the Royal French Navy and seconded to the Company of the Indies.[7] Even though the crude press gangs that had once closed down entire ports while they hunted down crews were a thing of the past, the draft system based on annual lists of all people in the maritime professions was efficient enough that few sailors could escape it.

All persons on the list were divided into four "classes" that took turns being on call for naval service for one year. After the class list was published at the beginning of each year, it was announced in the churches after mass and affixed on church doors. Those persons named were supposed to refrain from going to sea and to be on call for duty throughout the year. Although in theory any draftee in France could be sent to Lorient to serve on vessels of the Company of the Indies, there seemed to be resistance among many draftees, possibly because they were reluctant to undertake the long voyages to Asia. As a result, draftees for the company were recruited primarily in the nearby port cities of St. Malo, Brest, and Vannes.[8] This draft system proved inadequate for the company's needs, however, and the company had to recruit about a third of its crew members privately. Through a combination of the draft and private recruitment the company managed to man its ships and keep the sailors relatively content, or at least in line; the company was proud of the fact that it had only three desertions in 1730.[9]

When Durand asked the captain of the *Pontchartrain* about trading conditions in Whydah, he was told that that everything he had heard from the captain of the *Hirondelle* was true; not only were there no slaves to be had, but it was dangerous to go ashore. The crew of the *Pontchartrain* had lost two sailors in an attack on their tents, and the *Jason*, a private slaver sailing out of Nantes, had suffered a similar fate. Its captain, Mathieu Fillon, had died soon after the attack, and his ship had moved on to Jakin. Knowing that the European forts lacked the resources to ensure the safety of slave traders, the captain of the *Pontchartrain* had been counting on the Dahomian army to provide protection. But, he complained, the army of Dahomey had failed to ensure the safety of the European slave traders, and Assou had successfully shut down the slave trade at Whydah.

The attack on the tent of the *Pontchartrain* had taken place six weeks before the *Diligent* arrived. In the darkness of the early morning on July 17, six hundred raiders moved stealthily along the beach as the roar of the triple surf drowned out any noises that they made. Their objective was the series of large tents made from sailcloth that had been set up on the beach by the crews of the slave ships anchored in the harbor. As was customary for slave traders in Glewe, the tents served as a kind of way station between the ships and the European forts.[10] Trade goods from the ships were brought to the beach in large dugout canoes manned by African crews that could shoot through the treacherous triple surf. The goods were inventoried at the tents before being turned over to African porters who would

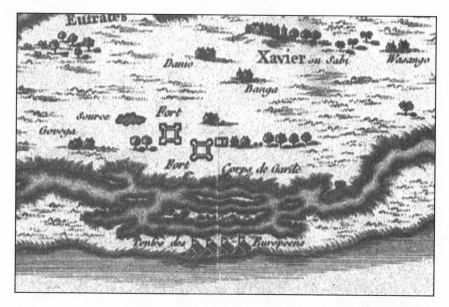

Figure 23.2   Des Marchais's 1725 map of the tents and forts on the coast of Whydah.

carry them the final three miles to be stored in the forts or in rented ware-houses in the town of Glewe. Slaves from the forts passed by the tents in the opposite direction. At the tents they were inventoried and loaded onto the canoes to be taken to the ship. For the slaves, the stopover at the tents represented their final steps on African soil.

The tents at Glewe beach were especially vulnerable to attack. To their south was the ocean with its deadly triple surf; to the north was the Glewe River, which was so wide and slow moving that it resembled a lake. The mud-walled forts of the French and English, as well as the largely aban-doned Portuguese fort, were nearly three miles away on the other side of the river. The English fort, whose mud walls and bastions had suffered ero-sion during the rainy season, was undergoing repair. It had thirty-two can-nons, and its military contingent consisted of a sergeant, a gunner, a corpo-ral, fifteen English soldiers, and ninety-four African soldiers. The French fort had also been undergoing repair since the arrival of the *Pontchartrain* in May. The ship had brought a new director, Achile de la Vigne, three assis-tants, a doctor, a priest, two coopers, and two masons for repairing the fort. It also brought a corporal and twenty-four French soldiers to boost the fort's military capacity.[11] Despite the repairs and beefed-up military capacity, the forts existed mainly to store trade goods and hold slaves. Their military posture was purely defensive, and they lacked the capacity for fighting outside their mud walls. In June 1731 both the British and the French directors had discussed plans for building "strong houses" on the beach for storing merchandise being unloaded from ships, but fear of attack had prevented them from doing anything.[12]

At the first light of dawn the African raiders raised their muskets and opened fire on the sentinels standing guard. Their plan was to move in quickly and overwhelm the opposition, but the first volleys raised the alarm. Soon musket fire was being returned from the direction of the tents. Realizing that they were outnumbered, many of the sailors in the tents fled for the Glewe River and the forts beyond it. The African attackers did not pursue them because their objectives were the tents and the trade goods inside, not the crew members themselves. They cut the tents to ribbons and then headed west with the merchandise toward Popo. In the remains of the tent belonging to the company ship *Pontchartrain*, they left the bodies of first pilot Jean Bourgeois, twenty-nine years old, and seaman Cado Dibredère, age twenty. Each of the tattered tents suffered casualties.[13]

When Noël du Rocher Sorin, the captain of the *Pontchartrain*, received the news at noon, he understood that the attackers were sending a message. The raid was much more than a simple act of pillage; it was an attempt to shut down the slave trade at Whydah. This was the second attack in eight days. The earlier attack had left two people in the *Pontchartrain* tent wounded and had pillaged the tent of the *Jason*, a private French slaver sailing out of Nantes, wounding two of its sailors. After the *Jason's* captain, Fillon, died on August 23 (of chagrin, it was reported), his ship fled Whydah for the safer harbor of Jakin.

When the news of those incidents reached the *Diligent* on September 1, Robert Durand had a ready explanation. Although he had never been to Africa before, he had formed opinions about local politics based on the rumors he had heard from other ship captains. The person behind the attacks, he wrote in his journal, was none other than Assou. Durand elaborated his analysis with a capsule history of recent events: "Whydah," he wrote, "has always been a great center of commerce where several ships at a time could purchase much gold and many slaves. The ruin of this trade cannot be blamed on anyone but Assou, the former protector of the French who was driven out of Whydah, along with his king, by the king of Dahomey. The king of Whydah and his subjects were forced to retreat to an island off Great Popo. Assou was disturbed at seeing himself reduced to a slavelike condition outside of his own country, whereas previously he had been viewed in Whydah as something like the king of the country and its trade. Jealous of watching trade flourish when he could not participate in it, he took it by the throat and decided to ruin it."

Of all the officials of the recently destroyed kingdom of Whydah who had been driven into exile on the island near Great Popo, the last person the French would have expected to orchestrate attacks on them was Assou. Prior to the destruction of Whydah, Assou had been governor one of the twenty-six tiny provinces that made up the kingdom. Europeans referred to him variously as a "prince," a "great captain," a "chief," and the "protector of the French," but usually they simply called him Captain Assou. His official titles concealed more than they revealed. Robert Durand was absolutely correct in his assessment that Assou had been the most powerful person in the kingdom of Whydah.

As early as 1702 Assou had been described by the French slave trader Damon as someone who could "accomplish anything with the court to further our interests."[14] When King Aisan of Whydah died in 1708, Assou was instrumental in lining up support for Aisan's son Huffon, who was still a minor, over the claims of the Gogon of Savi. After that, Assou emerged as the real power behind the throne. He was named the protector of the French, making him parallel with Captain Carter, who was the protector of the English. As one of the "great captains" of Whydah, Assou personally received customs payments from each slave ship that came to trade: sixteen thousand cowry shells, a length of silk cloth, and assorted goods amounting to the price of two slaves.[15] He also bought and sold slaves on his own account to become one of the wealthiest men in the country. He was, in short, a person born to a minor position who had risen to power and wealth through his association with the slave trade.

By the time the attacks on the tents occurred in 1731, Assou was in his sixties. In his younger days he had been described by Europeans as tall and heavy but well proportioned, with well-made facial features. He had spent part of his youth near the French trading compound in Savi and had learned to speak French so fluently that some Europeans were surprised to learn that he had never been to France. His impeccable French manners greatly impressed the European traders. The French slave trader Dralsé de Grand Pierre described him as possessing "all the merits of our most honest men of the first rank. He has grandeur and generosity along with polite French manners."[16]

Assou's two-story house with cannons in front of it was a landmark in Savi, Whydah's capital city. The floor and walls of Assou's master bedroom were covered with tapestries, and the room was furnished with stuffed chairs, stools, and a long table covered with a Turkish tablecloth. It also had a large mirror in an elaborately carved frame and a large imperial bed that was literally fit for a king. The house was part of Assou's larger compound, which contained five separate courtyards surrounded by long buildings containing apartments for his many wives. Although the apartments were not as impressive as Assou's bedroom, they were orderly and handsome, with walls covered by tapestries of beautiful cotton cloth. Some courtyards contained large furnaces where the wives worked to extract salt from seawater, prepare meat, bake bread, and brew beer. There was a separate and smaller courtyard where pregnant wives stayed while they were waiting to give birth to Assou's children.[17]

In his splendid house, Assou entertained frequently and lavishly. One evening he invited the officers of a French slave ship over for dinner. In his dining room, the table was covered with a beautiful tablecloth, on which were laid out knives, forks, and spoons of polished silver. On the buffet against the wall was a silver basin surrounded by gilded silver cups and crystal glasses. The French-style bread that he served, baked by his wives, was declared by the French visitors to be as good as any in Paris. Then he brought out the wine. First he served a Bordeaux, then a Madeira, then a Canary Island sweet wine, then a Canary Island dry. After that he brought out an assortment of French liqueurs. Toasts were exchanged as the men held up their glasses; each toast was accompanied by the boom of a small cannon.

The meal began with a rice soup with chicken in the middle and onions around the circumference of the bowl. Then came stews and delicacies. The main course included roast lamb, pork in a cream sauce, goose, pigeon, and a chicken liver pâté. Dessert included curds, almonds, hazelnuts, fruits of the country, pineapples, raw figs, and cooked figs. For entertainment there was a concert, complete with a trumpet player and a dance troupe. All in all, concluded the French officers, it was a most splendid evening.[18]

A short while later the French officers returned the favor by inviting Assou to visit their ship. When he boarded, he was saluted with seven cannon shots. After being greeted by all the officers, he was invited to spend the night aboard their ship. He declined, explaining that each night he slept with a different wife according to a fixed rotation schedule. If he stayed on the ship, then the wife scheduled for that night would become very distressed and raise a horrible fuss. Although the French officers were completely charmed by that explanation, there may have been another reason why Assou was reluctant to spend a night on a slave ship. He was given a seven-cannon salute when he departed.

Although Assou had embraced many of the elements of French culture, he found certain European religious practices repulsive. Various chaplains at the French fort had tried to convert him to Catholicism, but he had rejected it as illogical. He had no problem, he said, believing that God had been made flesh, had been humiliated, and had been put to death. But he had a great problem with the sacrament of communion and the accompanying doctrine of transubstantiation, which held that the communion bread and wine become the literal body and blood of Christ. Assou explained: "The proposition that one eats one's god fills me with horror and contradicts all sense and reason. I conceive that it is the most horrible thing in the world and, at the same time, the most useless. Why should one eat one's god? I find nothing in that belief except impiety, folly, superstition, and cruelty, for which we (whom you label as pagans and idolaters) would never be capable." Having finished his speech, Assou departed abruptly to show his indignation.

Assou knew full well that the Europeans had as much contempt for the religious beliefs of his country as he had for theirs, and he sometimes played on those differences to create elaborate jests. One evening when the slave trader and privateer Jean Doublet was at Assou's house for dinner, Doublet asked to be shown to the toilet. Assou led him to a row of privies and indicated which one he should use. No sooner had Doublet removed his trousers and underpants and sat down on the seat, than he spied an enormous snake in the corner. Terrified, he fled the privy with his underpants in his hands. Later, when he had retrieved his trousers and calmed down, he asked Assou if he had not sent him to that particular privy on purpose. As-sou burst out laughing, and in an instant Assou's brother, who was the high priest of the serpent cult, emerged cradling the snake in his arms like a baby. When Doublet again shrank back, Assou said, "Have no fear. This is our sacred animal."[19]

Religious differences could also turn deadly. A Frenchman at the Company of the Indies compound in Savi impudently killed a sacred snake that he found in his bed. Such an act was strictly prohibited throughout the kingdom, and culprits could be punished with death. When news of the killing spread through Savi, a crowd of over four hundred people gathered outside the com-pound and threatened to break down the gates unless they were let in to in-vestigate the matter and seize the culprit. When the director of the French company learned of the problem, he helped the man escape to the neighbor-ing English compound through a secret backdoor. Then he opened the gate to the crowd, who searched the compound for the remains of the serpent. Holding up the dead snake, they demanded that its killer be turned over to them immediately.

In panic, the French director sent for Captain Assou, who tried without success to appease the angry crowd. Finally, he promised them that if they would leave the compound and give the snake a proper burial, he would deliver the culprit to them later. The French director, who feared that all of the French in Savi risked being massacred, was ready to deliver his em-ployee to the mob. Assou, however, calmed the frightened director and said that he would work out a solution with the king. After delicate negotia-tions, the king agreed to allow the guilty Frenchman to be spirited out of the country as quickly as possible. For its transgression, the company paid a large quantity of merchandise and money to appease the popular outcry.

In a similar way, Assou intervened to save the French director in 1715, when the neighboring kingdom of Allada closed down the trade routes by which slaves came to Whydah. The king of Allada sent word to the French fort in Whydah that the ships currently in the harbor at Whydah should come to his country, where they would find plenty of slaves for sale. Upon hearing that news, two French ships in the Whydah harbor immediately set sail for Allada's port of Jakin. King Huffon of Whydah interpreted this action as extreme disloyalty, and he ordered the French director to leave the country before sunset. Getting the director safely to the harbor proved to be a problem, however, because the Whydah merchants were so outraged by this act of betrayal that they wanted to kill him. To solve the problem, Captain Assou came to the fort and personally escorted the director past the throngs of irate merchants to a canoe that carried him to the ship.

The French fully recognized how much their continued presence in Whydah depended on Assou. One French document noted that he was "the most honest, the best, and the most devoted. If the smallest problem for the French arises in the country, Assou is ready to sacrifice himself. It is Assou who represents the French in almost all disputes that go before the king."[20]

Assou also helped resolve quarrels among the European nations that traded at Whydah and is the most likely author of the 1704 treaty signed by all of them in which they promised to stop fighting with one another. The preamble to the treaty read: "The King of Whydah, having ordered the chiefs of the nations of Europe who have forts and posts in his kingdom and all the great men of the country to assemble at his palace, declares that irrespective of the wars that rage in Europe, or that they may have one against the other, they convene together in his presence a firm and durable peace in his harbor and even within sight of his harbor."[21] The treaty prohibited any ship from capturing any other ship; it prohibited ships from pillaging other ships; and it held that if a ship left the harbor during a time when the European nations were at war, no other ship could leave within twenty-four hours. This last measure was designed to prevent ships from acquiring cargoes of slaves by pursuing and attacking ships of rival nations. Each ship would at least get a twenty-four-hour head start.

Future events would sorely test the treaty. In 1715 a major conflict broke out among the English, Portuguese, and Dutch. The British director, Blaney, who was seeking exclusive access to the gold and tobacco that the Portuguese traders brought from Brazil, sent out eight of his African soldiers armed with pistols and sabers to find an old Portuguese trader with whom he had a quarrel. Finding the man beneath a tree in the trading square in Savi, the soldiers confiscated his hat and took turns urinating in it until it was full. Then they stuffed it back onto the old man's head. When a subsequent Portuguese ship, intimidated by Blaney's actions, agreed to trade exclusively with the English, the Dutch raided the ship and stole forty slaves. That infraction of the neutrality treaty made Blaney so angry that on November 18, 1714, he marched from the English fort to the Dutch compound in Savi with eighty African soldiers and four Europeans armed with muskets, pistols, and swords.

The sight of Blaney's armed men walking through the streets of Savi created a commotion in the city. Assou, who was at the French compound transacting business, heard the shouting and feared that war was about to break out among the Europeans. Asking the French director to round up some soldiers and come as quickly as possible, Assou rushed out to confront the English director. Soon twelve French soldiers marched into the street to see the Dutch director, Pieter Valckenier, being dragged feet first toward the English fort. Only when confronted by Assou and the French troops did Blaney release the Dutch director. Shortly thereafter King Huffon expelled Blaney from Whydah.[22]

Although Assou regularly performed delicate balancing acts in negotiating between the Europeans and the king, he remained loyal to King Huffon, whom he had helped put in power. In 1727, as the army of Dahomey was approaching Savi, Assou was one of only three captains who led his troops into the thick of the battle while the others held back and then fled. And it was Assou who organized the king's retreat to the island in the Glewe River near Popo.[23] Everything Assou had worked for in his life was destroyed in the Dahomian attack.

24

ONCE THEY HAD SETTLED on the island, Assou and King Huffon began to plan their return to power. Assou's power relative to the king became clear when the island began to be called "Assou Island." King Agaja of Dahomey could not pursue Huffon and Assou because his soldiers were not skilled in the use of canoes. Nevertheless, King Agaja was determined to capture Huffon. He told William Snelgrave that he would not rest until he had Huffon's head, but for the time being he had to be content with controlling the countryside by means of his army encamped at Savi.[1]

The fight between the king of Dahomey and the remnants of the defeated kingdom of Whydah created a situation that puzzled the British and French, who were huddled in their forts at Glewe. The continuing warfare should have yielded them a bonanza in slaves, but the large numbers of slaves that the Europeans eagerly anticipated did not appear to be forthcoming. This was partly because the major source of slaves in Whydah had always been the trade routes coming from inland areas, and those trade routes were now blocked by warfare and insecurity. Moreover, King Agaja had shifted the source of slaves from trade to warfare, and his wars of conquest could not produce the same number of slaves that the trade routes had formerly supplied. Observing the situation from afar, Mayor Gérard Mellier of Nantes wrote that the Dahomian conquest of Whydah "will set back our trade with Guinea for some time."[2]

King Agaja was certainly taking captives in his battles, but the European slave traders did not feel that they were getting a sufficient share. William

Snelgrave had gotten only six hundred out of the eighteen hundred captives that Agaja's army had brought in from Tofo, and even they were not the strong, healthy males that he had been promised. Many of the captives of Dahomey's wars were kept in Dahomey to work in the fields of King Agaja and his officers. Once a slave was put to work for the king, he or she could never again be sold. Nevertheless, large numbers of slaves were being delivered to the European forts at Whydah, and the constant complaints of the Europeans were in part the outcome of their own exaggerated expectations. In early 1728, for example, there were six French ships, five Portuguese ships, and three English ships waiting in the harbor beyond the forts,[3] and the competition among them had driven up slave prices by a third. The director of the French fort suggested that perhaps the real problem was too many ships instead of too few slaves. The long stay necessary for getting a full load provided an opportunity for the slaves on board the *Aurora*, a private slaver from La Rochelle, to revolt. In suppressing the revolt, the crew of the *Aurora* killed thirty-two slaves and badly wounded eight to ten others.[4]

The British and French directors came up with various theories as to what Agaja was doing with the slaves he captured. Their main theory was that he was selling them to the Portuguese. The reason for the Portuguese success in the slave trade was that many of the Portuguese ships did not sail from Portugal but from Brazil, where they did not have access to the usual assortment of trade goods. They therefore brought low-grade Brazilian tobacco that could not be sold in Europe and gold that had been smuggled out from the Minas Geraes in Brazil. Even though the king of Portugal had decreed the death penalty to anyone who shipped Brazilian gold to any country other than Portugal, the smuggling of gold to the Guinea coast was impossible to stop. One of the biggest smugglers of all was Joseph de Torres, who had built the Portuguese fort at Glewe in 1721. The theory propagated by the British, French, and Dutch was that King Agaja only wanted gold, and so he traded primarily with the Portuguese. The Portuguese had a similar advantage when trading with ordinary people in Whydah. Since the country was in a state of unrest, people had to be ready to flee their homes on short notice. Possessing large quantities of fine cloth or brandy was useless in such a situation, and people preferred to keep their wealth in the form of gold, which was easily carried if they had to flee.[5]

Even though the Portuguese obtained the choice slaves from King Agaja's wars, the fact remained that the warfare in Whydah was producing fewer slaves than the trade routes had produced prior to the fall of Savi. In 1728 even the Portuguese complained that ships from Brazil were now waiting up to a year to get a load of slaves, whereas formerly the entire round trip could be made in six or seven months. The viceroy of Brazil warned darkly of labor shortages in the gold mines, sugar mills, and tobacco plantations of Bahia. His own explanation was that formerly, "all of the slaves from the entire coast flowed into this place. The kingdom is now deserted because of the war waged against it by Dahomey. Because he is at war with all of the other kings, he does not send down slaves, and for this reason the ships are delayed."[6] For all the complaining by the European slave traders, the slave trade at Whydah was far from dead: over eight thousand slaves were shipped out of Whydah in 1728 and over nine thousand in 1729.[7]

There was another anomaly that puzzled the European slave traders: despite all the warfare, there was little demand for guns in 1728. The French director noted that there was no demand for gunpowder and complained that the Africans rejected French muskets. The reason, it appears, was that the French guns had a reputation for splitting when fired and injuring the shooter. At the same time, the director of the English fort begged the Royal African Company not to send him any guns because there had been no demand for them during the past ten months.[8] Perhaps the opposing armies had already obtained all the guns and ammunition they needed for the time being, or perhaps King Agaja was too much on the defensive to be in a position to build up his supply of arms.

Even though King Agaja appeared to the people of Whydah and Allada as a great conqueror, he was himself under attack from the kingdom of Oyo, which was located to his northeast. The army of Dahomey seemed invincible when fighting against the foot soldiers of Whydah and Allada, but it was far from invincible when fighting Oyo, which had a horse-mounted army. The foot soldiers of King Agaja could not repel the cavalry charges. But Oyo had two weaknesses. First, its horse-mounted army could come only during the dry season, when the rivers they had to cross were running low. Second, the dry season caused severe shortages of fodder for their horses. Even if they won the battle, they had to retreat before the fodder ran low or the rivers rose with the coming of the rains. The goal of the Oyo attacks was not to permanently occupy Dahomey, but rather to force King Agaja to restore the kingdoms of Whydah and Allada.

In March 1728 Oyo launched an invasion that would be repeated in 1729 and 1730. Each dry season the Oyo cavalry burned and looted King Agaja's capital of Abomey. Agaja fled to the countryside and played for time until the onset of the rains forced the Oyo cavalry to withdraw. The Oyo attacks and Dahomian retreats provided an opportunity for King Huffon and Assou to leave their island hideaway near Popo and try to restore the kingdom of Whydah. In early 1728, with the Dahomian army occupied by the Oyo invasion, Assou and a group of his followers came out of exile and settled near the European forts. Assou even tried to collect customs payments from the ships that anchored in the harbor, just as he had done before the destruction of Whydah.[9]

The Europeans, fearing that Assou's presence near their forts would invite an attack from the Dahomean army, began preparations to defend themselves. The English fort was in terrible shape. When the new director arrived in February 1728, he found that there was no gunpowder, and he had to use his limited supplies of gold to buy powder from passing ships. They were also short of lead shot for their guns, and they put the blacksmiths to work cutting up iron bars to use as bullets. The French fort was in even worse shape because the thatched roofs on its buildings had burned in a fire started by two slaves at the beginning of February.[10] The French director was trying desperately to get his fort repaired before the Dahomian army arrived.

The Portuguese fort was in such poor condition that its director had taken refuge in the French fort after the fall of Savi, and it was all but abandoned thereafter. A dispatch from Lisbon warned, "If the Portuguese fortress in Whydah cannot assure the protection of the Portuguese against the insults of the blacks of the king of Dahomey, it would be better not to possess it." The Portuguese director replied that *none* of the European forts at Glewe were capable of withstanding a sustained assault.[11] As the army of Dahomey approached, the Portuguese took refuge in the English fort, bringing the English garrison to forty Europeans and four hundred armed Africans.[12]

When the Dahomian army arrived at the European forts on April 30, it had been burning the countryside as it progressed. The British director sent out soldiers to burn all the African villages north of the British fort on

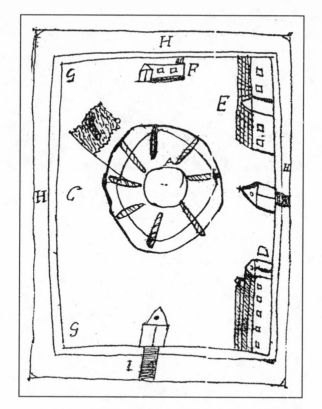

Figure 24.1   Portuguese sketch of Fort St. John the Baptist at Whydah, 1721.

an afternoon when a breeze was blowing from the ocean, reasoning that if Dahomians burned those villages on a day when the wind was blowing the other way, the fire might spread to the fort. He was using the African villages as a firebreak.

With the Dahomian army approaching, most of the Whydah forces fled toward their island at Popo, but Assou and his troops sought refuge in the French fort. In their pursuit of Assou, fifteen hundred Dahomian soldiers marched on the French fort. The bastions of the fort opened fire with their cannons, and 150 armed African soldiers stood outside the walls to protect the edge of the moat. The battle raged from 2:00 P.M. to 6:00 P.M. before the Dahomian army retired. Some of the attackers were caught between the English and French forts and were fired on from both sides. The British later tried to take much of the credit for the victory, but the French accused them of being cowards who fired only four cannon shots during the entire battle.[13]

Figure 24.2   English fort at Whydah in 1727.

During the battle Assou's leg was shattered by a musket ball when he went outside the French fort in a futile attempt to save five crew members from the slave ship *Charlemagne*, whose tent on the beach was being overrun by Dahomian soldiers.[14] That same evening the five captive French sailors were released and sent to the fort with the message that the Dahomian generals wanted the "little white man who spoke their language" to come out and talk to them.

The "little white man" to whom they referred was Etienne Gallot, twenty years old, who had arrived in Africa three years earlier. In the chaos following the fall of Savi, he had deserted the French fort and joined the army of Dahomey. He soon became a military adviser to King Agaja, and he taught the king how to construct certain types of fortifications that had been unknown in that part of the world. He also learned to speak the Gbe language. When he later returned to the French fort, the Company of the Indies wanted to fire him for desertion. But the director of the fort, Dupetitval, promoted him to assistant director because of his knowledge of the country and its people. Even though Etienne Gallot had served with the army of Dahomey, he did not support Dahomey's attempts to defeat Assou in 1728 because he had recently married Assou's daughter.[15]

The morning after the attack on the French fort, the Dahomians sent a dozen ambassadors to repair their relations with the French. They apologized for the attack, saying that they had mistakenly believed that the exiled "king of Allada" (perhaps the son of the slain King Sozo) was in the fort. The French director Dupetitval, for his part, gave the Dahomian ambassadors each a bottle of brandy, lengths of cloth, and gifts for their generals. He also promised to send Etienne Gallot to speak to the Dahomian generals. The ambassadors stayed at the fort till noon before departing with Gallot.

Following the battle and the withdrawal of the Dahomian army, Assou stayed on at the fort and tried to collect customs payments from the slave ships in the harbor. He also supplied the canoemen who ferried merchandise and slaves between ships and the beach. Although the Dahomians stayed clear of the fort after that, warfare continued to rage in the countryside, producing slaves that the companies eagerly loaded onto their ships. Most of the slaves coming to the forts at this time were from Whydah itself. Famine had engulfed the land, and people began for the first time to sell other inhabitants of Whydah to stave off starvation. In July the Dahomian forces captured three thousand villagers, mostly women and children, only two miles west of the English fort. The British director denounced the Dahomians for their "villainy" as he eagerly purchased the captives and loaded them onto waiting ships.[16]

In August 1728 King Agaja complained to the French director that Assou still had not submitted himself to the authority of Dahomey and that the French were selling gunpowder to supporters of the exiled King Huffon. He also complained that the French were watering down their brandy. On December 22 King Agaja sent another message ordering Assou and his followers to come before him, each one carrying a handful of straw to symbolize their submission. Otherwise, he said, there would be war. Two days after Christmas, the Dahomian army showed up at the gate of the French fort to enforce the king's demands. For its defense, the fort had only twelve working cannons and a total of nine Europeans (including three crew members from ships in the harbor). Assou contributed six hundred to eight hundred African soldiers.

The army of Dahomey attacked at eight o'clock in the morning. Three times they attacked, and three times they were forced to retreat in a hail of musket and cannon fire. They had lost nearly two thousand men, and still they regrouped for a fourth assault. This attack seemed as futile as the others, given that the muskets of the Dahomian soldiers could not penetrate the thick mud walls and they did not have any mobile cannons that they could bring in to support the assault. During the fourth attack, the flash from a French cannon started a fire that ran out of control along the thatched roofs of the fort toward the powder magazine. Seeing that the fire

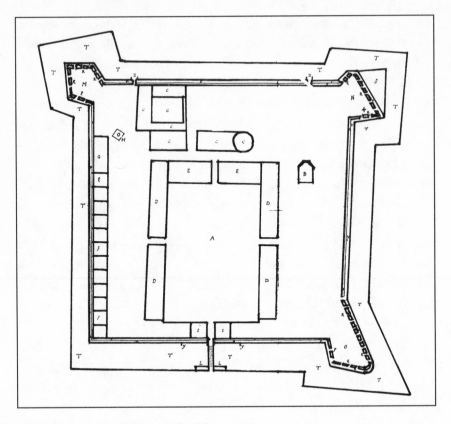

Figure 24.3   French fort at Whydah in 1718.

could not be put out, the Europeans and Assou fled to the nearby English
fort. Minutes later the blasts of the exploding powder magazine shook the
sky and reverberated over the ocean waves.[17]

When the French director Dupetitval came out of the English fort a
short while later, stillness had enveloped the countryside. The Dahomian
army had departed, taking their dead and wounded with them. Only one
fort employee had been killed, along with several of Assou's soldiers, but
two thousand African civilians who had sought refuge in the fort lay dead
from the explosions and the fire. With his fort in ruins, Dupetitval took
refuge on a ship in the harbor, and Assou returned to his island near Popo.
A few days later, ambassadors from the Dahomian army called Dupetitval
back from the ship to present him with a gift of ten slaves and a promise to
repair the fort. Once the fort was reestablished, the recriminations began

among the Europeans. The English believed that the French director, Dupetitval, had summoned the Dahomians in order to rid himself of Assou. Although the French director denied it, there was plausibility to the charge. Earlier that year Dupetitval had written to the company that if he had to choose between Agaja and Assou, he would prefer Agaja because the Dahomian king imposed order and discipline. Dupetitval argued that in Agaja's Dahomey a traveler would be safer than in Europe, and if a trader dropped something along the route, nobody would touch it until he returned to reclaim it. In his report on the explosion at the fort, Dupetitval argued that Assou was one of the major impediments to the return of peaceful trade.[18]

With the French back in their fort and Assou back on his island, the army of Dahomey withdrew, and for the next few months it was totally preoccupied with defending the heartland of the Dahomey kingdom from the 1729 dry-season assault by Oyo. As in the previous year, the people of the Dahomian heartland abandoned their villages and sought refuge in bushes and thickets, stripping the countryside of food. They knew that the horses of Oyo were suffering for lack of forage, and that the army would withdraw as soon as the rainy season began. During the Oyo invasion, contradictory reports arrived at the European forts at Glewe: that King Agaja had been killed; that he was still alive; and that he had lost most of his army.

Believing that Dahomey had been seriously weakened, the British director advised King Huffon to leave his island and take possession of his country again. With help from Assou and the king of Popo, King Huffon raised an army fifteen thousand strong. Although the king was a very obese man, he marched at the head of his army and camped near the English and French forts. The English fort fired cannon salutes in his honor, and Huffon and his chiefs were well entertained by the officers of the fort. This would be a staging area for preparing an assault on Savi, three miles away. Opinion in the French fort, however, was divided: the director, Dupetitval, wanted to have nothing to do with Assou's offensive, fearing that it would provoke another attack from Dahomey, but Etienne Gallot, Assou's son-in-law, wanted to support Assou and King Huffon.[19]

When King Agaja learned that King Huffon and Assou had returned to the forts, he knew that he could not raise enough soldiers to match their army, so he ordered a large number of women to be dressed and armed like regular male soldiers and placed in the rear of the column to prevent recognition of their sex. On July 5, 1729, the army of King Huffon was surprised to see such a large army coming toward them, and some of his officers advocated retreat to the island. Assou, however, insisted that they should engage the Dahomian army in battle. Although Assou's forces fought bravely, many of the soldiers under King Huffon deserted, giving the Dahomian army an opening to break through the lines and trap Assou's forces in their crossfire. Seeing that his cause was lost, Assou and his soldiers retreated toward their island.

King Huffon, who was too fat to flee, dived into the dry moat of the English fort and was helped over the wall by his two sons. This act created a dilemma for the English director, for he knew that as soon as the Dahomey army learned that King Huffon was in his fort, they would demand that the exiled king be given up. Although the Dahomian forces could not take the fort by outright attack, they could starve it out and they could block its trade. The director arranged for the king to escape during the night and be carried back to his island in a hammock.[20]

In the French fort, Etienne Gallot convinced his father-in-law, Assou, that Dupetitval was in league with King Agaja and was therefore Assou's enemy. During the night of July 23, 1729, Gallot secretly opened the gate to let in a band of armed supporters of Assou, who took Dupetitval prisoner. With a great celebration and several ceremonial cannon shots they proclaimed Assou's son-in-law, Etienne Gallot, the director of the French fort. Early in the following year, after their forces had again been defeated in a battle with the army of Dahomey, Assou and Huffon retreated to their island, taking Dupetitval with them. A short while later Huffon sent a message saying that Dupetitval had died of an illness, but rumors persisted that he had been executed.

The army of Dahomey, which was camped near the forts, now declared both the English director, Testefolle, and the French director, Gallot, to be enemies of Dahomey. When the English director left the fort to visit a friend, Dahomian soldiers captured him and took him to Savi, where he was executed. Etienne Gallot, afraid to leave the French fort in the daytime for fear that a similar fate awaited him, made a nighttime escape with all of the gold in the fort and managed to join Assou on his island. From there he boarded an English ship bound for London. The name of the ship was, appropriately enough, the *Happy Deliverance*.[21]

With all of the European directors who had supported Assou either dead or in flight, their successors promised King Agaja in August 1730 that they would no longer support Assou. To celebrate the agreement, the Portuguese and French came to the English fort, where three twenty-one-gun salutes were fired, and the English spent £18 on drinks. When Assou learned that he had been permanently frozen out of the European forts, he must have felt betrayed, especially by the French, whom he had protected for so many years. His only way to regain any of his former influence was to block their trade. King Agaja had decreed that all overseas trade in his kingdom should take place at Glewe, and so Assou's forces began attacking the tents of slave traders in an attempt to shut down, or at least disrupt, the trade that passed through the European forts. During the night of May 8, 1731, Assou's forces attacked the tents of the French slave ship *Aurore* and those of a Portuguese ship. The Portuguese fled, but the French fought off the attackers in a three-hour battle during which three of the French sailors were wounded. Further attacks on slave traders took place in June and July, and more were planned for the future.[22]

25

As the noonday sun beat down upon the harbor at Whydah on September 1, 1731, Robert Durand stood on the deck
of the *Pontchartrain*, where he was being detained by Captain Sorin, and
surveyed the beaches that were now empty of tents or any other signs of
active trade. His longboat, which had been commandeered by the
Pontchartrain, was approaching. A short while later Pierre Verger, the *Diligent's* passenger, emerged from the longboat in chains like a criminal, or
perhaps like a slave. When Verger was in custody aboard the *Pontchartrain*,
Robert Durand was allowed to return to the *Diligent* in his longboat.
Shaken by his experience, he told Captain Mary that they should under no
circumstances stop in Whydah. The captain was reluctant to abandon his
explicit orders and suggested that they should at least make an attempt to
trade in Whydah before continuing on. In that way they could claim to
have carried out their orders. The problem with that plan, Durand pointed
out, was that since they had harbored the fugitive Pierre Verger, they were
in danger of being arrested by the French director if they went to the
French fort. Persuaded by Durand's reasoning, the captain ordered his crew
to set sail for Jakin.

As the bow of the *Diligent* swung toward the east, Robert Durand took
in the panorama of the Whydah harbor. He gazed at the three forts that rose
up from the flat, nearly treeless coastal plain. The French fort was the most
impressive, he thought, and he dismissed the Portuguese fort as "no big
deal." All of the warehouses and trading lodges that had once been located

in Savi were now situated near the forts in the town of Glewe. Even though Durand had never seen Savi, he knew it by reputation and lamented its destruction. "In a land renowned for its great commerce," he wrote in his journal, "that city was great and contained an infinite number of inhabitants. It was the home of the king and of Captain Assou, who had a fortified house and soldiers who were always ready to take up arms at the least sign that the army of Dahomey was approaching."[1]

There was sadness in those words. Captain Assou, the legendary protector of the French, had now thwarted them completely. Robert Durand seemed to understand why. Knowing that he would not see Savi or visit the forts on this trip, he sketched the forts in his journal so that he would recognize them if he ever came back. At one o'clock in the afternoon, the sails picked up a brisk wind from the west-northwest, and the *Diligent* headed for Jakin.

PART 8

Jakin

26

AT 4:00 P.M. ON September 1, 1731, the *Diligent* fired seven of its eight cannons in a salute to announce its arrival at Jakin.[1] The harbor was crowded with a twenty-gun English ship belonging to the Royal African Company, a forty-gun Dutch ship belonging to the Dutch West India Company, two Dutch interlopers, eight Portuguese ships, and two French ships from Nantes: the *Jason* and the *Superbe*. With the trade at Whydah temporarily shut down, most of the slave traders had moved on to Jakin.

The *Jason* had come to Jakin after having its tent attacked in Glewe, and the *Superbe* was the ship that Pierre Verger, now in irons, had missed when it had sailed from Nantes in April. It had garnered a complete load of slaves in only two months and was ready to depart. Robert Durand and his companions quickly wrote letters that it would carry to Nantes after going first to Martinique to sell its cargo of slaves. The letters would take over seven months to get to Nantes.[2] Before departing, the *Superbe* sent the French canoe belonging to the Company of the Indies over to the *Diligent* for transporting merchandise.

The fifteen ships in the harbor were preparing to scatter slaves from Jakin all over the New World. The English ships carried their slaves to Jamaica, Barbados, Virginia, the Carolinas, and also to Rio de la Plata because England had the *assiento* contract for delivering slaves to the Spanish colonies. The Dutch ships took slaves to Dutch Guyana and the Caribbean. The Portuguese ships transported their captives to Brazil, and the French ships went to the French colonies of Saint Domingue, Martinique, and Guadeloupe.[3]

At eight o'clock the next morning Captain Mary entered the canoe to go ashore. He was accompanied by Devigne, the ship's doctor, and Dubourdieu, the passenger and Company of the Indies employee who would be useful for making contact with the company's trading lodge in Jakin. In addition to trade goods for paying customs and gear for their shore stay, they were carrying the twenty-one small cannons that Verger and Dubourdieu had brought along as a gift for the king of Jakin. The crew of the canoe was composed of Africans from Jakin, who were each given a hat and several flasks of brandy as payment for their services. As the canoe departed for the shore, the *Diligent* fired a seven-gun salute and its crew saluted the departure with a great shout of "Vivre le roi." With the ceremonies over, the canoe made its way toward the underwater sandbars that created the triple surf along the coast.

The waves began to form at the distance of a musket shot from the shore, where they encountered the first of two underwater sand bars that ran parallel with the shoreline. They formed in threes. The first wave was tall, the second was taller, and the third made an arc big enough to cover a canoe from front to back. In the early days of the trade at Whydah and Jakin, many European sailors had drowned trying to shoot the bank in their longboats. Consequently, they gave up and left the task of ferrying goods and people between the ships and the shore entirely to African canoemen. Carved from a single tree trunk, the African canoes were fifteen to eighteen feet long and three feet wide. The crew of a typical canoe numbered ten, with five paddling on each side. They paddled standing up and facing the the direction they were headed, as opposed to the European oarsmen, who rowed their longboats facing backward.[4]

William Smith, who had visited the area in 1727, described his experience with the waves. "I was amazed when we came among the breakers (which to me seemed large enough to founder our ship), to see with what wondrous dexterity they carried us through them, and ran their canoes on the top of one of those rolling waves a good way upon the shore. Which done, they all leaped out and dragged the canoe up the beach several yards from the power of the next returning wave. It is barely possible that a man may, if overset here, save his life by swimming, but it is not very probable, for there are such numbers of sharks here, and they follow a canoe to dry land in hopes of prey."[5]

As the canoe carrying Captain Mary, Devigne, and the passenger Dubourdieu headed toward shore, the oarsmen counted the waves of the triple surf. They let the first one pass, then the second. As the third wave rose up behind them, they dug in their paddles to catch it and ride it in to the shore. They had done it countless times before, but on this trip their timing was off and the canoe began to turn sideways and roll over as the force of the wave crashed over it. Captain Mary tried to hold on to the canoe, but eventually he lost his grip and swam for shore. Devigne rolled along the sandy bottom until he thought he was drowning, but eventually he surfaced in shallow water. The African canoemen, all good swimmers who were experienced in the surf, swam to shore. All the goods were lost: the provisions, Pierre Mary's silver snuffbox, Devigne's sword and cane. But the most serious loss of all was the twenty-one cannons destined for the ruler of Jakin. Whenever a canoe overturned, some whites suspected that the canoemen had done it on purpose so that they could return at night during low tide and dive for the lost goods.

The city of Jakin was only three miles from the seashore, but it took some time to get there because the landing party had to cross four streams on the way. Once there, Captain Mary went to the Company of the Indies trading lodge, manned by Mr. LaPierre. He needed LaPierre's help to secure a warehouse for storing his trade goods and negotiate the customs payment with the local rulers. Having lost all the goods and gifts for the ruler that his canoe had been carrying, he would have to wait for later canoes to bring more goods so that he could make the customs payments. In the meantime, he busied himself making the arrangements.

La Pierre explained to Mary that the port city of Jakin had formerly been part of the kingdom of Allada. But after Allada was captured by Dahomey in 1724, the ruler of Jakin submitted to King Agaja's authority and paid regular tribute to him.[6] Despite this tributary relationship, the ruler operated more or less independently in his dealings with European slave traders, a practice that would eventually get him into trouble with King Agaja. One result of this tributary arrangement was that European slave traders were obliged to make two sets of customs payments—one to the ruler of Jakin and one to King Agaja of Dahomey.

To the ruler of Jakin, Captain Mary promised two lengths of silk, one barrel of flour, and one barrel of wine. He then agreed to purchase five captives of "very bad quality" provided by the ruler. The Dahouin, a French-speaking local official who was in charge of French traders, was to receive a French hat and a keg of brandy. Captain Mary then signed a promissory note to pay the value of ten slaves to King Agaja of Dahomey and the value of eight slaves to the ruler of Jakin. After much discussion, the payments were fixed at a total of thirty kegs of brandy, forty lengths of salempouri cloth, thirty lengths of limancas cloth, two chests of smoking pipes, eighty thousand cowries, and forty lengths of linen cloth, to be divided between the ruler of Jakin and King Agaja.

A second promissory note was made out for customs payments to associates of the ruler of Jakin. The ruler's brother would receive two kegs of brandy and a barrel of gunpowder. The Dahouin would get a keg of brandy and a length of Indian cloth, either limancas or salempouri. The ruler's brokers and slave drivers would receive identical gifts. Finally, an official called Papagaye, who was the lord of the beach, was promised a similar payment. In return, Captain Mary received permission to begin trading and would be provided with warehouse and lodging space in the compound of the ruler's own palace.

Robert Durand had not been in the canoe with the captain on the day of the accident. Instead, he had been scheduled to go ashore the following morning in a canoe carrying goods for making the customs payments and sails for fashioning a large tent on the beach. He would be the commander of the tent. As Durand's canoe approached the shore, the canoemen found the waves so fierce that they turned back. The next day it was the same, and the day after that. Finally, on the ninth day, Durand got a ride with the canoe that served the English trading lodge and was manned by Mina canoemen from the Gold Coast. Eight times the canoe started toward shore and turned back. On the ninth attempt, the canoe caught the wave perfectly and went shooting in to shore.

The beach was littered with fourteen large tents fashioned from sailcloth, one for each ship anchored beyond the triple surf. To the west of the tents along the beach were the remains of the mud-walled Portuguese fort that Joseph de Torres had constructed so hastily that it was partially ruined by the action of waves at high tide. Because the English canoe that carried Durand to shore was already filled with English merchandise, he had to wait until the canoe of the *Jason* brought him the *Diligent*'s main topsail

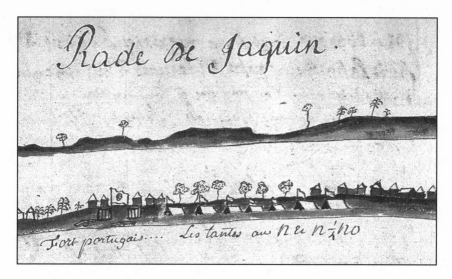

Figure 26.1   Durand's drawing of the beach at Jakin.

and a couple of its yards for making a tent.[7] By the end of the day the tent
was up and the French flag was flying.

Robert Durand woke up the next morning with the roar of the triple
surf in his ears. Stepping out into the morning mist, he surveyed the harbor,
which now had fifteen ships bobbing in the relatively calm waters just beyond the breakers. He fixed his spyglass on the *Diligent* and looked for any
signals to inform him of the day's activities. For the next month and a half,
he would be communicating with the *Diligent* largely through signals. The
sea was relatively calm that morning, and so he would be able to make good
use of the canoe belonging to the French trading lodge that had been
placed at his disposition. When the canoe arrived from the *Diligent* later in
the morning, it brought seamen Kanello, Bernard, Pascaud, and Goret, who
would help Durand man the tent, and it carried supplies that the crew
needed to set up operations on the beach. The canoe of the *Jason* helped
out by bringing the merchandise for making the customs payments.

That afternoon Durand had an audience with Papagaye, the lord of the
beach, whom the people on the shore treated like a king. With the help of
Papagaye, Durand hired servants, water carriers, and canoemen. He also
hired four personal servants who would be paid eighty cowries per day, and
he gave them European names. The three servants who assisted in ferrying

goods back and forth he named Jacques, Jeannot, and Le Breton. He named his cook L'Eveillé. Finally, he hired a young boy whom he called Joseph to be his personal valet. Joseph was paid forty cowries per day.

One of Durand's tasks was to oversee the replenishing of the ship's water barrels even though the water of Jakin had a reputation for being foul and unhealthy. The water rollers were paid 120 cowries for each barrel of water and a bonus of a bottle of brandy every Sunday. They had to take the empty barrels to a freshwater source and then roll them back to the beach. Because the large barrels, each one holding 480 gallons of water, were difficult to load onto longboats or canoes, the crew had simply lashed the barrels together to form rafts and floated them out to the ship on the heavier seawater in the early hours of the morning before the sea breeze made it impossible.[8]

The most crucial arrangements were with the local canoemen who would transport merchandise to the shore and carry slaves to the ship. They were promised a bottle of brandy each day, whether there was work or not, in order to keep them on call. On days when they transported merchandise or slaves, they were paid between two and four flasks of brandy depending on the amount of work they accomplished. Each Sunday they would be given a bonus of two thousand cowries and a flask of brandy. The job of transporting the trade goods from the canoes to the warehouse in Jakin, three miles away, fell to the porters, who were paid on a piece-work basis. Durand also hired hammock carriers to carry the *Diligent*'s officers between the tent and Jakin. He did not specify how many workers he hired, but with fifteen ships in the harbor, the total workforce servicing the slave trade in Jakin must have been considerable.

The job of the commander of the tent, wrote Robert Durand, "can certainly occupy the time of an honest man." Each day Durand received merchandise from the ship that he recorded in his account book and then sent on to the warehouse in Jakin. He watched for signals from the *Diligent* and sent signals back to indicate which merchandise he was sending to the ship or which goods he needed on land. He had to watch the merchandise closely to make sure that the canoemen and porters didn't steal anything, and he had to keep his servants happy so that they wouldn't quit and seek employment with the crew of another ship. Even though the main trading was being done at the warehouse in Jakin, Durand was constantly receiving African traders who came to the tent to purchase goods or sell slaves.

He had to keep meticulous records of each item purchased, paid for, delivered, sent, and received. There were a thousand tasks to be accomplished, and even the evenings provided just enough time to double-check the books against the remaining merchandise in order to correct any mistakes. For a month and a half this routine was repeated day after day.

Back on the *Diligent*, the crew was busy taking down the sails, topmasts, and yards. Then they lashed the yards lengthwise from mast to mast to form a ridgepole. They attached the largest sails to the ridgepole to make a kind of tent to shelter them from the hot sun and the September rains.[9] With the shipboard tent in place, the crew brought the trade goods up on the deck for inspection. When they opened the bales of Indian cloth that the Billy brothers had purchased from the Company of the Indies in Nantes, they discovered that their outfitters had been cheated. Opening a bale of limancas cloth, they found that each piece was only fifty-six feet long instead of a hundred, as written on the cargo list. This discovery prompted a complete inventory of the cloth, which revealed that fifty-six pieces of Indian cloth and sixty-three pieces of limancas were shorter than the cargo list specified. To protect themselves from being accused of stealing the missing cloth, all of the officers—Mary, Valteau, Durand, Laragon, Sabatier, and Leglan—signed a declaration swearing to the discrepancy.[10]

The tent on the beach served primarily as a way station between the ship and the warehouse at Jakin, but Durand also had authority to trade his merchandise for gold or slaves. During that month and a half on the beach he purchased only eighteen slaves. Given the large number of ships in the harbor—which reached eighteen at one point—it is surprising that he purchased any at all. Each day a number of slaves were brought to his tent by local Jakin merchants and officials, but Durand was determined to buy only the best ones. Most looked like the unsold remains from the slave baracoons in Jakin. Of the eighteen slaves that he purchased, he paid either seven or eight kegs[11] of brandy or forty-five to fifty-five pieces of linen platilles per slave.

Durand was also trying to obtain Brazilian gold from either Portuguese ships or Africans who had received gold from the Portuguese in exchange for slaves. He managed to sell twenty-nine kegs of brandy for one-half ounce of gold (eight ackies) each. The tent of the *Jason*, situated next to Durand's, was selling brandy more cheaply, and when the *Jason* departed for St. Domingue, Durand breathed a sigh of relief. With the *Diligent* being the only French ship in the harbor at the moment, it had a monopoly on eighty-five proof French brandy, and he could raise the price to ten ackies per keg. In his pleasure at the departure of the *Jason*, he could not have foreseen that the ship and its crew would never make it back to France.[12] Durand's price hike to ten ackies caused him to go for eight days without selling a single keg. The arrival of the *Nestor*, a French ship out of Nantes, on November 8 introduced new competition that forced Durand to lower the price of brandy to nine ackies.

At Whydah the *Nestor* had suffered the fate that the *Diligent* had avoided. When the *Nestor* had anchored at Whydah, its captain, Joseph Nègre, had been persuaded by the director of the French fort that it was safe to trade. No sooner had they set up their tent on the beach of Whydah than it was attacked by a group of four hundred armed men who knocked it down and cut it to ribbons. Ten days later, after a new tent had been erected from sailcloth and the goods to make the customs payment to the king of Dahomey had been unloaded, the crew was attacked by a force of five hundred armed men who seized the merchandise and captured Second Lieutenant Louis Beustier, Seaman Jean Bidot, and the pilot, Jean-Baptiste Erpin. The captives, along with the merchandise, were taken to Popo and presented to Assou, who held them until they were ransomed.[13]

The captain of the *Nestor*, who had a rather odd name for a slaving captain, "Nègre" (which could mean either "black person" or "slave"), brought in new merchandise to pay the customs to King Agaja. But after the payment had been made and twenty captives had been purchased, he found further trade impossible because Assou's forces were in control of the seashore. Finding himself cut off from his ship, he sent a letter to the *Nestor* ordering the ship to depart immediately for Jakin. Meanwhile, the captain, ten members of the crew, and twenty slaves tried to make the twenty-mile march to Jakin by land. On the way they were detained for seven days by the exiled "king of Allada" who had moved in to occupy the region while King Agaja's armies were engaged in fighting far inland with Oyo and Mahi. They were released unharmed after paying a ransom of brandy and cowry shells. Meanwhile, the *Nestor* was sitting in the harbor in Jakin under orders not to trade until the captain arrived. This delay provided Robert Durand with the opportunity to try to sell his French brandy before his new competitor entered the trade at Jakin.

27

*T*HE *DILIGENT* HAD BEEN at anchor in the Jakin harbor for
nearly two months when Robert Durand received a message
from Second Captain Pierre Valteau, who was supervising the purchase of
slaves at the *Diligent* warehouse located in the compound of the ruler of
Jakin. The warehouse had turned out to be a most unhealthy place, and all
of the crew members who were stationed there became seriously ill. Captain Mary had returned to the ship because of an illness on September 27,
after spending just twenty-six days in Jakin. He had been replaced by Second Captain Valteau, but on October 26 Robert Durand received a message that Valteau was sick and Durand should replace him at the warehouse. The only officer left on the ship who could replace Durand at the
tent was the first pilot, Sabatier. When the canoe carrying Sabatier arrived
at the beach, Durand turned over the account books and the remaining
merchandise in the tent and departed for Jakin.

Arriving in the city in his hammock carried by two porters, Durand
noted that it was very pretty and very commercial. Situated on flat land, it
contained houses built of earthen walls with bamboo and thatch roofs. The
countryside surrounding the city had earlier been described by another
Frenchman as "a very beautiful country, united like a hand and forested in
a very agreeable manner, situated between two beautiful rivers that make it
charming."[1] Despite the acknowledged beauty of the countryside, Durand
described it as the unhealthiest spot along the entire coast. The fact that

Jakin was situated between two rivers also meant that it was built on the plain of the coastal swamp.

Just beyond the city there was a large marketplace about a thousand yards square, which made it five times as big as the main market in Amsterdam. It was crisscrossed by streets twelve feet wide lined by merchants' stalls covered with woven mats. There were at least two hundred of these streets, all of which met in a central square. The market was subdivided into zones where different kinds of merchandise were sold. The diversity of merchandise was incredible. There were zones for merchants of pipes and tobacco, for colored cloth, for white cloth, for mats and baskets, for cooked fish, for palm oil, for dishes and clay pots, vegetables, fruits, lengths of cotton cloth, and lengths of bark cloth. In each zone there were five or six stalls offering food—pork, goat, chicken, or dog—and drink. The prices of each kind of meat were fixed, and buyers would make their choice and then hand over the cowry shell money with no discussion. Men and women ate in separate cafés. All together, there were at least ten thousand people at the market.[2]

To Durand, the most impressive European trading lodge in Jakin belonged to Hendrik Hertogh, the director of the Dutch West India Company's activities. After Savi fell in 1727, the Dutch had abandoned Whydah and concentrated their slave trading efforts on Jakin. Since the Dutch had never been permitted to build a fort at Whydah, they were in a better position than the other European trading companies to abandon the defeated kingdom and concentrate their efforts here. Since coming to Jakin, Hertogh had been twice promoted in rank until he was the second highest-ranking official of the Dutch West India Company on the Guinea coast, being subordinate only to the governor-general at Elmina.

Durand described Hertogh's trading lodge as a pretty house surrounded by a number of cannons that was sumptuously furnished with furniture and goods from Holland. Durand noted that Hertogh lacked nothing. "He brings from Europe everything that flatters his imagination. He has at his lodge a number of craftsmen of different professions who carry out his orders, and he brought several trumpets and players of musical instruments who fill his lodge with their concerts." Moreover, noted Durand, his warehouses were full of every sort of merchandise he had received from Dutch ships that had unsuccessful trading voyages. Durand learned about Hertogh's cache of merchandise from personal experience when Hertogh gave him a silver watch as a welcome gift.

Durand's assessment of Hertogh's wealth and influence was correct, for Hertogh had just received a promotion from his company and, more importantly, had forced his arch rival, the Portuguese slave trader Joseph de Torres, to depart from Jakin, leaving behind only a crumbling fortress on the beach. The rivalry between Hertogh and Torres had its roots in the permanent settlement between the Netherlands and Portugal in 1661, which had denied the Portuguese the right to trade along the Guinea coast. Although they were later permitted to trade provided that they received permission from the Dutch governor-general at Elmina and paid the 10 percent tax, the Portuguese were now attempting to implant themselves independently on the Slave Coast. The leader of that effort was Hertogh's rival, Joseph de Torres.

Torres was from Brazil, and he, more than any other Brazilian slave trader, had learned how to turn Brazil's commercial disadvantage into his own profit. Slave ships coming to Guinea directly from Brazil did not have access to the assorted European and Asian trade goods that were carried on ships sailing from Europe. Prior to the discovery of gold at Minas Geraes, Brazilian ships purchased slaves with third and fourth grade tobacco, which had no market in Portugal. By law, the higher grades of Brazilian tobacco had to be shipped directly to Portugal, but the *soca* (reject) tobacco was mixed with molasses to make a product that was in great demand along the Gold and Slave Coasts, though it was not popular in other parts of Africa. So great was the demand for their tobacco that the Portuguese felt they could use their monopoly on it to dominate the slave market in Whydah. The viceroy of Brazil wrote, "Whydah is the most famous port along this entire coast because of the great number and abundance of slaves which are traded there. Tobacco is the product that they value most and without which they cannot live. It is clear that since we are the only ones capable of bringing them this merchandise, we are also the most welcome among all the nations."[3] Even though there was a strong demand for the "reject" tobacco, a smuggling traffic in first grade tobacco developed in parallel with it. When a dispatch from Lisbon to Brazil demanded strict enforcement of the tobacco regulations, the viceroy of Brazil replied that the law was, for all practical purposes, unenforceable.[4]

The discovery of gold in the Minas Geraes in the 1690s added new complexity to the economics of the slave trade. Brazilian gold began to find its way to the Gold Coast and Slave Coast in the early eighteenth century despite the decree from the king of Portugal imposing the death penalty on anyone who shipped gold to any country other than Portugal. The viceroy of Brazil blamed the smuggling on the governor of Minas Geraes. Armed with gold dust, ships from Brazil bought their slaves directly from the Dutch, English, and French. In return, the European trading companies began to sell more and more of their slaves to the Portuguese in order to get their hands on Brazilian gold.

Joseph de Torres was the biggest smuggler of gold and first grade tobacco from Brazil to the Guinea coast in the first quarter of the eighteenth century. Evidence of his smuggling activities can be found in the ledger books of the Royal African Company fort at Whydah as early as 1718, and Torres was known to have made secret agreements with the Dutch and the English to bring gold to El Mina castle and Cape Coast castle in exchange for slaves and European goods. But Torres wanted more than just a lucrative trade, and in 1720, he convinced King Huffon of Whydah to give him permission to build a fort near the British and French forts at Glewe. Then he convinced the viceroy of Brazil to authorize him to build the fort, the walls of which were constructed in 1721. Upon his return to Brazil in 1722, he was arrested and sent to Lisbon because of the large amount of money he owed to the king's treasury. Even from prison he repeatedly, and unsuccessfully, sent out petitions to be named director of the fort.

After being released from prison, Torres returned to Brazil and requested support from the governor of Minas Geraes (who was himself under investigation for producing counterfeit gold coins) to launch an investigation into gold smuggling along the Slave Coast. He also wanted to rebuild the Portuguese fort, which had been largely abandoned since the Dahomian conquest of Whydah. Upon learning of Torres's scheme, the viceroy of Brazil complained that Torres was the biggest smuggler of all and wanted to conduct the investigation to cover up his own illegal activities. Nevertheless, the governor approved the project.

Arriving in Whydah in 1730 with materials to rebuild the Portuguese fort, Torres met great hostility from the local people at Glewe, who remembered his deceitfulness in his earlier dealings with them. Giving up on

Tiort portugais.....

Figure 27.1   Durand's drawing of Joseph de Torres's Portuguese fort at Jakin.

Whydah, he moved to Popo, where he planned to build a fort in the area controlled by the exiled King Huffon and Assou. But the tensions and continuing warfare between Huffon and King Agaja discouraged him from that project. Finally, he moved on to Jakin, where he received permission from the local ruler to construct a fort on the beach. He felled some palm trees, smoothed out the land, and covered it with bricks on which he constructed a bastion. He situated the fort on the beach so that its cannons could protect Portuguese ships anchored in the roadstead from attacks by the Dutch. Any Portuguese ship that failed to pay the 10 percent tax to the Dutch at Elmina—and there were many in that category—could be legally attacked by Dutch ships. The fort, Torres believed, would protect Portuguese ships at anchor in Jakin from such attacks. Shortly before the *Diligent* arrived in Jakin, the director of the Portuguese establishment at Whydah ridiculed Torres's fort, saying that "the fortification which Joseph de Torres began in Jakin is in the form of a bastion, but its construction will not last long. Six pieces of artillery are mounted, and he has begun another structure for ten other pieces. At present, they say that it has fallen into ruins."[5]

Hertogh had always been hostile to the efforts of the Portuguese to establish themselves on the Slave Coast. He had first arrived in Whydah in

1726, when the Dutch West India Company sent him to negotiate a treaty with King Huffon that called for, among other things, the demolition of the Portuguese fort at Glewe and the construction of a Dutch lodge near the French and English forts. When the Dutch compound at Savi was destroyed by the Dahomian invasion in 1727, Hertogh had already opened a trading lodge at Jakin. From the safety of Jakin, he was almost gleeful about the chaos in Whydah, and he wrote to the company, "Business looks so favorable that I would like to suggest building a lodge at Eppe, an island between Jakin and Appa. This is a place which is well situated for trade, and quite appropriate to retire to in times of emergency."[6] In 1730 the company promoted Hertogh from *commies* to *oppercommies*. Shortly thereafter a fire broke out in the Dutch West India Company lodge, which contained fifty-five slaves waiting to be loaded onto the ship *Waartwyk*. Most of them were burned alive, though a few managed to escape the fire. Surveying the damage and the charred bodies, Hertogh expressed relief that most of the trade merchandise had survived. In the wake of the fire, Hertogh toyed with the idea of rebuilding the lodge at Whydah, or even constructing a fort there, but by January 1731 he was rebuilding his lodge at Jakin.

Hertogh's motivation for rebuilding in Jakin was most likely to block Joseph de Torres, who by then had arrived in Jakin and started to build his fort. Hertogh complained that "by means of great expense, Torres has obtained much from the king; the foundations of the fort are ready, and now all available hands are involved in the construction of a redoubt." Hertogh boasted to the company, "I, on the other hand, let nothing be undone to prevent him from achieving such, and the presents which this gentleman is continuously offering are as much as possible neutralized by me with counter-presents, and I shall apply all my vigilance in order to thwart his intentions." To which the company replied, "If Hertogh does indeed see an opportunity to bring the progress of this work to a complete stop, or slow it off to such an extent that it will never be finished, we do give Hertogh permission to make some small expenditure to that end, but as economically as possible."[7]

It is hard to know exactly what kind of tactics Hertogh used against Torres, but in early 1731 he could boast that "Torres has left this place under the most shameful conditions in the world, without having done anything further on his fortress than building a simple bastion with a few beams and mud, which will soon collapse. Be assured that this gentleman will never again in his life build a fortress here, and that all his efforts and expenditure have been in vain." Not only did Torres leave Jakin a defeated man, but he feared imprisonment on returning to Rio de Janeiro because of all the money he had borrowed for the project. Having no means to pay his debts, he left Brazil for Lisbon on the India vessel *Santa Teresa* carrying nothing but the clothes on his back and documents from the fortress he had built at Jakin.[8] As Torres's fort was crumbling on the beach at Jakin, Hertogh was rebuilding his lodge and being promoted by his employers to the title of "governor of the Dutch West India Company."

A S SOON AS ROBERT DURAND had settled in to the warehouse in the compound of the ruler of Jakin, he sent the ailing Valteau back to the *Diligent*. It was partly a humanitarian move and partly a practical one: there was a law that captains of slave ships had to pay the ruler of Jakin the value of two slaves for any ship's officer who died on land, and the value of one slave for an ordinary sailor. It was economically advantageous to get sick officers back onto the ship before they died.

Both Whydah and Jakin had a reputation for being unhealthy places, and the reputation was proving true.[1] One theory of the time held that the danger came from the swamps which ran in a band over a mile-wide parallel with the coastline. The sun, it was believed, drew unhealthy vapors up from the swamps and the wind spread them over the whole country, causing violent stomachaches that degenerated into congestion of the brain with a severe burning fever. There was also bloody flux and raging colic that were blamed on the rawness of the fruits and the freshness of the water. The situation was summed up, with obvious exaggeration, by an English ditty:

> *Beware and take care of the Bight of Benin;*
> *There's one comes out for forty go in.*[2]

For Europeans to survive under such conditions, according to one theory, it was necessary "to eat little and often, to take strong drinks with

243

moderation, not to expose oneself to the evening damp or to the sun, to avoid the rain as much as one can, not to give oneself to the violent exercise of hunting, and to keep oneself covered at night because it is cool and damp." Another theory held that the water, being drawn from wells twenty to thirty fathoms deep, was unhealthy because it was "raw and cold as ice." The secret to staying healthy according to this theory was to mix water, which was too cold, with an equal quantity of local beer, which was too hot, in order to obtain a "pleasant and wholesome drink."[3] We don't know if Robert Durand held to any of those theories; the only theory that he noted in his journal was that the beach seemed to be a healthier place than the city of Jakin. Now he was stationed in the danger zone.

Despite all admonitions to moderation, Robert Durand and his companions undoubtedly indulged in the sort of drinking and whoring for which sailors in foreign ports were notorious. Durand, who always sought to portray himself as a sober and industrious individual, made no mention of any such activities in his journal, but they were readily available. Although the ship's stock of wine and brandy was strictly rationed, the local beer brewed from Indian corn was easily purchased, and prostitutes conducted their business in small huts—often no more than six feet wide by ten feet long—located near the main road and the market. A visit to a prostitute cost five cowries in the second decade of the eighteenth century, but by 1731, with the influx of slave ships into Jakin, the price must have risen rapidly. Some prostitutes even traveled out in canoes to visit the sailors on ship duty, even though such visits were forbidden by French maritime law.[4] Living in the compound of the ruler of Jakin, Robert Durand was undoubtedly furnished with a female companion during his stay and had no reason to trek out to the cluster of prostitutes' huts near the marketplace.

With Captain Mary having left the warehouse a month earlier and Second Captain Valteau now gone, First Lieutenant Robert Durand was now the highest-ranking officer of the *Diligent* on land, and he was directing the whole operation of choosing, buying, and loading the slaves. He was assisted by two crew members, one of whom fell ill soon after Durand arrived and was quickly removed to the ship. Durand still had his personal servants who had been furnished by Papagaye, and he also had other local African employees who worked in the warehouse. There were the porters, the washerwomen, the brokers, and the gatekeepers, all of whom were paid forty cowries per day. They were people who made their living working for slave traders; no sooner would the *Diligent* depart than they would be at work for another slave ship.

True to his profession as a merchant and a seaman, Robert Durand was far more interested in recording the prices, values, and profits of his trading activities than in the human tragedy that he was directing. Although he carefully recorded the gender and age category of each slave, he seemed to have little interest in where they came from, what their lives had been like before their enslavement, how they had become enslaved, or what ethnic and national groups they represented. The ethnic stereotypes that Des Marchais had sketched out in 1725 had once served as a guide to the different groups of captives who were brought from the interior along the trade routes, but that trading system no longer existed in 1731. Not only did the continual warfare make the trade routes unsafe, but King Agaja had also declared a monopoly on slave selling. The Portuguese complained in 1730 that Agaja "stops the passage of slaves and robs the Negroes who go into the interior to buy them." William Snelgrave, who returned to Jakin in 1730, noted that King Agaja "drives no regular trade in slaves, but only sells such as he takes in his wars."[5] Snelgrave knew that the only sure way to get a load of slaves was to go directly to King Agaja. Upon disembarking from his ship, he immediately requested an audience with King Agaja but learned that the king was currently located too far inland to be visited easily.

In the fall of 1731 the slaves being sold in Jakin came from two main sources. One was King Agaja's wars. Agaja was warring against the Mahi, Dahomey's neighbor to the northeast, and also against Mahi's ally Oyo. The campaign took an entire year, but the outcome was inconclusive at best, and some observers claimed that it ended in defeat for Agaja. In a full year of warfare he had taken a large number of captives. Since the trade at the forts in Whydah was more or less dead because Assou's forces controlled the beaches, Agaja sent his captives to Jakin, where the ships of all the European slave trading nations were now concentrated. From Agaja's point of view, it was a good commercial situation because slaves sent to Jakin sold instantly and fetched high prices. As for the captives of those battles, they arrived underfed, exhausted from days of forced marching, and possibly ill and suffering from festering wounds. Those who couldn't keep up the pace of the forced march were taunted, prodded, or beaten, and many who had started the journey sick and wounded had died along the way. By the time they reached Jakin, many had a vacant stare in their eyes of shock and resignation; others summoned all their courage to hold their heads high and watch for chances to escape or rebel.

The second source of slaves was the river that ran east from Jakin parallel with the coast to the Bay of Benin. Because this was a regular trade route that was not easily blocked by the army of Dahomey, it furnished people who had become enslaved in a variety of ways. Some were war captives from neighboring kingdoms; others had committed crimes and were unable to pay the resultant fines, and so they had been sold to pay the debt. Still others were ordinary debtors who had been seized and sold by their creditors. Snelgrave noted that such captives were usually sold to Africans and only rarely to Europeans. This was probably because of the belief that debt slaves should have a right to redeem themselves if they could find a way to repay the money that they owed. Finally, there were people who had been compelled by want or famine to sell a comrade or a relative, as happened in Whydah when the warfare destroyed the crops and left people hungry.[6]

Whether they were prisoners of war, convicts, debtors, or victims of famine, all of the captives who arrived in Jakin had become alienated from their birthright in one way or another. Being born as a member of a certain family, a certain kin group, a certain community, or a certain polity gave them a set of rights that inhered in the condition of belonging. In their own communities they were sons, daughters, brothers, sisters, mothers, and fathers, as well as citizens of larger communities. All of these identities had been rendered meaningless by the act of enslavement. To the African and European slave merchants alike, they had been reduced to commodities for sale. Their value was no longer their human worth as members of a family and community, but was based solely on Robert Durand's estimate of the worth of their labor to slave owners in Martinique.

Whether they had been brought down from a battlefield by King Agaja's agents or carried by private merchants in canoes along the river, the frightened, exhausted, captives—naked because their clothes had been stolen—were brought into the chief of Jakin's compound to be presented to Robert Durand.[7] Their hands were tied, and they were guarded by sentries with loaded muskets. To the indignities of capture and forced march was added the new indignity of inspection by a white stranger. To most of the captives, the Europeans in Jakin were the first white people they had ever seen in their lives, and they had heard rumors that whites were cannibals who bought slaves to use as food in their own country. As Robert Durand came over to inspect them, they must have felt like Hansel and Gretel being sized up for fatness and edibility by the wicked witch.

The preliminary inspection was devoted to classifying the group according to age, gender, and ethnicity. The best slaves, it was believed, were between ten and fifteen years old. The Portuguese had a reputation for buying only captives in that age range. The English factor at Whydah had once described the type of slaves that the Portuguese got in exchange for their gold as "without beard and as fine as waxworks." Older slaves, in contrast, were often referred to as "beard slaves."[8] Prior to the inspection, the African slave merchants would often shave captive men in their twenties as closely as possible to make them appear younger and would rub their chins with a pumice stone to make them smooth and soft. In order to detect any traces of stubble, Portuguese slave traders had a habit of running their tongues over the cheeks and chins of beardless male slaves. Captives younger than ten were considered children.[9]

The gender ratio of a slave cargo was an important consideration among slave buyers, though there were different opinions as to what was ideal. Snelgrave favored a ratio of three men for every woman, whereas Des Marchais counseled slave merchants not to have women make up more than a third of the cargo. The reason, he said, was that men were needed for the hard field labor on the plantations in the Caribbean. What he failed to understand was the prominent roles that women played in field labor in many parts of West Africa. The ethnic stereotypes described by Des Marchais in 1725 clearly referred to males alone.

Durand also checked the slaves for scarification, tattoos, and country marks that served as signifiers of ethnicity. The ethnic stereotypes that Chevalier Des Marchais had described in 1725 were no longer valid in 1731 because the wars and the closing of the trade routes had drastically altered the sources of slaves, but a new set of ethnic stereotypes had undoubtedly taken its place. Slaves at Jakin sent down by King Agaja in 1731 were likely to be Mahi or Oyo in ethnicity. Those who came in by canoe along the river were often what is called Yoruba today, but the trade routes often extended beyond Yoruba country, and so the slaves probably came from a variety of different ethnic groups.

After the cursory examination came the humiliation and degradation of the close physical examination. Any captives who had managed to retain some shreds of clothing were stripped naked. Normally it was the job of the ship's doctor to conduct the examination, but Devigne, who had come to Jakin along with Pierre Mary on the first canoe leaving the *Diligent*, had gone back to the ship with an illness after only seventeen days on shore. Durand was left to do the inspection himself. He would go up to the frightened and defiant captives and examine their eyes, teeth, and genitals. He would make them walk, run, wave their arms, stretch out their arms and legs in a grotesque caricature of the modern game Simon Says. Like modern-day doctors in a physical exam, he would put his hand on their groins and make them cough violently. Looking for symptoms of syphilis, gonorrhea, or yaws, he carefully examined the private parts of both men and women.[10]

Once Durand had made his selection, he began to bargain over the price. The price of the slave was set in terms of ounces of gold, even though the payment was made in trade goods. With the trade at Whydah shut down and all of the ships concentrated at Jakin, the price had risen. Even Hertogh, with all of his knowledge of the region and local contacts, was paying up to six ounces of gold for a male slave and four for a female slave.[11] Durand was still trying to stay within the guidelines that Pierre Mary had set: six ounces for a "Portuguese slave," five ounces for a common slave, and four ounces for all others. Once the price of the slave was decided on, the value of the trade goods carried by the *Diligent* had to be fixed in terms of ounces of gold: a keg of brandy, for example, was valued at eight to ten ounces; ten lengths of linen cloth went for one ounce, and a musket went for one-fourth of an ounce. The final stage of the bargaining consisted in determining which trade goods should be given to make up the agreed upon value. Because the *Diligent* carried a variety of trade goods, Durand's goal was to get rid of them all, even the ones that were not in demand. Therefore the bargaining began with Durand offering the least desirable trade goods. If they were refused, he would bring out more desirable merchandise.

What made the bargaining situation complex was that supply and demand conditions varied greatly between Vannes and Jakin, and therefore a trade item that was relatively expensive in France might be in low demand in Jakin and vice versa. An adult male slave, for example, sold for eight kegs of brandy, which had cost eighty-eight livres in Vannes. On the other had, if the same slave was paid for in lengths of linen cloth, the price was fifty lengths per slave, which cost 225 livres in France. If the slave was paid for in limancas or salempouri cloth, the price came to 180 French livres. The bargaining for a captive or a group of captives could take days, and it usually resulted in an assortment of high-value and low-value items being given in payment for the slaves.

The other major issue that had to be negotiated involved the relative prices of men and women, adults and children. As Robert Durand engaged daily in bargaining, he began to get a feel for the optimal price ranges. If a slave were paid for entirely in brandy, for example, an adult male would cost seven or eight kegs, an adult female would cost four or five, a young boy would cost three or four, and a young girl would cost two or three. That meant that a woman cost 50 to 70 percent as much as a man, and a girl cost between 50 and 100 percent of the price of a boy. The effect of age differences was clearly visible: a boy cost between 38 and 57 percent as much as a man, whereas a girl cost between 40 and 75 percent of the value of a woman. Durand also worked out the relative prices in terms of platilles, a kind of white linen: an adult male cost fifty, an adult female cost thirty-five, a young boy cost thirty, and a young girl cost twenty-five. Here the ratios were somewhat different: a woman was priced at 70 percent of a man, a girl was priced at 83 percent of a boy; a boy cost 60 percent as much as a man, and a girl cost 71 percent as much as a woman.

Durand dutifully recorded each purchase in an account book made of common paper and lacking a leather cover. Each person who assisted or directed the purchase of slaves at the warehouse wrote in this same book: Company of the Indies employee Dubourdieu, Captain Pierre Mary, Second Captain Pierre Valteau, Second Lieutenant Laragon, and now Robert Durand. For each captive purchased, Durand recorded the date, the name of the seller (but not the name of the captive), and the merchandise paid. In another part of the notebook was a series of columns, one for each type of trade goods, and he duly entered the different items paid for the slave in the appropriate places.[12]

After the purchase had been recorded, the captives were branded. Durand carried a branding iron bearing the mark of the *Diligent*, which he heated red-hot in a bed of burning charcoal. The captive was then brought up and held by several burly assistants. The spot on the body to be branded differed from nation to nation and even among individual slave traders— the French generally branded their captives on the fleshy part of the arm or the stomach—but the captives of the *Diligent* were branded on the right shoulder.[13] One of the assistants rubbed the spot with tallow and then placed a piece of greased or oiled paper over the spot, while another pressed the red-hot branding iron into the piece of paper. The captives struggled to avoid the hot iron, but to no avail. Some captives screamed in pain as the iron seared their flesh; others summoned their courage to maintain a stoic silence. Even after the hot branding iron was removed, the pain of the burn remained as the flesh started to swell in the form of the owner's mark.[14] As the burn slowly healed in the ensuing days, the mark remained.

Robert Durand's journal gives no hint about what he felt as he partici- pated in such activities. Did he feel compassion for his victims? Did he feel a sadistic sense of power? Or did he feel nothing at all? The only thought he reveals in his journal is his determination to do his job as well as possi- ble. "I am determined to spare no effort," he wrote, "in order to serve my employers in the way that duty requires of me." Whatever he may or may not have been feeling as the branding iron seared the flesh of the captives, he kept telling himself that he was simply doing his job.

The branded captives were then imprisoned in the rented warehouse in the compound of the ruler of Jakin. They were kept there for as long as possible because it was easier to supply them with food and water on land than on the ship. As the warehouse prison filled up, conditions for the cap- tives deteriorated rapidly. Space for sleeping or simply moving about be- came scarce. With sanitary facilities scarce or nonexistent, the omnipresent stench of feces, urine, and sweat permeated the warehouse. The captives were fed twice a day with meals largely composed of starchy foods that could be purchased cheaply. There was no meat or fruit. Durand recorded that the average meal for a captive cost thirty-five cowries, whereas one egg cost twenty cowries and one banana cost thirty.

As the warehouse prison filled up, captives were moved to the ship. In order to accommodate them, the *Diligent* itself was being modified. Little by little, the lower deck had been emptied of its merchandise, and the two carpenters, Colinbert and Mahé, were making it into a slave barracoon using the lumber that they had loaded at Fort Axim. The space between

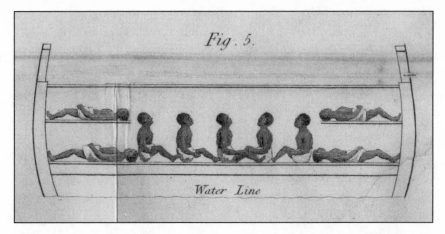

Figure 28.1   Cross section of a slave ship showing the platforms between the main and lower decks.

the decks was less than five feet high, and the carpenters reduced this further by building platforms along the sides in order to pack the slaves in a double-decker fashion.[15] Each captive would have about two feet of space between the wooden planks below and those above. They also built a partition across the lower deck to separate the front part from the rear part, in order to keep the men apart from the women. The women's section was located at the rear of the ship just under the officers' quarters.

The carpenters were also modifying the exterior of the *Diligent*. Across the deck just behind the mainmast they built a huge barricade of thick boards that separated the main deck from the quarterdeck. It rose above the quarterdeck and extended outward on the starboard and port sides of the ship so that nobody could get around it by going over the top or around the sides. The purpose of the barricade was to isolate the rear part of the ship, which contained the officers' quarters and the women's barracoon, from the front part of the ship, where the male captives would come up on deck to eat and exercise. Its other purpose was to provide a safe area where the crew could retreat in case of a rebellion. The barricade contained loopholes through which crew members could fire muskets or stab at rebellious slaves with half-pikes.[16] In addition to the barricade, the carpenters also constructed two platforms—one on each side of the ship— that would serve as toilets for the Africans, having holes in the floor through which waste could drop into the sea.[17]

Figure 28.2 Slave ship showing the barricade separating the front of the ship from the back.

Moving captives from the warehouse in Jakin to the newly constructed prison on the ship was a complex operation involving several local Jakin officials and great numbers of locally hired laborers. The guards were paid a bottle of brandy every time they escorted captives to the beach. The slave drivers received a bottle of brandy for every ten captives. The guards at the beach received 160 cowries per captive per day. When they were taken out of the warehouse, the captives were probably glad to get some fresh air. But they were apprehensive because they were not sure where they were going. From talking to the local guards and warehouse workers, they undoubtedly knew that they were destined for the slave ship. Many of them had never before seen the ocean, and thus the idea of disappearing over the horizon on a huge ship was extremely disconcerting. Some of the guards took sadistic delight in telling the captives that white people were cannibals and that they were being taken away to be eaten. The prospect of being eaten by whites so unnerved some of the captives that they would sometimes choke themselves to death by swallowing their tongues, or they would cut off one or more of their fingers in order to make themselves into "damaged goods" that would not be desired by the white slave traders.[18]

The atmosphere became tense when the captives were released from the warehouse to walk the three miles to the beach. The local slave drivers tied their hands behind their backs and roped them together two by two to make it difficult for one of them to run away. For the captives, it was their last chance to escape on African soil; for the local guards, it meant extra vigilance because the Dahouin of Jakin was financially responsible for any slaves who escaped on Jakin's soil. Once on the road, the captives were pushed and prodded to keep up the pace. Shouts pierced the air and scuffles broke out as the group made its way toward the *Diligent* tent on the beach, where the captives were recorded in the account books to make the transfer from shore to ship official. As the captives watched the white officer count them and write the number in his book, it was becoming clear to them that the stop at the tent was most likely their last stop ever on African soil. We can never know what thoughts formed in their minds, what feelings welled up in their breasts, or what images of home and family passed before them in kaleidoscopes of memory, but it was a moment they would never forget. Those who had never before seen the ocean stared at its endless expanse and watched the waves of the triple surf crash against the shore. They knew that soon they would be heading out into those waves, never to return.

The hired canoemen were waiting for them in the surf. In the lull after a large wave crashed into the beach, the captives were forced to wade into its wake and climb into the canoe, where they were told to sit in the bottom as low as possible to maintain the canoe's balance. There was water sloshing in the bottom of the canoe, but it made little difference to the captives, who were already wet from wading through the surf. As the canoe pushed off, it began to pitch violently, and its bow rose up to meet the approaching wave. The bow would rise rapidly and fall violently as the wave passed, throwing sprays of water into the canoe. As the canoemen paddled, they kept a lookout for any slaves who might try to leap overboard and drown themselves rather than be taken from their country. The canoe voyage was a long one because the ships were anchored as many as two miles from shore to avoid the pounding of the heavy surf.

For captives who had never before seen the ocean or experienced the power of the waves, the canoe experience was truly terrifying. Their stomachs, largely empty from the meager rations in the warehouse, wretched and heaved as the canoe pitched and rolled at the same time. The first wave was followed by the second, and then the third, which was large enough to swallow the canoe whole. The canoemen paddled in rhythm, occasionally pausing to wait for the right moment, then paddling hard to make as much progress as possible before the next wave came in. If the canoe was caught by a wave, it would be thrown backward toward the shore and the canoemen would be forced to begin the process again. The canoemen knew how difficult it was to traverse the waves, and they had arranged to be paid whether the canoe made it to the *Diligent* or not.

Finally, after endless pitches and rolls, advances and retreats, the canoemen grabbed hold of lines extending from the *Diligent* and steadied the canoe against the gentle bobbing of the ship. A rope ladder was extended from the ship, and the canoemen untied the hands of a woman captive and ordered her to climb it. One of the ship's officers was at the top of the ladder to supervise the operation, and several crew members waited there to grab the woman and pull her over the rail. Between the canoemen at the bottom and the crewmembers at the top, they were taking no chances that she might try to escape by jumping or falling from the ladder. The woman felt herself literally caught between the devil and the deep blue sea, but the sea was so terrifying that the devil seemed a better alternative. Reaching the top of the rope ladder, she was pulled onto the deck of the bobbing ship and taken down into the dark, cramped women's section of the slave deck, located at the rear of the ship and just below the officers' quarters. The air was dank and stifling hot because the refashioned cargo bay of the *Diligent* had not been built with ventilation in mind. After the women had all been loaded, the men were loaded onto the front part of the slave deck and shackled together two by two. The slave irons carried by the *Diligent*, which had been manufactured in Nantes, consisted of two U-shaped bars of iron held together by an iron rod that was passed through openings on the ends and locked into place. The slave iron bound the left ankle of one captive to the right ankle of another, making it difficult for either of them to walk unless they moved in perfect harmony. As their eyes grew accustomed to the semidarkness, they began to look around for comrades from the warehouse who had gone out before them.

*R*OBERT DURAND HAD SPENT less than three weeks at the warehouse at Jakin when the "malady of the country," as he called it, struck him on November 13. It started with a severe headache and pain in the kidneys. Each person who had worked at the warehouse, it seemed, had become ill within a few weeks. Robert Durand had hoped to escape the illness, but as he put his hands to his throbbing head, he knew he had been stricken. The next morning, Durand was carried in a hammock back to the tent on the beach to await a canoe to take him to the *Diligent*. There he greeted Sabatier, who had replaced him when he had left the tent for Jakin. They contacted the hired canoemen, who demanded an extra keg of brandy in order to paddle Durand through the surf. Because this payment had not been part of the agreement when Durand had first hired the canoemen, he refused to pay and vowed to find another means of reaching the *Diligent*. Shortly after noon he spotted the canoe belonging to the Royal African Company, manned by Mina canoemen, getting ready to "pass the bar" as they termed it. The English captain gave permission for Durand and Jean Mahé, the second carpenter of the *Diligent,* who was also sick, to ride with them in the canoe through the waves until they reached a point at which they could be picked up by the longboat of the *Diligent*.

Arriving on board, Durand felt better than he had the previous day, and he had hopes that he was beginning to recover. The next day, however, his fever was so high and his headache so severe that he requested a bleeding of his feet, a procedure that would be repeated eight times before his illness ran its course. He also had violent stomachaches and difficult breathing, symptoms that were treated by bleeding his arms on two separate occasions. For ten days the ship's doctor did not know whether Durand would live or die. Knowing no other treatment, he continued the bleedings and purgings. With his strength dissipated by both the illness and the treatment, Durand lay almost lifeless in the darkness to ease the ache in his head. On the slave deck just below him were several slaves suffering from similar illnesses, but they did not get the same level of medical attention. Perhaps, in this case, they were fortunate.

Captain Mary had recovered from his illness and arrived back at the warehouse in Jakin on November 10, three days before Durand's departure. Mary was eager to collect his cargo of captives and set sail. He knew that although the *Nestor* was anchored in the harbor, it was under orders not to trade until its captain, Joseph Nègre, arrived from Whydah by the overland route. With Captain Nègre detained by the exiled "king of Allada," and with both the French Company of the Indies representative, La Pierre, and the Dutch West India Company representative, Hertogh, working to negotiate Captain Nègre's release, Pierre Mary knew that he had to work quickly before he had some new competition.

The dismal tasks of inspecting, bargaining, branding, and transporting slaves for the cargo of the *Diligent* continued much as before, but now Pierre Mary was concentrating on his own personal trading. Before the *Diligent* had left Vannes, Mary had gone to Nantes to take out a *cambye*—a special kind of loan made to a ship's officer at interest rates as high as 33 percent on condition that if the ship became lost at sea, the creditor would absorb the loss.[1] Mary took out a loan for twelve hundred livres at 30 percent interest on April 12, 1731, and then returned on April 16 to take out a loan of seventeen hundred livres at the same rate. Second Captain Pierre Valteau took out three separate loans totaling four thousand livres on April 12. Robert Durand, in partnership with his wealthy father-in-law, Etienne Hascouet, borrowed fifteen hundred livres on April 25. Even the ship's doctor, Pierre Devigne, took out a five hundred livre loan on April 5.[2] The purpose of these loans was to allow the officers to obtain personal trade goods, known as *pacotilles,* that they would use to purchase slaves or gold in Africa. Durand's loan agreement specifically stated that he was to use the sum "for *pacotilles* for the voyage to the coast of Guinea." Being in charge of the warehouse in Jakin gave Captain Mary, Second Captain Valteau, and First Lieutenant Durand perfect opportunities to trade their *pacotille* merchandise for the best slaves. As a result, Pierre Mary bought twenty-six slaves for his own account, Pierre Valteau bought thirteen, and Robert Durand bought five.

The practice of private trading among officers was commonplace on private ships, and it helps explain how the outfitters of private slaving expeditions succeeded in securing qualified officers for their ships. The potential profit from private trading in slaves dwarfed the officers' meager salaries. Captain Pierre Mary, for example, received a salary of 120 livres a month, or 1,800 livres for the fifteen-month voyage. Although the captain's salary was more than ten times as high as that of the lowliest sailor, it was still meager in comparison with the potential profits from the sale of slaves. Captain Mary paid between 88 and 220 livres each for his adult male slaves, and he was expecting to sell them for 950 livres each in Martinique.[3] A modest calculation would put his expected gross profit margin at 700 livres per slave. The profit from just three slaves would thus be higher than his salary for the entire voyage, and the twenty-six slaves that he purchased could bring a gross profit of 18,200 livres, an amount that was roughly equal to the purchase price of the *Diligent* itself. Slave trading was much more profitable for ships' officers than it was for the outfitters of the voyages. The outfitters had to purchase the ship, hire the crew, provide food for the crew and the slaves, pay the insurance premiums, and pay the wages of local laborers when the ship was on shore, whereas the officers bore none of those costs. The profit for the officers was roughly equal to the difference between the purchase price and the selling price, minus the interest on the loan. Another advantage for the officers was that they could choose the best slaves and get the most advantageous gender ratios.

All together, more than a fifth of the space on the slave deck would be taken up by slaves who belonged to individual officers, and more than 10 percent of all the slaves on the *Diligent* belonged to Captain Mary. Before the ship had departed from Vannes, the officers had received a *port permis* document that gave them permission to bring along a modest quantity of private trading goods to exchange for a modest number of slaves, but Captain Mary had exceeded his *port permis* privileges. Not only were his private slaves taking up space in the *Diligent*, but they were also eating food that had been furnished by the outfitters—the Billy brothers and La Croix. The sailing orders given to Captain Mary outlined an elaborate system for identifying which captives belonged to which officer. Captives belonging to the ship's "cargo" were branded on the right shoulder; those belonging to the captain were branded on the left shoulder. The *pacotille* slaves of the second captain were branded on the right side of the chest, while those belonging to the first lieutenant were branded on the left side of their chest. Those captives purchased by lower officers were branded on right and left hips and buttocks.[4]

Although private French slave ships could legally carry modest amounts of *pacotille* goods and modest numbers of *pacotille* slaves openly, ships belonging to the great trading companies carried on a similar *pacotille* trade in secret. The director of the French fort at Glewe believed there was no captain or officer of the Company of the Indies who did not bring a *pacotille*, even though the practice was clearly illegal.[5] Carrying private trade goods was officially forbidden by the company, which limited each captain to one trunk three and a half feet long, sixteen inches wide, and sixteen inches high, and each officer to a similar trunk three feet long.[6] The company was nevertheless alarmed by the quantity of private goods being stowed away on ships. In 1724 the director of the company lamented, "That which is brought back in the *pacotilles* of the ships is without question robbery. Soon the officers will cancel out the sales of the company if each ship carries two hundred bails of merchandise as *pacotille* for them and their consorts."[7] That same year the commander of the port of Lorient professed to be "frightened by the quantity of *pacotilles* that are smuggled aboard company ships."

The company's efforts to stop private trading were as continuous as they were ineffectual. In 1725 the company ordered soldiers traveling aboard company ships to police the ships for *pacotilles*. Two years later it announced that any official who seized a *pacotille* could keep half of it, and that any sailor who informed an official of the whereabouts of a *pacotille* would get half of the official's share. Despite these measures, however, it remained commonplace for officers on ships of the Company of the Indies to carry private trade goods and conduct private trade.[8] The company tried to discourage the practice of *pacotilles* by paying a bonus for each slave delivered alive to the islands on behalf of the company. On the Senegal circuit, the company paid ten livres per slave: the captain got five livres, the first lieutenant got one livre, and the rest of the officer corps got proportionally smaller bonuses. Company ships that made the longer circuit to Whydah received a larger bonus of fifteen livres per slave: the captain got seven livres, the first lieutenant got two, and so on down the line. Under this system, the captain would lose bonus money each time a *pacotille* slave was substituted for a company slave, but the bonus was so small in comparison to the profits to be made from privately owned slaves that the measure had little effect.[9]

By 1728 the *pacotille* problem had attracted the attention of the director of the French fort in Whydah.[10] The Company of the Indies, he complained, was less vigorous in taking measures against *pacotilles* than it had been previously, and it was completely failing to prevent the practice. Some company captains were going as far as to appropriate brandy and cowry shells belonging to the ship's cargo and cover the loss with a false declaration. If the captains would go that far, noted the director of the fort, they were likely to do almost anything to obtain and protect their *pacotilles*. In general, he believed, there was no captain or officer who did not bring a *pacotille*. Although the company ships were inspected before they left the company port of Lorient on the Brittany coast of France, they would stop during the night at the nearby port of Pen-Mane and load their *pacotilles* in secret. Once they arrived in Whydah, they no longer made any attempts to hide their personal goods and personal commerce.

Private trading was also common on slave ships of the Dutch West India Company. Despite company regulations that allowed captains (but no other officers) to take along small amounts of merchandise for their own use, private trading among all officers became widespread. The company council complained that so much private merchandise was being carried on slave ships that there was not enough space for the slaves.[11] Similar conditions reigned on English ships, as Jean Barbot noted:

> It also concerns the adventurers in Guinea voyages for slaves not to allow the commanders, supercargo, or officers, the liberty of taking aboard any slaves for their own particular account, as it is too often practiced among European traders, thinking to save something in their salaries by

the month: for experience has shown that the captain's slaves never die, since there are not ten masters in fifty who scruple to make good their own out of the cargo; or at lease such license-slaves are sure to have the best accommodations aboard, and the greatest plenty of subsistence out of the ship's stock: and very often those who were allowed to carry but two slaves have had ten or twelve, and those the best of the cargo, subsisted out of the general provisions of the ship, and trained up aboard to be carpenters, coopers, and cooks, so as to sell for double the price of other slaves in America, because of their skills.[12]

Portuguese captains sailing from Brazil were free to load as many private slaves as they wished, both for themselves and their friends.[13]

While Captain Mary was exceeding his legal *pacotille* privileges in trading for slaves, he was also making shady deals for Brazilian gold and tobacco. Recovering from his illness on board the *Diligent* during the month of October, he learned that the crew of an English ship anchored nearby was running short of meat, and so he traded them four barrels of the *Diligent's* salted beef and one barrel of flour for four eighty-pound rolls of Brazilian tobacco. Later, when a nearby Portuguese ship wanted to use the *Diligent's* longboat to load fresh water, Captain Mary charged them one eighty-pound roll of tobacco for each trip. The longboat made six trips.[14] In the two transactions Pierre Mary had personally garnered ten rolls of tobacco weighing a total of eight hundred pounds. The captain engaged in other dubious transactions as well. Although Robert Durand turned over to Captain Mary all the gold he had received from selling French brandy at the tent on the beach, the captain would later be unable to account for it. The captain had also obtained a gold ring and a hunting knife from the passenger Pierre Verger in exchange for a bedspread of limancas cloth belonging to the cargo.[15] In the bizarre world of slave traders, in which death and captivity were part of their everyday business, it was seemingly minor transactions such as these that would eventually get Captain Mary into serious legal trouble.

With Captain Mary on shore to finish the trade, things were not going well on the *Diligent*. On November 17 second carpenter Jean Mahé, who had returned to the ship sick along with Durand on November 14, died of bloody flux. Mahé was thirty-seven years old. When his clothes and the other items in his sea chest were auctioned off to the other members of the crew, they brought a total of forty-one livres.[16] On November 18 a slave imprisoned on the slave deck died. Durand, who lay very sick in the officers' quarters keeping the room as dark as possible to reduce the throbbing in his head, recorded the death without giving any indication of the cause.

As the slave deck of the *Diligent* gradually filled up and became more cramped, the crew became tense because they knew that shipboard slave revolts most often took place while the ship was in sight of land. Sentinels guarded the hatchway to the slave deck twenty-four hours a day, and there was a chest of small arms loaded and primed on the quarterdeck. The swivel guns on the quarterdeck were aimed at the main deck near the hatchway. The tensions mounted at mealtimes when the slaves were brought up to the main deck to be fed, since this was their best opportunity to revolt. All crew members who were not busy distributing food stood guard with arms loaded with case shot. Some slaving captains even purchased a small number of Gold Coast slaves who were instructed to serve as informants and report any plans for rebellion or escape while the ship was at anchor.[17]

The other worry of the crew was that some captives would try to commit suicide by jumping overboard while they were on deck at mealtimes. The words of the Englishman Phillips that some slaves had a "greater apprehension of Barbados than we can have of hell" were borne out by captives' frequent attempts to escape overboard, even though it meant certain death in the turbulent and shark-filled waters. Perhaps they did it to avoid a lifetime of slavery; perhaps they did it out of fear of being eaten by white cannibals; or perhaps they did it out of a belief that death would return them to their own country. In any case, the captives seemed to view suicide more as a form of martyrdom and an affirmation of their faith than as simple escapism. The decision of whether to attempt suicide or try to reconcile oneself to slavery was agonizing and intensely personal. On the French ship *Courrier de Bourbon* two women captives managed to get to the rail but were captured when they hesitated: one woman was still trying to convince her uncertain comrade to jump.[18]

The officers and crew on the *Diligent* were nervous because they had heard stories about ships such as the *Junon*, on which six enslaved women managed to jump into the sea at Whydah and were quickly eaten by sharks. "It is a frightening thing," wrote the captain of the *Junon*, "to see the sharks around the ship. There were thousands of them." Some slave traders believed that if sharks gathered around a ship while it was in the port, they would follow it all the way across the ocean in anticipation of future meals. To prevent the sharks from gathering, crew members on the *Diligent* stood at full alert to prevent any escape attempts.[19]

One theory current among European slaving captains was that suicides could be discouraged if the crew punished attempted suicides by cutting off a limb. According to the theory, Africans committed suicide so that their spirit would return home, but the spirit could return home only if the body was intact. Dismemberment, went the theory, would defeat the whole purpose of the suicide and discourage others from trying it. Captains who considered themselves "humane slave traders" rejected the practice as cruel and barbaric, but it was apparently followed by other captains who were less fastidious.[20]

On November 26 Captain Mary and his aides returned to the ship. They had finished their slave trading, vacated the warehouse in Jakin, and taken down the tent on the beach. The captain had made his decision about how many captives constituted a full load. By packing 256 slaves onto a ship of ninety-five registered tons burden, he was creating a ratio of 2.7 captives per ton, which was considerably higher than the 1.9 captives per ton average ratio for French ships leaving the coast of Africa in 1731.[21] It was the smaller ships such as the *Diligent* that were the tightest packers: the sixty-ton *St. Dominique* carried 201 captives for a 3.35 per ton ratio, and the ninety-five ton *Ceres*, which was the same tonnage as the *Diligent*, carried 283 captives for a ratio of almost three captives per ton. The relationship between crowding on slave ships and mortality of the captives has often been misunderstood. It was not the crowding itself that caused the deaths of slaves, though it certainly caused misery and discomfort. The real problem was that the ship's capacity to carry food and water was more or less fixed, and so more captives meant less food and water for each one. With its ratio of 2.7 captives per registered ton of burden, the *Diligent* was skirting the danger zone.

By the end of the day the last of the slaves had been crammed into the slave deck, and the unspent trade goods had been returned to the ship. In the final days before departure, the crew had dismantled the tent that sheltered the deck and had returned the yards and sails to their sailing positions. Millet and other foodstuffs had been purchased in Jakin, and the replenished water barrels had been safely stored in the hold. Eager to flee Jakin before any more crew members or slaves died, the captain ordered the *Diligent* to prepare for departure. The very next day Pierre Mathieu, an officer in training who was twenty years old, died of a high fever.

With the ship ready to depart, Robert Durand felt well enough to make a list of the slave cargo that the *Diligent* was carrying. There were 201 captives belonging to the outfitters in Vannes—the Billy brothers and La Croix. Durand listed those slaves as belonging to the "cargo." He did not list their names or places of origin, but he did group them by gender and age class (captives under the age of ten were considered boys and girls). Durand's list totaled 109 men, 71 women, 17 boys, and 4 girls. Overall, there were 1.7 males for every female. This was far from the three to one ratio that William Snelgrave had requested from King Agaja and closer to the two to one ratio recommended by Des Marchais.

The captives that Durand listed as *pacotilles* had a different age and gender composition entirely, demonstrating how the slave traders could take advantage of their position of being on the spot to get the most economically advantageous slave cargo. Of Captain Mary's twenty-six personally owned slaves, twenty-three were men and only three were women. He had purchased no children. Similarly, Second Captain Valteau purchased nine men, two boys, and two women, and Robert Durand purchased five men, no women, and no children. Lower-ranking officers also tried to purchase slaves with their *pacotilles,* but their relative lack of resources and access affected their purchases. Second Lieutenant Thomas Laragon purchased three women; the ship's doctor, Devigne, purchased three men and two women; First Mate Leglan bought one girl; the pilot, Sabatier, bought one man, and the second doctor, Touchard, bought one woman slave.

All together, 256 people—201 belonging to the outfitters and 55 belonging to the ship's officers—were packed onto a slave deck that was only sixty-three feet long and twenty-one feet wide at its widest point. Some of the space on the slave deck was taken up by the thick, coiled anchor ropes and the sail lockers. Even counting the additional space created by the platforms, each person got a space about one foot wide by five feet long, which required the captives to lie on their sides with only about two feet between the deck and the platform above it (or between the platform and the deck above it).[22] Even in the center of the slave deck, where the headroom was not truncated by platforms, the space was only about four and a half feet high. Because there was more headroom in the middle, the captives were placed in a squatting position with their knees against their chins. The *Diligent* had been built as a grain ship, and thus ventilation on the slave deck was extremely poor and the heat could become stifling.

At eight o'clock in the morning on Tuesday, November 27, almost three months after their arrival in Jakin, the crew of the *Diligent* set its sails and caught a light breeze from the northwest. From his vantage point on quarterdeck, Durand sketched the crumbling Portuguese fort, the tents of the slave traders on the beach, and the city of Jakin in the background. Like the rest of the crew, he was eager to get away from Jakin as quickly as possible. As the *Diligent* moved away from the shore, it gradually picked up speed. Soon it was running ahead of the breeze in full sail. Instead of heading west and slightly north toward the island of Martinique in the Caribbean, which was its ultimate destination, it was moving in a southeasterly direction—straight for the Portuguese islands of Principe and São Tomé.

PART 9

Atlantic Islands

30

$\mathcal{A}$s THE AFRICAN COASTLINE receded and finally disappeared from view, the *Diligent* seemed to enter another world.[1] In Jakin, the officers of the *Diligent* had lived as guests in the compound of the local African ruler. They had given the proper gifts, paid the proper customs duties, and showed polite deference in dealing with African officials. They had bargained patiently with African slave merchants and had carefully negotiated wages and working conditions with their hired African laborers. All of those measures had been necessary in order to acquire their shipload of captives. But once the ship left the Jakin road, all of that began to change. In the small wooden world ruled by Pierre Mary, Pierre Valteau, and Robert Durand, the lines of race and station quickly converged.

A cold war reigned on the ship. The crew felt it, especially during the early days at sea. To them, every African captive regardless of age or sex was a potential rebel. Children carried messages, and their sharp eyes sometimes found small metal objects such as loose nails that could be used to pick locks or make weapons. Women used their limited freedom of movement and their access to the officers' quarters to study the operations of the crew to detect opportunities for rebellion. On the slave ship *Annibal* in 1729 a group of women forced themselves into the great room of the officers' quarters, probing for weak spots in the crew's defenses.[2] Women also carried messages and helped plan rebellions; that is why the partition between the men's quarters and the women's quarters was made as soundproof as possible. Modern statistical studies confirm that the greater the percentage of women on the ship, the greater the likelihood of rebellion.[3] To the crew of the *Diligent*, the women and children were to be watched as closely as the men.

The crew had another reason to be wary of the women: they suspected that some of them might be sorceresses. They had heard the stories like the one recorded by Father Labat of the French ship heading out from Gorée Island with a sorceress among the captives. She made the water and food disappear and caused deaths among her fellow captives. When the ship's doctor did an autopsy on one of the deceased slaves, he found the heart and liver dry and hollow like a balloon. The doctor whipped the sorceress unmercifully, but she claimed that she felt no pain. She also swore revenge. Two days later the doctor died in great pain. When his body was opened up for the autopsy, it was discovered that his testicles were as dry as parchment. Finally the ship returned to the African shore and set the woman free. Several British officers who were prisoners on that French ship, claimed Father Labat, had signed a deposition swearing that the story was true.[4]

Among the Africans, some of whom had been on the ship for over two months before it sailed, a series of informal and largely hidden social networks were developing as each captive discovered which captives spoke a language that he or she could understand. In the ensuing conversations, they learned who was highborn and who was common, who had been wealthy and who had been poor, who had held positions of authority and who was a follower. Comparing stories about how they had become enslaved, they discovered who had been captured in warfare, who had been kidnapped, who had been sold because of debt or famine, and who had been sold for criminal activities. But questions about the past were not as important as questions about the present and the future. Would they survive? If so, what would become of them? As the language-based networks coalesced, leaders emerged and began making plans for rebellion or escape.[5]

At five o'clock in the morning on November 29, just before the first light of dawn, a man on the slave deck—we don't know his name—began to stir. He lay naked on the rough boards with only about two feet between the deck below him and the platform above him. It was difficult to sleep with his leg locked to the leg of another captive by slave irons; even chains would have been preferable. The air had grown stale during the night, and the lower deck radiated stored-up heat despite the relative coolness of the night. The man had most likely been a soldier in the army of Mahi or Oyo. He had stoically endured his capture by the army of Dahomey, his forced march to the coast, the humiliating inspection by one of the *Diligent's* officers, and the terrifying canoe ride through the towering waves. He was not sure where he was being taken or for what purpose, but he had heard many times that the whites were cannibals who bought African captives for food.

Now, in the stale darkness of the slave deck, he could take it no more. He began to exhort his fellow captives to immediate rebellion. They should rise up as one and try to break out through the barred hatch cover. The other captives immediately recognized the plan as foolhardy. To have any chance of success, a rebellion needed to be carefully planned and based on sound intelligence. Weapons needed to be found, actions had to be coordinated, and the move had to be timed perfectly. Seeing the other captives reject his plan, the man became enraged. He had to act now, and if his comrades would not join him in rebellion, he would lash out in whatever way he could at whomever was nearby. Lacking any weapon other than his teeth, he bit his thumb until blood spurted from it. Then he bit one of the captives lying near him.

Hearing the shouts from below, the night guards opened the hatch and entered the slave deck. Despite the crowded conditions, the other slaves had managed to pull back to give the man room. He was not mobile because his leg was still locked to that of his partner in irons, but he crouched defiantly under the low ceiling. When anybody, black or white, tried to approach him, he bared his teeth and tried to bite them. As more crew members rushed down to the slave deck, they eventually managed to subdue the man and free his partner from the irons that bound them together. They took the man to the main deck, where they pinned him down and tied his hands behind his back. Then they began to beat and kick him.

Captain Mary had been fearing a revolt ever since the ship left Jakin. He was aware that the first days out of port, when it was still possible for rebellious slaves to force the ship to return to the African coast, were likely times for a rebellion. With each day that passed, the possibility of return seemed more and more remote. Mary had not experienced a shipboard rebellion on his two earlier voyages to Guinea, but he had come close. Just after his initial slaving voyage on the *Marie* in 1720–1721, he took an assignment on another ship. The *Marie* returned to Guinea and suffered a revolt in which as many as forty of the African captives were killed.[6] His former comrades on the *Marie* had recounted that story to him many times.

This one-man minirevolt gave Pierre Mary an opportunity to get rid of a potential troublemaker and intimidate the rest of the captives at the same time. He ordered the captives brought up on deck. With the Africans looking on, several sailors tied a rope around the man's chest and hoisted him up to the yard of the foremast. At first the African onlookers were relieved to see that the rope was not around the man's neck. As the man was raised into the air, he shouted his defiance into the southwest wind. Then a firing squad commanded by gunner Charles Auger stepped up to the quarterdeck. With muskets aimed at the body dangling from the yard, they shot the man over and over as his blood spattered on the deck. This was done, wrote Robert Durand in his journal, "to teach a lesson to all the others."

The possibility of rebellion was never far from the minds of slave ship officers and crews when they swapped stories in slaving ports. There had been at least seventeen shipboard slave revolts during the 1720s on French ships alone. On the *Excellent*, seventy-four captives lost their lives during a revolt; many of them died fighting for their freedom, but others took advantage of the confusion to commit suicide by jumping overboard. Revolt and suicide—two ways to escape captivity—seemed to go hand in hand. On the slave ship *Amériquin* some slaves got hold of an ax and wounded three crew members before they were subdued. The captives on the slave ship *Dauphin* revolted just as the ship was preparing to leave the harbor of Whydah. When the revolt was suppressed, the ship sailed, but the captives revolted again on the first day at sea. Their leader was hung from the yard and shot, but six days later his followers staged a third revolt. On the *Annibal* the captives succeeded in obtaining axes, cutlasses, scissors, hammers, fingernail files, and even two pairs of pistols. By the time the revolt was crushed, forty-five captives were dead and another forty-seven wounded. Five of the wounded captives who were believed to be the leaders of the revolt were hung from the yards. The most successful revolt of the time took place on February 11, 1732—shortly after the one-man revolt on the *Diligent*—when the captives on the *Parfait* revolted at Great Popo and manage to sink the ship before swimming for shore.[7]

Slave traders had a variety of theories about what caused revolts and how to prevent them. After William Snelgrave had crushed a rebellion on the *Henry* in 1721, he interrogated the leaders as to why they had rebelled. They replied that Snelgrave "was a great rogue to buy them in order to carry them away from their own country; and that they were resolved to regain their liberty if possible." True to their word, they began plotting a new rebellion a few days later.[8] Even though Snelgrave had personally crushed three slave rebellions on three different ships, he still believed himself to be a model slave trader. He considered revolts to be caused by the "sailors' ill usage of these poor people." He argued that treating the captives with "humanity" and "tenderness" would keep them from rebelling. The most important point, he argued, was to tell the captives through an interpreter that they were not going to be eaten by white cannibals; rather, they were being taken to till the soil for white masters in a faraway country. Whether or not any of the captives believed him is an open question.[9]

Similarly, Des Marchais, who also believed himself to be a model slave trader, had a theory that rebellions were caused by bad food and by the captives' fear of being eaten. To avoid exacerbating that fear, he ordered the doctors on his ship never to perform an autopsy on a slave who died; the sight of a partially dissected cadaver would be taken as proof of the captors' intentions. It was important, Des Marchais believed, to reassure the captives that when they arrived in the Caribbean they would work the land and learn to know the true God. Such reassurances would be believed, he thought, if they were accompanied by humane treatment of the sick.

Still, Des Marchais did not rely on "humane" treatment alone to prevent rebellions. He advised his fellow slave traders always to be on guard, especially during the night when rebellions were most likely to occur. To guard against plots, slave traders should identify those slaves who seemed most "indifferent about their liberty" and give them preferential treatment to turn them into informers. He also advised slaving captains to keep the hatch closed with iron bars at night and to leave only a small hatch opening for those who had to come up, shackled two by two, to relieve themselves. There should never be more than two or three pairs of captives on deck at night, he advised, and they should return before others were allowed to come up. If the guards heard a noise on the slave deck at night, they should not go down themselves to check it out, but should send some of the captives whom they had selected to command the others. The crew members on night watch should always be armed in case the slaves tried to force open the hatch cover.[10]

When faced with the threat or reality of a shipboard uprising, most, if not all, slaving captains followed the theory that brutal intimidation was the best course of action. Such a theory had been expressed earlier by Jean Barbot, who wrote that if a rebellion occurs, the captain should "spare no effort to repress their insolence and, as an example to the others, sacrifice the lives of all the most mutinous. This will terrify the others and keep them obedient. The way of making it clear to them, I mean the form of punishment that scares the Africans most, is by cutting up a live man with an ax and handing out the pieces to the others."[11]

Even William Snelgrave, for all his claims to being a "humane" slave trader, could be brutal in the face of rebellion. In 1721 Snelgrave's ship was in the road of the British fort at Anamabu. After a failed rebellion in which a white sailor was killed, Snelgrave informed the captains of the eight other ships in the Anamabu road that he was about to execute the rebel leader and that all of them should bring their captives up on the decks to watch. With his own captives and those from the eight surrounding ships looking on, Snelgrave's men tied a rope around the rebel leader's chest and hauled him up the fore yardarm. Then ten sailors fired on him with muskets and killed him instantly.

After the execution, the sailors lowered the man's body to the deck. In front of all the horrified onlookers they cut off his head and threw it into the shark-infested sea. This was done, Snelgrave explained, in accordance with the theory current among slaving captains which held that Africans in that region believed that dismemberment prevented the spirit of the person from returning home after death. Snelgrave not only wanted to execute the rebellious man, but he also wanted to prevent his spirit from returning home. By so doing, he hoped to intimidate the African captives sufficiently to prevent future acts of rebellion.[12]

On the *Diligent*, the brutal bluster that Captain Mary so publicly displayed could not quite hide the fact that he was scared to death of losing control, since the captives outnumbered their jailers by nearly seven to one. When the naked and bloody body of the man who had staged the personal rebellion was hauled down from the yard, the sailors threw it into the sea with no ceremony. Robert Durand didn't record whether or not he saw any sharks.

The *Diligent* was sailing south-southeast even though its destination, Martinique, was located across the Atlantic to the west-northwest. The reason for this seeming anomaly was the Guinea current, which flowed east past the Gold Coast, Whydah, and Jakin all the way to Gabon. The only way to escape it was to drop down to the equator. The second reason for sailing south-southeast was that they were headed for the Portuguese-controlled islands of Principe and São Tomé, where they hoped to restore the health of the sick crew members and slaves and stock up on food and good water for the middle passage. The two Portuguese islands were standard stops for ships leaving the Gold and Slave Coasts, and many ships stayed as long as six weeks before attempting the Atlantic crossing. Of the nine French slave ships that left the Slave Coast in 1731, six of them stopped in Principe and one stopped in São Tomé. [13]

The currents determined the route: ships leaving from the Gold Coast could sail directly for São Tome, whereas those leaving from Whydah and Jakin had to go first to Principe because the current carried them east of São Tomé. If the currents were especially strong and the winds contrary, ships had to make their way toward Principe by following the African coast as it curved south, anchoring during the day and sailing at night to take advantage of the land breeze. Under such conditions, it could take up to thirty days to reach Principe from Whydah or Jakin. Ships headed for Principe could get trapped in the Guinea current for as long as five months. [14]

Since its departure from Jakin on Tuesday, November 27, death had stalked the *Diligent*. Mathieu Kanelo, the twenty-year-old officer in training from Vannes, had died of a "hot fever" only one hour after the ship left Jakin. The next day the second doctor, René Touchard, died from an injury he had suffered earlier when his canoe overturned while crossing the bar. Among his possessions that were auctioned off were two medical books, which were purchased by first surgeon Devigne. On Saturday, December 1, a captive belonging to the cargo died of what Robert Durand called the "malady of the land." On Sunday Pierre Thaubier of Le Croisic, a twenty-one-year-old seaman, died of "hot fever, the ordinary disease of the country." Over the next five days three more captives died: one man and two women. Durand did not record the cause of their deaths, but he noted that they had died "suddenly and unexpectedly."

Burials at sea were becoming an almost daily occurrence. The death of a crew member was handled very differently from the death of a captive. When a crew member died, his *matelot* (counterpart on the other watch team) was in charge of the funeral arrangements. The doctor and the *matelot* wrapped him in his blanket or, if blankets were scarce, in a mat and tied it securely. The wrapped body was then carried to a spot on the main deck accompanied by the two cabin boys, one carrying a wooden cross and the other carrying a burning torch. The entire crew gathered while the captain said prayers, and then each crew member in turn sprinkled holy water on the body. Finally, a cannonball was tied to the feet of the corpse, and the body was thrown overboard. A single cannon shot was fired in salute for an ordinary sailor (several cannon shots for an officer) as the body disappeared beneath the waves.[15]

Africans who died received no such ceremony. Since they were not Christians, prayers and holy water were irrelevant, and the crew did not want to use up blankets, cloth, or cannonballs in disposing of the bodies. The crew waited until night when no slaves were watching and then threw the naked body overboard to bob in the water as the ship continued onward. That is why sharks followed the slave ships.[16] If the deceased African had countrymen or comrades aboard, they undoubtedly fashioned a ceremony as appropriate as they could make it on the slave deck at night when there were no crew members watching. There was a strong belief that the spirit of the deceased went home after death, and the surviving Africans did what they could to help the deceased on his or her journey.[17]

The presence of two doctors on the *Diligent*, required by French law on all long-haul voyages, apparently did not do much good. The doctors were referred to as "surgeons" because they amputated limbs, pulled teeth, and administered bleedings. In the seventeenth century many ship's surgeons had started out as barbers and learned surgery "on the job." The French government tightened up the regulations in 1717, forcing shipboard surgeons to take an apprenticeship in a hospital in the port and then pass an oral examination held at the Admiralty Court by a jury of licensed surgeons. Not until 1767 were ship's surgeons required to undertake serious medical studies.

Even with the tightened regulations of 1717, Des Marchais had nothing but scorn for the doctors on French slave ships, who barely knew how to bleed a patient and were ignorant of the basic medicines. They got hired largely because they worked so cheaply.[18] A similar sentiment was expressed by the English surgeon T. Aubrey. In his 1729 manual for slave ship doctors he noted, "Abundance of these poor creatures are lost on board ships to the great prejudice of the owners and the scandal of the surgeons merely through the surgeon's ignorance, because he knows not what they are afflicted with, but supposing it to be a fever, bleeds and purges, or vomits them, and so casts them into an incurable diarrhea, and in a few days they become a feast for some hungry shark."[19]

Given the ineffective medicines and poorly trained doctors, Captain Mary knew that the best way to preserve the lives of crew members and captives was to get the ship to a healthier environment. There seemed to be a general agreement among slaving captains that Whydah and Jakin were unhealthy places with bad air and bad water. The only solution was to get to the Portuguese island of Principe as quickly as possible. Even Des Marchais, for all his cynicism about doctors, recommended the food and water on Principe.[20] With crew members and captives alike sick and dying, Captain Mary was heeding this advice and trying to get to Principe as quickly as possible.

31

$\mathscr{A}$T NOON ON DECEMBER 6, 1731, the lookout spotted the jagged peaks of Principe Island, and two days later the *Diligent* lay at anchor in the port. They had made excellent time, crossing from Jakin to Principe in just twelve days. Normally, ships left Whydah and Jakin with enough food and water for at least three weeks in case they ran into contrary winds or had trouble finding the island. Death rates were high on this stretch of the voyage because many of the slaves and crew members were sick when they boarded the ship. The key to keeping death rates down, given the ineffectiveness of the doctors, was to get to Principe quickly.

The consequences of getting there slowly were demonstrated by the ship *St. Michel*, which had passed that way just a year before the *Diligent*. The trip from the Guinea coast to Principe had taken over a month, and by the time the ship arrived, thirty-two Africans had died and the rest were sick. The ship's doctor was a young man who was incapable of treating any of the sick and didn't even know which medicines to give for which disease. At Principe the governor provided them with a more competent doctor, but thirty-three more of the captives died soon after. Departing Principe for its sister Portuguese island of São Tomé, the *St. Michel* was again slowed down by contrary winds and calm. With the captain very sick and his first lieutenant blinded by an eye disease, nobody was capable of commanding the ship. Many of the Africans died from disease and lack of food. By the time the *St. Michel* arrived in São Tomé, four and a half months after leaving the Guinea coast, only thirty-eight Africans out of the original 202 were still alive.[1]

Figure 31.1   Durand's drawing of the harbor at Principe.

For the *Diligent*, things went somewhat better, although another African woman died suddenly at seven o'clock on Friday morning, December 7. Coming into the harbor at Principe, Durand recognized two ships that he had encountered earlier on the Guinea coast: the *Pontchartrain* and the *Hirondelle*, which had left the Guinea coast three months earlier. The letters they had earlier sent with the *Hirondelle* did not precede them. An English ship and two Portuguese ships were also in the harbor.

Because Durand and Valteau had been sick throughout the passage to Principe, they immediately left the ship to recuperate in a rented house on shore. Ordinary crew members who were sick were taken ashore and put up in a tent on the beach a mere rifle shot from the ship. The captain rented a warehouse for the slaves and immediately brought the sick captives to shore. Even so, another woman slave died on the second day in Principe. Seven African captives and four French crew members had died so far.

While the sick were recovering, the rest of the crew was very busy. Principe had a calm harbor that Durand described as "like a pond." Because the harbor was deep, ships could anchor close to shore, which made it easy to load and unload the people and the merchandise. The healthy captives were moved into a rented warehouse on shore that contained separate facilities for men and women and had fenced-in yards where they could get fresh air and exercise without being able to escape. Their shackles were removed for the duration of the stay on land, and each morning and evening they were taken to a nearby stream where they could bathe. The men and women were always kept separate because slave traders believed that the separation prevented certain kinds of quarrels from arising. It also kept men and women from getting together to plot rebellions to be carried out on the Atlantic crossing. The captives were watched closely in the warehouse yard during the day and were locked inside the warehouse during the night, in part to make sure that they were not stolen by local slave owners, but also out of fear that they would escape and join maroon communities in remote parts of the island.[2]

On the *Diligent* the crew unloaded the merchandise and supplies and stored them in a separate warehouse on shore so that they could clean the ship from bottom to top. They emptied the water barrels containing water from Jakin and refilled them with fresh water from the island because Europeans believed that the water of Whydah and Jakin caused worms and scurvy. Robert Durand did not report how much water they loaded into the hold of the *Diligent*, but a reported rule of thumb was to load one *barrique* of water (sixty gallons) per captive. The water was generally loaded in large wooden barrels, each containing eight *barriques* of water. If the *Diligent* followed this rule, then it would have loaded 249 *barriques* of water for the slaves, which would have filled thirty-two barrels. With each *barrique* containing about sixty gallons of water, this would have meant three quarts per person per day if the voyage lasted eighty days. Some of the water would go into the souplike gruel that the slaves ate, and the rest would be for drinking.[3]

The *Diligent* also used the occasion to stock up on inexpensive food. Selling foodstuffs to passing slave ships was, along with the warehousing of captives, the mainstay of the island's exchange economy. Durand noted that the Portuguese governor had declared a monopoly on the sale of food to foreigners, and so they bought everything from the governor at fixed prices. The price was set in ackies of gold and then translated into equivalent amounts of limineas cloth that was left over from the trading in Jakin. They bought chickens, goats, ducks, lemons, bananas, figs, and coconuts. They bought a thousand plantains, seventeen hundred coconuts, and sixty bushels of manioc flour. The manioc flour would be added to the millet that they had purchased in Jakin as food for the captives. A gruel made of fava beans, millet, and manioc flour would be the staple food for the slaves.

Durand took an inventory of the fava beans and found that they had 1,026 buckets, each containing half a bushel.[4] Slaving captains were of differing opinions about the effects of the beans. The English Captain Thomas Phillips believed that they had a "binding quality" that made them effective in preventing diarrhea, but some French captains worried about the "insipid flatulence" caused by the beans and recommended that they be seasoned with peppers and salt to make them more digestible. Chevalier Des Marchais agreed that the fava beans, when cooked only with water and a little salt, could be disgusting and indigestible. He recommended a more diversified diet of one-quarter fava beans, one-half rice, and the remaining quarter a mixture of peas and cassava. To make the food more digestible, it should be cooked with lard.[5] The *Diligent* was following Des Marchais's advice in making provision for a diversified diet. As a general rule of thumb, they needed one ton of foodstuffs for ten captives, or about twenty-six tons of food for the middle passage.[6]

By Christmas Day the *Diligent* was scrubbed, provisioned, and ready to leave. Nobody had died since December 10, and the slaves and crew seemed to be recovering their health. Robert Durand had been feeling better for a while, but his fever returned on December 24. With all else ready, it was time to reboard the African captives. Whereas their original embarkation had taken place over a period of weeks, with the captives brought out a few at a time in canoes that fought the triple surf of Jakin, here it could be done in calm waters with the longboat and the skiff. The crew was again tense because they knew that reboarding and departure were prime occasions for rebellions. They boarded the men first and shackled them in the men's area of the slave deck as soon as they arrived. Then they loaded the women into the women's part of the slave deck but did not shackle them. They would, however, be locked below deck until they were out of sight of land. This precaution, they believed, would make a revolt less likely. Once the ship was out of sight of land, the crew would bring captives up to the main deck a few at a time while staying on full alert for any signs of rebellion.[7]

Principe Island was located one degree, thirty-seven minutes north of the equator. Robert Durand calculated its latitude at two degrees, which was pretty close given the crude instruments he was using. After leaving Principe, the *Diligent* headed west-southwest toward the Portuguese island of São Tomé. On Saturday, December 29, Durand recorded his latitude as zero degrees, thirty minutes north; on Sunday it was zero degrees, fourteen minutes north. Then, on New Year's Day, he recorded his latitude as seven minutes south. The ship had crossed the equator with the turn of the year. Unlike the crossing of the Tropic of Cancer, this crossing triggered no special ceremony or even any particular mention. The only indication that they had crossed the equator at all is Durand's notation: "Lat. Obs. S: = 7m." On January 3 they spotted São Tomé, which touched the equator. Seamen commonly believed that the Aqua Grande River, which ran through the city of São Tomé near the northern end of the island, marked the equator. By walking across the bridge that spanned the river, it was believed, one could cross from the northern hemisphere to the southern hemisphere. It was an intriguing, but inaccurate, tale; mapmakers already knew that the equator actually ran through the *southern* tip of the island.[8]

Captain Mary had not planned to stop in São Tomé because he had already restocked the supplies and rested the crew and captives on Principé. But as they approached the island, he noted that the winds had become very still, and he could feel the tug of the Guinea current trying to carry the ship back toward the African coast. After consulting with officers Valteau, Durand, and Laragon, as well as with the first pilot Sabatier and first mate Leglan, he decided to stop at São Tomé to wait for better winds to carry them through the equatorial doldrums.[9] Taking advantage of their unplanned stopover, they bought 132 bushels of manioc flour, four bushels of peas, and some plantains for the captives. Avoiding the Aqua Grande River, where people were continually bathing and washing their clothes, they found a clear stream with good water for topping off their water barrels.

"The city," wrote Durand, "is very pretty. The governor-general of the islands makes his residence here. There is a bishop here, and they produce a great many black priests." In making this latter observation, Robert Durand did not know that a bitter racial struggle had been taking place on the island between the descendants of former black slaves who had worked in the cane fields in the heyday of sugar production and the *mestiço* and mulatto priests who were proud of their Portuguese blood. At the center of that particular struggle was a black priest named Manuel do Rosário Pinto. We can pick up his story in the year 1710.

32

*T*HE BLACK PRIEST LOOKED through a crack in one of the shuttered windows of the Cathedral of Nossa Senhora da Graça and waited while his eyes adjusted to the glaring sun outside. December 5, 1710, was a hot day, but the coolness of the cathedral afforded substantial relief from the tropical heat. A simple stone building with a single bell, Nossa Senhora da Graça was not impressive, but it was nevertheless the tallest building in São Tomé City and the seat of a diocese that had authority over the islands of the Gulf of Guinea and the African mainland from Cape Palmas to Mount Cameroon.[1] Looking beyond the shallow waters of Ana de Chaves Bay, Father Pinto's eyes focused on a ship in the distance. Perhaps it was bringing his salvation.

Father Pinto's struggle to become archdeacon of the diocese had been long and hard. Now that he had finally accomplished his goal, he found himself a prisoner in his own cathedral. The church had been turned into a fortress: the doors were barred, the windows were shuttered, and Pinto and his fellow black deacons were heavily armed. Outside, armed factions loyal to Pinto's rival, the *mestiço* priest Jerónimo de Andrade, controlled the city and the beach. Although there was little danger that those factions would actually try to storm the cathedral, neither Pinto nor his fellow black priests could leave it without endangering their lives.

Manuel do Rosário Pinto was born in the parish of Trinidade, south-west of the capital. Like most free blacks on São Tomé, he was a descendant of slaves. As the middle part of his name, "do Rosário," suggests, his

Figure 32.1   Durand's drawing of São Tomé City. Note the cathedral beside the Aqua Grande River. Sailors believed that the river was the dividing line between the hemispheres.

family had been involved with the religious brotherhood for Africans in São Tomé: Irmandade de Nossa Senhora do Rosário. In the sixteenth century King Dom Joao III had given the brotherhood the right to demand freedom for any black man or woman who was a member of the order. Equally as important as its role in obtaining freedom for black slaves, the church owned large estates of land in Trinidade Parish that it parceled out to freed slaves.[2] With the Pinto family owing both its freedom and its livelihood to the church, it is not surprising that the young Manuel decided to enter the priesthood.

As a young man, Pinto studied in either Brazil or Portugal—no one knows which—to become a priest of the Habit of Saint Peter. In 1696, at the age of thirty, he became the parish priest in his hometown of Vila da Trinidade. Located inland from the capital and away from the fertile coastal plain, Trinidade was a poor parish whose parishioners eked out a subsistence on church-owned lands. After only one year as parish priest, he was imprisoned for a month by the deacons of the diocese because they found the four-cornered hat that he wore to be offensive and he refused to stop wearing it. After his release, he journeyed to Lisbon to plead his case before the king of Portugal. He not only defended himself brilliantly, but he secured a nomination to become one of the deacons of the cathedral, thus joining the group that had recently put him in prison. In 1706 he was elected visitor of the diocese and traveled throughout the island visiting the different parishes. But in his zeal to root out errors of belief and practice, he offended some of the most powerful people on the island.[3]

Pinto's fight with the mulatto priest Jerónimo Andrade started in 1707, when there was a vacancy in the senate of the diocese. At the time the senate was composed of four black members and five *mestiço* members. Pinto nominated his fellow black priest, Father Campos, for the position. The election of Campos would deprive the *mestiço* priests of their majority.

To prevent that from happening, Jerónimo Andrade, who was the treasurer of the diocese, and his fellow *mestiço* deacons wrote a letter to the king of Portugal, arguing that formerly only whites and *mestiços* had been considered eligible to serve in the senate of deacons. The Bishop Dom Bernardo Zuzarte had named the first black deacons only in 1684. "By the experience we have had with these people," wrote Andrade, "it is not conducive to the tranquility of this senate that they should be made deacons. Seeing themselves made deacons even though they are unworthy of this honor, they will become proud and accomplish nothing except the sowing of dissension."

Learning of the letter, Father Pinto and his fellow black priests immediately wrote to the king charging that the *mestiço* priests were motivated by jealousy and pride in their exalted offices. After arguing that "the black priests are those who best keep their obligations, attend the supplication, and are legitimately born," Pinto urged the king to reward those who had done well without regard to color. The king decided in favor of the black priests and awarded the position to Father Campos, bringing the membership in the senate of deacons to five black priests and five *mestiço* priests.[4]

As the greatest historian from the island of São Tomé in the eighteenth century, Manuel do Rosário Pinto certainly understood that his personal battles were related to the shifting fortunes of the island in the larger Atlantic world. The island was uninhabited when Portuguese explorers discovered it in 1470. It quickly became a transshipping point for slaves from Kongo and Old Calabar, many of whom were shipped on to the Gold

Coast to be exchanged for gold, while others were shipped to Portugal and later to the New World. It also became one of the world's major sugar producers with Portuguese-owned plantations worked by African slaves. At the height of the sugar boom in the sixteenth century it had a population of a hundred thousand, over three thousand of whom were Portuguese, and it had as many as two hundred sugar mills.[5]

The sugar boom was short-lived because the sugar did not crystallize well in the humid climate. Even at the peak of its sugar boom, São Tomé sugar was selling for a half the price of early Brazilian sugar and one-fourth the price of Madeira sugar. As sugar production developed in Brazil, it drove São Tomé sugar off the market. As early as 1550 some planters began moving to Brazil with their slaves. Of the seventy-two private sugar estates on the island in 1575, fifty-nine of them were abandoned by 1615.[6] In the seventeenth century, after the Dutch had briefly occupied the island, 350 white and mulatto planters moved to Brazil.[7] Plantation owners who departed left their land in the hands of the local free black and mulatto population, and they often sold their slaves or gave them to local free blacks.

By the end of the seventeenth century, the former sugar plantations were mostly abandoned. The final blow came in 1716, when the municipal council rebelled against the governor, and thirteen sugar mills in the vicinity of São Tomé city were destroyed. By that time the sugar produced on the island could be described as "very coarse and dirty, and seldom well cured," and the island actually *imported* sugar from Brazil. The rum produced from local sugar was described as "sad, stinking, raw stuff."[8]

With the decline of sugar production, and with the slave trade from Angola now bypassing São Tomé entirely, the island focused its economy on providing food, supplies, and warehouse facilities to passing slave ships. The currents of the Gulf of Guinea had made Sao Tomé an almost required stopover for slave ships sailing from the Gold and Slave Coasts to the new world.

From its very beginning, São Tomé had been a multiracial society. Because few Portuguese women were willing to migrate to the island in the sixteenth century, the Crown encouraged interracial coupling by bringing in slave women from Kongo for purposes of breeding. In 1515 the king proclaimed that all African slave women who had been given as wives or concubines to Portuguese settlers were free, as were their offspring. Two years later the king granted freedom to all slaves given to early settlers or purchased by them. In making these decrees, the king was drawing a distinction between those Africans who had been originally brought in to help populate the island and those who were later brought in to labor on plantations as slaves.[9] The decrees of 1515 and 1517 created the nucleus of a free African population whose descendants proudly referred to themselves as *filhos da terra*, or "sons of the land."[10]

Already by 1539 the Portuguese Crown had recognized the right of free blacks and *mestiços* to vote and hold office in the municipal council, which frequently governed the island during long periods when there was no governor. Only landowners could vote, but many blacks and *mestiços* were amassing substantial landholdings, especially after the departure of the Portuguese sugar planters in the seventeenth century. By the beginning of the eighteenth century the landholdings of certain *filhos da terra* families, such as Cunha-Caravalho, D'Alva, and Chaves, far exceeded those of the church.[11] By the time the *Diligent* arrived in 1731 there were about two hundred whites on São Tomé out of a total population of about ten thousand, and the island's economy was in the hands of blacks and *mestiços*.[12] With sugar production largely abandoned, most of the remaining slaves lived in their own houses and raised food crops on their own farms, giving a certain percentage of the produce to their owner. They were more like sharecroppers than plantation slaves.

The one structure that resisted efforts by free blacks to penetrate positions of authority was the Church. Although there had been black priests early on and a special religious order for blacks had been established in 1526, blacks were kept out of the senate of deacons until 1684. Mulattos had been admitted early on, and they soon dominated the senate of deacons, but people who could claim no Portuguese blood faced an uphill battle. After Father Andrade's attempt to keep black priests out of the senate of deacons had been defeated by Father Manuel do Rosário Pinto, Andrade continued to show his resentment of the black priests. When the office of archdeacon became vacant, Andrade named himself to the position. Pinto challenged this, and, sitting as the head of the senate of deacons, he publicly censured Andrade.

Enraged at being humiliated by a black priest, Andrade sought the assistance of the municipal council. There was no governor on the island at the time (Governor Diniz Pinheiro had died in 1709 and would not be replaced until 1715), and so the municipal council was the governing authority. It was dominated by members of black *filhos da terra* families with large landholdings and slaveholdings, and by landholding *mestiço* families whose pigmentation was darkening with each generation. Both groups looked down on people like Pinto, who was descended from plantation slaves and whose family had eked out a living on Church-owned land. The upstart black priest had to be stopped, they decided, and so the municipal council ordered Father Pinto's arrest and authorized Father Andrade to take up arms. It was at that point that Pinto and the other black priests took refuge in the cathedral.[13]

Pinto was watching the harbor so intently from the cathedral window on December 5, 1710, because he was looking for a particular ship. News had come of the imminent arrival of the new bishop, João Sahagum, a member of the "Shoeless Augustinian" order. He had studied philosophy for three years and theology for four years at the *collegio santatanensi* in Portugal and had also lived in São Tomé, where he served as director of the hospice in São Tomé City and became a good friend of Pinto.[14] The ship had been expected since mid-November, and Pinto knew that it could come any day. With the arrival of the new bishop, Father Andrade and the municipal council would not dare arrest him. His eyes focused on a ship in the distance. As it came closer, Pinto noticed that it was flying a Portuguese flag. That was a good sign. Late in the afternoon Bishop João Sahagum descended from the ship.

The arrival of the new bishop on December 5, 1710, ended the siege of the cathedral, and over the next few weeks Pinto resumed his regular duties. The bishop investigated the whole affair and was preparing to take action against the municipal council and Father Andrade. Suddenly he fell ill, and he asked the black deacons led by Pinto to govern the diocese in his place. That very same day, while going to visit the sick bishop in his wooden house near the cathedral, Pinto was ambushed by partisans of Andrade's faction. They attempted to kill him, but he managed to escape. Seven days later, a member of Pinto's faction was captured by Andrade's faction, beaten until he was nearly dead, and locked in the dungeon of the Portuguese fort. He arrived at the fort so near death that he was given last rites. Fearing for their lives, Father Pinto and his allies fled to a forested area in the mountains outside of town.[15]

What saved the black deacons was that the bishop recovered from his illness and excommunicated the four members of the municipal council who played a role in capturing and beating the black priest. In return, the municipal council threatened prison and exile to anyone who had played a role in the bishop's decision to excommunicate them. Given that there was no governor in place to adjudicate the matter and that the municipal council was the chief political authority in the absence of a governor, the bishop backed down and decided not to pursue the matter further.

Things remained stalemated until March 1714, when an arcane legal dispute regarding a will reopened the battle between the bishop and the municipal council. The council ordered the ecclesiastical authorities, including the black priests Pinto and Campas, to leave the city. Pinto, Campas, and the bishop retreated, hoping that matters would cool down, but as soon as they left the cathedral, the municipal council closed down the diocese and declared the see to be vacant. Unable to return to São Tomé City, Bishop Sahagum, Campas, and Pinto boarded a ship bound for Lisbon to take their case directly to the king. After hearing the case, the king sided with Pinto and promoted him to archdeacon of the diocese. But he also gave Pinto a strong rebuke: "I give you notice, Manuel do Rosário Pinto, archdeacon of the See of the Island of São Tomé, that I am informed that by your pride you have perturbed and troubled these people in great disservice to God and myself."[16]

The royal rebuke notwithstanding, Pinto had won. He had earlier defeated Father Andrade and his *mestiço* followers, and now he had defeated the *filhos da terra* who dominated the municipal council. He had been officially appointed archdeacon of the diocese. Since the bishop had stayed behind in Lisbon when he returned to São Tomé, Pinto was the acting bishop of a diocese whose authority stretched from Cape Palmas to Mount Cameroon. He also became the counselor to the new Portuguese governor, Bartholomeu da Costa Ponte, who arrived in 1715. So close was the relationship that when the governor became ill, he convalesced at Pinto's house. As archdeacon of the diocese and counselor to the governor, Manuel do Rosário Pinto had become one of the most powerful people on the island.

Soon, however, a rift over the slave trade developed between the governor and the municipal council that would test Archdeacon Pinto's loyalties. The slave trade had always been the mainstay of the island's economy: during the fifteenth century São Tomé had served as a transshipment point for slaves; during the sixteenth century the importation of slaves had animated the island's sugar plantations; and more recently the provision of foodstuffs for slave ships had become São Tomé's major economic activity. The church was involved in the slave trade in two ways. First, the clerics of the Cathedral of Nossa Senhora da Graça had been granted the right to trade freely in slaves in order to support themselves, and the black brotherhood of Irmandade de Nossa Senhora was given the right to tithe the slave trade and to engage in slave trading with its own agents. The second form of involvement was that church lands produced foodstuffs that were sold to slave ships. Even the black religious brotherhood with which Archdeacon Pinto's family had been involved was authorized by the Crown to trade freely in food and spices. The result was that the church and the secular authorities competed fiercely with each other to trade with passing slave ships.[17] As both archdeacon of the diocese and a friend of the governor, Pinto was in a delicate position when it came to matters of commerce.

In 1716 the governor received a request from a treasury official in Brazil to censure the Crown magistrate of São Tomé for buying slaves from French and English ships. The problem was not that the judge had been dealing in slaves—that was perfectly legal and even encouraged—but that he had dealt in slaves with the French and the English, thus violating the Portuguese monopoly on the slave trade to the island. Although English and French slave ships could stop in São Tomé to purchase food or water, they were strictly forbidden from trading in slaves with local officials. Moreover, by purchasing slaves from French or English ships, the Crown magistrate avoided the customs payments that all Portuguese slave ships that stopped in São Tomé paid to the Portuguese Crown.[18] The governor's censure of the Crown magistrate angered many members of the municipal council because they too had undoubtedly made some lucrative deals trading slaves with the English and French, and they were not about to give up their potential profits.

With the governor and the municipal council at an impasse over enforcing the Portuguese monopoly on the slave trade, the municipal council stirred up an insurrection against the governor. As the rebellion spread, the governor was forced to take refuge in the fort São Sabastão. As it became clear that the people had turned against the governor, even the deacons of the diocese abandoned him. When the governor asked them for their help, they offered him only their prayers.

Figure 32.2   Durand's drawing of the fort at São Tomé.

With the fort surrounded by five thousand armed rebels, the governor sought a means of escape. Here is how Archdeacon Pinto recounted the event. "With the governor caught in this bind, redemption arrived in the form of an English ship. The captain of the ship, having news that Governor Bertholameu da Costa Ponte was in the fort, which was surrounded by rebels, went to the fort in his longboat to offer the governor his services. The governor, seeing himself abandoned by the fort's soldiers, who had joined the rebels, resolved to secure all of the fort's artillery, and in effect he succeeded. Closing the door on the artillery, he leaped from the wall and descended by a rope. Reaching the beach, he embarked in the longboat to the English ship, which quickly set its sails and departed."[19]

After Bishop Sahagum returned to São Tomé in 1719, things calmed down somewhat for Pinto. The two clerics were good friends, and Pinto had even provided a member of his own family—either his daughter or his sister—to be the bishop's mistress. From this union the bishop fathered a daughter who was given the name Domingas Pinto.[20] The archdeacon, Manuel do Rosário Pinto, was named to a variety of ecclesiastical offices, including visitor to the rural parishes in 1725 and visitor general for the whole diocese in 1728. In his spare time, however, he was working on his life's greatest and most ambitious work: a history of the island of São Tomé. It began with the Portuguese discovery of the island in 1471 and continued through the death of Bishop João de Sahagum in 1730 and the arrival of Governor Lopo de Souza Coutinho in 1731.[21]

Curiously for a history written by a descendant of slaves, it contained no commentary on the slave trade. It barely mentioned slavery at all, except to discuss the major slave rebellions in the island's history. Pinto showed little sympathy for rebellious slaves. His description of the Amador rebellion of 1595 shows clearly that he identified with the civil authorities. In describing one battle, he wrote, "We were afraid as our army caught sight of the enemy, but as God was on our side, we took courage. Our army marched into battle; the enemy soon entered the fight." Discussing the aftermath of the rebellion, he commented, "At the conclusion of these events there was sorrow because seventy-odd sugar mills had been burned. There were not enough lashes that could be meted out to the guilty to compensate for the loss. And with this, the island rested quiet and secure, there remaining in use twenty-four or twenty-five sugar mills."[22]

Pinto struck a similar tone in describing the 1709 slave rebellion that he himself had witnessed. The rebellious slaves "caused great damage to their masters and to their masters' estates, robbing some persons of gold, silver, and clothes." Describing the fate of the rebels, he wrote that their leaders "fled in a canoe by sea with the stolen goods that they had taken; and wishing to avoid capture, they voluntarily drowned themselves. And the rest who remained alive were brought as prisoners to the city and were carried before the governor, who commanded that they be returned to their masters on condition that they should be quickly sold to Brazil."[23] Pinto, who was a member of the college of deacons when the rebellion broke out, seems to imply that the rebellious slaves had received their just punishment.

During the time when the *Diligent* was anchored in the harbor at São Tomé, Archdeacon Pinto was working on the final chapters of his *History of the Island of São Tomé*. Each time he stepped out of the cathedral and looked at the ships in the harbor between January 4 and January 10, 1732, he would have seen the *Diligent*, with its load of slaves, rocking gently in the waves. Perhaps, in passing the cathedral, Robert Durand saw a seventy-six-year-old black priest, his body bent and his hair white, standing in the doorway and gazing over the harbor. Durand could not have known or even suspected that this man was writing the greatest work of scholarship that São Tomé would produce in the entire eighteenth century.

PART 10

The
Middle Passage

33

THE SOUND OF ACCORDION music flooded the deck of the *Diligent*. It was six o'clock in the evening, and the 248 remaining African captives were all on deck. They had just finished their evening meal, and now it was time for exercise. At the front of the ship, some of the African men were standing on the forecastle while the others found places among the cannons, the pumps, and the longboat on the main deck. The men were shackled two by two, the right foot of one man shackled to the left foot of his partner, an arrangement that made walking awkward and sometimes painful. At the rear of the ship behind the barricade, the women were on the quarterdeck. They were not shackled, and they moved around freely.

We can scarcely imagine how the high-pitched screeches and shrieks of the accordion sounded to the ears of the African captives. Music in the Whydah/Dahomey region was principally vocal music accompanied by drums, rattles, and gongs. The instrumental music came primarily from two-toned trumpets made from elephants' tusks that were used to announce the presence of royalty, and from three-holed flutes made from iron or reeds that were held like a clarinet.[1] Although the accordion must have sounded shrill to the Africans, it could have been worse; many English ships used bagpipes. Some slaving captains, aware of the clash of musical tastes, advised their fellow slavers to purchase musical instruments from the captives' home regions before departing from Africa.[2]

Nevertheless, accordion players had become standard accoutrements on French slave ships. The reason was explained in Savary des Bruslons's

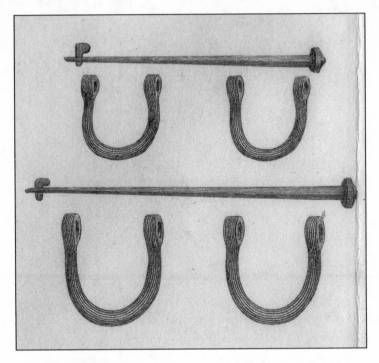

Figure 33.1   Slave irons that bound the right leg of one captive to the left leg of another.

Dictionnaire universel de commerce, published in 1723. Savary warned that slaves were often seized by sadness and despair because of their love for their homeland. Sadness, he wrote, makes them vulnerable to the diseases that kill a great many captives during the middle passage, and despair leads many of them to attempt suicide. The secret for battling both sadness and despair, and keeping the captives alive until the ship landed in the New World, Savary believed, was to play musical instruments such as the hurdy-gurdy or the accordion.[3] The Billy brothers had taken this advice seriously, paying 195 livres in salary to Noël Magré, the accordion player. Given that a prime slave could sell for over nine hundred livres in Martinique, they had reasoned that the accordion player would more than earn his salary if his music saved even one captive.

The immediate purpose of the music, however, was to animate the evening exercise session in which the slaves were ordered to dance to maintain their health. The exercise partially compensated for the physical immobility caused by the crowding below decks, and some Frenchmen even believed that it helped prevent scurvy.[4] The problem for the men on the main deck and forecastle is that they were shackled two by two with rigid slave irons, making dancing impossible. Instead, they swayed to the music while crew members prodded the shackled partners to jump up and down in unison. Dancing on the decks of the small ship was not easy in any event, given the constant pitching and rolling of the vessel. Even standing still on a moving ship was a dynamic exercise as muscles tightened and relaxed to compensate for the movement.[5] The Africans could easily lose their balance if the ship pitched suddenly in the middle of a jump. Those who stood about or moved listlessly to the music were prodded or lashed with the short whip.

The women on the quarterdeck, in contrast, were unshackled because crew members believed there was little chance that they would stage a rebellion. Naked under the setting tropical sun, some of the women moved listlessly with signs of depression showing on their faces and in their movements. Crew members shouted at them or prodded them to move faster and to dance with kicks and leaps. If the prodding didn't work, they used the short whip or the lash. Other women, wanting to take full advantage of every moment of temporary freedom, moved their limbs gracefully in an effort to forestall the cramps that would build up in their muscles during the long night of imprisonment below the deck, or they writhed and twisted their bodies to give expression to their pain. In their current state of captivity, the dance gave them a rare form of personal expression.[6] As the women moved to the music, some of the sailors pointed, leered, and jeered.

In the eighteenth century, the practice of "dancing the slaves" was a common, though not universal, feature of the middle passage. As a combination of drill and performance, forced movement and self-expression, slave dances were open to a variety of interpretations. The French slave trader Jean Barbot described them as "full of jollity and good humor," and the captain of the Danish slave ship *Fredensborg* wrote in his logbook that "the female slaves enjoyed dancing their Negro dances on the quarterdeck." A more chilling description was provided in 1789 by the British slave-ship surgeon James Arnold. "It was usual to make them dance in order that they might exercise their limbs and preserve their health," he wrote. "This was done by means of a Cat of Nine Tails with which they were driven about one

298 | THE DILIGENT

among the other, one of their country drums beating at the same time. On these occasions they were compelled to sing, the Cat being brandished over them for that purpose. It was the business of the chief mate to dance the men, and of [myself] and the second mate to dance the women. The men could only jump up and rattle their chains, but the women . . . were driven among one another."[7] On the *Diligent*, the accordion music created a festive-sounding atmosphere, but the results were scarcely any different.

Like the music, the dancing revealed a clash of cultural tastes. European crew members did not understand the athletic dance moves that were popular among Africans. This misunderstanding was highlighted by a Dutch visitor to King Agaja's court in Dahomey who recounted that after dinner the king danced by "jumping about in the strange manner of this land." The Dutchmen, in turn, entertained King Agaja with a French minuet, followed by a Polish one.[8] One can only wonder what the king thought of the minuets. On board the *Diligent*, however, the athleticism that went into some of the African dance moves was exactly what the crew wanted to see because physical exercise was the purpose of the whole event. Despite the festive music, the joyless dance was the shipboard equivalent of exercise in a prison yard.

When the song he was playing on the forecastle of the *Diligent* came to an end, Noël Magré had to decide what to play next. Robert Durand did not record what he played, but it is likely that his repertory included "The Short Straw," a popular French sea song about a ship that had run out of food. According to the song, the crew members must draw straws to determine which one of them will be eaten by the others. Hearing the tune, the sailors recall the words.

> They must draw the short straw,
> To decide who will be eaten.
> The mate who distributes the straws
> Discovers that the shortest remains.
> He cries, "Oh Virgin Mary,
> It is I who will be eaten."[9]

The Africans heard only the tune, but if they had heard the words, they might have taken them as proof certain that the rumors of white cannibalism were true.

In an atmosphere charged with brutality and inhumanity, accusations of cannibalism were manifestations of the animosity that the African captives felt for their European jailers. By conjuring up images of white cannibalism, the Africans were saying, in effect, that Europeans did not abide by the normal rules of civilized societies. They viewed their European jailers as witches and not ordinary humans. Nor were Africans the only ones to spread stories about white cannibalism. Father Labat believed that English, Dutch, and Portuguese slave traders had spread the word that the French were cannibals. They did it, Labat claimed, because they were jealous of French commercial success.[10]

There were also rumors circulating among white slave traders about a grisly incident that took place in 1724 on an English slave ship commanded by Captain John Harding. Believing that the slaves onboard his ship were plotting a revolt, Harding ordered the arrest of the man whom he believed to be the ringleader. In front of the other captives, the man's throat was slit and his heart and liver were cut out. Then Captain Harding ordered the bloody heart and liver to be cut into three hundred pieces, and he forced each of the horrified captives to eat a piece by threatening to do the same thing to them if they refused. The experience so traumatized and disgusted the captives that many of them refused all food after that and gradually starved to death.[11]

Aware of the implicit and sometimes explicit accusations of white cannibalism, Europeans often retaliated with countercharges that some of the African captives on their slave ships were probably cannibals themselves. William Snelgrave accused King Agaja's Dahomian soldiers (but not King Agaja) of practicing cannibalism, though he admitted that he had no proof, and Father Labat, who had never been to Africa, made wild charges that entire countries in Africa maintained butcher shops that sold human flesh.[12]

The mutual images of cannibalism that were commonplace on slave ships mirrored the kinds of accusations that had long been exchanged between notables and peasants in France. In 1580 rebellious French peasants had frightened the burghers of Romans by marching through the streets announcing, "Before three days are out, Christian flesh will be selling at six deniers a pound." After the rebellion was crushed, the victors reportedly butchered the peasants "like pigs" and congratulated themselves on eating the poor villagers before they themselves were eaten. Throughout the French wars of religion in the sixteenth century, there were stories of eating hearts and livers and of children and adults cooked for cannibal feasts. During the French Revolution, new accusations of cannibalism erupted, and the Revolutionary Committee of Nantes was accused of holding cannibalistic rituals in which they drink from cups filled with human blood. To the crew of the *Diligent*, the implicit accusations of white cannibalism had a deep resonance within France itself.[13]

The *Diligent* had been transformed into a floating prison, and the crew members did double duty as prison guards and sailors. As in any prison where the inmates vastly outnumbered the guards, the captain tried to use a combination of punishments and rewards in order to keep the captive population under control. On the third day out of Jakin he executed a man for trying to bite his fellow prisoners, but later in the voyage he distributed tobacco to the captives from his own personal stock.[14] In this regard, he was following a strategy that had earlier been outlined by Jean Barbot. In his advice to slave traders, Barbot urged butchering mutinous slaves alive, but in the very next paragraph he recommended giving the slaves occasional gifts of tobacco and brandy. "Above all, wrote Barbot, "make plenty of friendly gestures toward them and often jest with them."[15] But whether the carrot or the stick was used to achieve it, the goal was always the same.

Captain Mary was under strict orders from his employers to deliver his human cargo to Martinique alive and healthy enough to fetch high prices at sale. This meant sufficient food, water, and exercise for all concerned, along with rudimentary hygienic measures to keep epidemics from breaking out on board. The crew members were especially afraid of epidemics because they knew that they were vulnerable to the same diseases that plagued the Africans. The professional reputations of the officers depended on getting their captives across the ocean alive, and captains who experienced high death rates felt compelled to defend themselves by arguing that they were not at fault. Des Marchais, who was full of advice on measures that slave traders should take in order to preserve the health of their human cargoes, lost over half of his captives to disease during his 1725 crossing. Writing about that voyage, Father Labat defended Marchais's reputation by claiming, "Despite the care that that Chevalier Des Marchais gave unceasingly to avoid that catastrophe, he couldn't escape losing a great many blacks."[16] Even amid the death and brutality of the slaving business, professional reputations had to be protected.

Ordinary crew members, however, had no such incentives. Like the captives, they ate bad food and slept in cramped quarters. So crowded were their quarters in the bow of the ship that many were forced to sleep on deck or even in the longboat. The crew members were the ones who had close physical contact with the captives in the daily battle for control that took place above and below the decks. Such a situation often produced hostility on the part of the crew members, who carried all of the prejudices of their time and were convinced that their African captives would slit their throats in an instant if they got the chance. That latent hostility of the crew members explains why ship owners gave repeated instructions that ordinary sailors were never to strike the slaves.[17] Instead, sailors were ordered to report any problems they had with the slaves to the officers, who would decide on the appropriate punishments. Such rules were undoubtedly honored more in the breach than in the application, but they nevertheless reflected the view of the ship owners that ordinary sailors were brutish fellows who could not be trusted to maintain control in a calculated manner.

They key to getting a cargo of slaves across the Atlantic with a minimum loss of life, slaving captains agreed, was to make the crossing as quickly as possible. Because São Tomé was located on the equator, Captain Mary had been worried about getting becalmed in the equatorial doldrums. A former employee of the Nantes outfitter Montaudoin, he had heard stories about Montaudoin's ship the *Maréchal d'Estrées*, which fell becalmed near the equator and spent fourteen weeks on the middle passage instead of the expected ten. The ship ran out of food and 202 out of 525 captives died, for a mortality rate of 38 percent.[18] But the *Diligent* was lucky. Although the winds near the equator were light and variable, the ship had been able to drop down to nearly three degrees south latitude with the aid of a south-flowing current.

The *Diligent* was bound for the French island of Martinique. Having signed a subcontracting agreement with the Company of the Indies, it was legally bound to deliver its slaves to one of France's Caribbean colonies. The most popular destination for French slave ships in 1732 was Saint Domingue, which received two-thirds of all slaves carried on French ships. Thirty percent went to Martinique.[19] Pierre Mary had experience in both places, as did Robert Durand, but the Billy brothers had chosen Martinique because all of the direct trade from Vannes had gone there and Saint Domingue was unfamiliar to them.

The standard strategy for crossing the Atlantic from São Tomé to Martinique called for dropping down to three and a half degrees south of the equator to catch the southeast trade winds that would carry them across the Atlantic. Under normal circumstances they should have been able to make the crossing in fifty days.[20] But the winds they were encountering on this voyage were coming from the south-southwest, impeding their westward progress. Unlike ships with triangular sails, square-riggers such as the *Diligent* were not very good at sailing against the wind, and eighty degrees from windward was as close as they could get. Bracing the sails to go as close to the wind as possible, the *Diligent* was able to hold a westward course at between two and three degrees south latitude despite the southwest winds.[21] The ship was helped somewhat by the west-flowing south equatorial current, but progress was nevertheless slower than expected.

It was not until January 31—three weeks out from São Tomé—that the winds turned around and began to blow from the southeast. These were the southeast trade winds that they had been looking for. Now they could begin to make better time. With steady winds, the ship could go for days with almost no changes in the set of the sails. From January 20 to January 29 the wind had blown steadily from the south-southwest, and from January 31 to February 11 it would blow from the southeast. With few adjustments to be made to the rigging, the crew members busied themselves with guarding and managing the African captives.

Now recovered from his illness, Robert Durand carefully recorded the ship's position, the weather, and any unusual events in his journal. Here is how he described the last day of January, when he first recorded southeast winds, and the beginning of February:

Thursday, January 31. Lat. 2° 47″ S. Long. 9° 56″. Since yesterday noon the winds from the S. and SSE. Pretty seas. We steered to W1 1/4 NW. Under full sail.

Friday, February 1. Lat. 2° 39″ S. Long. 8° 11″. Since yesterday the winds from the SSE and SE. The sea pretty. Under full sail. Studding sails high and low. We steered NW. In the morning we sighted a ship behind us following the same route and gaining on us.

Saturday, February 2. Lat. 2° 13″ S. Long. 5° 56″. Since yesterday noon the winds from the SE. The sea pretty. Under full sail. We steered

W $^1/_3$ NW. At two o'clock in the afternoon the ship we had spotted in the morning came alongside to windward. They said that they had left São Tomé one day after us. Good sailing ship and interloper with 22 cannons going to Europe. Because they had caught a lot of fish, they lowered their skiff and rowed over to our ship to get some salt. Mr. Mary wrote a letter to send to France with that ship. This morning we spotted it ahead of us.

Curiously, Durand mentioned the African captives only twice during the entire sixty-six days of the middle passage, and then only to record deaths. One of the deaths was recorded with nothing more than a skull and crossbones drawn in the margin of the page. Neither did he record any of his own thoughts or feelings about being on officer on such a ship. Was he trying to pretend that this was an ordinary voyage of an ordinary merchant ship? Had the daily routines of a slave ship become so familiar to him that he felt them hardly worth recording? Was he in denial? Was he becoming hardened? The English slaving captain John Newton would note later in the century that participation in the slave trade "gradually brings a numbness upon the heart, and renders most of those who are engaged in it too indifferent to the sufferings of their fellow creatures."[22] Was that why Robert Durand didn't write about conditions onboard the *Diligent*?

In any case, we will have to depend on other documents from the period to give us hints about how life was most likely lived on this floating prison. Historians have uncovered records of 17,108 slaving voyages during the eighteenth century, but they have found only a handful of brief accounts of daily life on eighteenth-century slave ships. Even former slaves who later wrote accounts of their captivity gave few details of the middle passage.[23] It seems to have been an experience so awful that perpetrators and victims alike were inclined to suppress it or gloss over it. What emerges from the surviving accounts (many of them written by slaving captains trying to justify the slave trade or by abolitionists trying to stir up the public against it) is a general agreement on how slaves should ideally be treated in order to deliver them alive to the New World and then the wide variations in actual practices aboard different ships. The hierarchical command structure on ships meant that much depended upon the will, personality, competence, and sanity of the captain.

By all appearances, Captain Mary was certainly sane, at least in comparison to his fellow captain Jean Bonneau, whose mad follies he would encounter in Martinique. None of Mary's crew—not even those who would later testify against him at his trial in Vannes—ever accused him of cruel or sadistic behavior toward them. Mary was corrupt, but in a calculating sort of way that sought to maximize his personal profits. He could be hard or he could be kind, but he was unlikely to engage in any kind of behavior that would undermine the order of the ship or the profits of the voyage. Each African captive was worth up to a thousand livres if delivered to Martinique in healthy condition. Pierre Mary was well aware of that figure because twenty-six of the captives onboard the *Diligent* were his own personal property. Given these considerations, we can speculate that his ship probably ran pretty much according to its owners' instructions.

34

*T*HE EVENING DANCE PERIOD over, the Africans were ordered to return to the slave deck for the night. First carpenter Joseph Colinbert and first surgeon Devigne had just finished inspecting the slave quarters to make sure that nobody had hidden a potential tool or weapon, and they gave the signal that all was in order. After the captives had descended to the lower deck amid shouts, shoves, and blows from the crew, they twisted and maneuvered as well as they could (given the confines of their irons) to slip into the tiny spaces on or below the platforms where they were to spend the night. Sometimes fights broke out as captives struggled for the best spots.[1] Sleeping in such a space was difficult. The captives had to lie on their side on the hard planks because there wasn't even enough space to lie on their back or stomach. The British called such packing "spooning" because it resembled the stacking of spoons. The rocking and pitching of the ship made people periodically slide or tumble into one another.

The discomfort of lying in awkward positions on the rough boards of the horribly overcrowded lower deck was matched or exceeded by the problems from the heat and lack of air. The only air in the lower deck went through hatches in the main deck. Because the *Diligent* had been built as a grain ship, its hatches were smaller than those on ships built for carrying slaves, and its lower deck was stifling. The heat that built up under the equatorial sun was oppressive, and the deck was so tightly packed that the captives sucked the oxygen out of the air at night. The French slave

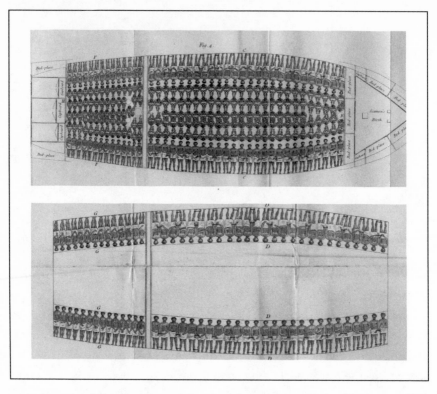

Figure 34.1   These drawings of the slave ship *Vigilante* from Nantes show the arrangement of the captives on the slave deck and the platforms.

trader Jean Barbot noted that sometimes the heat and lack of oxygen on the lower decks of slave ships were so excessive that "the surgeons would faint away and the candles would not burn."[2]

If the captives needed to relieve themselves during the night, they were supposed to ask the sentinels to open the hatch and let them come up on deck to use the toilets. Some ships placed tubs on the slave deck that were coated on the inside with tar and filled with about six inches of seawater. They were supposed to be emptied twice during the night. Given the severely overcrowded conditions on the slave deck, getting to the tubs or the stairway was a major challenge. The man needing relief and his partner-in-irons had to move together, frequently tripping over or stumbling into their fellow captives in the darkness. Such accidents gave rise to shouts and quarrels. Prevented by the dense mass of bodies from making progress,

Figure 34.2   Slaves on the deck during the day.

some captives just gave up and relieved themselves where they lay, bringing shouts of protest from their near neighbors.[3] Given the diarrhea and
vomiting that afflicted many of the captives, it was impossible to avoid a
buildup of filth during the night.

Silence was supposed to be the order of the night, but it was never total.
There were the groans of the sick, the shouts of the angry, the weeping of
the depressed, and the hysterical laughter of those who were losing their
emotional equilibrium. When disputes arose, there were slave "quartermasters" who were supposed to order everybody to be quiet and report
the dispute to the captain the next morning. Crew members were afraid to
enter the slave deck at night lest they be taken hostage. Even the ship itself
added to the noise by its constant creaking as the individual timbers that
made up the hull slid back and forth against one another.[4] Because the
Diligent was an aging ship, the creaking of the timbers was increasing, as
was the leaking of the hull. The pumps were worked regularly to keep the
hold relatively dry. When the slaves were locked below, the crew washed
down the main deck, quarterdeck, and forecastle. After the cleaning, they
inspected the decks to make sure that nobody had left a tool or utensil of
any kind lying around that a slave might use as a weapon.

Around nine o'clock in the morning, after the morning dew had dried from the decks, the men were brought up on the main deck and forecastle two at a time. The carpenter and another officer stood at the hatchway to check their shackles. This was done partly to make sure nothing had been cut or opened during the night, but also to remind the captives that the crew was ever vigilant. On the decks the Africans could relieve themselves in the makeshift toilets and wash themselves with seawater.

Around ten o'clock they were served their first meal. The souplike gruel made of fava beans, millet, peas, or manioc flour was served in buckets, with ten persons squatting around one bucket and eating with a wooden spoon. Each person got one quart of gruel for each meal.[5] Prior to their captivity, the Africans had been used to eating meals that contained generous amounts of meat and fish cooked in a sauce made from palm oil and sea- soned with peppers. They had also eaten a lot of fruit, especially oranges and lemons. Once they became enslaved, all of that changed. The English slave ship surgeon T. Aubrey, writing in 1729, complained that on English ships the Africans were "scarcely allowed two spoonfuls of oil amongst a whole mess, which serves ten, and then for peppers they must shift with a very small quantity." As a result, the Africans found the food tasteless and disgust- ing. Those who refused to eat were "abused by sailors, who beat and kick them to that degree that sometimes they never recover." Aubrey recom- mended that palm oil and peppers be distributed at each meal so that each African could season the gruel as much as he or she liked. Similarly, Des Marchais noted that Africans found fava beans cooked only with water and salt to be disgusting and indigestible. He urged each slave ship to carry five or six barrels of lard to flavor the beans.[6]

Even if the food supply was adequate, getting it was a daily struggle. With ten people sharing each bucket of food, the strong took more than their al- lotted share and the weak got less. People who lost their wooden spoons were often refused new ones. They just had to eat with their hands.[7]

Along with the meal, each African was given water to drink. A second drink of water came at noon, and a third came with the evening meal. A rule of thumb on French slave ships was to load one *barrique* (sixty gallons) per captive, which would allow three quarts per captive per day for an eighty-day voyage. If one quart of water went into the soup each day, that left nearly two quarts for drinking.[8] We don't know how much water the

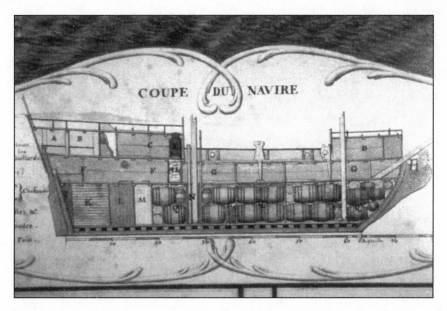

Figure 34.3   Cutaway view of a slave ship showing food and water storage.

Diligent actually loaded in Principe and São Tomé, but we do know that another French ship, the *Jeannette*, loaded 268 *barriques* of water for 246 captives and a crew of nineteen. That came to slightly more than one *barrique* of water per person.[9]

If the rule of one *barrique* per captive was actually followed on most French slave ships, then their water ration would have been significantly higher than that on the slave ships of other nations. The English surgeon T. Aubrey noted in 1729 that on some English ships slaves were given only a spoonful of water with each meal. The problem was not lack of water, but a theory current among some ship's doctors that drinking too much water caused diarrhea. But later in the century a survey of seven Liverpool slave ships showed that they carried two quarts of water per person per day.[10] The Danish doctor Paul Erdman Isert reported that captives on Danish slave ships received only twenty-four ounces (three English pints) of water per day, whereas he believed that sixty-four ounces were necessary in the tropical heat.[11] Portuguese ships were required by law to carry three pints per person per day, which was only half the amount that had been required prior to 1684.[12] If the *Diligent* actually loaded one *barrique* of water per captive, then each one would have received the sixty-four ounces a day that Isert recommended.

Because crew members walked among the slaves to serve food, all available hands were on alert at mealtimes in case a revolt broke out. Captain Mary had no doubt heard the story of the English ship *Ferrers Galley*. The captain, Francis Messervy, used to walk among the captives at mealtime and personally put palm oil and peppers into the buckets of rice. He did this thinking that he was ingratiating himself to the captives, but in the process he forgot that a major objective of any rebellion was to seize or kill the captain. One day as he passed with oil and peppers among the men eating on the forecastle, they picked up their buckets on a prearranged signal and hit him over the head until he was dead. This was the opening gambit in a rebellion that resulted in the death of eighty slaves.[13]

After the meal came the morning session of dancing and exercise. Then the captives were put to work scraping the slave deck clean under the supervision of crew members. Even if the night buckets had been emptied twice during the night, as they were supposed to have been, the stench must have been unimaginable in the almost airless compartments. The disagreeable odors affirmed the opinion stated by Sir Dalby Thomas in 1706. "Your captains and mates must neither have dainty fingers nor dainty noses," he wrote. "It's a filthy voyage as well as laborious."[14] After the deck was cleaned, it was "perfumed" by passing through the compartments with a vinegar-soaked sponge.

Two or three times a week the slaves were put to work scrubbing down the slave deck with water. One group of them worked hauling as many as three hundred buckets of seawater up by pulleys, while another group washed down the lower deck. Because the water ran down into the hold through the cracks in the lower deck, a third group of slaves manned the pumps to keep the hold as dry as possible. In all of these tasks, they were supposed to sing while they worked. After the lower deck was washed, it also was perfumed. Captives passed through the compartments with buckets of vinegar into which had been plunged a red-hot cannonball or red-hot bullets. The thick and penetrating odor of the vinegar was supposed to chase the stale air out of the slave quarters. After the "perfuming," the deck was scrubbed with cold vinegar.[15]

Such cleaning routines, while considered standard practice on well-run slave ships, were not always honored. Jean Barbot, who had been involved in both French and English slaving expeditions, noted that "some French and English ships in these voyages for slaves are slovenly, foul, and stinking, according to the temper and the want of skill of the commanders." Portuguese ships, he believed, did not even come up to the standards of English and French vessels.[16] Similarly, the Dutchman William Bosman bragged that Dutch slave ships were "for the most part neat and clean," whereas those of the French, English, and Portuguese "are always foul and stinking."[17]

At noon, when the cleanup was finished, the Africans were given their second drink of water, after which they were allowed to relax on deck. At about five in the evening it was time for their second meal of the day. Again, fava beans made up the essential diet, but the monotony was broken by the addition of cassava, peas, and plantains purchased in Principe and São Tomé. After the evening meal, there was a second session of dancing. Then, after the officers had inspected the slave deck for any weapons, nails, or pieces of metal that a slave might have hidden, the captives were ordered to return below deck and their irons were checked for the night.

Certain small changes broke the monotony of the daily routine. Each captive was bathed twice a week if time and weather permitted. At bath time, each African was placed in a tub and several bucketfuls of cold seawater were poured on his or her head. Such a practice might have felt refreshing on hot days, but captives who were sick with fever and chills sometimes tried to refuse the bath. They were then forced into the tub with "blows and kicks and Cats."[18] Other slaves were put to work hauling up the buckets of water for the baths. Every two or three weeks the captives had their beards, heads, underarms, and pubic hair shaved to prevent lice, and their fingernails and toenails were trimmed. On special occasions they were given small amounts of brandy, and Captain Mary would sometimes distribute Brazilian tobacco from the personal supply that he had obtained in Jakin. Many of the captives were used to smoking from childhood, and so the tobacco was considered a treat.[19]

Women followed a similar daily schedule, but with certain modifications. For one thing, they were not put in irons because the slaving captains believed that they lacked the physical strength to overpower the crew members. They were not allowed on the main deck or forecastle to mingle with the men; rather, they ate, danced, and washed on the quarterdeck, separated from the men by the barricade. To get from the slave deck

to the quarterdeck, they climbed a staircase that went through the officers' quarters. Because of the easy access between the women's quarters
and the officers' quarters, the women were often put to work cleaning the
officers' quarters or doing other work. Brought naked onto the ship, some
women would remain in a squatting position all day long to preserve
their modesty.[20] If they were lucky, they would be given a quarter of an
aune of cloth with which to fashion loincloths and perhaps another small
piece of cloth to use as a tampon during menstruation.

Given the officers' easy access to the women's compartment, the women
were easy prey for sexual advances. The French documents of the period
are almost completely silent on this subject, but they contain a couple of
clues worth noting. Outfitters of French slave ships instructed their officers
that ordinary sailors should not be allowed to enter the women's quarters
of the slave deck. If they needed access to the sail lockers or did cleaning
and repairing in the women's prison, they were to do it during the day
when the women were on the quarterdeck. If a sailor found it necessary to
enter the women's quarters at night, he was supposed to take an officer
with him.[21]

Although there is no way of knowing if the policy was actually enforced,
its very existence carries two implications. First it implies a belief among officers—probably based on experience—that sailors would rape the women
if given a chance. The other implication is that the policy gave officers free
access to the women's quarters away from the prying eyes of their crew. The
owners of the La Rochelle ship the *Bonne Société* counseled their captain to
"prevent encounters of the whites with the women slaves because it often
leads to unfortunate results." Nevertheless, the normal practice was probably
closer to that described by the New Rochelle slave trader Proa, who wrote
in his memoirs that each officer chose a female slave to serve him "at the
table and in bed." The captain on the Nantes ship the *Jeannette* went even
further when he passed the women around to his crew "given the custom
among them that each one should have a woman."[22]

There is only one known case of a rape on a French slave ship that got officially reported in the eighteenth century. The captain's report provides a
rare window into an otherwise unspoken sphere of shipboard crime. According to the report, Second Captain Philippe Liot "mistreated a very
pretty Negress, broke two of her teeth, and put her in such a state of languish

that she could only be sold for a very low price at Saint Domingue, where she died two weeks later. Not content, the said Philippe Liot pushed his brutality to the point of violating a little slave girl of eight to ten years, whose mouth he closed to prevent her from screaming. This he did on three nights and put her in a deathly state. This slave girl finally admitted that the said Philippe Liot had descended into the hold and had forced her by putting his hand over her mouth to prevent her from screaming, and that he had done this for three nights. This mistreatment and violence did so much damage to the girl that she was sold in Saint Domingue for only 800 livres instead of the 1,800 she would have been worth."[23] In this case the incident was reported because it had reduced the profitability of the voyage. We will never know how many similar incidents went unreported.

A more general picture of the treatment of women on eighteenth-century slave ships was provided by the English slaving captain John Newton, who noted later in his life, "When I was in the trade I knew several commanders of African ships who were prudent, respectable men, and who maintained a proper discipline and regularity in their vessels; but there were too many of a different character. In some ships, perhaps in most, the license allowed in this particular was almost unlimited." Newton later elaborated by describing what the sailors did when women and girls were first brought naked and frightened aboard ship. "In imagination," he wrote, "the prey is divided upon the spot, and only reserved until opportunity offers. Where resistance or refusal would be utterly vain, even the solicitation of consent is seldom thought of."[24] Newton's fellow Englishman Alexander Falconbridge had a somewhat different take on the issue. He noted that on board some English ships the sailors were allowed to have intercourse with "such of the black women whose consent they can procure." The officers, on the other hand, were permitted "to indulge their passions among them at pleasure, and sometimes are guilty of such brutal excesses as disgrace human nature."[25]

The daily routines of the middle passage—eating meals, washing, and dancing on the decks—could be followed only during good weather. On rainy days the grates of the hatches were covered with canvas to keep out the water, rendering the interior stifling. Sometimes when the weather was continually bad, the captives were not allowed on deck for weeks at a time. Under such circumstances the lower deck did not get cleaned, and there were only feeble attempts to deodorize it by passing through with sponges that had been dipped in vinegar. The smell must have been unimaginable. The *Diligent* was lucky to have only four days of rain and encounter only seven squalls during the entire sixty-six-day middle passage. On most days, the hatches were uncovered and the captives were allowed on deck.

Even with good weather, the standard routines of food, exercise, and cleaning were not followed by all slaving captains. Jean Barbot noted that "some commanders, of a morose peevish temper are perpetually beating and curbing the slaves even without the least offense, and will not suffer any upon deck but when unavoidable necessity to ease themselves does require."[26] Barbot urged such captains to consider the humanity of the captives; if that argument didn't move them, he said, they should consider the profits of their ship's owners. Another witness of the period, Father Laurent de Lucques, traveled on a Portuguese slave ship with 742 slaves who were apparently kept below deck for the entire voyage. "The blacks were lying like animals amid dirt and filth," he wrote. "Someone cried on one side; someone on the other. There were some who cried and lamented, others laughed. In sum, all was confusion. The space was so restricted for the multitude of blacks that it was almost impossible for them to change places. The stench was intolerable. Sleep was brief because they could barely close their eyes. Because of the multitude of people, it was almost impossible for them to bring food to their mouths, and what little food there was proved to be badly prepared. I don't know if we should characterize that ship as hell or purgatory." Father de Lucques decided to characterize the middle passage as "purgatory" because it was a temporary condition. Hell, apparently, would begin for the slaves after the ship reached Brazil.[27]

Now that they were on the high seas, the crew of the *Diligent* became less strict about shackling the men. Many slaving captains believed that the captives were unlikely to rebel on high sea because they would be unable to sail the ship back to land if the rebellion succeeded. Even if the rebellious slaves kept some crew members alive to sail the ship, they could not trust them to actually sail to their desired destination. Although there were many revolts on high sea, the captains believed that they usually took place on ships whose crews had been decimated by disease, were negligent, or were drunk. In reference to slave ships on high sea, Thomas Phillips wrote, "I have never heard that they mutinied in any ships of consequence that had a good number of men and the least care." But John Atkins disagreed, observing, "When we are slaved and out to sea, it is commonly imagined that the Negroes' ignorance of navigation will always be a safeguard, yet as many of them think themselves bought to eat, and more, that death will send them to their own country, there has not been wanting examples of rising and killing a ship's company distant from land."[28] Modern statistical studies show that about 30 percent of shipboard rebellions took place on high sea, a higher percentage than either Phillips or Atkins imagined.[29]

There was a wide divergence among slaving captains on the issue of shackling their captives during the middle passage. Captains such as William Snelgrave, Thomas Phillips, and Jean Barbot claimed that they removed all shackles from the captives once the ship was on high sea. Others, such as John Newton and Alexander Falconbridge, kept their captives in chains throughout the voyage.[30] Perhaps the most common practice among slaving captains, however, was to watch the captives closely and reward the ones who seemed most cooperative by removing their shackles.[31] Such a strategy created powerful incentives for captives to comply with the ship's regulations and daily routines. Those slaves who were not suicidal knew that they depended on the crew to get them safely across the ocean. Listening to the timbers groan and creak during the long nights, they were constantly reminded that nothing but the thin wooden hull separated them from the sharks.

Gradually, a rudimentary form of social organization developed on the ship, based on a chain of command that ran from the captain to the youngest captive. Several of the most compliant Africans had been appointed "quartermasters," or overseers of the men's and women's quarters. Their job was to settle quarrels that arose among the captives, organize the captives into groups of ten for eating, and supervise the work parties that cleaned and washed the lower deck. They were also to report any discussion of rebellion among the slaves. In return for performing those tasks, they received some extra freedom, perhaps some clothes, and occasional gifts of brandy and tobacco. Most of the captives began to fall in line with the ship's routines because they knew that cooperation was the best way to assure themselves of adequate food, fresh water, and perhaps even freedom from their shackles. After a few weeks at sea, the daily routine became almost automatic as each captive learned where to go at mealtime, where and when to wash or bathe, when to dance, and which tasks to carry out when cleaning the ship.

Below the decks at night there reigned a hidden and less formal social organization that had been created by the leaders who tried to organize rebellions. Now, however, the hope that such an action could be accomplished had faded. If the crew had been decimated by illness or if the sentinels had gotten sloppy, perhaps hopes of rebellion might have revived. As neither of these circumstances had come about, there was most likely a gradual shift in the nature and structure of the informal networks. The firebrands of rebellion gradually lost their followings, and a more moderate leadership emerged that focused on such issues as helping the sick, encouraging the depressed, mediating disputes, and performing nighttime funeral ceremonies.

35

$\mathcal{O}$N February 28 a slave died. Robert Durand did not record the cause, but five days later, when another slave died, he did: scurvy. The scurvy frightened Captain Mary because it was a major killer of both slaves and crew on the middle passage. The previous year the Dutch ship *Beekesteyn* had lost 150 slaves to the disease. What made it so frightening was that nobody knew what caused it or how to cure it. Doctor Aubrey's 1729 manual for surgeons on English slave ships did not contain any discussion of the causes and cures for scurvy. In the absence of authoritative medical opinion, all kinds of theories abounded. Des Marchais believed that it was caused by bad water. Father Labat believed that it could be prevented by rubbing palm oil on the skin of the captives. Other captains believed that dancing prevented the disease.[1] It would not be until 1754 that Dr. James Lind identified the value of oranges, lemons, and limes in preventing scurvy.

Captain Mary had been lucky. Since the ship left São Tomé on January 10, only two slaves had died. The total number of deaths among captives since leaving Jakin was now nine, which came to less than 4 percent of the human cargo. By the standards of slave ships, they were doing remarkably well. The judge and consuls of Nantes estimated in January 1732 that the death rate on slaving voyages from Nantes was 20 percent, and so Captain Mary's toll was only one-fifth of the average. Modern statistical data show that for the Atlantic slave trade as a whole during the first quarter of the eighteenth century, the death rate was just over 16 percent.[2]

Had Captain Mary been working for the Company of the Indies, he would have earned a fat bonus. When the company had reclaimed its monopoly on the slave trade in 1723, it gave its captains a bonus of six livres per slave if they had less than 5 percent mortality, three livres for less than 10 percent, two livres for less than 15 percent, and one livre for less than 20 percent.[3] The message was clearly that a 20 percent death rate was worthy of a bonus, albeit a small one. With a slave death rate of 4 percent, Captain Mary would have been eligible for the Company of the Indies's highest bonus. The death rate of his crew, in contrast, was over 10 percent, but there were no bonuses given for crew survival. The deaths of crew members saved the owners money because the deceased wouldn't have to be paid for months when they didn't work.

Captain Mary had good reason to believe that the Billy brothers would be pleased by the high survival rate among the slaves, but he also knew that there were two problems on the ship that could get him into deep trouble with his employers. When Mary had received his sailing instructions from the Billy brothers and La Croix before leaving Vannes, he had received permission to purchase a certain number of slaves on his own account. The problem was that the twenty-six slaves he had purchased in Jakin exceeded his authorization, and the discrepancy would be difficult to hide. His sailing orders provided severe penalties for exceeding his quota: he could be fined up to a thousand livres per excess personal slaves, or the excess slaves could be confiscated and sold for the account of the ship's owners.[4] Pierre Mary's second problem was that the slave who had died on December 3 between Jakin and Principe was one of the slaves he owned. Yet he had recorded the death as that of a slave belonging to the *Diligent's* outfitters: the Billy brothers and La Croix.

To protect himself and better conceal his fraud, Pierre Mary drew up a declaration that significantly undercounted his personally owned slaves and called the other officers into his cabin one at a time to sign it. Second Lieutenant Laragon, who had argued with Mary several times, refused to sign, saying that committing a fraud would endanger his eternal soul. On a ship full of imprisoned and dying Africans, he chose this issue to battle for his eternal salvation. Laragon and the ship's doctor Devigne later had a heated discussion on the quarterdeck and agreed not to sign the declaration. Devigne then went to Durand in his cabin and recounted

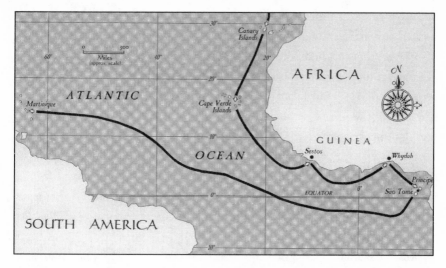

Figure 35.1   Redrawn version of the Pieter Goos map showing the *Diligent's* route from Whydah to Martinique.

the story. Soon after Devigne left, Durand heard Laragon swear again that he would not sign the false declaration because it went against his conscience.[5]

Robert Durand had not been asked for his signature. He was already at odds with Mary because he had noted in his personal journal on December 3 that a slave belonging to Captain Mary had died. Since the captain had declared the dead slave to belong to the cargo, Durand's journal entry was evidence of fraud on the part of the captain. Mary had not seen the journal entry, but he must have sensed Durand's hostility and for that reason did not ask him to sign the declaration. The only signature that he could count on was that of his brother-in-law, Valteau, but without the signatures of the other officers, the declaration was worthless. Pierre Mary would have to find another way to conceal his fraud.

The matter was not talked about further as the *Diligent* continued to head west and slightly north day after day. Throughout the month of February 1732, its latitude had climbed slowly from four degrees north latitude to thirteen degrees. Martinique was located at fourteen degrees north latitude, and the plan was to get on the same latitude as Martinique and sail west right into it. Because longitude measurements were so unreliable, getting on the right latitude was the safest way to avoid overshooting the island. By March 1 they were at fourteen degrees, and the task before them was mainly to sail straight west.

As they approached Martinique, the treatment of the slaves changed. The amount of food given at each meal increased, and each male captive was shaved, head and beard. The captives were given palm oil to rub on their skin, and the music and dancing increased.[6] Everything possible was being done to increase the selling price once they reached land.

By now the *Diligent* was thousands of miles away from the port of Jakin, where it had sat throughout September, October, and November to purchase its load of slaves. Many of the captives still carried vivid images of Jakin because it was the last time they had seen African soil. Robert Durand and the crew probably thought about Jakin very little, as their minds were focused on their approach to Martinique. Neither the crew nor the captives would have imagined that Jakin was about to be destroyed by the army of Dahomey.

36

*A*T 11:00 A.M. ON April 2, 1732, a messenger arrived at the Dutch trading lodge in Jakin with the news that the army of Dahomey was approaching. The Dutch director, Hertogh, sent his assistant, Hoffmeester, to find out what was happening. Hoffmeester quickly mounted a horse and rode north for half an hour to ascertain the whereabouts of the Dahomian army. Seeing a huge cloud of dust in the distance and hearing the sound of drums, he continued at a full gallop for another half hour. By then he was close enough to see a few flags flying above the marching army, but the dust prevented him from determining its size. When he decided to ride a little closer, he noticed a party of Dahomian soldiers armed with muskets advancing toward him. He instantly whirled about, put the spurs to his horse, and fled before a volley of musket fire.[1]

Arriving back in Jakin an hour later, Hoffmeester went to the Dutch trading lodge to get a fresh horse. He found that Hertogh and the African employees of the lodge had all left, leaving the six Dutchmen behind. Soon he heard gunfire coming from the west side of town. A Dahomian army ten thousand strong was attacking the city! Hoffmeester told his companions to lock the front and back doors of the lodge, and then he set out on a fresh horse to look for Hertogh. When he reached the great tree, he suddenly found himself surrounded by Dahomian soldiers, who captured him and took him to their camp outside the city.

The next morning Hoffmeester made a tour of the prison camp. It contained about four thousand men plus women and children. Among them he discovered the director of the Portuguese trading lodge with seven Portuguese employees, the English slaving captain Robert More with his overseer and a seaman, the director of the French lodge with three Frenchmen, and the five Dutch employees whom he had left at the lodge. The Portuguese director, De Pinto, was engaged in a long conversation with the Dahomian General Agau, after which he was allowed to return to his lodge. The remaining white captives were ordered to march fifty miles to Allada to be presented to King Agaja. When the Dutchmen received an audience with King Agaja several days later, the king gave them liquor to drink and asked where Hertogh was. Upon learning that Hertogh had escaped, the king appeared annoyed. He informed the captive Dutchmen that Hertogh was the cause of the war. King Agaja had attacked Jakin because he had heard that Hertogh sent gifts to the Asante caboceer Amoe of the Gold Coast in order to convince him to attack Dahomey.

To the rulers and traders in Jakin, the attack could not have come as a complete surprise. The ruler of Jakin had long run his city more like an independent port of trade than a subordinate division of the Dahomian state. The fact that the *Diligent* had paid two sets of customs duties—one to King Agaja and one to the ruler of Jakin—hints at the awkward coexistence of the two polities. King Agaja, having finally defeated the kingdom of Mahi after a year of fighting, was finally free to turn his army to other matters. His top priority was Jakin. Even though he had declared a monopoly on the slave trade in the lands under his control, he knew that the ruler of Jakin was working with Hertogh to bring in slaves from the east along the river that ran behind Jakin. Agaja had also heard rumors that Hertogh had encouraged Oyo to attack him and had supplied ammunition to the king of Weme in order to encourage him to attack Dahomey.[2]

When the army of Dahomey attacked Jakin, Hertogh was having his noon meal at the Dutch trading lodge. Upon hearing the news, he ordered his Dutch employees to stay at the lodge to protect the trade goods stored there while he departed for the river with his armed African retainers. They guarded the riverbank and fought off the Dahomian soldiers while he entered a canoe and fled down the river. The ruler of Jakin and his principal officials also escaped in canoes and went with Hertogh to an island in the river that they had fortified ahead of time for that very purpose.[3]

Both Hertogh and the ruler of Jakin fled so quickly that they left many important people behind. Hertogh left his six Dutch employees; the king left behind his mother. Once the army of Dahomey was in control of Jakin, the plundering and burning of the city began. The conquerors took 4,538 African prisoners and twenty Europeans. They seized the merchandise in the trading lodges and confiscated the artillery pieces that were mounted in Joseph de Torres's crumbling fort on the beach. Losses from the lodges were estimated at the value of 600 captives for the Dutch, 150 for the French, 80 for the captain of an English ship, and 20 for various individuals.

Hertogh and the ruler of Jakin both fled to the island of Lebee, which lay in the middle of the river and was therefore safe. After a week in Lebee, Hertogh moved on to Apa, a coastal island about thirty miles from Jakin, where he hoped to establish a new trading lodge. "I am now on a safe island," he wrote to the Dutch governor-general at Elmina, "where no enemy can ever come." Although King Agaja's English, French, and Portuguese captives were released three days after arriving in Allada, the Dutch captives were held for over a year while King Agaja negotiated with the Dutch West India Company. By the time the Dutchmen were released in July 1733, two of them had died miserably in captivity.

The English naval surgeon John Atkins, who became an opponent of the slave trade after observing it firsthand during his trip to Whydah in 1721, later wrote a book in which he interpreted King Agaja's destruction of Whydah (1727) and Jakin (1732) as blows against the slave trade. Explaining the destruction of Whydah in 1727, he wrote, "The victorious king of Dahomey, turning things topsy-turvy and entirely destroying our slave trade, deserves some remarks. This prince was probably incited to the conquest from the generous motive of redeeming his own and the neighboring country people from those cruel wars and slavery that was continually imposed on them by these snakes and the king of Ardra." Of the destruction of Jakin, Atkins wrote that King Agaja had "surprised and plundered all the European merchants at Jakin, finishing in that the destruction of the slave trade." He added, "The king's actions carry great reputation, for by the destruction of this trade, he relinquished his own private interests for the sake of public justice and humanity."[4]

Contrary to Atkins's portrayal of King Agaja as a great humanitarian crusading against the slave trade, the king himself was soon trying to repair his relations with the Dutch West India Company. He made it clear that he hated Hertogh, but he wanted to reestablish trade with the Dutch. He offered to build them a new lodge at his own expense, provided that someone other than Hertogh directed it. At the same time he sent an army of three thousand to camp on the beach near the island of Apa, where Hertogh had relocated. They would seize Hertogh if he ever set foot on the mainland. Hertogh, for his part, opposed the company's efforts to mend its relations with King Agaja. He threatened to resign from the company if it tried to reestablish trade with the Dahomian king. In response the company's Elmina Council judged that "it would by no means be beneficial to the company to reject such an advantageous offer made by the king of Dahomey just because of one single servant."[5] Rebuffed by his own company, Hertogh backed down.

After the destruction of Jakin the slave trade shifted back to the French, English, and Portuguese forts in Whydah. King Agaja had declared in 1730 that the port of Jakin should be closed and all slave trading was to take place at the forts in Whydah.[6] The destruction of Jakin in 1732 paved the way for the implementation of that policy. When Captain Assou died in June 1733 and the exiled King Huffon died two months later, King Agaja could finally consolidate his control over the former kingdom of Whydah. During the second quarter of the eighteenth century, the slave trade from Whydah averaged nearly twelve thousand captives a year.[7] Still, the wars and upheavals had taken their toll, and Whydah would never again dominate the Atlantic slave trade as it had done prior to the destruction of Savi.

*A*T TWO O'CLOCK IN the afternoon on March 11 the lookout on the *Diligent* spotted a vessel ahead of them to the leeward. Like the *Diligent*, it was steering straight west toward Martinique, but it was moving so slowly that the *Diligent* would soon overtake it. When the ship spotted the *Diligent*, it clewed up the main course in order to slow down and wait for the *Diligent*. Seeing this maneuver, the *Diligent* changed direction to pass the ship on the north side. At 6:00 P.M. they were close enough to the strange ship to see its flag flying without being able to distinguish its colors. The other ship apparently had ideas of accosting the *Diligent* because it kept to windward. During the evening, seeing that the *Diligent* was a much faster ship, it fired a blank cannon shot to indicate that it wanted to talk. When the shot brought no response, it fired again and lit several lanterns. During the next two hours it fired cannon shots at regular intervals and lit more lanterns. Captain Mary decided to try to pass it on the south side with all cannons armed in case it was a pirate ship. As the two ships got closer together, Robert Durand counted thirty lanterns hanging from the shrouds, whereas the *Diligent* was sailing in the darkness using only the light of the full moon.

When the strange ship continued to fire cannon shots to signal the *Diligent* to stop, Captain Mary had to make a decision. If it was a friendly ship calling for help, he reasoned, there was little that that the *Diligent* could offer, given that it was very large and the *Diligent* was near the end of its provisions. If, on the other hand, it was a pirate ship, it would overpower them and they would be lost. The two ships were now only a musket shot apart. The *Diligent* turned to pass the ship on the north side. Seeing the maneuver, the other ship put itself on a collision course with the *Diligent*, forcing it to again change course to stay parallel with the other ship. Even after the *Diligent* moved ahead, the other ship continued to keep its lanterns lit and fire blank cannon shots. By 10:30, when the other ship was practically out of sight despite the full moon, the cannon shots stopped and the lanterns went out. The next morning the ship was nowhere to be seen, and the crew members began to debate their actions of the previous night. Some thought it had been a pirate ship; others believed it was simply a ship in trouble calling for help.

This was the second potential pirate ship that the *Diligent* had encountered since leaving São Tomé. The first encounter had taken place on the sixth day out from São Tomé, when they had spotted a ship flying the English flag. Seeing the ship change course to approach them, the crew of the *Diligent* feared that it might be a pirate ship flying the English flag as a ruse. They scrambled to prime and arm the cannons. By eleven o'clock the two ships were within hailing distance, and the English ship lowered its longboat to come aboard the *Diligent*. The English officer, who spoke French, explained that the purpose of his visit was to learn the *Diligent's* latitude and longitude. The English slaver had been three months on the route from England to Angola, and it was unsure of its bearings.

Despite the false alarm, Captain Mary had been right to exercise caution in approaching the English vessel. This was the same region where Des Marchais had encountered a pirate ship in 1725. That ship flew white flags with red sabers, leaving no doubt as to its identity, and it fired blank cannon shots to request their surrender. As the pirate ship got closer, it lowered the white flags and raised black ones, signaling that the chance for surrender was over. Now it would give no quarter. The two ships exchanged cannon fire for over two hours as the pirate ship tried to maneuver close enough to board Des Marchais's vessel. Then a cannon shot hit the foremast of the pirate ship, causing it to fall in such a way that it knocked down the main mast as well. With the pirate ship unable to maneuver, Des Marchais and his crew were saved.[1] The slaves on board might have been better off had the pirates succeeded because pirates often set slaves free or invited them to join their crew.

The *Diligent's* encounter with the strange ship in Caribbean waters near Martinique required great caution because the early eighteenth century was the heyday of pirates in the Caribbean. By 1718 piracy had so interrupted France's trade with its Caribbean colonies that the French government, lacking the naval resources to combat the pirates directly, offered a general amnesty to all French pirates for a period of one year, after which all those who refused the amnesty would be punished by the full rigor of the law. There were few takers. It was not until 1726 that a French naval fleet, led by M. de la Jonquière, made an unsuccessful attempt drive pirates from the waters off Martinique. The situation was still so bad in 1729 that the governor of Martinique issued an order forbidding any ships to sail until the danger of being seized by pirates had passed. The slave ship *Charlemagne*, among others, was prevented from sailing for nearly a month because of reports that there were pirates in the area.[2] Piracy had become so open around Martinique that in 1731 a group of six men were caught trying to recruit young men to steal a ship and form a pirate band. They even tried to tempt soldiers to desert and join their group. After the plot was discovered, the leader was given a life sentence as a galley slave in the Mediterranean waters off Marseille.[3]

In addition to their general appreciation of the insecurity of the area, the officers of the *Diligent* had a very personal reason to fear pirates in the Caribbean. In 1728 a captain named Pierre Valteau, almost certainly a relative of the *Diligent's* second captain,[4] was sailing from Guadeloupe to Martinique in the slave ship *Expedition*, owned by René Montaudoin of Nantes. He had sold his cargo of slaves in Guadeloupe and was making the very short trip to Martinique to join up with the *Fidelité*, a slave ship also owned by Montaudoin. On the way to Martinique he was attacked and captured by the pirate Jean-Thomas Dulaien, who had been born in Guérande, only a few miles from Captain Valteau's town of Le Croisic. Captain Valteau was sailing a small, thirty-ton corvette with a crew of twelve. Because trying to fight off a pirate attack in such a small ship was foolhardy, he had removed the cannons from the deck of his ship and placed them in the hold as ballast before leaving Guadeloupe. The pirates seized all his merchandise but left his ship and crew intact. With no merchandise to carry back to France, Captain Valteau's ship was sold, and he traveled back to France on the *Fidelité*.

Soon after his attack on Captain Valteau's ship, the pirate Dulaien returned to Nantes and requested amnesty. It was granted on condition that he turn over his ship, the *Sans Pitié* (No pity), and all its cargo and treasures to the admiralty court. Having already hidden the most valuable of his treasures, he turned over his ship along with a little gold and fifteen slaves, who were subsequently imprisoned in the castle in Nantes. They were later shipped to Martinique to be sold, but two of them died in the meantime. As a free man in Nantes, Dulaien would stroll along the Quai de la Fosse past the houses of merchants whose ships he had plundered. They had agreed to his amnesty in hopes of recovering their merchandise, and now they realized that they had been tricked. Disappointed, they hurled insults at him as he strolled past their houses with a long sword hanging from his belt, and he responded with threats and crude gestures. On the very day that the *Diligent* arrived in St. Pierre, Martinique, the governor of Martinique was writing his final report on the disposition of the thirteen surviving slaves.[5]

On March 13 at two o'clock in the afternoon the lookout at the top of the mast spotted the mountain peaks of Martinique about seventy-five miles ahead of them. By the time the sun had set, the mountains could be seen from the lower mast as well. Sailing by the light of the nearly full moon, the *Diligent* made good progress during the night.

When the sun rose at six o'clock the next morning, Robert Durand could distinguish the outlines of the islands of Guadeloupe, Dominica, Marie-Galante, and La Désirade, and he sketched them in his journal. By noon the *Diligent* was in the channel between Dominique and Martinique, and their destination was in plain view. Martinique was one of the Lesser Antilles. It was a small island—roughly forty miles long and sixteen miles across at its widest point—that stretched from north-northwest to south-southeast. As a volcanic island, it had a terrain that rose steeply from the seashore to the mountainous interior. The relatively flat land near the shore occupied only 10 percent of the island's surface; the rest was steep and hilly.[6] In 1732 Martinique was home to 11,377 European settlers, 43,751 black and mulatto slaves, and 1,152 free blacks and mulattos. Slaves outnumbered free people by nearly four to one. The island had 471 sugar mills. Since each plantation had its own sugar mill, that meant roughly 471 sugar estates.[7]

Throughout the day the *Diligent* headed toward the northern tip of Martinique. It would round the tip and then follow the shoreline southeast

Figure 37.1   Harbor of St. Pierre, Martinique, with Mount Pélée in the background.

to land at St. Pierre, on the west side of the island. Encountering a strong current during the night that hindered their advance, they dropped anchor at two o'clock in the morning to wait for daylight. The next morning they sailed southeast along the shoreline and anchored at St. Pierre at eleven o'clock. Only five other slave ships arrived in St. Pierre in 1732. Three of them sailed from Nantes and two from St. Malo.[8] The *Diligent* was the first slave ship ever to arrive from Vannes.

The middle passage was over. Nine captives and four crew members had been lost. The voyage had taken sixty-six days, and Robert Durand complained that it had been hampered by contrary winds and currents. Under ideal conditions, they could have made it in fifty. Compared with other French ships at the time, however, their voyage was about average. Of the five French ships for which we have accurate records of the crossing from the Portuguese Islands to Martinique in the years 1731–1732, the times were forty-three days, fifty-one days, sixty-two days, sixty-four days, and seventy-five days.[9] When the *Diligent* arrived in Martinique, it still had reserves of food and water, and only two slaves had died since leaving Principe Island. By the standards of slave traders, the crossing had been a success.

PART II

Martinique

38

HE SUN SHONE BRIGHTLY on March 18, 1732, as crew members prepared the *Diligent* to receive visitors. They had scrubbed
the decks early to give them time to dry before the visitors arrived and
stretched a canopy made of sailcloth over the quarterdeck. A table covered
with white tablecloths was set up in its shade, and they set out the finest wine
and brandy that Captain Mary had to offer. The most elaborate preparations,
however, concerned the captives. Ever since the *Diligent* had arrived in St.
Pierre, Martinique, four days earlier, the crew members had bathed them,
shaved them, and rubbed them with palm oil to make their skin glisten.

The harbor of St. Pierre was dominated by the imposing heights of
Mount Pelée, a flat-topped volcano that rose from the seashore to a height
of 4,583 feet, with the summit only about three and a half miles from the
sea. On most days the summit was hidden by clouds. The slopes of the volcano were covered with the debris of pulverized pumice that made the
hoofbeats of horses ring hollow when they crossed it. The volcanic soil was
easy to cultivate, and the lower elevations of the mountainside were planted
in vegetables and cassava to provide food for the inhabitants of St. Pierre.
The cassava was eaten mostly by slaves. On the other side of the mountain
were large sugar plantations.[1]

Sandwiched between the seashore and the mountainside, the city of St.
Pierre stretched along the shoreline at the foot of the volcano for about a
mile. With 9,382 inhabitants (2,691 whites, 324 free blacks, and 6,367 black
slaves),[2] St. Pierre was by far the largest city on the island, nearly three

times as large as Fort Royal, Martinique's capital, and slightly larger than Vannes, the *Diligent's* home port. The *intendant* of Martinique had proclaimed in a burst of local pride that St. Pierre was "comparable to the largest third-class cities in France."[3]

Several longboats approached the ship carrying finely dressed men in broad-brimmed hats: representatives of the governor and other officials who were coming to get their first pick of the African captives. After being greeted by Captain Mary and the officers of the *Diligent*, they were ushered up to the quarterdeck for food and drinks. Then they began to wander about the ship to examine the captives on display. Following the usual routine, the women captives were on the quarterdeck, and the men were on the main deck and the forecastle.

No one has recorded what the Africans thought of all this. Did some of them think that they were finally about to be eaten? Did others hope they would be purchased and taken off the ship? Did they feel hope? fear? indifference? or just overwhelming embarrassment when the well-dressed officials looked them over, examined their teeth, felt their arms and legs, touched their genitals, and ordered them to walk, turn, or jump to show their physical dexterity? Certainly the ritual reminded them of the day in the courtyard of the ruler of Jakin when they had been examined in a similar manner by Pierre Mary or Robert Durand.

Mary was hoping to get 950 livres for each adult male African, and proportional prices for women and children. It would be a significant markup, given that the value of the goods that they had paid for adult male slaves in Jakin had averaged about two hundred livres. He was especially hoping to get that much for the twenty-six slaves who belonged to him personally. Two of them bore the mark of the *Diligent* on their right shoulder, indicating that they belonged to the ship's owners, instead of brand marks on their left shoulders indicating that they belonged to the captain. One of them had come into the captain's possession after being switched with one of the captain's slaves who had gone mad during the middle passage; the other had been substituted for the captive belonging to the captain who had died on December 3. Pierre Mary's substitutions bore out the statement of the French slave trader Jean Barbot that "the captain's slaves never die."[4]

It had become customary for government officials to get first pick of the slaves before the sale was opened to the general public. According the established practice, the governor-general got to choose twelve slaves, often at bargain prices, his lieutenant got eight, and the *intendant* got six. Merchants complained bitterly that this practice was costing them a lot of money. In 1715 Captain Mary's former boss René Montaudoin had complained that government officials "swooped down on the slave ships like hungry vultures." Royal decrees abolished the practice in 1715 and again in 1721, when it became apparent that the first decree was being ignored. Instead of taking their choice of slaves, the local officials would get to divide up a 2 percent royalty on all slaves sold.[5]

Despite all that legislation, the merchants of Nantes complained bitterly in 1732 that the governor and his commandants were still taking "an arbitrary number of slaves" in "contravention of the orders of His Majesty." Back in the days when the Company of the Indies had a monopoly on the slave trade, the merchants argued, no gratuities had been given. But as soon as the trade was opened up to private merchants, the governor and officers began to reclaim their former privileges. The merchants insisted that all gratuities should be voluntary, should be in cash instead of in slaves, and should in any case be limited by law to 2 percent of the value of the cargo. As things now stood, slaving captains were giving up at least 4 percent of their cargo and often much more.[6] Despite the complaints, the governor and the *intendant* got first pick of the captives on the opening day of the *Diligent*'s sale; the planters and merchants would have to wait until later.

It was easy for the governor and his aides to enforce their privileges because their official permission was needed before the sale could begin. As soon as the *Diligent* anchored in St. Pierre on March 15, Captain Mary sent Robert Durand to Fort Royal to get permission from the governor-general to open the sale.[7] Fort Royal was the political capital of the island, even though St. Pierre was the island's major port and commercial city. Traveling by longboat, Durand and his crew rowed sixteen miles along the rugged coastline to the capital.[8]

With Robert Durand away on his mission, Captain Pierre Mary called on the clerk of the admiralty in St. Pierre. He showed the clerk the papers he had received from the admiralty bureau in Vannes before his departure, and he gave a report on his voyage.[9] Most of the information in the report was routine, but there were a couple of striking anomalies. When reporting slave deaths during the middle passage, the captain reported eight, all of them belonging to the owners of the ship. He had left out the ninth slave death, which involved a slave of his. Pierre Mary also reported that the *Diligent* had left Jakin with 252 slaves on board, whereas Robert Durand's journal clearly listed 256. The four slaves that Mary failed to report were almost certainly his personal slaves above the limit of his port permit. Was the captain planning to hide them on the ship? Was he planning to smuggle them to shore at night? Given that Durand clearly knew that Captain Mary's figures were false, it is no wonder that he was sent off to Fort Royal to be well out of the way when Mary made his declaration.

After Robert Durand and Pierre Mary had made the proper declarations before the government officials, the health inspector came out to the ship. Local officials in Martinique were worried that newly arriving slaves might bring epidemics to the island, and so the inspector had the right to quarantine the entire ship or to order that slaves suffering from scurvy or smallpox should disembark outside of the city of St. Pierre.[10] Although the health inspectors could on occasion be bribed to overlook small health problems, they took major health problems very seriously.

Only a year before the arrival of the *Diligent*, the Company of the Indies ship *St. Louis* arrived at St. Pierre on its way to Louisiana with 340 slaves. A great many of them had become ill with a variety of diseases, and the illnesses were exacerbated when the ship ran short of food. Fearing that he might lose all of his captives, the captain stopped in Martinique to give the slaves a chance to recuperate before heading on to Louisiana. The health inspector determined that ninety-two of the slaves were not fit to travel, and he ordered them to be brought ashore to recover. During the next week he ordered another ten Africans ashore. When the sick slaves on shore showed no signs of recovery, the captain of the *St. Louis* continued on to Louisiana with the 229 slaves remaining on board. When the company agent in St. Pierre requested permission to sell the remaining slaves cheaply so that he could recover some money before they died, the governor refused because the inspector had judged that they were not in good enough condition to be sold.[11] There is no record of what happened to the sick captives; most likely they died.

With the formalities out of the way, the sale of the *Diligent*'s captives opened on Tuesday, March 18. After a long and careful examination, the white officials claimed ten to twelve of the strongest and healthiest slaves as

Figure 38.1   Slave buying on the deck of a slave ship.

their personal gratuities. Then some of the officials on board began discussions with Captain Mary about purchasing certain of the remaining captives. By the end of the day, Mary had sold several Africans for 950 livres each. As the last longboats departed with the confiscated and purchased slaves, the unsold slaves were fed, exercised, and sent below the deck for the night. They would be put on display again the next morning.

Wednesday was a repeat of the previous day, except that this time local slave merchants came aboard. They were wholesalers who tried to buy slaves in large lots for low prices and then resell them a few at a time at higher prices. The reselling business had been controversial in the French West Indies ever since it was first outlawed in 1665. When the government was unable to stop the practice, it declared that slaving captains could not sell their full cargo until after the sale had been open for fifteen days.[12]

Despite the legislation against them, the resellers stayed in business by taking advantage of three factors. First, slave ship captains were eager to sell their cargo quickly and return to France. If a wholesaler could purchase the entire cargo, then the ship could make a quick turnaround. Second, the planters who lived far from St. Pierre found it difficult to get to the port quickly after receiving news that a ship had arrived. The rugged mountains of the island kept some parts isolated and made travel extremely slow. In

1718 the government had undertaken an ambitious project to build roads into the heart of the island to accommodate the small planters, but the project would not be complete until 1739.[13] The wholesalers could provide slaves to those planters who couldn't get to the port on time. Third, the planters didn't always have the resources to purchase slaves, especially in the months prior to the sugar harvest, whereas the wholesalers seemed to have adequate resources to bridge the lean times.

The dealers came aboard and inspected the slaves much as the government officials had done the day before, except that they had to pay for the slaves that they chose. When Pierre Mary told them the price he was asking, they would offer much less in order to begin the process of bargaining. But this time things went badly for the captain. When Mary held out for high prices, hoping to end up somewhere in the neighborhood of 950 livres for a male slave, the dealers abandoned the bargaining process. Mary had decided that he would rather let the buyers walk away than lower the price. At the end of the day Robert Durand wrote in his journal that many merchants had come aboard, but few had purchased any slaves.

When word got out in St. Pierre of the high prices that were being demanded on the *Diligent*, the slave dealers who had flocked aboard on Wednesday melted away. A few buyers—some of them dealers, some of them planters—came out in boats on Thursday, Friday, and Saturday, but they purchased very few slaves. On Sunday, not a single buyer rowed out to the ship. We can only wonder what kind of obsession with huge profits had gripped Pierre Mary's mind. A report put out by the judge and consuls of Nantes on January 30, 1732, just six weeks before the *Diligent* arrived in Martinique, estimated that the average selling price for a slave in the islands was five hundred livres.[14]

Captain Mary realized that his chances for selling his cargo of slaves were slipping away quickly. He also knew that sitting in port for a long time in the cramped ship was not good for the health of the Africans; melancholy would grip them and they would start to die. Therefore on Sunday, eight days after arriving in St. Pierre, he rented a fortified warehouse near the mercantile exchange. The rest of the day was spent unloading the captives into the longboat and rowing them up the river to the warehouse. The slave warehouses of St. Pierre were notoriously stinking, overcrowded, and insufficiently sheltered from the rains and had been the subject of royal ordinances in 1708, 1718, and 1723 that called for reforms. The reforms were largely ignored.[15]

Because the warehouse was more accessible than the *Diligent,* sitting out in the St. Pierre harbor, the move to shore brought out new buyers who came to look over the Africans. During the first few days on land, Mary sold the best of the remaining slaves at nine hundred or even eight hundred livres, although some sold for much less. Captain Mary was gradually lowering his asking price, but he had done so too late. He had held out for high prices because there was no competition. The only other slave ship in the harbor, the *Renée Françoise,* had been there since January 24.[16] It had already sold its slaves and was waiting to load sugar. Nevertheless, many potential buyers had already left town to wait for news that a new ship had arrived.

There were two reasons why the African captives on the *Diligent* were not selling at the prices that Captain Mary had expected. First, the number of slaves being delivered annually to Martinique had skyrocketed since the slave trade had been opened to private traders. In 1726 fewer than a thousand slaves had been delivered, but by 1729 the number had risen to over two thousand. Then in 1730 the number more than doubled to nearly five thousand.[17] The rapid increase in the supply of slaves was having the predictable effect of driving down prices. Second, just as slave deliveries were increasing, the economy of Martinique was going through a crisis. Most economic crises build up gradually and dissipate gradually, but everybody in Martinique knew the precise minute when this one began—12:43 P.M. on a clear, sunny day in November 1727.

39

$\mathcal{A}$T FORTY-THREE MINUTES past noon on November 7, 1727, the ground trembled. Then it shook as three successive shocks, each more violent than the last, hit at one-minute intervals. In the harbor of St. Pierre, the water level dropped precipitously and the sea turned to foam as if it were boiling in a cauldron. The ships shook so violently that their cannons were thrown into the air. Cattle grazing along the seashore stampeded in fright and tumbled down amid the shocks. On the mountain slope above St. Pierre, a stone the size of a navy warship loosened and slid into the city.[1]

When the ground stabilized after the earthquake, most of the wooden houses in St. Pierre were still standing, but the stone houses were so badly damaged that their inhabitants were afraid to stay in them. The churches and government buildings sustained heavy damage, and the prison was destroyed. Inmates who were not killed or wounded in the quake fled. The Jesuit house in St. Pierre was badly damaged, and the Dominicans' was uninhabitable; the building of the religious order of Charity was in ruins.[2] People barely had time to flee from their houses when the sky opened up with torrential rains and winds that reminded them of a hurricane. The mountain streams and rivers quickly turned into raging torrents.[3]

The damage was less visible in the countryside, but its consequences were equally serious. On the sugar estates, the flash floods drowned a large number of slaves, whose quarters were often built by the waterways. The cane fields remained intact, but the sugar mills, boiling houses, curing buildings, and distilleries were badly damaged. Thousands of clay pots for cooling the sugar and clay forms for making sugar loaves were broken. The high sugar season, which began in January, was jeopardized for lack of pots and forms. To aid the sugar plantations to repair the damaged buildings and equipment in time for the sugar harvest, the Church suspended several saint's holidays so that the slave owners could keep their slaves working without a break.

There was a second reason why the Church was willing to cancel state holidays: they were worried about a potential slave rebellion. On November 20 a priest heard the confession of a slave who mentioned that a general uprising all over the island was being planned.[4] The inspiration behind the movement was a young prophet who, it was said, had accurately predicted the earthquake. Rumors were rife that the uprising would break out on the festival of St. Thomas, December 21. When nothing happened on that day, a new set of rumors held that it was set for the festival of St. Stephen, December 26. The day came and went without any sign of an uprising, but the island's officials remained nervous. Canceling religious holidays, claimed the *intendant* Blondel, was "necessary to curb the excess liberty of the slaves and to take away from them any and all means to assemble and hatch plots."[5]

Although the *intendant* himself doubted the capability of the slaves to unite in an island-wide rebellion, given the diversity of the languages that they spoke and the isolation of many plantations from their neighbors, he took no chances. In the cities of Fort Royal and St. Pierre he set up special army encampments along the streets and proclaimed curfews after eight o'clock in the evening. Because runaway slaves living in free maroon communities in the hills were presumed to be major organizers of the rebellion, he ordered a general hunt for maroons and runaways throughout the island. No maroons were captured, but some camps were found and some old clothing was confiscated. Blondel also ordered all planters to inspect the dwellings of their slaves to see if there were any maroons or runaway slaves hiding there. The search turned up no runaways, but many plantation slaves were accused by their owners of voicing seditious opinions and sent to the dungeon at Fort Royal. Blondel also delivered gunpowder at greatly reduced prices to the rural planters and even gave it away free of charge to those who could not afford it. Above all, he asked the white planters to calm down. A "terror and panic" had gripped the island, he complained.[6] We will never know whether his measures to prevent the rebellion were effective or whether the rumors of rebellion were just the nightmarish fantasies of white planters. In any event, no rebellion materialized.

Throughout the lowland coastal regions of Martinique, where the sugar was grown and processed, the sugar mills and processing buildings were damaged, but the cane itself remained unharmed. It would soon produce a bumper harvest that would go a long way toward paying for the damage done by the earthquake. Higher up the mountain slopes in the regions above a thousand feet, where cocoa trees dominated, the earthquake had a very different effect. After the shocks had subsided, over 8 million cocoa trees lay uprooted on the mountain slopes.[7] They could not be replanted. Cocoa growers knew that the trees took a lot of nutrients out of the soil, and so land that had once supported a stand of cocoa trees would be too depleted to nurture new ones. Only three weeks after the earthquake, Blondel wrote, "it is impossible to continue to grow cocoa in Martinique."[8]

Although the earthquake struck rich and poor planters alike, it did not affect them equally. The planters of tree crops such as cocoa were hit much harder than the planters of sugar. Sugar, which grew along the coastal plain at altitudes below a thousand feet, was a crop that only substantial planters could grow. Each sugar plantation included cane fields, a sugar mill, a boiling house, a curing house, and a distillery, all of which required substantial amounts of labor. Local planters estimated that it was impossible to run a sugar plantation with fewer than fifty slaves. Father Labat, who outlined the operations of his own sugar plantation in great detail, needed 120 slaves to work a sugar holding of thirty hectares.[9]

The small-scale planters, in contrast, lived inland on steep mountainsides at elevations above a thousand feet, where they cultivated cocoa trees and foodstuffs instead of sugar cane. Rather than maintain a plantation-style organization, cocoa planters allowed their slaves to live in their own huts surrounded by their own gardens. Prior to the earthquake, it was the cocoa farms that had created much of the demand for slave labor. With the sugar-producing parts of the island more or less filled up by the early eighteenth century, the sugar sector was not expanding. Sugar planters purchased only enough slaves to replace those who died or grew too old to work in the fields; the death rate among slaves exceeded the birthrate, creating a continuous, but relatively stable, demand for new laborers. Of new slaves imported into the island, half of them would be dead eight years later. With an overall annual death rate above 6 percent and a birthrate of less than 3 percent, over thirteen hundred slaves were needed annually just to keep the slave population of Martinique stable.[10] The real growth area for slave sales was the mountainous interior, where a small-scale cocoa planter could establish an estate with perhaps ten or fifteen slaves.

It was those small-scale plantations in the interior that were ruined by the destruction of the cocoa trees. The planters were in despair because they counted on sales of their cocoa to pay for the salted beef and other imported items that they depended on for survival. Even King Louis XV recognized the severity of their losses by distributing salted beef to them as charity and exempting them from the capitation tax for several years. The charity was too little and came too late. When a ship from Nantes loaded with barrels of salted beef arrived at one rural port, a mob of five hundred pillaged everything in its hold and then burned it. Rumors abounded that groups of cocoa planters were planning to attack and pillage large sugar estates.[11]

In despair, many of the small planters left Martinique. Some went to islands belonging to the English or the Spanish. Some went to Sainte Alourzie, an island belonging to France but never colonized because of an ownership dispute with the British. Others went to the nearby island of Dominica, also owned by France but inhabited by the indigenous Caribs. Like the Caribs, the refugees lived by hunting, fishing, gardening, and cutting wood. The French in Martinique characterized them as living "without discipline, without morals, and perhaps without religion." Others went to St. Vincent, another uncolonized island inhabited by indigenous Caribs. The governor tried to keep them from leaving by making all sorts of grand promises, but he could not offer them a way to make a living.

Advocates for the small planters estimated that over a thousand people—including planters, their families, and their slaves—had gone to Sainte Alourzie and Dominica alone. They estimated that two-thirds of the small planters on Martinique—over two thousand of them—had been harmed by the cocoa disaster and would soon leave if they did not find an alternative way to make a living. If they left with their wives, children, and slaves, over fourteen thousand people would stage a mass exodus from Martinique.[12] Not only would their departure shrink the market and make Martinique a less desirable trading partner, but these were the very people who grew most of the food that fed the island. To prevent such a disaster, an alternative livelihood needed to be found for the small-scale planters.

The solution, the planters believed, was coffee. It grew well on the mountainsides that had lost the cocoa plantations. It was a hardy plant that could thrive in poor and exhausted soils. It could be grown, harvested, and processed by smallholders with a few slaves. It would have a market in France because it would be produced at nearly the same latitude as the Mocha coming from the Levant. The only hindrance to coffee planting was that the Company of the Indies had a worldwide monopoly on the coffee trade to France, and the company would not permit coffee growing in Martinique. The company argued that the market for coffee in France was almost saturated by its imports from the Levant. Any future growth would be met by coffee plantations that the company was planning to establish on the island of Bourbon (now known as Réunion) in the Indian Ocean. Coffee production in Martinique was simply out of the question.[13]

In the early eighteenth century the secrets of growing coffee were guarded as closely as nuclear secrets are today. In 1719 the *intendant* of Martinique had come up with the idea of sending a spy to Mocha in the Levant during the coffee-harvesting season to buy or steal some live seeds that could germinate and reproduce in Martinique. There were two obstacles to the plan. The first was that officials in the Levant kept close watch to make sure that not a single coffee seed fell into the hands of strangers. An equally daunting obstacle was that the Company of the Indies, which had a royal monopoly on French trade with the Levant, found out about the plan and opposed it. Nevertheless, the Council of the Marine promised the *intendant* that it would do everything in its power to furnish some coffee seeds or plants to Martinique.[14]

There was an alternative to smuggling coffee beans from the Levant. In the king's garden in Paris were several coffee plants that had been given to King Louis XIV by the government of Holland. In 1721 Gabriel de Clieu, an army captain at Fort Royal, Martinique, was given the mission of taking a single coffee plant from the king's garden in Paris to Martinique. The story of his voyage that is told in Martinique to this day is that with his ship was running short of water, Clieu used a substantial portion of his own meager daily ration to keep the plant alive till he reached Martinique. Although there is no documentary evidence other than Clieu's own testimony to back up the story, it is nevertheless credible. Direct trade captains from Nantes had a reputation for being so stingy that they would rather load an extra bale of merchandise than an extra barrel of water, and they had nothing to gain by keeping their passengers happy or even alive, since they had paid their fares in advance. So it is not impossible that Clieu really was kept on short water rations throughout the voyage.

By November 7, 1727, when the earthquake shook Martinique, an estimated 100,000 coffee plants were under cultivation. Since exporting coffee was illegal, most of it was sold locally. The governor predicted that when all the bushes that had been planted began to produce, the result would be almost sufficient for the needs of the island. In the wake of the cocoa disaster, the governor tried to stem the exodus of small planters by visiting the ruined cocoa farmers and promising that they would be allowed to grow coffee. He even promised them subsidies and distributed seeds free of charge. Still, his actions did not solve the immediate crisis, since newly planted coffee bushes don't began bearing fruit for three years.

In 1729 the Company of the Indies reacted swiftly to protect its monopoly. Under pressure from the company, the French minister of the marine, Maurepas, ordered the island's administrators to stop the spread of coffee planting and uproot existing coffee bushes. This order caused an uproar among the small planters, who again threatened a mass exodus. At the same time, they continued to plant coffee and tried to find ship captains who were willing to smuggle it to France. By 1731 nearly 2 million coffee bushes had been planted. Caught in the middle, Maurepas fashioned a compromise between the planters and the company: Martinique could export coffee to the major Atlantic ports in France, provided that they reexported it to other European countries in the same sacks. It could not be sold in France.[15]

The victory for the small planters was announced on September 27, 1732. It was received, in the words of the governor, "with universal joy throughout the island."[16] By then, however, the Diligent was already back home in Vannes. In March, when Captain Mary had been trying to sell his cargo of captive Africans for high prices, the small planters were not in a mood to buy. Their cocoa plantations had been destroyed, and their coffee bushes did not yet have a legal market. Under the circumstances, it is not surprising that Captain Mary's hopes for enormous profits were quickly dashed.

40

On SUNDAY, APRIL 13, almost a month after the *Diligent* had arrived in St. Pierre, a male slave died in the warehouse. The death did not come as a total surprise to Captain Mary because he knew that the health of the captives in the warehouse was deteriorating. Alarmed by this development, Robert Durand wrote in his journal that even though the Africans had been in magnificent condition when they arrived in Martinique, their health was deteriorating each day. Durand believed that chagrin was overtaking the captives now that they had arrived at their destination and were languishing in the warehouse. Durand's other theory was that the physical deterioration was caused by the food. The fava beans had run out, and the slaves were now being fed bread, which disgusted them.

Three days later a second slave died. This time Durand noted the cause as "bloody flux," a disease that we now call amoebic dysentery. The man who died—we don't know his name—had been hovering near death for days before he finally expired. With great courage and perseverance, he had survived his capture in Africa, the forced march to the coast, and the stale confinement of the middle passage. The strength of his character had sustained him all the way across the Atlantic Ocean, and now he had died lying in a pool of bloody filth in a warehouse in Martinique. From the looks of his comrades, others would soon follow. The situation echoed one that an administrator in St. Pierre had observed when he visited several slave warehouses in 1724 and wrote that they "presented a revolting picture of the dead and the dying thrown helter-skelter in the gutter."[1]

Neither Robert Durand nor the ship's doctor, Pierre Devigne, understood much about bloody flux. It would be much later in the eighteenth century when the Bordeaux slave trader Brugevin would describe it with amazing accuracy and clearly distinguish it from the more ordinary bacillary dysentery. "This catastrophic disease," Brugevin wrote, "is known on the Guinea coast by the name of dysentery, but it is of a different nature than ordinary dysentery. It becomes putrid and in a very short time epidemic and incurable. When it reaches a certain degree of decomposition, those who have been attacked soon perish. If the disease attacks a person with a robust constitution, sufficient strength, and the courage to withstand this cruel disease, the strength of their character could perhaps triumph, but I can attest that not one person in twenty-five will survive. No known treatment can cure those who are attacked, once the disease has progressed to a certain degree."[2]

The doctors were of little help. They withheld solid food from the patients, administered frequent enemas, and gave them medicines that annoyed and disgusted them—while the sick became weaker. Captain Brugevin's experiments in the 1780s would show, on the contrary, that patients with amoebic dysentery needed solid food, especially fava beans. On that point, at least, Robert Durand had it right.

The man who died had most likely picked up the disease through contaminated food and water. After an incubation period of eight to ten days, the man was struck with violent headaches and severe stomach cramps. Soon he had a raging fever and unremitting stomach pains, and he passed up to forty bloody stools a day. Death, when it came, was usually the result of cardiac failure and exhaustion or a perforated colon.[3] Durand didn't report what they did with the body. Given the high death rate in the slave warehouse district of St. Pierre, there was almost certainly a local undertaker who made daily rounds of the warehouses with his oxcart to pick up bodies and bury them in a common grave outside the city. For the citizens of St. Pierre, the sight of the oxcart carrying bodies stacked like cordwood was disturbingly familiar.

The crowded and filthy warehouse was an ideal place for the disease to spread, though its effects would not be seen right away because of the incubation period. Two days after the man had died from bloody flux, a woman slave died of the same disease. For the next three days nobody died, and

Robert Durand began to have hope. Then on Monday another slave died—a man. The following day a male slave died of bloody flux, the fifth death in ten days. Durand noted each death by sketching a skull in his journal.

Captain Mary was worried, but he did not panic. He had left Jakin with 201 captives belonging to his employers, and 192 of them had been alive when he arrived at St. Pierre. He had sold seventy-one of them. Five had now died. That left 116 slaves for him to sell. Mary tried to keep the deaths of the slaves in the warehouse a secret because he knew that the information would only encourage the wholesale dealers to hold out for bargain prices, but word quickly spread. A certain Mr. Dubot, a slave reseller, appeared and offered to buy all 116 of the remaining slaves as a lot for fifty-six thousand livres, half to be paid immediately and half in six months. That amounted to about 483 livres per captive, about half of what Captain Mary had originally hoped to get. Still hoping that the slaves and the prices would recover, Mary refused the deal.

Over the next few days no more slaves died, and Captain Mary managed to sell a few slaves from the warehouse, but at prices much lower than he had wanted. It must have started to dawn on him that since the day of his arrival in St. Pierre things had grown progressively worse. He was now thinking less about making profits than about cutting his losses. Gradually, panic set in. He was cutting his losses too late.

In the meantime, a slave dealer in St. Pierre named Lamy was getting regular reports about the state of affairs in the *Diligent*'s warehouse. We know almost nothing about him except that in 1725 he was one of the twenty-five "first-class *négociants*" who signed a petition requesting the *intendant* of the islands to move to St. Pierre.[4] Lamy waited until the deteriorating situation in the warehouse had caused Mary to rethink his position. Timing was everything in the reselling business. Just when Captain Mary was about to despair, Lamy showed up and offered to purchase the remaining ninety-six captives for four hundred livres apiece, half now and half in one year. That was eighty-three livres apiece less than Dubot had offered only a short while earlier, and the wait for full payment was now a year instead of six months. This time, however, Captain Mary took the deal. Eager to shed his responsibilities for his human merchandise, Mary turned the slaves and the warehouse over to Lamy and moved with his officers to a house near the hospital that belonged to a certain Mr. Poirier.

Figure 40.1   Slaves doing laundry in St. Pierre.

Lamy had bought the slaves at less than half the original asking price. Did he think that he could restore them to health after Captain Mary had failed to do so? Did he calculate that given the bargain price he had paid, he could afford to lose a certain percentage of them and still make a profit? Did he calculate that the prices would rise in the coming months? Was he planning to take them to remote parts of the island and sell them to planters who lacked easy access to the slave markets in St. Pierre? Was he planning to ship them to Guadeloupe or St. Domingue in hopes of getting better prices there? Such questions must remain unanswered because Robert Durand never again mentioned the captives after the day of their sale.

As for the rest of the *Diligent*'s captives, we can speculate. We know that between the time of the *Diligent*'s arrival in St. Pierre on March 15 with 247 slaves and the time Mary sold the final lot of 96 slaves to Lamy, five slaves had died. It follows that 146 slaves had been given to local officials as gratuities or sold as individuals or in small groups to local planters and dealers. Those slaves most likely stayed on the island of Martinique. Perhaps as many as 10 percent of them ended up in urban centers such as St. Pierre or Fort Royal, where they worked as household servants or in the service of local *négociants*, small merchants, artisans, or government officials.[5] The rest ended up on the plantations of the countryside. Given the poverty of the small planters who grew cocoa and coffee on the hillsides of the mountainous interior, it seems most likely that the majority of the 146 slaves were purchased by sugar planters living along the coastal plain.

We have a firsthand description of life and work on a sugar plantation at the beginning of the eighteenth century because Father Jean-Baptiste Labat, who had managed plantations for ten years, wrote about his experience in great detail. One reason why Father Labat was willing to describe his operations so minutely was that he fancied himself a model plantation owner who was setting a good example for all the other planters on the island. It was a sign of his times that Labat did not seem at all embarrassed at being a slave owner, but he became extremely upset when people accused him and his fellow priests of dabbling in commerce.[6] In 1705 Labat described his vision of an ideal plantation. If some of the slaves were lucky, they might have ended up on a plantation like the one described by Labat. For the rest, conditions were far worse.

Labat has left us a detailed account of how he inducted newly purchased slaves into the work routines of his sugar plantation. He freely acknowledged that his approach was far from typical, and he noted that many planters were so hard and avaricious that they threw the new slaves into the thick of the work before they even had time to catch their breath. Such planters had forgotten, Labat explained, "that these poor people are tired from a long voyage during which they were attached two by two with iron anklets. They are exhausted by hunger and thirst, which never fails to make them suffer tremendously during the crossing, not to mention the unhappiness that comes from being torn from their country with no hope of ever returning."[7]

When new slaves arrived at his plantation, claimed Father Labat, he ordered them to be fed, allowed to rest a few hours, and then taken to the sea to bathe. Their heads were shaved, and they were given palm oil to rub on their skin. If they had scurvy, the palm oil was thought to cure it or at least keep it from spreading. For the first two or three days the new slaves got olive oil in their food. They ate several small meals a day instead of two large ones, and they bathed every morning and evening. The doctor then bled them to release the bad humors and gave them enemas to purge their intestines. Such measures, believed Labat, would keep them from succumbing to the diseases that attacked slaves who were newly arrived on the island.

Labat estimated that a third of the newly arrived slaves died within the first year because of new diseases, the change in climate, and the heavy work regimen. That astonishingly high death rate was part of a widely recognized phenomenon that the English referred to as "seasoning" and the French called *acclimatization*. Slaves who survived the *acclimatization* period on the islands sometimes went on to live long lives. The 1732 census of Martinique listed 12 percent of the slave population as "infirm or elderly." Of the 132 adult slaves on the Belin plantation in Saint Domingue in 1762, thirty-three of them were in their fifties and twenty-six of them were over fifty-nine.[8]

After a week of food and rest, the newly purchased slaves were ready to begin light work. Each one was placed in a house with an older slave who knew the ways of the plantation. If there was somebody on the plantation who spoke his or her native language, so much the better. The elder slaves often acted like surrogate parents to the newly arrived slaves and taught them the routines of life on the plantation. The heavy work would come later.

Even though the Code Noir required that slaves be baptized within seven days of arriving in Martinique, the rule was usually ignored, even on plantations run by religious orders. Father Labat had newly arrived slaves eat and sleep alone so that they would feel socially ostracized. When they asked why they were not allowed to eat with the others, they were told that it was because they were not Christians and had not been baptized. Soon they would ask for baptism in order to end their social isolation. At that point Father Labat would give them some rudimentary instruction in the faith and baptize them. At the time of baptism, each slave was given a Christian name that was written down in the special parish register book that was reserved for slaves. They were not entered into the regular parish register, which was reserved for whites and free blacks.

Labat's ideal sugar plantation included 120 slaves. Twenty-five of them were cutters of cane who worked in the fields from 6 A.M. to 6 P.M. with a two-hour break at noon. Eight additional slaves transported the cut cane to the mill in ox wagons. Work in the fields stopped around 6 P.M. as darkness approached, and the workers then returned to the house to work another two to three hours preparing manioc flour or doing other tasks.

Five slaves, usually women, worked full-time in the sugar mill crushing the cane and extracting the juice. The cane needed to be processed immediately after being cut, and so the mill ran twenty-four hours a day during

Figure 40.2   Horse-driven sugar mill.

the cutting season, which extended from January through May. The crew worked from six in the morning to midnight without a break for meals. The slaves were supposed to bring their lunches with them and eat in rotation so that the mill never stopped turning. At midnight they were relieved by the workers of the night shift, who worked until six in the morning. Labat recommended that the mill workers be divided into two teams, each of which worked eighteen-hour days in the mill for one week and then six-hour days in the mill the following week, with the rest of their working hours spent stoking the fires in the boiling house.[9] By alternating the schedules of the two teams, the mill could run nonstop.

If a sugar plantation was lucky enough to have a stream running through it, the mill could be driven by waterpower; otherwise it was driven by teams of horses, mules, or oxen walking round and round a tight circular path. Of the 471 functioning sugar mills in Martinique in 1732, 296 of them relied on animal power, 13 were wind driven, and 162 were powered by water. Labat's mill was driven by water; otherwise he would have needed extra workers to drive the animals.[10]

Figure 40.3   Working in the boiling house.

The sugar was milled by a bank of three vertical wooden rollers with steel blades. Each cane had to be fed into the mill twice: once between rollers one and two, and then back between rollers two and three. Workers who were tired from long hours and lack of sleep would sometimes get their fingers caught in the rollers, and so a hatchet or a billhook was kept handy to chop off the hand or arm of the worker so caught. Labat recounted the story of one young slave woman belonging to the Jesuits whose entire body, except for her head, was crushed between the rollers.[11]

Six slaves worked at the boiling house—which contained six enormous red copper kettles sitting over brick fireplaces—to reduce, clarify, and crystallize the cane juice that had been extracted at the mill. Each batch of cane juice had to be boiled up to six times at different temperatures. Sugar boilers were highly skilled artisans who had to know just when to skim off the impurities and when to stop the boiling at each stage. During sugar season they worked long hours in the overwhelming heat of the boiling house. So furious was the pace that six workers were needed to cut wood for the boilers, and another three workers kept the boilers going by stoking them with wood and dried cane. Like the mill, the boiling house operated twenty-four hours a day during the sugar season. In describing the work during sugar season, Labat noted, "One can see what the work regimen of a sugar plantation is and how difficult it is for the slaves, who are often malnourished, to withstand it without succumbing."

Not all the slaves worked in the cane fields or the sugar mills. Labat's plantation had a range of skilled tradesmen: coopers, blacksmiths, wheelwrights, carpenters, joiners, masons, and others who kept all the machinery and equipment in good repair. Labat recommended that skilled tradesmen should get extra meat and other amenities so that young slaves would be eager to learn the trades. The herdsmen who watched the oxen and horses, he believed, should come from the Senegal and Gambia regions of West Africa because people from those regions had been accustomed to cattle herding before being enslaved. Perhaps the most important worker on the plantation was the foreman who oversaw the work of the slaves. On some plantations the foreman was white, but Father Labat, like many other planters, preferred to use a black slave as foreman.

Women, like men, worked at a variety of tasks. Labat asserted that women made the best workers in the sugar mill. He advised placing a woman be in charge of the distillery because he believed that she would drink less of the brandy than would a man. A wise and intelligent woman, he advised, should be chosen to run the infirmary and take care of sick slaves. Two other women should be put to work making the cassava flour that served as the staple of the slaves' diet.

All together, Labat calculated, seventy-four slaves were required to produce the sugar. Then he added four servants for the planter's house. There were always some slaves sick at any given moment who needed to be replaced; Labat estimated the number of replacement workers at seven. Then there were twenty-five children and ten invalids or elderly people.[12] What is striking about Labat's figures is the small number of children and elderly people in a system that continually brought young workers in their prime from Africa to labor on the plantations. His figures corresponded roughly with the demographic profile of Martinique as a whole. Thirty percent of the slave population in 1732 was made up of children, and the elderly and infirm made up only 12 percent.[13] Under the difficult conditions of plantation life, not many slaves lived to old age.

With 120 slaves, the sugar plantation was like a small village. Labat's plantation overlooked the sea, where it stretched out for a thousand paces along the shore and extended back for three thousand paces on the gently sloping ground. It included the house of the planter, made of stone and facing the sea; a mill to grind the cane and extract the juice; a boiling house where the juice was reduced, clarified, and crystallized; a curing house to drain the molasses and dry the sugar heads; a storehouse for the raw sugar; and a distillery for making brandy. Downwind from the main house (so that fires in the slave quarters would not spread to the main house) were the houses of the 120 slaves, lined up along two streets. Labat described the slaves' houses as "no big deal" *(très peu de choses),* but he suggested nevertheless they should be lined up in an orderly fashion. The corrals in which the oxen and horses were kept at night were located near the slave houses so that the slaves could keep watch over them. Altogether, the houses and buildings occupied a space three hundred paces by three hundred paces.

On each side of the buildings were cane fields, and behind the buildings were more cane fields. They were divided into squares one hundred paces by one hundred paces by eight-foot-wide paths so that the ox wagons could pass.[14] Thus the fields behind the house, which occupied an area a thousand paces by four hundred paces, were divided into forty separate squares. Behind the cane fields were fields for cassava, sweet potatoes, millet, and yams to feed the slaves.

Because the cane had to be milled within twenty-four hours after cutting, the work went on at a fever pitch during the sugar season. Sugar was harvested from January through May, and some planters tried to plant different fields at different times to keep the harvest going throughout the year. It took fifteen to eighteen months for newly planted cane to reach maturity. Then it was cut and would regrow to produce another crop twelve months later. After two or more second-growth crops had been harvested, the field would be left fallow to regenerate before a new crop of cane was planted.[15] Each field therefore had a life cycle of about five years. Planters tried to stagger their planting so that the fields would not all reach maturity at once, and at any given moment a planter might have six separate cane crops at different stages of maturity. But the cane had to be planted during the rainy season, which limited the planters' flexibility, and January through May was the main sugar season. During the rest of the year the pace of life was less feverish, as the slaves worked in the gardens, weeded the cane fields, and repaired the equipment.

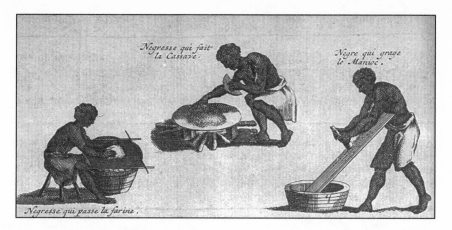

Figure 40.4   Slaves preparing cassava.

To sustain the slave laborers on the plantation, the Code Noir (1685) prescribed that each slave should receive two and a half pots of cassava per week. Labat preferred to give three, and he advised planters to plant three or four times as much cassava as they thought they needed. Clearly that advice was not being heeded, and an ordinance of 1726 required all planters to plant five hundred stalks of cassava per slave, a substantial increase over the two hundred stalks per slave that had previously been required. The island's census takers took the requirement so seriously that they actually made counts or estimates of the number of cassava plants on each plantation. In 1732 they found that the island was nearly 2 million plants short of the legal minimum.[16]

For meat, the Code Noir required that each slave should receive two pounds of salted beef or three pounds of fish per week. The salted beef was mostly imported from Ireland, and Labat advised that during times when France was at war on the seas and salted beef became scarce or expensive, sweet potatoes and yams could be substituted for meat. Generally the rations were distributed on Monday of each week.

The fact that slaves depended on salted beef imported from Ireland reveals one of the strange anomalies of Martinique's export-oriented economy: the island produced almost no meat. Labat's model plantation reserved the first three hundred meters inland from the seashore as pastureland for the oxen and horses, work animals that could not be slaughtered for meat.

Labat estimated that his model plantation required forty-eight oxen for pulling the wagons. If the sugar mill was powered by horses, fifty were needed to keep it going. In addition, Labat recommended a herd of about fifty cows to provide milk and replacements for oxen that died. That came to 150 animals that needed to be pastured but could not be slaughtered for meat.[17]

As early as 1680 the *intendant* of Martinique had complained that there was no place left for pasturing cattle because all of the seashores had been planted in cane. By 1721 the *intendant* complained that no beef was available except "old ox-team oxen whose only value lies in their skin and bones; their meat is worthless and cannot nourish a human body." Although there were 14,270 cattle and oxen on Martinique in 1732, very few of them were available for slaughter.[18] As befits an export-oriented, monocropped economy, the answer was for merchants from Nantes to bring in salted beef from Ireland.

Getting a sufficient supply of Irish salted beef to feed the slaves of Martinique was a continuing headache for the governor, especially after non-French ships were forbidden from trading there in 1727. The meat supply therefore relied largely on the merchants of Nantes, and they were not delivering beef in quantities anywhere close to sufficient. In June 1730 the French minister of the marine complained that the merchants of Nantes were only sending a fraction of the beef that was needed. If the situation did not change quickly, he warned, there would soon be a total beef famine in Martinique. The merchants of Nantes replied that they were losing money on every barrel of Irish beef that they carried to Martinique, and that the meat trade would soon collapse altogether unless it became profitable for them.[19] The problem was partially alleviated in 1731, when the French Council of State allowed French ships to go to Ireland to stock up on salted beef and then travel directly to Martinique. During the month prior to the arrival of the *Diligent*, six hundred barrels of Irish salted beef had arrived in this fashion.[20]

Even when sufficient food was available on the plantation, slaves faced the problem of finding enough time to prepare and eat it. Labat noted that many planters didn't adequately staff their cane mills and boiling houses, and so during sugar season many of the slave workers did not have time to eat.

As for clothing, the Code Noir stated that each slave should be furnished with two sets of clothing per year. Labat furnished his male slaves with two pairs of shorts and two shirts made from the rough cloth of Brittany each year, and women slaves got two skirts and two blouses made from the same cloth. Labat noted that less conscientious planters gave their slaves only one outfit per year, and still others merely gave them pieces of cloth out of which to fashion their own clothing.

All in all, Labat calculated that the cost of keeping 120 slaves was 6,610 livres per year. About a third of that was for salted beef, and five hundred livres went for medicines and doctor's fees. Those 120 slaves, he estimated, would produce sugar and brandy worth 44,640 livres, or about seven times as much as the cost of their yearly upkeep.[21] His calculations did not include the capital costs of obtaining land, constructing buildings, and purchasing equipment and slaves, but his calculations give a rough idea of the profits that the planters could expect after recovering their initial capital outlays.

The slaves who ended up on Labat's plantation were the lucky ones; their circumstances were not typical of life on sugar plantations in Martinique. People who ran more brutal plantations did not write descriptions of them. But Blondel, the *intendant*, gives a glimpse of the harsher realities of plantation life in Martinique. He was investigating the high mortality rate among slaves in 1725, although he did not specify what the mortality rate was.

"This slave mortality," he wrote, "appears to be caused by the heavy labor that the planters make them perform without adequate nourishment. Some planters give them nothing except to let them work for themselves on Saturdays in order to earn their sustenance for the rest of the week; others give them only half the rations that are required by the ordinances of the king; and others give them even less. Still others give them neither the half rations nor the free Saturday. To be fair, there are some planters who give their slaves everything that is required by the Code Noir, but such planters are rare. The others, in contrast, are very numerous."[22]

41

ON MAY 21, 1732, crew members aboard the *Diligent* watched the 270-ton ship *Phénix* glide into St. Pierre's harbor. The long-boat was lowered, and a dozen seamen rowed for shore. They were not crew members of the *Phénix*; rather, they were men who had been stranded in Cayenne when their own ship, the *St. Jean-Baptiste,* had departed at midnight on May 4, leaving them on shore. After arriving in St. Pierre on the *Phénix*, the twelve men went straight to the office of the admiralty to make a deposition. The man who spoke on behalf of the group was Pierre Bernard, second captain of the *St. Jean Baptiste*. It was a strange, nightmarish tale that he told.[1]

The *St. Jean Baptiste*, a ninety-ton ship with a crew of eighteen, was owned, outfitted, and captained by a certain Jean Bonneau from Nantes. To finance the trip, Bonneau had borrowed 28,966 livres as a *cambye* loan at 33 percent interest, a loan that amounted to 60 percent of the total cost of outfitting the voyage. Bonneau had served as captain on at least four previous trips to Guinea, and he was also a combat-hardened veteran of the French Royal Navy, having lost a hand in the service of the king. He was listed in the admiralty records in Nantes as an invalid.[2] Bonneau's problem, it turned out, was not with his hand but with his mind.

Bonneau's ship, the *St. Jean Baptiste,* had left Nantes on August 19, 1731, nearly three months after the *Diligent* departed from Vannes. His plan was to buy slaves in the area around Cape Mesurado, the region where the *Diligent* had made its first landfall on the West African coast. Because there were no European forts or lodges in the region, he planned to cruise the coastline and buy small batches of slaves here and there until his load was complete.

The *St. Jean Baptiste* reached Cape Mesurado on October 23, 1731, and Captain Bonneau went ashore to buy rice and bargain for captives. Nobody knows what happened on shore that day or even *if* anything happened, but when he returned to the ship that night he began mistreating and abusing the crew. The abuse worsened day by day. On the fifth day it exploded. Trembling with rage, Captain Bonneau became extremely abusive toward some African merchants who had come aboard to collect payment for captives they had sold him. He was equally abusive toward the crew, hitting the ship's carpenter, Yves Soyer, with a wooden club so hard that he broke the carpenter's arm. Approaching Second Captain Pierre Bernard, he hit him on the head with the club, ordered him arrested, and relieved him of his office.

Second Captain Bernard was under arrest until the next day, when Captain Bonneau ordered him to leave the ship and take refuge on a British ship anchored nearby. No sooner had he arrived at the British ship than Captain Bonneau followed him in another boat and begged him to return. The captain said that he had struck Bernard by accident when he was really aiming at another seaman standing nearby. Although Second Captain Bernard was not convinced by the explanation, he reluctantly agreed to return to the *St. Jean Baptiste* with captain Bonneau; otherwise he could be charged with desertion.

No sooner had the two men returned to the *St. Jean Baptiste* than captain Bonneau ordered his second captain to fetch his sword. Believing that he was being sent ashore on a mission, he obeyed the order. On returning to the deck, he found Captain Bonneau armed with a sword that he had removed from the trunk of his ensign. The captain ordered the deck cleared and challenged Bernard to a sword fight. Bernard refused, citing the law that a second in command was forbidden to strike his captain. Furious, the captain attacked Barnard and forced him to defend himself. After a few bouts of sword thrusts and parries, the captain backed off and ordered Bernard arrested for a second time.

The next day, October 29, a canoe with three African merchants approached Jean Bonneau's ship. Knowing how the captain had mistreated their comrades a few days earlier, they came aboard with some hesitation, but they wanted their payment for a canoe load of captives that they had delivered a few days earlier. As they approached the captain, he ordered them to be seized. The order caught the crew by surprise, and their moment of hesitation gave the African merchants a chance to dive over the side of the ship and swim to their canoe.

That incident came at a delicate time because the local Africans at Cape Mesurado were holding the ship's ensign hostage on account of the captain's earlier mistreatment of local African merchants. Instead of bargaining to get his ensign back, Captain Bonneau ordered his ship to cruise back and forth firing cannon shots in the direction of the town. Although the ship could not get close enough to the town to actually do any damage, the cannon shots apparently intimidated the local chief into sending out two canoes, one of which carried the ensign. When the canoes arrived, the captain invited the Africans to come aboard to guide his ship to the town of Petit Jonque. Seeing the captain with sword in hand and two pistols in his belt, they refused, but the captain eventually persuaded one of them to come aboard and guide the ship.

After leaving Cape Mesurado, the captain focused his rage on the crew. He severely wounded several seamen with sword and knife attacks, and he even threw boiling water onto one of them. One evening he ordered his major, Jacques David, to retire for the night. A few minutes later he became furious when he called for the major and learned that he was sleeping. When David appeared, the captain gave him some blows with the sword and threatened to hang him from the main yard for sleeping on the job. Then he turned his fury toward Second Captain Bernard. Finding Bernard on the forecastle, the captain approached him sword in hand and ordered him put in irons.

The crew could take it no more. Up to this point they had been reluctant to mutiny because Jean Bonneau was both the captain and the owner of the ship. If they mutinied, they could expect little sympathy from the courts in France. But given that the captain was in a continuous state of fury and that he had threatened many times to kill all the crew members, they decided that the risk of continuing on with the mad captain was greater than the risk of mutiny. Accordingly, they descended on the captain as one, took away his sword, and put him in the very irons that he had designated for Second Captain Bernard. They carried him to his bed in the captain's cabin and left him in irons and under guard. A few days earlier he had tried to set the ship on fire, and if left alone, he was likely to try something like that again.

Having disposed of their captain, the crew unanimously chose Second Captain Pierre Bernard as the new captain of the *St. Jean Baptiste*. Bernard at first refused the honor, knowing that he risked being hanged back in France, but when the crew insisted, he reluctantly accepted the assignment. To protect himself from the legal repercussions of his actions, the new captain drew up a deposition explaining the events and had it signed by all the members of the crew.

The crew was now safe from the fury of their captain, but a greater danger lay before them. Would they ever be able to return to France? Would the French navy pursue them? Would they become outlaws or pirates? Spotting an English ship near Jonque, Pierre Bernard and his crew rowed over in the longboat, told the English captain their story, and asked advice on what to do. The English captain was reluctant to help a group of mutineers, but he remembered a Dutch ship anchored at Bacha that had been at Cape Mesurado, whose crew might know of the incidents. The English ship then left for Bacha, followed by the *St. Jean Baptiste*.

A few days later the *St. Jean Baptiste* met up with the English and Dutch ships at Bacha. Pierre Bernard asked the captains of the two other vessels to come aboard the *St. Jean Baptiste* to see the deposed captain Jean Bonneau and hear the stories of the crew members. After a long meeting on board the *St. Jean Baptiste*, the English and Dutch captains recommended that captain Bonneau remain in irons. They each wrote out a written attestation, later translated into French, as to what they had heard and what they had recommended.

Jean Bonneau remained in irons for almost a month while the *St. Jean Baptiste* continued to trade for slaves along the windward coast. On November 25, Pierre Bernard spotted the French ship the *Grand Phénix*. He went on board the vessel to ask its captain to pass judgment on Captain Bonneau. Although the *Grand Phénix* was a private ship, it was armed and commissioned for war, a situation that gave its captain official standing to pass such a judgment. Captain Tessier of the *Grand Phénix* was ill, but he sent his officers plus the chaplain and the surgeon to visit the *St. Jean Baptiste* and take depositions from crew members.

Pierre Bernard had never been comfortable with his new role as captain of a mutinous crew, and the visit of the French officers gave him a way out of his predicament. As the visitors were about to leave his ship, he announced that he was leaving the *St. Jean Baptiste* and would go along with the visitors to the *Grand Phénix*. Once he was gone, Captain Jean Bonneau should be released from his irons and given command of the ship. The other crew members were so distraught at the prospect of again being under the command of Jean Bonneau that they entered the longboat to join Pierre Bernard on the *Grand Phénix*. When the captain of the *Grand Phénix* saw that the *St. Jean Baptiste* was about to be abandoned by its crew, he ordered Pierre Bernard back to his ship. Back on the *St. Jean Baptiste* he found that Captain Bonneau was still in irons. When he requested the consent of the crew to release the captain, he met with unanimous opposition. Jean Bonneau would remain in irons.

All the while, the *St. Jean Baptiste* was purchasing slaves. The lower deck was starting to fill up with captives who, like Jean Bonneau, were also in irons, but with little hope of being released. When the ship reached the vicinity of Cape Palmas on December 5, Captain Bonneau threatened to sue the crew for twenty thousand livres if they didn't stop at the cape. In his continuing fury, he didn't realize that they were already fifteen leagues past Cape Palmas. The next day, just beyond Cape Palmas, the *St. Jean Baptiste* encountered the *St. Marc,* a private ship out of Nantes that was armed and commissioned for war. When Pierre Bernard asked if it was possible to turn the ship around and return to Cape Palmas, he was told that it was not possible because the Guinea current was too strong. Captain Bonneau then demanded that he be released from his irons. The request was put to a vote of the crew, who rejected it unanimously.

On December 9 the ship stopped at a village that had captives for sale. When canoe loads of captives were brought out to the ship, Pierre Bernard was too sick to meet with the African merchants. The highest-ranking officer on the ship was now the ensign, a young man on his first trip to Guinea who was not capable of conducting the complex negotiations necessary for buying slaves. The ensign suggested that Jean Bonneau be released from his irons in order to conduct the negotiations, and he even promised to ask the captain of a nearby English vessel to oversee the release. Captain Bonneau, for his part, turned conciliatory. He promised that if released he would not mistreat the crew. Even if a crew member deserved to be punished, he vowed, he would not punish him without the consent of all the other officers on the ship. Despite their reservations, the crew voted to release the captain from his irons and restore to him all his former authority over the ship and crew. On December 10 Captain Jean Bonneau was again in command of his ship.

For the next two months the ship resumed slave trading along the Ivory Coast without further incidents between the captain and the crew. We can only imagine how the African captives were treated, given that they were under the control of a mad captain and an angry crew. Because of all the turmoil and confusion, the ship's supplies and merchandise were running low, and so the officers, such as Second Captain Pierre Bernard, spent goods from their personal *pacotilles* to purchase slaves and food for the ship. On February 7, 1732, the *St. Jean Baptiste* set sail for the Americas with a full load of 160 slaves.

The Atlantic crossing did not go well. The *St. Jean Baptiste* encountered contrary winds and deadly periods of calm. Eventually, they made landfall along the coast of Brazil, where they were not allowed to sell their slaves because they were in Portuguese territory. Since the ship was running short of food and they had nothing to sell except their slaves, the officers again reached into their personal *pacotilles* to allow the captain to purchase food for the journey to Cayenne. Up to this point Captain Bonneau had more or less kept his bargain with the crew. But he became violent and abusive on the trip to Cayenne, attacking crew members for no apparent reason.

On April 28 at 3 P.M. Second Captain Bernard was up on the foremast with one of the seamen. The seaman told a joke that made Bernard laugh. Hearing the laughter and thinking that he was the butt of the joke, Captain Bonneau ordered Pierre Bernard to descend. In front of the entire crew he relieved the second captain of his command and promised to put him off the ship at the nearest port. Bernard would be replaced by the inexperienced ensign. He needed only one officer to run his ship, Bonneau declared. During the next few days he became excessively violent, throwing any object at hand at any crew member who happened to be nearby. He gave one seaman a cut that went all the way to the bone and would not allow the ship's doctor to treat the wound. A few days later Captain Bonneau entered the cabin of Pierre Barnard and furiously searched it for arms while cursing and waving a loaded pistol in the air. He ordered Bernard placed under arrest and put an armed sentinel at the door. Thirty minutes later the captain allowed Bernard to leave his cabin provided that he promised to say nothing about the incident.

On May 2 the *St. Jean Baptiste*, still carrying its load of captives, anchored in the harbor of the French colony of Cayenne (French Guyana). For the first time since the mutiny, the ship was in French territory. The captain went ashore and returned two days later without visiting the admiralty office or undertaking the official formalities necessary for selling the slaves. Seeing an opportunity, Pierre Bernard requested permission to go ashore that evening so that he and the other crew members could report the bizarre happenings to the admiralty judge. The captain allowed Bernard and eleven seamen to go ashore. At midnight the seamen on shore received a message that the *St. John Baptist* had set its sails. They ran outside in the pale light of the moon just in time to see the dim outline of the ship sailing out of the harbor. It was heading for Martinique, Bernard was told.

Stranded in Cayenne, Pierre Bernard and his eleven comrades told their story to the judge at the admiralty court. The judge declared Jean Bonneau a fugitive and ordered his longboat, which had been left behind with the shore party, sold for ten livres. The twelve stranded crewmen managed to hire the *Phénix* to take them to Martinique in search of Jean Bonneau and the *St. Jean Baptiste*. They told their stories again at the admiralty office of St. Pierre. They had expected to find the *St. Jean Baptiste* in St. Pierre, but it was nowhere to be found.

Much later the crew would learn that the ship was in Surinam. It had sailed out of Cayenne with a crew of only four. The captain could not help them with the ropes because of his missing hand. Under the circumstances, the crew of four did not believe themselves capable of sailing to Martinique. They were also terrified that the reduced crew might invite a shipboard slave revolt. Instead of going to Martinique, the ship headed for the Dutch colony of Surinam, only thirty-six miles from Cayenne. The captain, the crew of four, and 153 captives arrived the next day. When the Dutch asked them to leave, the four sailors complained that the ship was not seaworthy, but after a cursory inspection by four Dutch carpenters, it was ordered to sail to Martinique. The Dutch were less interested in the safety of the ship than in getting rid of Jean Bonneau.

Upon leaving Surinam, the *St. Jean Baptiste* struck a shallow shoal, where it sat for two days before the currents forced it to roll over and break up. Somehow, the crew and the captives made it to shore, where they were rescued and taken back to Surinam. Captain Bonneau locked up the captives in a warehouse belonging to the Dutch West India Company and sold forty-four of them—mostly young boys and girls—in order to purchase a small English ship. The governor of Surinam ordered Bonneau to leave with his four crewmen and his remaining slaves, and he even posted guards on his ship to monitor its activities. But the captain was in one of his periods of fury, and so violently outrageous were his excesses that the government ordered him arrested and locked in the Dutch fort. His new ship and the remaining captives were sold.

In Martinique, Pierre Bernard and the eleven other stranded crew members found passage to Nantes on a two-hundred-ton ship that was captained by Pierre Chalet and owned by Pierre and Jean Charon of Nantes. The direct-trading vessel left St. Pierre on June 21, 1732, bound for Nantes with 546 barrels of sugar and 88 bales of cotton. Oddly enough, the ship was named *St. Jean Baptiste.*

42

*S*EVEN CANNON SHOTS SHATTERED the morning stillness in St. Pierre's harbor on June 29, 1732. Robert Durand had given the order to fire a salute to Captain Mary in celebration of the feast of St. Peter, sometimes referred to by the crew as "Captain's Day." They had celebrated the previous Feast of St. Peter just as the *Diligent* was crossing the Tropic of Cancer. They had now been away from Vannes for nearly thirteen months. Captain Mary and Second Captain Valteau were not on the *Diligent.* The crew was now divided between those on the ship and those who were loading merchandise into the warehouse that they had rented on shore.

After the slaves had disembarked on March 23, the ship's carpenter, Joseph Colinbert, had been busy reconfiguring the ship to make it a merchant vessel. The work would have gone faster if his colleague, second carpenter Jean Mahé, had not died in Jakin. First Colinbert dismantled the *barricado* that had separated the male captives on the main deck and forecastle from the women on the quarterdeck. Below the deck he took down the thick barrier that divided the men's slave quarters from the women's quarters, and then he took down the platforms that had divided the cramped deck into two levels. The ship was being emptied of its remaining cargo and supplies, which was not a difficult job since the food and water that the ship had been carrying were mostly used up. After the ship had been completely emptied, it was scrubbed clean using hundreds of buckets of water that were then pumped out of the hold. The carpenter was caulking and repairing the wooden hull and was checking and tuning the rigging so that the ship could pass the safety inspection and be allowed to return home.

Captain Mary was ashore in the warehouse with the ship's coopers—Jean Carry, René Botterel, and Joseph Pasco—and other members of the crew. The slave warehouse had been given up in April, when Lamy had purchased the last ninety-six captives, and the captain had rented a merchandise warehouse to receive the sugar, cotton, and rocou that they would receive in exchange for the slaves. As soon as the *Diligent* was reconfigured, they would start loading. But this was Captains' Day, and Pierre Mary had brought some wine and food from the ship for the celebration. Robert Durand and the other officers who were still on the ship celebrated with cannon salutes in the morning and evening.[1]

On shore, the coopers had been especially busy, taking the barrels apart, scrubbing the staves, and putting them back together for reuse. Their main job, however, was to inspect the barrels of sugar that came into the warehouse to make sure that the sugar was protected for the journey back to France. Although the captives of the *Diligent* had been sold for prices fixed in French livres, the prices were merely units of account, and the payments themselves were always made in the products of the island such as sugar, cotton, and rocou. Because the necessary products were not always on hand in sufficient quantities, the standard contract called for 50 percent of the payment for the slaves to be made immediately and the rest to come in six months or a year. Such contracts were not necessarily detrimental to the ship's captains because a load of captives would normally bring about twice as much merchandise as the ship could carry. The balance had to be carried back to France little by little on direct trading vessels, which always had some extra room in their cargo holds. Captain Mary had sold his last ninety-six captives to Lamy on terms that called for the final 50 percent of the payment to be delivered in one year. In effect, Mary had given him an interest-free loan for a year. Such practices cut into the profits of the outfitters. Merchants in Nantes were well aware of the interest losses in such transactions, and they estimated the loss at 6 percent per year.[2]

Most of the payments for the captives came into the warehouse in the form of sugar. Martinique produced two main kinds: raw and clayed. Raw sugar was made by pouring the thick liquid syrup from the boiling house into uncovered pots that had holes in the bottom through which the liquids drained away in about three weeks. The sugar produced by this method was "raw, greasy, brown, and soft."[3] It was the cheapest and poorest-quality sugar produced in Martinique. In 1732 raw sugar made up less than 10 percent of the sugar exported from Martinique.[4]

The bulk of the sugar produced in Martinique was clayed sugar, which was produced by a much more elaborate process. After the sugar had been boiled and cooled, it was placed in cone-shaped molds that were placed over pots like funnels. Wet clay imported from Rouen was then placed over the sugar at the wide end of the cone. The water in the clay passed through the sugar and drained out the narrow end of the cone, taking the impurities with it. This process took nine or ten days and was repeated with a new layer of clay. The loaves of sugar were then placed in the drying room. When the fires of the drying room had accomplished their mission, the sugar loaves were broken open and separated into different grades. The sugar at the narrow end of the cone was the least pure and was called "head sugar." The best sugar was called white sugar, and the grade in between was known as common sugar. The different grades of sugar sold for varying prices: head sugar sold for eighteen livres per hundredweight, common sugar sold for twenty-four livres, and the best white sugar for as much as fifty livres. The best white sugars that emerged from the claying process were so good that they were often mistaken in France for refined sugar, and it was only in April 1731 that the French Council of Commerce clarified the difference.[5]

Whether head, common, or white, the loaves were put into mortars, broken up with iron hoes, and pounded with pestles until the grains separated. Only then could the sugar could be weighed and packed into barrels. The packing process provided ample opportunity for fraud. Some planters tried to pack common or even raw sugar in the middle of the barrel and hide it by putting white sugar at the top and bottom. Other planters used extra-thick barrel staves so that there was less room for sugar inside.[6] Pierre Mary had ordered all three of the *Diligent*'s coopers to be at the warehouse in St. Pierre to open the barrels of sugar that came in and repack the faulty or suspicious ones. The barrels weighed between fifty and sixty livres when empty, and contained about eight hundred livres of sugar apiece.[7]

All together, Pierre Mary purchased 251 barrels of white and common sugar, amounting to 20,800 livres, and ten smaller barrels known as *quarts*, containing about 200 livres of sugar each, bringing the total weight of the sugar to 202,800 livres. Since prices were always quoted in *quintaux*, or hundredweights, the *Diligent* was loading 2,028 hundredweights of sugar.

Because much of this sugar was not completely dry at the time it was loaded, it would lose 13–15 percent of its weight during the Atlantic crossing.[8] The *Diligent* would arrive in Vannes with approximately 1,724 hundredweights of sugar.

Durand did not mention how much of that total was made up of clayed white sugar and how much was clayed common sugar, but we know that in 1732 twenty livres of clayed common sugar entered Nantes for every livre of clayed white sugar.[9] We can reasonably assume that white sugar made up about 5 percent of the total. The *Diligent* was most likely carrying 203 hundredweights of white sugar and 1,825 hundredweights of common sugar. The sugar, Robert Durand noted in his journal, had been purchased at higher prices than they had expected to pay. Because they had sold their captives at low prices and were now purchasing sugar at high prices, they would receive far less sugar for their cargo of African captives than they had anticipated.

The second commodity that Pierre Mary was purchasing was cotton, which was grown in small patches on the mountainsides on land above a thousand feet in elevation. He purchased twenty-three bales of cotton, each weighing about four hundred livres.[10] As with sugar, there was ample opportunity for fraud in the transactions. Some planters soaked the cotton balls that were in the middle of the bale to make it heavier, and the soaked cotton would then rot during the voyage to France. So serious had the problem become that in 1729 the Council of State in France had passed a law mandating a hundred-livre fine for each bale of cotton that contained soaked balls. Each planter was supposed to stamp his name and address on the bales so that he could be pursued if the bale was later found to be faulty. To this the planters protested that the rotten cotton was the fault of ship's captains who stored the bales in leaky warehouses or allowed them to get wet when carrying them to the ship in their longboats.[11] As with the sugar, Robert Durand noted that cotton had cost them dearly.

The final item that Pierre Mary purchased was rocou. A plant native to Martinique, the paste made from its seeds was used to prepare white cloth to receive dyes of various colors. Cloth that had been "rocoued" displayed greater consistency of color than untreated cloth. The rocou bushes were generally planted from March to May. Once a bush reached maturity, it could produce two crops annually for many years: a crop in June and another in December. Like sugar, rocou required complex and intensive processing, making its production a combination of agriculture and industry. After the seeds were removed from the fruit, they were allowed to ferment in calabashes for eight days, after which they were crushed in a mortar to detach the husks from the seeds. The husks were strained and boiled in vats until foam appeared on the surface. The foam was boiled for twelve hours in another vat while being stirred vigorously. Then it was poured into basins to cool into a paste and packed into small barrels called "quarts."[12] Pierre Mary purchased thirteen barrels of rocou, each weighing nearly two hundred livres.[13]

As the sailors at Captain Mary's warehouse ate their holiday meal and drank the ship's red wine, the warehouse looked nearly empty. They had started loading the *Diligent* on May 20, about a month after selling their final lot of slaves to Lamy, and by now they were nearly six weeks into the loading process. Just a few more days and the ship would be ready to sail for France.

Sitting in the harbor bobbing gently on the waves, the *Diligent* had been given the responsibility of commanding the harbor. As many as a hundred ships were sometimes in the St. Pierre harbor at a time, and somebody had to organize the comings and goings and enforce the rules. Normally that job would go to a French Royal Navy vessel or a ship of the Company of the Indies, which sailed under the authority of the king of France. In the absence of such vessels, the command of the harbor was entrusted to a private merchant vessel such as the *Diligent*.[14] The crew was to fire a cannon shot every morning and evening to remind the other ships of their special role. On May 3, when they first raised the banner indicating their command of the harbor, the other vessels in the harbor gave them twenty-one-gun salutes. Their job was to arrest anyone who caused disorder in the harbor. They could put people in irons, tie them to the cannon and whip them, or lock them in the hold, according to the infraction committed. Nevertheless, the job was something to be avoided because enforcing the rules took up the officers' valuable time and firing the cannon shots twice a day used up their gunpowder.

Throughout most of the *Diligent*'s stay in Martinique, Robert Durand had neglected his journal. But with the ship preparing for departure, he tried to sum up his impressions of the island. "Martinique is the American island," he wrote, "that carries on the most beautiful commerce as judged by the large number of vessels that always abound here and by the fertility of its land, which produces beautiful sugar, cotton, coffee, etc. This island furnishes all the other windward isles of America and gives them an outlet for all that they produce. It also commands them in all matters because it is the headquarters of a general and a powerful governor, one at Fort Royal, the other at St. Pierre. St. Pierre is a place so famous for its commerce that each year more than three hundred ships arrive in this harbor loaded with merchandise that sells so well that they return to France loaded with sugar and cotton."

The last of the sugar, cotton, and rocou was removed from the warehouse on July 5 and loaded onto the ship. The barrels of sugar had been packed into the hold where the water barrels had been during the middle passage. With only thirty-three people on board, the water supplies on the *Diligent* took up very little space. The bales of cotton were stacked on the lower deck, where the captives had been imprisoned during the middle passage. This was the driest part of the ship. Even with the twenty-three cotton bales, there was now ample room for the crew to hang their hammocks on the lower deck for a decent night's sleep. Robert Durand understood that the cargo on the *Diligent* represented only half the value that the Billy brothers would receive in exchange for the African captives, because the sale contracts had called for 50 percent of the payment to be made immediately and the remaining 50 percent payable in six months or a year.

By the morning of July 12 the *Diligent* was ready to sail. The merchandise, food, and water had been loaded, and the sailcloth awnings that had sheltered the deck were removed and reattached to the yards. But the departure did not go smoothly. When Pierre Mary gave the order to weigh anchor, the crew discovered that the *Diligent's* anchor line had become entangled with that of the ship *Renommé*, and it was not until two o'clock in the afternoon that the anchor was freed. With all sails furled, the ship drifted in the harbor as the crew worked to haul up the longboat and place it in its position on the deck. Captain Mary was not on the *Diligent* because he had gone over to the *Renommé* to discuss the anchor problem and had stayed for lunch. Because of their fear of pirates, the *Diligent* would be traveling back to France in a convoy together with the *Renommé* and the *St. Anne*.

By four o'clock in the afternoon Captain Mary was back on board the *Diligent* ordering the crew to prepare for departure. A longboat arrived carrying a soldier who had been sent by Mr. Begue, the commandant of St. Pierre, with a request that Captain Mary go ashore to discuss certain matters. The same soldier had come out that morning with the same request, and Captain Mary had refused to go. After refusing a second time, Captain Mary ordered the sails set immediately in order to move the *Diligent* out of cannon range of the fort.

Seeing the *Diligent* preparing to depart, the soldiers at the fort fired a cannonball that made a huge splash just short of the ship. It had come too close! The *Diligent* was now moving out of cannon range, and the fort did not fire a second shot. Writing in his journal later that day, Robert Durand described the events but did not provide answers to any of the questions that the incident raised. Why was Captain Mary summoned by the commandant of St. Pierre? Why did he refuse to go? Why did he hastily set sail in anticipation of cannon shots from the fort? Had he been involved in some shady deals in St. Pierre? We will never know. "I am in the dark as to the cause of the cannon shot," Durand wrote in his journal.

PART 12

The Return

43

*A*T 7:00 A.M. ON September 22, 1732, eleven sailors from the *Diligent* filed into the indoor food market in Vannes. Thirty butcher shops filled the southern portion of the building, sellers of white bread occupied the central part, and merchants selling rye bread filled the western part. The east side of the market housed the cloth sellers and haberdashers.[1] Bypassing the crowds, smells, and shouts of the market, the sailors climbed the stairs to the courtroom on the second floor.

Less than three weeks had passed since the *Diligent* had returned to the Gulf of Morbihan and anchored off the island of Bouëdec. The crew had been busy unbending the sails and striking the yards and upper masts. Small boats had begun unloading the barrels of sugar and rocou and the bales of cotton to carry them to Nantes, where they would be sold. As soon as the sailors were released from the *Diligent*, they received subpoenas to appear at the admiralty court. The Billy brothers and their partner La Croix had filed a lawsuit against Captain Mary.

Lawsuits by ship owners against their captains were not unknown in Vannes, and the admiralty court averaged about one such case per year. Usually they involved captains who didn't deliver their grain on time or failed to pay adequate shares to the investors. Robert Billy, the father of the Billy brothers, had once sued the captain of a grain ship that sank in the Gulf of Morbihan.[2] This was the first time, however, that a slaving captain was being sued in the admiralty court of Vannes.

The charges against Captain Mary fell into three general areas. First, he had squandered the ship's supplies in unnecessary extravagance. Second, he had traded merchandise belonging to the ship on his own account. The third area was the most serious: Captain Mary had on two occasions switched one of his personally purchased slaves for one belonging to the outfitters of the voyage.

When the eleven witnesses entered the courtroom, they were greeted by Pierre Jarno, the attorney for the Billy brothers and La Croix, and sworn in by the presiding officer, Charles-Louis Chanu.[3] When neither Captain Mary nor his lawyer, François Pihan, had arrived by 7:30, the court sent a bailiff to find the lawyer. Pihan told the bailiff that he had no witnesses and would not be present at the depositions. The judge declared Pihan in default and proceeded without him.

During the depositions, several sailors testified that the captain had received six to ten rolls of Brazilian tobacco, each weighing sixty to eighty pounds, by trading four of the *Diligent*'s barrels of salted beef to an English ship and hauling fresh water in the *Diligent*'s longboat for two Portuguese ships. Most of the tobacco had been distributed to the crew and the slaves during the middle passage, but the captain had sold two rolls on his own account in Martinique. Just before the ship anchored in the Gulf of Morbihan, Captain Mary had thrown the remaining tobacco—about a third of a roll—into the sea. Several of the sailors reported hearing rumors that the captain had tried to force the officers to sign an attestation regarding the number of slaves they were carrying, but none of them had seen it themselves. Several sailors also confirmed that among the seven or eight slaves who died during the crossing between Jakin and Martinique, one of them had belonged to Captain Mary.

As the sailors testified, the clerk wrote down their statements. Then he read back the depositions and asked the witnesses to sign them. Of the eleven witnesses, only five could sign their names. When the last deposition was finished, the presiding officer called a recess of one hour to wait for Pierre Mary or his lawyer to appear. When neither of them showed up, Charles-Louis Chanu closed the proceedings for the day.

No officers had yet testified. Second Captain Valteau was a tainted witness because he was the captain's brother-in-law. The ship's surgeon, Devigne, had left soon after the *Diligent* landed. First Lieutenant Robert Durand

and Second Lieutenant Thomas Laragon had been subpoenaed, but they had already left the *Diligent* and were unavailable on September 22. They were sworn in on Wednesday, September 24.

This time François Pihan, the lawyer for Captain Mary, was present. He protested that the lawsuit was frivolous and should be dismissed immediately. He also complained that he had not been given enough time to brush up on the relevant laws and ordinances. When those motions were denied, he requested that Laragon should be removed from the witness list because he was prejudiced against the captain. During the voyage Laragon had had several public arguments and confrontations with the captain, and he had displayed a general lack of respect for his superior officer. Like the other motions, this one was denied. The lawyer raised no objection to the testimony of Robert Durand. Because of the lateness of the hour, the presiding officer ordered the proceedings suspended until one o'clock the next afternoon.

Durand testified on Thursday, September 25.[4] He raised his right hand and swore that none of the parties in the dispute were his relatives or partners. He also swore that he was no longer in the service of the Billy brothers nor was he under the command of Captain Mary. As a free agent, he swore to tell the truth.

Pierre Jarno, the lawyer for the Billy brothers and La Croix, began the questioning. "During the time when you commanded the tent on the beach at Jakin, did you obtain any gold?"

"Yes, Monsieur," Durand replied. "I sold brandy and smoking pipes for a total sum of fifteen ounces and eight ackies of gold, which I turned over to Captain Mary. I have a receipt for it in the form of a letter signed by the pilot, Sabatier, because Captain Mary was sick on board the ship at the time. During the entire period that I was at the tent, I kept a daily account book, which I turned over to Captain Mary when I left the tent to command the warehouse in Jakin."

"While you were in Jakin, did Captain Mary trade merchandise belonging to the ship's cargo for personal items?"

"I have no personal knowledge of these things because I was at the tent on the beach. But I have heard that Captain Mary ordered the *Diligent's* longboat to haul water for a Portuguese ship, and I heard that he received Brazilian tobacco in return. I also heard that he purchased a knife and a gold ring from Mr. Verger and paid for them with a length of limancas cloth belonging to the ship's cargo."

"What did Captain Mary do with the tobacco he received from the Portuguese ship in Jakin?"

"He sold it in Martinique to a Mr. Thuillon for liqueurs. I don't know how much tobacco he sold or how many bottles of liqueur he received in exchange."

"Did you purchase any captives when you were at the tent on the beach in Jakin?"

"Yes, I purchased eighteen captives for the account of the cargo."

"How many captives in all were purchased at Jakin?"

"By my best recollection, there were 201 captives belonging to the cargo, plus fifty-six belonging to the *pacotilles* of the officers. Captain Mary had twenty-seven, Second Captain Valteau had thirteen, I had five, Laragon had three, Dr. Devigne had five, and Jean Leglan had one. I believe, though I cannot be certain, that Sabatier had one, and that Captain Mary purchased one captive from René Touchard, the second surgeon who died soon after we left Jakin."

"Why aren't you sure?"

"I recorded all those figures in my personal journal, which I kept for my own use, but I don't have it with me right now. I am giving you my best recollection of the numbers of captives."

"How many captives died during the Atlantic crossing?"

"Eight captives died. Seven of them belonged to the cargo. The other one belonged to Captain Mary. I saw the brand mark on the left shoulder of the dead captive. I wrote it down in my personal journal."

"Isn't it common practice that when a slave dies, the captain should write out a declaration signed by the officers of the ship verifying the marks on the dead captive?"

"Yes. That is correct."

"Was such a declaration drawn up in the case of the captive that you claim belonged to Captain Mary?"

"No. There was no verification and no declaration. I only know that I saw Captain Mary's mark on the shoulder of the slave."

"Did any of the other captives who died carry the marks of any of the *Diligent's* officers?"

"Not to my knowledge."

"Did Captain Mary ask the officers to sign a declaration relating to the number of captives that the officers were carrying as *pacotilles*?"

"Yes. Captain Mary prepared a declaration to deal with the issue of the slaves that he and the other officers had purchased above the number permitted in our port permit. The declaration gave a reduced figure for the slaves belonging to himself and the officers. Mary tried to force Dr. Devigne and Second Lieutenant Laragon to sign it, but the doctor left without signing. Later I heard Laragon swear that he would not sign the false declaration because it would weigh too heavily on his conscience."

"Did Captain Mary ask you to sign the declaration?"

"No. I never saw or read the declaration myself."

Pierre Jarno paused, looked at his notes, and continued the questioning. "Do you know of any other fraud that Captain Mary committed with regard to the African captives?"

"Yes, monsieur. One of the slaves belonging to Captain Mary went mad during the middle passage. That slave had been purchased for the captain by Sabatier and branded on the left shoulder to indicate that he belonged to Captain Mary. The captain replaced the mad slave with one in excellent condition who belonged to the ship. The mad slave, who still bore Captain Mary's mark, was sold along with the ship's slaves in the warehouse in St. Pierre."

"Did you see any other captives in the warehouse who bore the mark of Captain Mary?"

"Three or four of the slaves in the warehouse bore Captain Mary's mark, but I cannot say if they had been exchanged for slaves belonging to the ship."

Jarno had elicited the information he wanted. He would seal it with a final question: "Can you verify the information that you have given us?"

"While I was commanding the warehouse in Jakin, I kept careful records in an account book. All of the different transactions made by the different officers are recorded there in their own handwriting. I gave that book to Captain Mary."

After Robert Durand was dismissed, it was the turn of Second Lieutenant Thomas Laragon. He was the last of the thirteen witnesses. Laragon's testimony was generally consistent with that of Durand, but he added a few details. He testified that the *Diligent* had left Jakin with 250-something slaves: 201 or 202 belonged to the ship, and the rest belonged to the *pacotilles* of the officers. Eight captives had died during the Atlantic crossing: seven of them belonged to the outfitters and one belonged to Captain Mary. In addition, five captives had died in Martinique. Of the *pacotille* slaves, twenty-six belonged to Captain Mary, thirteen to Second Captain Valteau, five to First Lieutenant Durand, five to Dr. Devigne, and three divided among Sabatier, Touchard, and Leglan. In Martinique the captain had exchanged his *pacotille* slave who had gone mad for one or two slaves belonging to the ship.

Unlike Robert Durand, who had never seen the declaration that Captain Mary tried to persuade the officers to sign, Laragon had seen it with his own eyes. The purpose of the declaration, he testified, was to justify the fact that the ship was carrying more *pacotille* slaves than their port permit allowed, while at the same time understating the true number of *pacotille* slaves on board. According to the declaration, the ship was carrying only six more *pacotille* slaves than it was allowed, whereas the true number was much higher. Despite the heavy pressure that the captain put on him, he had refused to sign the false declaration.

The only way to verify the truth of his recollections, Laragon explained, was to examine the account book that had been kept by the various officers who had conducted transactions at the warehouse in Jakin. That notebook could clear up all discrepancies in the testimony of the various witnesses. The problem, the court understood very well, was that the account book had been turned over to Captain Mary. It would have to be found before the matter could be cleared up.

44

ITH THE TRIAL IN recess while the court tried to obtain Pierre Mary's account books, the Billy brothers occupied themselves with unloading the *Diligent* and selling the sugar, rocou, and cotton in its hold. Only after the merchandise was sold would the Billy brothers know if they had made a profit on the voyage and if so, how much. The calculations of profits and losses did not depend on Pierre Mary's account books because the *Diligent*, like other merchant ships in the early eighteenth century, conducted its trade largely by barter. Money served only as a unit of account to determine how many barrels of sugar or how many bales of cotton would be received for each African captive sold in Martinique.

Ascertaining the bottom line of the barter accounting systems was relatively simple. First, the Billy brothers determined how much money they had received for their sugar, rocou, and cotton after customs duties, barge, and warehousing costs had been deducted. That was their return on the voyage. Their outlay was the sum listed in the original *mise-hors* plus the wages paid to the crew members, insurance premiums, and interest on their loans. They also had to pay the Company of the Indies ten livres for each slave delivered to Martinique, as specified in their subcontracting agreement.[1] The costs were then subtracted from the returns to determine profit and loss. The situation would have been relatively straightforward were it not that the *Diligent* had brought back only half the merchandise that was owed to the Billy brothers. Only after the last grain of sugar had been sold could the final reckoning take place.

Despite all the talk in Nantes about the values of free enterprise, the financial structure of the slave trade favored large traders who outfitted several different ships over small traders with their investment sunk into a single ship. Large traders had sufficient capital to finance the delays in the returns. They could use the late returns from previous voyages to finance new ones, and losses from any single voyage would be offset by profits from others. For small traders such as the Billy brothers the total profit and loss balance rested on a single voyage.

Once the Billy brothers saw what the *Diligent* had carried back from Martinique, they knew that the huge profits they had anticipated would not be realized. In discussions that turned into shouting matches, Pierre Mary had tried to explain that with the trade at Whydah shut down by Assou and with fifteen slave ships anchored at Jakin, the prices they had paid for African captives were higher than they had anticipated. He also tried to explain that the destruction of the cocoa trees and the small estates in Martinique had driven slave prices down. He had tried to sell the captives for 950 livres each but had been forced to settle for 450. Knowing that their profits would be meager at best, the Billy brothers took out their anger and disappointment in their lawsuit against Pierre Mary.

The evidence presented against Mary so far had made it clear that the captain had cheated his employers, but some of the charges were nevertheless extremely petty. Mary was accused of using food from the ship to provide a meal for the crew at the warehouse in St. Pierre, Martinique, on the festival of St. Peter. He was also accused of using the ship's gunpowder to fire cannon salutes on the morning of the festival. Another charge was that he had used a piece of cloth belonging to the ship to barter for a knife belonging to Pierre Verger, the ship's passenger. If the profits from the voyage had been as high as the Billy brothers had anticipated, they might have been willing to overlook the captain's small infractions. Under the present circumstances, however, they were squeezing every *sou* out of the shady captain.

Unloading and selling the sugar, cotton, and rocou that the *Diligent* had brought back from Martinique was neither a simple nor an inexpensive process. The products were loaded onto small coasting vessels to be taken down the coast and up the Loire River to Nantes. The transportation cost at least four *sols* (20 sols = 1 livre) per hundredweight. When the boats arrived in Nantes there were costs for unloading, wheelbarrow transport, weighing, barrel work, and storage that came to nearly half a livre per hundredweight. The transporters had a reputation for breaking the barrels and damaging the contents. "You would not believe," wrote a *négociant* to his correspondent in the islands, "the losses that we suffer in discharging a ship at the mouth of the river and then at our quays. When the staves of the barrels give way, one is often obliged to reload the sugar into new barrels."[2]

Right at the Quai de la Fosse in Nantes was a customs office of limited authority. Ever since its incorporation into France in 1532, Brittany had maintained a certain degree of independence with regard to tariffs and customs duties, and it was characterized for customs purposes as "so-called foreign province." Goods from Brittany did not officially enter the French customs union until they passed through the customs office at Ingrande, some thirty miles up the Loire from Nantes, at the point where the Loire left Brittany and entered into the provinces of the French Customs Union. Sugar, cotton, and rocou that came into Nantes from the Caribbean had to pay duty to the *Domaine d'Occident*, which had authority over trade with France's Caribbean islands, and they also had to pay municipal duties called *droits de prévoté et ville*.[3] At that point the goods could be reexported to other countries without having officially entered the French Customs Union.

The cotton industry in Nantes had taken advantage of its customs privileges to develop the first modern factory ever built in the city. Whereas the traditional weavers of flax still worked with home looms as individual artisans, the cotton cloth factory had a hundred looms and employed about a thousand workers who lived in company-built quarters. Most of the rough cotton cloth produced at the factory was sent to West Africa to be traded for slaves, and the rest was sent directly to the West Indies to be used as clothing for slaves.[4] Little did the slaves in Martinique who worked in cotton fields suspect that their product would be used to purchase other captives to join them in their fields.

In a similar way, the sugar merchants of Nantes tried to take advantage of the customs situation to reexport two-thirds the sugar that came in from the West Indies to Holland, Germany, Spain, and Italy. French sugar exports dominated the European market in the eighteenth century. In 1730 France exported about 35 million pounds of sugar, whereas its nearest competitor, England, exported only 20 million pounds. England received almost twice as much sugar from its colonies as did France, but its high rate of domestic consumption left little for export. The profits from French exports of sugar and other colonial products were the key to maintaining a favorable balance of trade with their European neighbors.[5]

The sugar that was not reexported was refined in Nantes or sent up the Loire through the customs station at Ingrande to be refined in Orleans, Angers, Saumur, and Tours. At the end of the seventeenth century, Nantes had thirteen sugar refineries. But after the French Customs Union slapped a duty of fourteen livres per hundredweight on refined sugar entering the French Customs Union through the customs post at Ingrande, the Nantes refining industry declined. In 1732 there were only three or four refineries left in Nantes, and cities that were located up the Loire and inside the French Customs Union became the centers of sugar refining in France. Since raw sugar could be imported into the French Customs Union for 2.5 livres per hundredweight, it was far more economical to ship raw sugar through the customs post at Ingrande and have it refined in Orleans, Angers, Saumur, and Tours.[6]

Refined sugar was then sent to Paris and other cities, where apothecaries used it for making medicine and grocers sold it for sweetening food and drink. It was probably consumed mainly by the nobles and the bourgeoisie; the vast majority of rural Frenchmen probably never tasted sugar. Even with sugar consumption increasing steadily from 1730 on, per capita sugar consumption in France was only about one-tenth that of England. One scholar has theorized that the French had less interest in sugar because they drank so much wine, whereas the English, who drank mostly beer and ale, were developing a taste for sweetened tea. As for desserts, the French maintained a stronger taste for cheese than for sweets.[7]

An added incentive for shipping raw sugar up the Loire to be refined was that sugar obtained in exchange for slaves could pass the customs port at Ingrande for only half the normal duties, whereas sugar that had been obtained in the direct trade with France had to pay full duties. Since both categories of sugar looked exactly alike, the only way to differentiate them was by means of the exemption certificates issued to slave traders. That customs differential gave rise to the bizarre situation in which direct traders found it advantageous to claim that sugar they had received in exchange for the wines of Brittany and the salted beef of Ireland was actually the fruit of the slave trade. The best strategy for the direct traders was to send their sugar through the customs post at Ingrande under the exemption certificate of a slave trader.

According to the customs officials, the fraud was carried out in the following way: If a slave trader arrived in Nantes with eight hundred barrels of sugar, accompanied by an exemption certificate for eight hundred barrels, he might immediately reexport four hundred of them to Holland. He would then replace them with four hundred barrels of sugar belonging to direct traders and send all eight hundred barrels up the Loire through the customs post at Ingrande. In return for smuggling sugar belonging to the direct traders through customs under his exemption certificate, the slave trader collected a 15–20 percent commission from the direct trader.[8]

The slave traders of Nantes vigorously denied the charges. They claimed that most of the sugar the customs agents found suspicious was actually late-arriving sugar from previous slave trading transactions, and therefore it could legitimately enter France under the exemption certificates. Despite the denials, the customs officials seized several cargoes of sugar in 1731.[9] Given that all sugar from the slave trade was exempted from half of the duties charged at Ingrande and that two-thirds of the sugar that arrived in Nantes was reexported and never arrived at Ingrande, it would be surprising if the customs collectors at Ingrande ever received full customs payments on any sugar at all.

The sugar scandal at Ingrande underlined the close relationship between the slave trade and sugar. The main purpose of the suffering and death experienced by African captives who had been forced onto the *Diligent* was to keep the sugar plantations of the West Indies producing at a feverish pitch. That sugar, in turn, was sold to the upper classes in France, Holland, Germany, Spain, and Italy. It would not be far-fetched to conclude that the main reason for the misery and death of the *Diligent* captives was to supply wealthy Europeans with sugar for their tea and cakes.

It was not until over a year later, after the *Diligent* returned from Martinique with the rest of the goods, that the Billy brothers could draw up the final balance sheet of the slaving voyage of 1731–1732. If the planters and slave resellers of Martinique paid their debts in a year as promised in the sales contracts, then the Billy brothers were lucky. Debts could drag on for up to ten years in the island trade.[10] Assuming that the second half of the cargo came in on time and was sold under similar conditions to the first half, then we can imagine the look of consternation on the face of the Billy brothers and La Croix when their clerk added up the total figures. The voyage had cost eighteen lives and had resulted in a net loss of over two thousand livres.[11] Under the circumstances, it is not surprising that the Billy brothers never sent the *Diligent* on a slaving voyage again.

ROBERT DURAND WAS BACK in the courtroom on February 28, 1733, five months after his previous appearance. Since the original depositions, the case had focused on the missing account books. The most important evidence was in the register kept at the warehouse in Jakin, where most of the captives had been purchased. Several different officers had been in command of the warehouse at different times, and each had written in that same register. By the testimony of all concerned, the accounts had been left in the hands of Pierre Mary, and so the court ordered him to produce them.

Mary at first claimed that no account books had been kept. But under continued pressure from the court, he produced two sets of papers in November.[1] The first comprised five pieces of paper attached together with the title: "Rough draft of the merchandise and that which I received from the ship to send to the warehouse in Jakin, and at the same time to account for the trading that I did here for the account of the ship *Diligent* either in gold or in captives, to aid me, Robert Durand, officer of the tent of the *Diligent*." It was the personal scratch pad that Robert Durand had used while he commanded the tent on the beach of Jakin from September 13 to October 23, 1731. As the officer of the tent, he had recopied the figures into a proper account book, but that book was nowhere to be found. Durand had given the draft pages and the account book itself to Captain Mary when he had left the tent on October 24 to take command of the warehouse in Jakin.

Pierre Jarno, the lawyer for the Billy brothers and La Croix, had examined the pages with great skepticism. They were a rough draft of the accounts and not the accounts themselves. More telling was the fact that many of the numbers had been altered in different ink. Jarno strongly suspected that it was Captain Mary who had altered the figures. The main problem with the document, however, was that it contained accounts from the tent on the beach and not from the warehouse in Jakin, where the bulk of the slave trading had taken place.

The second document was even less helpful than the first. It was a single piece of paper with numbers on both sides. One side contained the title, "Merchandise sent to the warehouse, October 26." At the top of the other side was written, "Notes of what I received at the tent, belonging to the ship, beginning October 26, 1731," and at the bottom was the date November 14 and the signature of François Sabatier, the *Diligent*'s pilot, who had replaced Robert Durand at the tent. These were clearly the rough notes of Sabatier at the tent from October 26 to November 14. Like the earlier document, it showed signs of having been altered: on the second side were several numbers in the handwriting of Captain Mary. The two documents, even though altered, provided a general indication of the activities at the tent, but the accounts of slave trading at the warehouse in Jakin were still missing.

It was not until mid-February that Pierre Mary turned over an account book that he claimed was the one the court had been seeking. Ever skeptical, the lawyer for the Billy brothers and La Croix demanded an evidentiary hearing to authenticate the evidence. Robert Durand and Thomas Laragon, both of whom had written in the account book at the warehouse in Jakin, were quickly called in to testify before the *Diligent* departed for the Mediterranean.

The hearing was presided over by Noël Bourgeois, the judge from the présidial court who also served as lieutenant general of the admiralty court. Pierre Jarno, the attorney for the Billy brothers and La Croix was present, but François Pihan, the attorney for Captain Mary, was not. Because this hearing concerned a potentially crucial piece of evidence, the judge decided to wait while a bailiff went to look for attorney Pihan. The attorney finally arrived three hours late.

Jarno, the lawyer for the Billy brothers and La Croix, began questioning Robert Durand.[2] "When you were trading on the coast of Africa, was there a register book in which the accounts of slave purchases were kept?"

"Yes, monsieur. There was a register book of approximately forty or fifty pages of common paper with no cover, which never left the warehouse at Jakin. This book was used by different officers who took turns commanding the warehouse. When one officer would become ill, he would go back to the ship to recover in the healthy sea air, and would be replaced by another."

"Did you write in that book? And do you have knowledge of other people who wrote in that register book?"

"Yes, monsieur. Mister Dubourdieu, a passenger on the *Diligent*, served as assistant to Captain Mary when we first arrived in Jakin. He was the first to write in it, and it was he who set up the columns and their headings. He became ill after seven or eight days at the warehouse and retired to stay with a friend. After his departure, Captain Mary kept the accounts. He fell ill about fifteen days after the departure of Dubourdieu, and so Second Captain Valteau left the ship to replace Captain Mary. Valteau kept the accounts in the register for about a month before he fell ill and returned to the ship. I replaced Second Captain Valteau at the warehouse. For fifteen days I kept the accounts in the register book, and after that Captain Mary returned to the warehouse, having recovered from his illness. During the next eight days Captain Mary sometimes wrote in the register and sometimes I wrote in it. Then I became ill and returned to the ship. Captain Mary remained in charge of the account book until the trade was concluded."

"Did anyone else write in the account book?"

"Second Lieutenant Thomas Laragon was at the warehouse from the very beginning. Sometimes he aided Captain Mary, Mr. Dubourdieu, and Pierre Valteau by writing down certain transactions in the book."

"Can you describe the account book in which you and the other officers wrote down records of their transactions while purchasing slaves at the warehouse?"

"Yes, monsieur. The register contained the date of the purchase of each slave, the name of the person who sold the slave, and the merchandise that we gave in exchange. We also recorded the gold that we purchased. The last third of the register book contained separate columns for each kind of merchandise—brandy, limancas cloth, linen cloth, cases of smoking pipes, cases of muskets—that went on for six or seven pages. Each time a transaction was recorded in the first part of the register, goods spent in the transaction were also noted in the appropriate columns at the back of the register."

At this point the account book that had been submitted by Captain Mary was shown to Durand. It contained about seventy-five sheets of paper. The cover consisted of a large piece of parchment. On one side was written the title "The loading of the ship *Diligent* commanded by Mr. Mary." On the back cover were the words, "Consumption, 1731." Durand paged through the register book and nodded to indicate that he has finished his examination. The lawyer continued his questions. "Is this the account book that you have been telling us about?"

"No, monsieur. This is not the register book that I have been telling you about. This is a register kept by Second Captain Valteau, the brother-in-law of Captain Mary. It contains records of the loading of the *Diligent* in Vannes and the consumption of food during the voyage. It contains nothing about the trade in slaves that we conducted in Jakin."

Thus ends the official record of the court case against Captain Pierre Mary, a man accused of defrauding his employers, but not of playing a key role in the deaths and ruined lives of 256 Africans. The final disposition of the case took place sometime later, when the judge, Noël Bourgeois, pronounced his judgment in the civil suit. The judgment was duly recorded in the Register of Audiences. That register book was still intact seventy-six years later when someone made an inventory of the admiralty records. At some point after that—we don't know when—all of the Registers of Audiences from 1689 to 1780 disappeared.[3] We will never know what Judge Noël Bourgeois pronounced on the fate of Pierre Mary.

We have ample grounds for speculation. Given that thirteen officers and sailors testified against the captain and nobody testified in his defense, it seems certain that the judge found in favor of the plaintiffs. But for how much? Of the various charges against Pierre Mary, the ones most amply proven by the testimony were that he had sold two rolls of tobacco in Martinique for bottles of liqueur and that he had used a piece of cloth belonging to the ship to purchase a knife and a ring. More seriously, he had switched a healthy slave belonging to the ship for his own personal slave who had gone mad and would therefore have fetched a lower price, and he had switched a slave of the cargo for his own personal slave who had died. On these charges, the judgment against Captain Mary would have come to a couple of thousand livres at the most. In addition, he was probably fined several thousand livres for carrying personally owned *pacotille* slaves in excess of his authorization.[4] Given that he had made substantial profits from the sale of his personally owned captives in Martinique, the judgment would not have done him serious financial damage. Perhaps that is why he did not mount a vigorous defense.

There is one thing that we know for certain about the outcome of this case: that Captain Mary never again commanded a slaving vessel. The court case may not have ruined him financially, but it did end his career. In addition to having the civil judgment go against him, Pierre Mary was probably found guilty of violating book 2, title 1, article 20 of the Ordonnance de la Marine, which stated that any captain who sold merchandise belonging to the outfitters must pay for the goods out of his own funds. Then he should be "declared unworthy of being a captain and banned from the port of the city where he lives."[5] By the strange ethical standards of slaving ports, Pierre Mary had been declared dishonorable.

46

*B*ARELY TWO WEEKS AFTER his testimony at the admiralty court in Vannes, Robert Durand was on his way to the Mediterranean as second captain of the *Diligent*. His promotion had come about partially because Pierre Valteau, who had been the second captain during the slaving voyage, was now off the crew because of his close association with Pierre Mary, but it was also a reward for his testimony against his former captain. In preparing for this voyage, the Billy brothers fired most of the crew. They replaced Pierre Mary with Captain Louis Jugan, who recruited a new crew from his hometown of Saint-Malo. The only three people from Le Croisic who were on the *Diligent* when it sailed on March 15 were Second Captain Robert Durand, Lieutenant Thomas Laragon, and a young man named Pierre Durand—almost certainly a relative of Robert—who came along as an officer in training. Two years earlier Pierre Mary had demoted Robert Durand in favor of his brother-in-law Pierre Valteau. Now Durand was getting his revenge.

The Mediterranean trip marked a clear shift in the commercial strategy of the Billy brothers. The first leg of the trip carried grain from Vannes to Marseille. Although grain exports from Brittany to other provinces of France had been forbidden by law since 1724, a series of bad harvests in Provence beginning in 1730 had forced the government to allow grain exports to Marseille. This meant that the Billy brothers could fill the *Diligent* with grain produced in the hinterland of Vannes instead of relying on imported trade goods purchased in Nantes.

The grain that the *Diligent* carried to Marseille was exchanged for olive oil, soap, and other products that were then taken to Martinique to be exchanged for sugar and cotton. Since the value of a shipload of goods from France was rarely enough to fill up more than half the ship with sugar and cotton from Martinique, the trip would also give the *Diligent* a chance to pick up the remaining cargo that was owed to it from the sale of the slaves in 1732. From Martinique the *Diligent* returned to Marseille, sold the West Indies cargo, and loaded up with Mediterranean products to carry to Nantes.[1]

The *Diligent*'s return trip met with bad luck. Sometime after leaving Marseille on April 4, 1734, with a load of olive oil, soap, and other merchandise, several large waves slammed into the ship. So great was their force that Captain Jugan feared that some of the olive oil barrels had broken and that the combination of oil and water in the hold had ruined much of the merchandise. After he had anchored at Paimboeuf (which served as the mooring area for Nantes) on May 7, he immediately took a boat to Nantes and filed a declaration of the damage.[2] The document would be useful if the Billy brothers tried to collect insurance on their losses.

The *Diligent* did not stay long in Nantes. On June 30, 1734, less than two months after its arrival, it departed for Cadiz, Marseille, and other Mediterranean ports. It would not cross the Atlantic on this voyage. This time there was a new captain—a certain Jacques Coedel—and Robert Durand served as first lieutenant. This was not a demotion for Durand; the Mediterranean voyage did not require a large crew and therefore the ship was sailing without a second captain. The ship returned to Nantes on March 26, 1735.[3]

By December the *Diligent* was back in the Gulf of Morbihan, loaded and ready to depart. But this time it was a simple grain ship, and the Billy brothers were back to being simple grain merchants. Robert Durand was no longer on the crew, and it had a new captain, Jacques le Boda. Carrying 129 tons of wheat, the *Diligent* ran aground off the point of Long Island before it ever got out of the Gulf of Morbihan. After repeated attempts to free the *Diligent*, the Billy brothers went to court to request permission to dump the wheat into the gulf in hopes of salvaging the ship. The court appointed two experts—Dubodan and Desruisseaux—to visit the ship and make a recommendation about what to do with the grain. When the two men visited the ship on December 27, they found that the wheat was rotten and emitting a foul odor. It was good for nothing except to be thrown into the sea.[4]

Here the record of the *Diligent* ends. It seems likely that the ship was too badly damaged to be used again. As befits a ship that had been the site of so much human misery, our last glimpse of the *Diligent* in the documentary record shows it making a great stink in the Gulf of Morbihan.

Robert Durand was not on the *Diligent* when it ran aground because he had left the crew in March 1735. His four voyages on the *Diligent* had given him the experience he needed to apply for certification as a captain. After being examined for his knowledge of navigation, winds, tides, and currents by a panel of experts at the admiralty court in Nantes, he received his official certification as a captain on October 22, 1736.[5]

As a certified captain, Robert Durand was eager to command a slave-trading voyage to Africa, where he had not been since the slaving voyage of the *Diligent* in 1731–1732. The detailed drawings of the castles and shoreline of West Africa and the careful records of prices and merchandise that he had kept in his private journal in 1731 and 1732 would serve him well if he went back to Guinea. He was soon hired as a captain by G. Bouteiller and Son, *négociants* from Nantes who would outfit eight slaving voyages between 1739 and 1749.

His first voyage was a near disaster. Leaving Nantes in October 1739, he sailed his 160-ton ship, the *Valeur*, to the area near the mouth of the Congo River, where he purchased 547 slaves. After a smooth middle passage in which there were very few deaths, the ship approached Cape Français in St. Domingue. Twelve miles from the harbor the *Valeur* ran aground and sank. Fortunately, all of the slaves and crew made it safely to shore. Despite the loss of the ship, the venture nevertheless turned out to be profitable for the outfitters. Durand would get another chance. His next slaving voyage left Nantes in October 1741 in the 160-ton ship the *Perle*, and the destination was Whydah. Durand purchased 451 captives but had a disastrous Atlantic crossing in which ninety of the captives died. Durand also lost seven crew members on that voyage.[6]

Durand's next, and last, slaving voyage left Nantes on April 29, 1746. It was a dangerous time to undertake a voyage because France had declared war on Britain on March 15, 1744. Britain's naval strategy was to shut down the French slave and colonial trades by blockading the English Channel, the Loire estuary, the Gold Coast of West Africa, and the approaches to St. Domingue. No sooner had the war been declared than the British captured the Nantes slaver *Concorde*, which didn't yet know that

Britain and France were at war. During the rest of 1744 the British attacked the Nantes slavers the *Sainte-Anne* and the *Prudent* near Martinique, the *Finette* and the *Badin* along the African coast, and the *St. Charles* within sight of the French coast.[7]

When news of the British blockade reached Nantes, preparations for slaving voyages came to a near standstill. Thirty-four slaving voyages had left Nantes in 1743, but after the war was declared on March 15, 1744, the number of sailings dropped precipitously. The *Providence* and the *Jeune Flore* left in April and made successful voyages, but the *Aventurier*, which left in May, the *Prudent*, which left in June, and the *Galathée*, which left in July, were all captured by the English. The last slave ship to leave Nantes in 1744 was the *Union*, which sailed in August. It was owned and outfitted by G. Bouteiller and Sons. Its fate remains unknown. The following year only two slave ships left Nantes: the first was captured by the English, and the second disappeared without a trace.[8]

In 1746 G. Boutellier and Sons decided to try to run the British blockade. They would send out the *Perle*, a 160-ton ship armed with eighteen cannons. Robert Durand would be its captain. Because of the wartime conditions, the ship was outfitted with an extraordinarily large crew of sixty-four men, and Robert Durand was given a Letter of Mark, which allowed him to attack and capture any British ships that he might encounter. The *Perle* was to travel with an armed convoy for safety.[9]

The *Perle* left Nantes on April 29, 1746, for its rendezvous with the convoy and on May 2 joined a fleet of seventy-two warships and merchant ships that would travel together. For seven weeks the *Diligent* waited with the other ships until the fleet was ready to depart on June 22. Such a large fleet was very cumbersome, and it moved slowly. By July 15, when the fleet was still off the French coast near Bordeaux, Robert Durand decided to separate his ship. For three days the *Perle* sailed alone without incident, and by the time the sun rose on July 18 it was off the coast of Portugal. At eight o'clock in the morning they spotted a strange ship approaching them. Durand put his ship at full sail, but throughout the day the ship kept closing in on him. At about five o'clock in the afternoon Durand ordered the *Perle* to raise its French flag and fire a cannon shot to warn off the other ship.

James Osborn, captain of the HMS *Shoreham*, had been stalking the *Perle* all day in hopes that it would turn out to be a French ship. Now that the

Perle had shown its colors, he was free to launch an attack. He had no doubt about the outcome of the battle. His ship was a British war frigate of the sixth rate, armed with twenty-four cannons and carrying 160 men. Osborn had been promoted to captain less than two years earlier, and taking a French prize would look good on his record.[10]

As soon as he saw the French flag, Osborn gave the orders to engage the *Perle* in battle. During the next hour the English ship fired forty-five nine-pound cannonballs, twenty-five loads of grapeshot, seventy-one rounds of double-headed shot, and twenty-three musket shots. One of the cannon shots shattered the foremast of the *Perle* eighteen inches above the cap; another broke the main mast at a spot eight feet below the main yard; and another cannon shot pierced the *Perle's* hull just above the waterline. About an hour after the battle had begun, a cannonball from the *Shoreham* made a direct hit on Robert Durand, who was directing his crew from the quarterdeck of the *Perle*. The force of the blow hurled Durand's body across the deck. With the captain dead and the *Perle* badly damaged, Lieutenant Pierre Le Ray raised the white flag of surrender.[11]

*A*FTER THE 1731–1732 voyage of the *Diligent,* the Billy brothers did not outfit any more slaving voyages, but they remained invested in the slave trade. They each owned one-seventh of the *Concorde,* a ninety-eight-ton ship that first left Vannes on a slaving mission on December 13, 1731, less than six months after the *Diligent.* After loading 510 captives along the Guinea coast, it experienced a major revolt in which 196 of the captives were killed. Only 266 out of the original 510 Africans were still alive when the ship reached Martinique. Joseph-Ange Dubodan was the outfitter of that voyage, and he played that role when the *Concorde* set out on its second slaving voyage in 1735. In 1742 the *Concorde* set out on its third slaving voyage, captained by Dubodan's son, François Barnabé. The ship was still on the high seas when the Anglo-French war broke out on March 15, 1744, and it was captured by the English less than two months later. Captain Dubodan was held prisoner by the English until the Peace of Aix-la-Chapelle ended the war in 1748.[1] With the loss of the *Concorde,* the Billy brothers' involvement in the slave trade came to an end.

Although their slaving venture in 1731–1732 did not bring them the huge profits they had hoped for, fortune was kind to them in other ways. In 1726 the price of grain in Vannes started to rise, beginning a long-term trend that continued until 1789, driven by a general rise in grain prices throughout France and western Europe.[2] As the Billy brothers began to gain confidence that the trend would continue, they gained a new interest in the grain trade. The government permitted grain exports to Provence after 1730 and exports

Figure 47.1   Port of Vannes showing the new Billy mansion (with two figures in front).

to the other provinces of France after 1744. The trade in grain, not the trade in slaves, became the key to their prosperity in Vannes.

As the Billy brothers grew prosperous in the grain trade, Guillaume tore down his father's house overlooking the port and replaced it with a much larger mansion that held business offices and warehouse space on the ground floor, living spaces on the second and third floors, and accommodations for servants on the fourth floor.[3] As before, he shared the house with his younger brother, François. Guillaume never remarried after the death of his wife, Catherine Fournier, in 1729. He devoted himself to his business, local politics, and his daughter, Jeanne-Agathe, who married a ship's captain sailing for the Company of the Indies in 1752. François's wife died on April 4, 1750, while giving birth to their twelfth child, Vincent-Olive Billy. In 1761 his oldest daughter, Marguerite, married a lieutenant sailing for the Company of the Indies.[4]

With prosperity came the status and respect that the bourgeoisie of Vannes had always sought. Guillaume served as a judge on the consulate court between 1726 and 1734, and François served between 1735 and 1740,

Figure 47.2   The port of Vannes in the late eighteenth century.

and then again between 1753 and 1755. In 1758 Guillaume was named Garde-Marteau of the royal waters and forests in the region of Vannes, one of three officers who administered the royal domains and rendered justice. The Billy brothers' partners in their slaving ventures also did well in local politics. Michel Buat de la Croix, their partner in the *Diligent* venture, served a term as judge on the consulate court, and their partner in the *Concorde* slaving expeditions, Joseph-Ange Dubodan, purchased the office of mayor in 1748.[5]

Guillaume Billy's dream of emulating the commercial success of Nantes and Lorient did not materialize. Rather than become an entrepôt for merchandise from around the world, Vannes continued to service the production of the peasants in its hinterland. The bold plans that the municipal council had approved in 1727 for refurbishing the port were only partially realized. Almost nothing was done until 1743, when the municipal council decided to extend and reconstruct the quay that Guillaume's father had built in 1697. The project required Guillaume to cede the land between his house and the quay to the city, something that he did only after a long and bitter fight.[6] Perhaps the most noticeable change in the appearance of the port during the three decades after the slaving voyage of the *Diligent* was the construction of the Billy mansion.

During that same period the neighboring city of Nantes grew and changed visibly. Completion of the new merchant quarter that had originally been planned in the 1720s for the Ile Feydeau was stalled for years because of the shifting subsoil and unsure foundations, but it gained new life when the architect Pierre Rousseau solved the problem by borrowing some techniques from the Dutch. The slave trader Guillaume Grou built a large mansion there beginning in 1747, setting off a new flurry of construction and growth. About half of the inhabitants of the new development were slave traders. With their newfound wealth, the moneyed classes of Nantes were beginning to yearn for high culture. In 1765 the architect Ceinray presented his plans for constructing a municipal arts center that included a theater and a concert hall.[7] During that same year thirty slave ships left Nantes bound for Africa.

Lorient also experienced new growth. Between 1732 and 1745 the Company of the Indies invested nearly 3 million livres in rebuilding its compound. In addition to refurbishing the existing facilities, the company built a new sales showroom, warehouse, directors' offices, quay, and back warehouse. After 1734 the company no longer ferried its goods to Nantes to be sold but conducted all sales in Lorient.[8] With all that growth and prosperity, company officials in Lorient found it irritating that their activities were under the control of the admiralty court in Vannes. The commerce of Vannes, they scoffed, "is nothing other than that which its hinterland furnishes: a few small ships that leave filled with grain and a few others that arrive with wines from Bordeau and Nantes. So much for the city that tried to emulate Lorient, a city that receives warships of eighty cannons and sends out commercial vessels of thirteen hundred tons. Where are the great ships that stop at, or are outfitted in, Vannes?"[9]

Vannes never became a commercial city in the mode of Nantes and Lorient, but its grain trade got a major boost in July 1764, when the government of France lifted its prohibition on exporting grain to foreign countries.[10] Advis Desruisseaux developed a thriving trade with Spain, and other local grain merchants followed suit. After the harvest of 1765, much of the grain produced in the hinterland of Vannes was shipped out of the country while local prices rose from 10.5 livres per *perrée* to 12 livres in August and 12.3 livres in September. The members of the artisan and working classes, who had to purchase their bread and flour from merchants, began to fear that they would not be able to feed themselves

Figure 47.3   The Billy mansion.

through the winter. On September 10 the house of the merchant Danet, who had been accused of trying to buy up the local grain supplies on speculation, was stoned and his windows were broken. Danet suspected that it was the work of certain local artisans who had been seen huddling together earlier that day. On September 11 a wine merchant who was mistaken for a grain merchant was attacked by a mob and nearly killed.[11]

The outpouring of popular anger reached its climax on Friday, September 13. A crowd of artisans marched through the central city past the houses of the nobles and city officials, seizing carts filled with grain that belonged to tenants of local nobles and tithe farmers. Another crowd—this one made up mostly of women—headed outside the city gates toward the port, where the grain merchants lived. Marching down Lower Calmont Street, they begin to attack the houses of the major grain merchants.

When they arrived at the Billy house, the women picked up rocks and begin to hurl them at the windows. First one, then two, then a torrent of rocks came crashing through the glass. In between the sounds of window-panes being smashed, the women were shouting that their children were starving because the Billy brothers shipped their grain out of town. Others shouted that the grain merchants were bringing famine to the land. The rocks kept coming until two dozen large windows and nearly a hundred small panes in different parts of the house were broken. The crowd seemed to know exactly where to aim their rocks. They broke two large panes and eighteen small panes in Guillaume Billy's office on the ground floor, and sixty-six small panes in Guillaume Billy's sitting room on the second floor.[12]

We have no way of knowing how many of the 242 captives sold by the *Diligent* in Martinique in 1732 were still alive on September 13, 1765. Given the high mortality rate on the islands, their number could not have been great. During more than thirty years of slavery in Martinique they must have wondered who sent that ship to carry them in irons across the ocean, and who received the money that was paid to purchase their labor. Perhaps they dreamed of retribution, or at least of expressing their anger at the persons who had ruined their lives for reasons of profits. But not in their wildest fantasies would they have ever guessed that there would be an outburst of popular anger against the very people who were behind their torment. Nor would they have imagined that when it came, it would be orchestrated and administered by the poor women of Vannes.

Afterword

$\mathscr{I}$N A STATE OF great anticipation, I set off for Martinique in March 1997 during spring break at Yale. As a historian whose knowledge of Martinique was largely limited to eighteenth-century documents, I was eager to discover how much had changed since the *Diligent* fled the port of St. Pierre with a cannonball splashing in its wake. Slavery was finally abolished in 1848, and Martinique became a *département* of France in 1946. When I arrived at the airport in Fort-de-France, Martinique, I was as much in France as if I had arrived in Paris. The city had been called Fort Royal in the days of the *Diligent*, but the name was changed when the French Revolution began eliminating all traces of royalty. The city of St. Pierre, where the *Diligent* sat at anchor for four months, was completely destroyed by a volcanic eruption of Mount Pelée in 1902. The modern city bears little resemblance to the old.

My goal was to find out what had become of the 242 Africans who survived the voyage of the *Diligent*. They were the raison d'être for the *Diligent*'s voyage and they were its victims, and yet they were the least documented of all those who became involved in one way or another with the *Diligent*. When small crimes are recorded, it is usually by their victims, but when enormous crimes are recorded, it is almost always by their perpetrators. Although Robert Durand carefully recorded the age category and gender of all the captives, he did not record their names.

Because the laws governing slavery in France's Caribbean colonies prescribed that all slaves had to be baptized, I hoped to at least find their Christian names in parish records in Martinique. Then I could learn if they married, if they had children, and when they died. What I discovered, instead, was that slave baptisms, marriages, and burials had been recorded in separate registers. Although most of the parish registers for whites and free blacks survived, the slave registers had long since vanished. The only reference to slaves that I found in the surviving parish registers of the period was from April 1714. The priest of the parish of Our Lady of Caze Pilote wrote the heading, "Baptisms of whites found among those of Negro slaves," and then he proceeded to list several whites whose baptisms had been inadvertently entered into the slave register.[1] That was the only concrete proof I found that the slave registers I was looking for had ever existed.

My second goal was to find the Lamy plantation. Robert Durand had written in his journal that the *Diligent* had sold the last ninety-six slaves to a certain Mr. Lamy. My first hypothesis was that Lamy must have been a very large sugar planter if he could afford to purchase ninety-six slaves at a time. My search through the land records and parish records in the rural parishes surrounding St. Pierre led nowhere. At that point, I took a bus to the University of the Antilles to look for Professor Mireille Mousnier. She and her colleague Brigitte Caille had written a wonderful book with pull-out maps showing the locations of all the sugar mills in Martinique during the seventeenth, eighteenth, and nineteenth centuries.[2] If anybody could find the Lamy plantation, it was she.

I eventually found her, and she invited me to her home on a mountainside overlooking the sea. She told me at the beginning that she had never heard of a Lamy plantation, and at any rate no plantation in Martinique in the early eighteenth century was wealthy enough to purchase ninety-six slaves at a time. After several hours of looking through her research notes and photocopied documents, she found a mention of Lamy in a footnote to a book on the Gaoulé revolt in Martinique in 1717.[3] Several months later in Paris I found the document referred to in the footnote. Lamy was a *négociant* living in St. Pierre. He was a reseller of slaves. Given his profession, he could have sold the slaves to anybody, even planters on other islands. The trail had come to a dead end.

Walking down the crowded streets of Fort-de-France the next day, I could not help but wonder if perhaps one of the people whom I was passing was a descendant of one of the African captives who had come over involuntarily on the *Diligent*. Although the names of those Africans have been forever lost to history, somewhere in Martinique their descendants have survived, endured, and perhaps triumphed.

Appendix A

Reconstructing the Balance Sheet of the Diligent

I. Merchandise Brought from Martinique

Sugar

The *Diligent* loaded 251 *barriques* of clayed white and clayed common sugar @ 800 livres/*barrique*,[1] yielding 200,800 livres of sugar.

The *Diligent* also loaded 10 *quarts* of clayed white and clayed common sugar @ 200 livres/quart,[2] yielding 2,000 livres of sugar.

Total sugar carried equals 202,800 livres.

1 quintal *(cent pesant)* equals 100 livres, so the *Diligent* carried 2,028 quintals of sugar.

Durand reported that the *Diligent* carried clayed white and clayed common sugar, but he did not give the proportions.

Based on the relative proportions of the two kinds of sugar arriving in Nantes in 1732, I am assuming that 5 percent was white and 95 percent was common.[3]

Clayed white sugar, 101 quintals, minus 15 percent weight loss in transit = 86 quintals.[4]

86 quintals sold at 37 livres/quintal.[5]	3,182
Second shipment: 86 quintals arriving year later.	3,182
Total for clayed white sugar	6,364

Clayed common sugar, 1,927 quintals, minus 15 percent weight loss in transit = 1,638 quintals.

1,638 quintals sold at 30 livres/quintal.[6]	49,140
Second shipment of 1,551 quintals arriving a year later.	49,140
Total for clayed common sugar	98,280
Total for clayed white and clayed common sugar	104,644

Cotton

The *Diligent* carried 23 bales of cotton weighing 400 livres each = 9,200 livres, or 92 quintals.[7]

92 quintals sold at 75 livres/quintal[8]	6,900
Second shipment of 92 quintals arriving a year later	6,900
Total for cotton	13,800

Rocou

13 *quarts* of rocou each weighing 200 livres yields 2,600 livres (or 26 quintals) of rocou.[9]

26 quintals @ 35 livres/quintal[10]	910
Second shipment arriving a year later	910
Total for Rocou	1,820

Total returns from Martinique

Sugar	105,862
Cotton	13,800
Rocou	1,820
Total	121,482

II. Costs of Recovering Second Half of Goods

1 sol/livre (20 sols = 1 livre) shipping charge on 2,028
quintals of clayed white and clayed common sugar.[11]   10,140

1 sol/livre shipping charge on 92 quintals of cotton.   460

1 sol/livre shipping charges on 26 quintals of rocou.   130

Total   10,730

III. Outfitting Costs

Trade goods[12]   37,782

Mise-hors (including 18,500 cost of ship)[13]   43,990

Insurance on trade goods, 8 percent[14]   3,023

Insurance on *Diligent* (18,500 livres), 8 percent   1,480

Total outfitting costs   86,275

IV. Expenses in Selling Goods

Gabare transport from Vannes to Nantes: 3,684 quintals
of goods @ 6 sols/quintal = 22,104 sols, or 1,105 livres.[15]   1,105

Unloading, wheelbarrow transport, and barrel work in Nantes:
3,684 quintals @ 9 sols/quintal = 33,156 sols or 1,658 livres.[16]   1,658

Droits de prévoté et ville: 3,684 quintals @ 5 sols
and 4 deniers per quintal.[17]   982

Droits de domaine d'occident: 3,684 quintals @10 sols per quintal.[18]   1,842

Total expenses for selling merchandise   5,587

V. Other Expenses

Interest on 4,500 livres of *cambaye* loans at 30 percent.   1,350

Wages for *Diligent* crew:

1,266/month times 13 months (2 months were paid in
advance) = 16,458.

16,458 minus wages saved by deaths of Mahé (34/mo.), Touchard
(36/mo.), Lethiris (12/mo.), and Thaubier (30/mo.).[19] Ten months
of wages saved for each = 1,120 saved. Total wages   15,338

13 livres per slave paid to the Compagnie des Indes for
244 slaves.[20]   3,172

Total other expenses   19,910

VI. BALANCE

Returns from Martinique

Sugar   104,644

Cotton   13,800

Rocou   1,820

Total returns from Martinique   120,264

Expenses

Outfitting costs   86,275

Second half return costs   10,730

Selling costs   5,587

Interest on loans   1,350

Wages to crew   15,338

Fee to Company of the Indies   3,172

Total expenses   122,502

Loss   2,238

This reconstruction is based on several assumptions. First, I am assuming that all slaves were sold on terms that called for half the payment due immediately, and the other half due a year later. Therefore, the cargo carried by the *Diligent* from Martinique to Vannes in 1732 represents one-half of the total cargo paid for the slaves. This assumption gives a maximal figure for the return on the slave sales. If some of the slaves were paid for in full immediately, then the second shipment would have been smaller. Second, I am assuming that the ratio of common sugar to white sugar carried by the *Diligent* was the same as the average ratio coming into Nantes in 1732—twenty to one. Third, I am assuming that the second half of the cargo, which was brought back from Martinique in 1733, was sold for a sum identical to the first half, even though it was sold in Marseille instead of Nantes. Fourth, I am assuming that the Billy brothers followed the standard accounting practice of their time by including the purchase price of the *Diligent* in the *mise-hors* but not counting the loss of 6 percent interest on the goods that were delivered a year later. By allowing half of the goods to be delivered a year later, the *Diligent* was giving the slave buyers an interest-free loan.

Appendix B

Abbreviations Used in Notes

ADLA—Archives Départmentales de Loire-Atlantique, Nantes, France

ADMF—Archives Départmentales de la Martinique, Fort-de-France, Martinique

ADMV—Archives Départmentales du Morbihan, Vannes, France

AHU—Arquivo Histórico Ultramarino, Lisbon, Portugal

AMN—Archives Municipales, Nantes, France

AMV—Archives Municipales, Vannes, France

AN—Archives Nationales, Paris, France

AOM—Archives d'Outre-Mer, Aix-en-Provence, France

AR—Algemeen Rijksarchief, The Hague, Netherlands

ASV—Archivo Segreto Vaticano, Vatican City

BA—Biblioteca da Ajuda, Lisbon, Portugal

BLY—Beinecke Library, Yale University

BM—Bibliotheque Mazarine, Paris, France

BN—Bibliotheque Nationale, Paris, France

MD—Musée Dobrée, Nantes, France

NMM—National Maritime Museum, Greenwich, England

MSA—Maryland State Archives, Annapolis, Maryland

PRO—Public Record Office, Kew, England

SHML—Service Historique de la Marine, Lorient, France

NOTES

PREFACE

1. On the Vinland Map controversy, see Laurence C. Witten II, "Vinland's Saga Recalled," in R. A. Skelton, Thomas E. Marston, and George D. Painter, eds., *The Vinland Map and Tarter Relation*, new ed. (New Haven, 1995), pp. xli–lxiii; Kirsten A. Seaver, "The Vinland Map," *Mercator's World*, March–April 1997, pp. 42–47; Paul Saenger, "Review Article: Vinland Re-read," *Imago Mundi* 50 (1998): 199–202; Douglas McNaughton, "A World in Transition: Early Cartography of the North Atlantic, in William W. Fitzhugh and Elisabeth I. Ward, eds., *Vikings: The North Atlantic Saga* (Washington, D.C., 2000), pp. 267–269.

2. W. C. McCrone and L. B. McCrone, "The Vinland Map Ink," *Geographical Journal* (1974): 212–214.

3. T. A. Cahill et al., "The Vinland Map Revisited: New Compositional Evidence on Its Inks and Parchments," *Analytical Chemistry* 59 (1987): 829–833.

4. Robert Harms, *River of Wealth, River of Sorrow: The Central Zaire Basin in the Era of the Slave and Ivory Trades* (New Haven, 1981).

5. The journal is now housed in the Beineke Rare Book and Manuscript Library at Yale University. It is catalogued as Durand, Robert, Journal de bord d'un négrier, Gen Mss, vol. 7.

6. These documents are found in Vannes in the Archives Départmentales du Morbihan, 9B 208.

7. Witten, "Vinland's Saga Recalled," p. lv.

8. This brief history of the Atlantic slave trade draws heavily from Hugh Thomas, *The Slave Trade* (New York, 1997).

9. The figures are taken from David Eltis, "The Volume and Structure of the Atlantic Slave Trade: A Reassessment," *William and Mary Quarterly*, 3d ser., 58 (2001): 17–46.

10. The figures were calculated using David Eltis, Stephen D. Behrendt, David Richardson, and Herbert S. Klein, *The Trans-Atlantic Slave Trade: A Database on CD-ROM* (New York, 1999).

11. Arthur Young, *Travels during the Years 1787, 1788, and 1789* (London, 1794), 1:103.

PART 1 MATTERS OF MORALITY
CHAPTER 1

1. Robert Durand, Journal de bord d'un négrier, 1731–1732, BLY, Gen Mss, vol. 7, p. 1.

2. Jean Ehrard, "L'esclavage devant la conscience morale des lumières françaises: Indifférence, gêne, révolte," in Marcel Dorigny, ed., *Les Abolitions de l'esclavage* (Paris, 1995), pp. 143–152.

3. Gilles Bienvenu, *Nantes: Plans commentés* (Nantes, 1994), p. 17.

4. Gaston Martin, *Nantes au XVIIIe siècle: L'administration de Gérard Mellier* (Paris, 1928), p. 10; Plan de Nantes par De Fer, 1716, MD, 956.1.776; Musée Dobrée, *Iconographie de Nantes* (Nantes, 1978), p. 72.

5. Marie-Christine Hervé, "Le couvent des Bénédictines de Notre Dame du Calvaire de Nantes de son origine à la révolution, 1623–1799" (Mémoire de Maîtrise, Université d'Etudes Régionales, Nantes, 1985), pp. 118, 130.

6. Livre des délibérations capitulaires de la communauté . . . 1684–1789, ADLA, H 447, p. 318; Gérard Mellier, Réponses au mémoire . . . concernant les nègres esclaves, 1716, ADLA, C 742, p. 2.

7. The descriptions of the layout of the convent come from Hervé, "Couvent des Bénédictines," pp. 118–119, 144.

8. Joseph du Tremblay, *Constitutions de la congrégation des religieuses bénédictines de Notre-Dame du Calvaire* (1634; reprint, Lille-Paris, 1902), p. 196.

9. Du Tremblay, *Constitutions,* p. 130; Hervé, "Couvent des Bénédictines," pp. 33–34.

10. Hervé, "Couvent des Bénédictines," pp. 171–173. On the use of the term "noble man," see Paul Devolant, *Recueil d'arrests rendus au Parlement de Bretagne sur plusierus questions célèbres* (Rennes, 1722), 2:239.

11. Mellier, Réponses au mémoire, p. 2.

12. Déliberation capitulaires, pp. 298, 318.

13. Etat tamporel fidelle, November 1715, ADLA, H 446.

14. Délibérations capitulaires, p. 318; Propositions que font les négotiants de Nantes, November 12, 1714, ADLA, C 751; Jean Mettas, *Répertoire des expéditions négrières françaises au XVIIIe siècle,* ed. Serge Dager (Paris, 1978), 1:75, 90, 92; Jean Meyer, *La noblesse bretonne au XVIIIe siècle* (Paris, 1966), 1: 356–357.

15. Sue Peabody, *"There Are No Slaves in France":The Political Culture of Race and Slavery in the Ancien Régime* (Oxford, 1996), pp. 12–13.

16. Moreau de Saint Méry, *Loix et constitutions des colonies françoises de l'Amérique sous le vent* (Paris, 1784–1790), 1:579, 2:99.

17. Despite repeated attempts, I was unable to locate the présidial court's records of the case. I am therefore relying on Gérard Mellier's summary in Réponse au mémoire, pp. 2–3. Mellier does not give the girl's name, and the records of the convent do not identify Pauline Villeneuve as a black slave. However, given the chronology and the fact that the convent had only one member from the Caribbean in its entire history, it seems certain that they are both referring to the same person.

18. Du Tremblay, *Constitutions*, pp. 177–178.

CHAPTER 2

1. Mémoire concernant les négres esclaves que les officiers et habitans des colonies française de l'Amérique meridionale amenent en France pour leur service, n.d., ADLA, C 742.

2. Martin, *Gérard Mellier,* pp. 59–80.

3. One of those manuscripts, completed in 1719, was later published as Gérard Mellier, *Essai sur l'histoire de la ville et du compté de Nantes* (Nantes, 1872).

4. Bechameil de Nointel, Mémoire concernant la province entière de Bretagne, 1698, BN, Manuscrits, FF 8149, pp. 82–87.

5. Mémoire sur le commerce qui se fait à Nantes et sur les moyens de l'augmenter, 1714, AMN, HH 228, no. 3.

6. The translation of the line of poetry comes from *Horace: Odes and Carmen Saeculare,* translated and annotated by Guy Lee (Leeds, 1998), p. 55.

7. Guillaume Delìsle, Africa, c. 1700, map in the possession of the author; Delìsle, Carte d'Afrique dressé pour l'usage du roy, 1730, Map Collection, Sterling Memorial Library, Yale University.

8. Pierre H. Boulle, "In Defense of Slavery: Eighteenth-Century Opposition to Abolition and the Origins of a Racist Ideology in France," in Frederick Krantz, ed., *History from Below: Studies in Popular Protest and Popular Ideology in Honor of George Rudé* (Montreal, 1985), pp. 221–241.

9. Simone Delesalle and Lucette Valensi, "Le Mot 'nègre' dans les dictionnaires français d'Ancien Régime, histoire et lexicographie," *Langue Française* 15 (1972): 88, 93–94.

10. Jean Gallet, *Seigneurs et paysans bretons du Moyen Age à la révolution* (Rennes, 1992), pp. 165–167, 188, 220; James B. Collins, *Classes, Estates, and Order in Early Modern Brittany* (New York, 1994), pp. 267–268.

11. On the reputed criminality of Breton peasants, see Jean Le Tallec, *La vie paysanne en Bretagne centrale sous l'Ancien Régime* (Spézet, 1996), pp. 180–183.

12. Musée Dobrée, *Iconographie de Nantes,* pp. 53, 59.

13. Observations sur la liberté que l'on pretend être acquise en France par la seule entrée dans le royaume, BN, Manuscrits, Collection Joly de Fleury, vol. 315, fol. 117v.

14. *Le Code Noir* (1767; reprint, Fort-de-France, Martinique, 1980), pp. 30–31, 36.

15. John Thornton, *The Congolese Saint Anthony: Dona Beatriz Kimpa Vita and the Antonian Movement, 1684–1706* (Cambridge, 1998), p. 204; Mettas, *Répertoire,* 1:54–55.

16. For modern scholarly analyses of this line of argument, see Abd Ahed, *Contribution à une théorie sociologique de l'esclavage* (Paris, 1931), pp. 182–246; Orlando Patterson, *Slavery and Social Death* (Cambridge, Mass., 1982), p. 5.

17. Savary des Bruslons, *Dictionnaire universel de commerce* (Paris, 1723), 2:858.

CHAPTER 3

1. Pierre Bonnaise, *From Slavery to Feudalism in South Western Europe,* trans. Jean Birrell (Cambridge, 1991), pp. 1–59, 288–313; Marc Bloch, *Rois et serfs* (Paris, 1920), pp. 47–48; Bloch, *French Rural History,* trans. Janet Sondheimer (Berkeley, 1966), pp. 104–105.

2. Sydney Herbert, *The Fall of Feudalism in France* (London, 1921), pp. 2–3.

3. Bloch, *French Rural History*, pp. 83–109; William Phillips, *Slavery from Roman Times to the Early Transatlantic Trade* (Minneapolis, 1985), pp. 43–59; Bloch, *Rois et serfs*, 60–70, 94–98; Pierre Bernard, *L'etude sur les esclaves et les serfs d'eglise en France du VIe au XIIIe siècle* (Paris, 1919).

4. Arthur Young, *Travels During the Years 1787, 1788, and 1789* (London, 1794), 1:98.

5. Gui Alexis Lobineau, *Histoire de Bretagne* (Paris, 1707), 1:851–852. On the "year and a day" and *mottiers*, see Gallet, *Seigneurs et paysans bretons*, pp. 150–167.

6. Ch.-L. Chassin, *L'église et les derniers serfs* (Paris, 1880), pp. 22–29, 188–191; Herbert, *Fall of Feudalism*, p. 6.

7. Edit du roy concernant les esclaves nègres des colonies, October 1716, ADLA, C 742.

8. Sue Peabody, *"There Are No Slaves in France": The Political Culture of Race and Slavery in the Ancien Régime* (Oxford, 1996), pp. 19–20.

9. Dale Van Kley, *The Jansenists and the Expulsion of the Jesuits from France, 1757–1765* (New Haven, 1975), p. 1; Alexander Sedgwick, *Jansenism in Seventeenth-Century France: Voices from the Wilderness* (Charlottesville, Va., 1977), p. 189.

10. Van Kley, *Jansenists*, pp. 1, 23; Sedgwick, *Jansenism*, pp. 189–191.

11. Peabody, *No Slaves in France*, pp. 19–20.

12. J. Rennard, *Histoire religieuse des Antilles françaises des origines à 1914* (Paris, 1954), pp. 41–42.

13. Jacques Petitjean-Roget, *Personnes et familles à la Martinique au XVIIe siècle* (Fort de France, Martinique, 1983), 1:xxi.

14. Jean-Baptiste Labat, *Nouveau voyage aux îles d'Amérique* (Paris, 1722), 3:464.

15. Rennard, *Histoire religeuse*, p. 68.

16. Cited in Lucien Peytraud, *L'esclavage aux Antilles françaises avant 1798* (Paris, 1973), pp. 172–173.

17. Peytraud, *L'esclavage aux Antilles*, pp. 147–149, 172–173.

18. Ibid., pp. 153–163.

19. Peabody, *No Slaves in France*, pp. 19–21; *Biographie universelle, ancienne et moderne* (Paris, 1811–1862), 24:46–47.

20. Lemerre's memorandum is: Observations sur la liberté que l'on prétend être acquise en France par la seule entrée dans le royaume, BN, Manuscrits, Collection Joly de Fleury, vol. 35, fols. 113r–127r.

21. There is some ambiguity as to whether the edict was ever registered. Here I am following the arguments of Peabody, *No Slaves in France*, pp. 19, 21, 146–147, 149–150.

22. Ehrard, "L'esclavage devant la conscience morale," p. 143; Boulle, "In Defense of Slavery," p. 226.

23. Edward Derbyshire Seeber, *AntiSlavery Opinion in France During the Second Half of the Eighteenth Century* (Baltimore, 1937), p. 31.

PART 2 THE FINANCIERS
CHAPTER 4

1. Madeleine Delpierre, *Dress in Eighteenth-Century France*, trans. Caroline Beamish (New Haven, 1997), pp. 23–24.

2. Extrait des registres du greffe civil et criminel de l'isle Martinique, November 19, 1729, ADMV, 9B 208.

3. Joseph C. Miller, *Way of Death: Merchant Capitalism and the Angolan Slave Trade, 1730–1830* (Madison, Wis., 1988), p. 577.

4. Dernis, *Histoire abregée des compagnies de commerce qui ont esté établis en France depuis 1626,* 1742, AOM, col. F 2A 12.

5. The king's edict of December 1701 defined *négociant*s as "all those who conduct their commerce in warehouses, selling their merchandise in bales, cases, or whole pieces, and who have no shops open nor any window display or sign on their doors or houses." ADLA, C 695.

6. A. M. de Boislisle, *Correspondance des contrôleurs généraux des finances avec les intendants des provinces* (Paris, 1883), 2:495–496; Emile Gabory, "La marine et le commerce de Nantes au XVIIe siècle et au commencement du XVIIIe," *Annales de Bretagne* 17 (1901–1902): 262–265.

7. Thomas Schaeper, *The French Council of Commerce, 1700–1715* (Columbus, Ohio, 1983), p. 52.

8. Jacques Saint-Germain, *Samuel Bernard: Le banquier des rois* (Paris, 1960), pp. 103–107.

9. The memorandum was erroneously attributed to John Law and published in Paul Harsin, ed., *John Law: Oeuvres complètes* (Paris, 1934), 2:67–259. It is now believed to be largely copied from a memorandum written by Jean Le Pottier. See Edgar Faure, *La banqueroute de Law* (Paris, 1977), p. 694.

10. Tom Kemp, *Economic Forces in French History* (London, 1971), p. 49.

11. Arthur Young, *Travels During the Years 1787, 1788, and 1789* (London, 1794), 1:103.

12. Edward Fox, *History in Geographic Perspective: The Other France* (New York, 1971), pp. 34–38, 64–68.

13. Ernest Labrousse and Fernand Braudel, eds., *Histoire économique et sociale de la France* (Paris, 1970), 2:505.

14. Lettres patentes du roy pour la liberté du commerce de la coste de Guinée, January 1716, ADLA, C 740; Gaston Martin, *Nantes au XVIIIe siècle: L'ère des négriers, 1714–1774* (Paris, 1993), pp. 177–178.

15. Mémoire sur la liberté du commerce de Guinée (no date, but clearly written soon after the expiration of the *assiento* contract), AOM, col. C 6 25.

16. Boislisle, *Correspondance des contrôleurs généraux,* 3:507.

17. Ibid., 3:507; Observations sur le mémoire de Monsieur Raudot; Mémoire pour faire connaître la nécessité d'accorder des permissions pour la commerce de Guinée, May 1714, AOM, col. C 6 25.

18. Mémoire sur la Guinée, 1716, AOM, col. C 6 25.

19. Mémoire pour faire connaître la nécessité d'accorder des permissions pour le commerce de Guinée, May 5, 1714. AOM, col. C 6 25.

20. Observations sur le mémoire de Monsieur Raudot.

21. Gaston Martin, *Nantes au XVIIIe siècle: L'administration de Gérard Mellier* (Paris, 1928), pp. 145–146.

22. Lettres patentes du roy pour la liberté du commerce de la coste de Guinée, January 1716, ADLA, C 740; "Declaration du roy concernant la Guinée," December 1716, ADLA, C 740.

23. Lettres patentes du roy pour la libérté du commerce de la coste de Guinée; Arrest du conseil d'estat du roy du 25 Jan. 1716, ADLA, C 741.

24. Lettres patentes du roy portant règlement pour le commerce des colonies françoises, April 1717, AN, Marine A 1 54.

CHAPTER 5

1. Jacques Cellard, *John Law et la régence* (Paris, 1996), pp. 41–42, 65–70.

2. Rochelle Ziskin, *The Place Vendôme* (Cambridge, 1999), p. 32.

3. Harsin, *John Law: Oeuvres complètes*, 1: xxxii; Maurice Dumolin, "La Place Vendôme," Annexe au procès-verbal de la séance de 26 mars 1927, in *Commission Municipale de Vieux Paris, procès-verbaux, année 1927* (Paris, 1731), pp. 29–52.

4. Janet Gleeson, *Millionaire* (New York, 1999), p. 99.

5. Ibid., 63–65; Gray, *The Memoirs, Life, and Character of the Great Mr. Law* (London, 1721), p. 10.

6. *London Gazette*, January 3–7, 1694–1695, quoted in Edgar Faure, *La banqueroute de Law* (Paris, 1977), p. 632.

7. A. W. Wiston-Glynn, *John Law of Lauriston* (Edinburgh, 1907), pp. 29–33; Le Baron Albert de Montesquieu, *Voyages de Montesquieu* (Bordeaux, 1894) 1:64.

8. Harsin, *John Law: Oeuvres complètes*, 1:xxxi–xxxvi; Cellard, *John Law et la régence*, p. 42.

9. Harsin, *John Law: Oeuvres complètes*, 1:xxvii.

10. Wiston-Glynn, *John Law of Lauriston*, p. 34.

11. Harsin, *John Law: Oeuvres complètes*, 2:266.

12. Cellard, *John Law et la régence*, pp. 57, 74–76.

13. Ibid., pp. 7, 21, 79–80.

14. Ibid., pp. 92–96; Philippe Haudrère, *La Compagnie française des Indes au XVIIIe siècle, 1719–1795* (Paris, 1989), 1:48–54.

15. Cellard, *John Law et la régence*, pp. 154–160; Haudrère, *Compagnie française des Indes*, 1:55–57.

16. Haudrère, *Compagnie française des Indes*, 1:56–58; Wiston-Glynn, *John Law of Lauriston*, p. 75.

17. Gérard Le Bouëdec, *Le port et l'arsenal de Lorient* (Paris, 1994), 2:163.

18. Claude Nières et al., *Histoire de Lorient* (Toulouse, 1988), pp. 50–51.

19. Le Bouëdec, *Port et arsenal de Lorient*, 2:214–216.

20. Ibid., 2:216.

21. Ibid., 2:162–163.

22. Cellard, *John Law et la régence*, p. 288.

23. Georges Cain, *La Place Vendôme* (Paris, 1908), p. 10.

24. Maurice Quénet, "Un example de consultation dans l'administration monarchique au XVIIIe siècle: Les nantais et leurs députés au Conseil de Commerce," *Annales de Bretagne et des pays de l'ouest, Anjou, Maine, Touraine* 85 (1978): 454–455.

25. Arrest du conseil d'estat du roy, ADLA, C 738.

26. Haudrère, *Compagnie française des Indes*, 1: 64–65; Jean Tarrade, *Le commerce colonial de la France à la fin de l'ancien régime* (Paris, 1972), p. 90.

27. Jean Mettas, *Répertoire des expéditions négrières Françaises au XVIIIe siècle*, ed. Serge Daget (Paris, 1978), 1:88–109.

28. Haudrère, *Compagnie française des Indes*, 1:124–126.

29. Charles Becker, "Note sur les chiffres de la traite atlantique française au XVIIIe siècle," *Cahiers d'etudes africaines* 26 (1986): 653, 658; Haudrère, *Compagnie française des Indes*, 1:124; Martin, *Gérard Mellier*, p. 149.

30. Edgar Faure, *Banqueroute de Law*, 477–489; Gleeson, *Millionaire*, pp. 209–211.

31. Faure, *Banqueroute de Law*, pp. 477–486; Cain, *La Place Vendôme*, p. 12; Cellard, *John Law et la régence*, pp. 141–145, 385.

32. Quénet, "Exemple de consultation," p. 453; Laurent Roblin, "Le commerce de la mer: Nantes 1680–1730" (doctoral thesis, University of Paris IV, 1987), pp. 508–509.

CHAPTER 6

1. Martin, *Gérard Mellier*, p. 149.

2. *Biographie universelle, ancienne et moderne* (Paris, 1811–1862), 27:543.

3. Blondel, January 14, 1725, AOM, C 8A 34, fols. 133r–134v.

4. Maurepas, Commerce de Guinée, mémoire, n.d., AN, M 1026.

5. For the memoranda and the responses, see Extrait de deux mémoires presentés au nom des actionnaires sur le commerce de Guinée et des reponses des directeurs de la compagnie article par article à ces deux mémoires; Extrait du 1er et 2e mémoires des actionnaires; Mémoire sur la manière dont la Compagnie des Indes peut exercer son privilège de Guinée, en cas qu'elle ne continue pas à le faire en entier par elle-même; Les deux mémoires. All of these documents are found in AN, M 1026.

6. Jean Meyer, *L'armement nantais dans la deuxième moitié du XVIIIe siècle* (Paris, 1969), p. 228.

7. Feuquières and Blondel, July 21, 1725, AOM, C 8A 34, fol. 50r-v.

8. Haudrère, *Compagnie française des Indes*, pp. 124–125, 159 n. 442; Robert Stein, *The French Slave Trade in the Eighteenth Century: An Old Regime Business* (Madison, Wis., 1979), pp. 19–20.

9. Becker, "Note sur les chiffres," pp. 653, 658; Mettas, *Répertoire*, 2:575–586.

10. Haudrère, *Compagnie française des Indes*, 1:125–126.

11. Ibid., 1:160 n. 450; Becker, "Note sur les chiffres," p. 658.

PART 3 OUTFITTING A SLAVER
CHAPTER 7

1. On the order of setting sail, see John Harland, *Seamanship in the Age of Sail* (London, 1996), pp. 271–272.

2. H. du Halgouet, "Commerce de Vannes avec les îles d'Amérique," *Bulletin de la Société Polymathique de Morbihan*, 1940, p. 6.

3. Chevalier de Tourville, *Exercice en général de toutes les maneuvres qui se font à la mer* (Havre de Grace, 1643), pp. 3–4.

4. Robert Durand, Journal de bord d'un négrier, 1731–1732, BLY, Gen Mss, vol. 7, p. 5.

5. T. J. A. Le Goff, *Vannes and Its Region: A Study of Town and Country in Eighteenth-Century France* (Oxford, 1981), pp. 14–15, 154–163, 172, 202; Arthur Young, *Travels During the Years 1787, 1788, and 1789* (London, 1794), 1:99–103, 450.

6. Jean Meyer, *La noblesse bretonne au XVIIIe siècle* (Paris, 1966), 1:520.

7. L'aposition des sceaux après le décedes du feu Sr. Billy, November 16, 1722, ADMV, B 637; Musée de la Cohue, *Vannes, une ville, un port* (Quimper, 1998), p. 20; AMV, parish records, St. Paterne, October 24, 1695; July 8, 1705.

8. AMV, parish records, St. Paterne, September 26, 1727.

9. Vannes, Rôle de capitation, 1731, AMV, CC 4.

10. Quoted in Le Goff, *Vannes and Its Region*, pp. 71–72.

11. Edit du roy, December 1701, ADLA, C 695.

12. Meyer, *Noblesse bretonne*, 1:137–139.

13. A. M. de Boislisle, *Correspondance des contrôleurs généraux des finances avec les intendants des provinces* (Paris, 1883), 2:485.

14. Meyer, *Noblesse bretonne*, 1: 245–252; A. Perret, "René Montaudoin: Armateur et négrier nantais," *Bulletin de la Société Archéologique et Historique de Nantes et de Loire-Atlantique* 88 (1949): 86–91; Guy Richard, *Noblesse d'affaires au XVIIIe siècle* (Paris, 1974), p. 84; Olivier Pétré-Grenouilleau, *L'argent de la traite: Milieu négrier, capitalisme et développement: Un modèle* (Paris, 1996), pp. 147–148.

15. Paul Devolant, *Receuil d'arrests rendus au parlement de Bretagne sur plusieurs questions célèbres* (Rennes, 1722), 2:239.

16. Le Goff, *Vannes and Its Region*, pp. 11, 30, 32, 42–46.

17. Bechmeil de Nointel, Mémoire concernant la province entière de Bretagne, 1698, BN, Manuscrits, FF 8149, pp. 95–98; J. Letaconnoux, *Les subsistences et le commerce des grains en Bretagne au XVIIIe siècle* (Rennes, 1909), pp. 176–187.

18. Délibérations de la communauté de ville de Vannes, November 10, 1728, AMV, BB 14, fol. 25 r-v.

CHAPTER 8

1. H. du Halgouet, *Nantes: Ses relations commerciales avec les iles d'Amérique au XVIIIe siècle* (Rennes: 1939), pp. 27–28; Du Halgouet, "Commerce de Vannes," p. 4.

2. Du Halgouet, "Commerce de Vannes," pp. 3–6.

3. Conseil de Commerce, November 25, 1728, AN, F12 75, pp. 898–901.

4. Arrest du conseil d'etat du roy, December 21, 1728, ADMV, 9B 4.

5. Lettres patentes, March 21, 1730, AMV, HH 1.

6. Extrait des registres du greffe civil et criminel de l'isle Martinique, November 19, 1729, ADMV, 9B 208.

7. Montaudoin négociant de Nantes, n.d., ADLA, C 741; Jean Meyer, *L'armement nantais dans la deuxième moitié du XVIIIe siècle* (Paris, 1969), p. 228.

8. Commerce de Nantes in 1731, January 30, 1732, ADLA, C 740.

9. Actes de Propriété, 1724–1735, ADMV, 9B 57, fol. 41r-v. On the shipbuilder Rollando, see Acts de Propriété, 1714–1724, ADMV, 9B 56, fol. 54r.

10. Armement, *Le Diligent de Vannes*, February 14, 1730, ADMV, 9B 208.

11. Etienne Raut and Léon Lallement, "Vannes autrefois: La traite des nègres," *Bulletin de la Société Polymathique de Morbihan*, 1933, p. 63; Thomas-Lacroix, "Constructions et ventes de navires," p. 95; Thomas-Lacroix, *Répertoire numérique*, p. 11; Armement, La *Concorde* de Vannes, June 17, 1730, ADMV, 9B 208.

12. Actes de Propriété, 1724–1735, ADMV, 9B 57, fols. 50v–51r; Thomas-Lacroix, "Constructions et ventes de navires," p. 97. The commission is calculated on the basis of the commission that Joseph-Ange Guillo Dubodan received for serving as outfitter

on the *Diligent's* sister ship, the *Concorde*. Compte de l'armement, missehors, et cargaison du navire *La Concorde de Vannes*, January 7, 1732, ADMV, 11B 52.

CHAPTER 9

1. The confusion was not cleared up until the Arrest . . . du 30 septembre, 1741, ADLA, C 740.

2. Arrêt du 26 fevrier, 1726, ADLA, C 740. The actual forms filled out by the owners of the *Diligent* have not survived, but this document contains copies of the standard forms.

3. Martin, *L'ere des négriers*, p. 180; Elizabeth Donnan, *Documents Illustrative of the History of the Slave Trade to America* (Washington, D.C., 1930–1935), 2:449–450.

4. Armement, *Le Diligent de Vannes*, 1731, ADMV, 9B 208.

5. David Eltis, Stephen D. Berendt, David Richardson, and Herbert S. Klein, *The Trans-Atlantic Slave Trade: A Database on CD-ROM* (New York, 1999); Guinée, c. 1724, AOM, C 6 10.

6. On the trade goods in the Company of the Indies warehouse in Nantes, see Gaston Martin, "Les ventes de la Compagnie des Indes à Nantes (1723–1733)," *Revue de l'histoire des colonies françaises* 13 (1925): 490–491, 506–507. On cowry shells, see Jan Hogendorn, *The Shell Money of the Slave Trade* (New York, 1986).

7. Réponse au mémoire des négociants de Nantes, May 29, 1718, ADLA, C 571.

8. Arrest du conseil d'estat du roy, December 29, 1718, AMN, HH 236, no. 22; see also X. du Boisrouvray and M. Konrat, eds., *La traite des noirs à Nantes du XVIIe au XIXe siècle* (Nantes, 1980), fol. 67v.

9. The thirty barrels is derived by analogy to a similar weight in cowries on the *Concorde*.

10. The *Diligent's* sister ship, the *Concorde*, carried brandy from both Nantes and Bordeaux; Compte de l'armement, missehors, et cargaison du navire *La Concorde de Vannes*; Jean Boudriot, *Compagnie des Indes, 1720–1770* (Paris, 1983): 1:139.

11. Boudriot, *Compagnie des Indes*, 1:140.

12. Durand, Journal de bord d'un négrier, p. 3. The supply list is based in part on the *mise-hors* of the *Diligent's* sister ship, the *Concorde*, because the *mise-hors* of the *Diligent* has not survived. The *Concorde* was the same size as the *Diligent* and the Billy brothers were part owners. It started loading two weeks before the departure of the *Diligent*, and it seems reasonable to assume that the two ships were similarly equipped. Compte de l'armement missehors et cargaison du navire *La Concorde de Vannes*.

13. For an analysis of the accounting system, see Meyer, *L'armement nantais*, pp. 143–165.

14. Based on the example of the *Concorde*. The *mise-hors* always included the purchase price of the ship, even if it had already been amortized on a previous voyage. See Meyer, *L'armement nantais*, pp. 154–155.

15. Contrôlle des Actes, April 17 and 20, 1731, ADLA, IIC 2679, fols. 48v, 56r.

16. In his study of Nantes, Jean Meyer noted, "We have not found a single case of a long-distance voyage that did not take out insurance." Meyer, *L'armement nantais*, pp. 148–149.

17. Jacques Ducoin, *Naufrages, conditions de navigation et assurances dans la marine de commerce du XVIIIe siècle* (Paris, 1993), 1:159, 198–199; 2:648–656. The figures for direct voyages were calculated by taking the average of the outbound and the return voyages, which Ducoin lists separately.

18. Ducoin, *Naufrages*, 1:237–239; 2:666–668.

19. Jean Mettas, *Répertoire des expéditions négrières françaises au XVIIIe siècle*, ed. Serge Daget (Paris, 1978), 1:153–154; 2:587–588.

CHAPTER 10

1. Durand, Journal de bord d'un négrier, p. 5.
2. Gallois de la Tour, Mémoire sur la Bretagne, fol. 258r.

PART 4 SAILING SOUTH
CHAPTER 11

1. René-Josué Valin, *Commentaire sur l'ordonnance de la marine du mois d'aout 1681* (Poitiers, 1828), 1:50.

2. Jean Merrien, *La vie des marins au grand siècle* (Rennes, 1995), pp. 101–102.

3. Part 4 of this book is based on Robert Durand, Journal de bord d'un négrier, 1731–1732, BLY, Gen Mss, vol. 7, pp. 6–25.

4. Bouguer, *Traite complet de la navigation* (Paris, 1706), pp. 100–104; and pl. 4, fig. 17.

5. Ibid., pp. 117–118, and pl. 4, fig. 27.

6. De Radoüay, *Remarques sur la navigation et moyens d'en perfectionner la pratique* (Paris, 1727), p. 17; John Atkins, *A Voyage to Guinea, Brasil, and the West-Indies* (London, 1735), pp. 203–204.

7. Dava Sobel, *Longitude* (New York, 1995), p. 132.

8. De Radoüay, *Remarques sur la navigation*, p. 13.

9. Pas Caart vertoonende West-Indische als ook de Westelyske Custen van Europa en Africa. Eertyds in't ligt grbracht door wijlen Pieter Goos enz. Door Joannes Van Keulen en Zoonen, 1759. Gerard Hulst Van Keulen. AR, 4 VEL 96.

10. Calculated using figures in David Eltis, "The Volume and Structure of the Atlantic Slave Trade: A Reassessment," *William and Mary Quarterly*, 3d ser., 58 (2001): 17–46.

11. Le Croisic, Capitation, 1720, ADLA, B 3502, fol. 43; Le Croisic, Capitation, 1731, ADLA, E Dépôt 38, CC 1, fol. 5.

12. Gérard le Bouëdec et al., *Le Morbihan de la préhistoire à nos jours* (Saint-Jean d'Angély, 1994), p. 210.

13. Gallois de la Tour, Mémoire sur la Bretagne, c. 1733, BN, Manuscrits, FF 8153, p. 61; Fernand Guériff, *De poudre, de gloire, et de misère* (Nantes, 1980), pp. 196, 201, 213.

14. Estat des voyages de long cours faits par le Sr. Robert Durand, 1734, ADLA, B 5001; Lettre de capitaine et pilote, October 22, 1736, ADLA, B 4494, fols. 104v–105v; Robert Durand in Journaliers des officiers-mariniers et matelots (Le Croisic, Batz, Le Poulinguen), 1730–1732, ADLA, 120J 32.

15. *L'Espérence*, August 11, 1729, ADLA, B 4584, fol. 44r.

16. Parish records, Le Croisic, January 22, 1729, and September 10, 1730, ADLA, 1 Mi ec 303 R 12.

CHAPTER 12

1. Le Bouëdec, *Le Morbihan*, pp. 217–218.

2. Capitation, Le Croisic, 1730, ADLA, E Dépôt 38, CC 1, fol. 25v; Registre, capitaines, maîtres, ou patrons et pilotes, Département de Nantes, Quartier du Croisic, ADLA, 120J 33.

3. Pierre Mary in Journaliers des officiers-mariniers et matelots (Le Croisic, Batz, Le Poulinguen), ADLA, 120J 32; Capitation, Le Croisic, 1720, ADLA, B 3502, fol. 14r; Capitation, Le Croisic, 1730, ADLA, E Dépôt 38, CC 1, fol. 25v.

4. *La Marie Heureuse de Nantes*, August 1, 1721, ADLA, B 4580, fols. 62r, 64r-v.

5. *La Marie Heureuse de Nantes*, August 22, 1727, ADLA, B 4582, fols. 193v–194r; Pierre Mary in Journaliers des officiers-mariniers et matelots.

6. Procès verbal, March 11, 1730, ADMV, 9B 208; Extrait des registres du greffe, April 24, 1730, ADMV, 9B 208.

7. Pierre Valteau, May 15, 1722, parish records, Le Croisic, ADLA, Mi ec 303, R 12.

8. Valin, *L'ordonnance de la marine*, pp. 50–65.

9. Memoire de la course des forbans, February 6, 1722, AOM, col. C 6 25, no. 11.

10. Léon Vignols, "La piraterie sur l'Atlantique aux XVIIIe siècle," *Annales de Bretagne* 5 (1889–1990): 200–203.

CHAPTER 13

1. Alain Cabantous, "Espace maritime et mentalités religieuses en France aux XVIIè et XVIIIè siècles," *Mentalities/Mentalités* 1, no. 1 (1982): 4–5; testimony of Jean Carry, September 22, 1732, ADMV, 9B 208.

2. Edouard Richer, *Voyage pittoresque dans le département de la Loire-Inférieure* (Nantes, 1823). A facsimile copy was published as *Description du Croisic* (Paris, 1993), p. 87.

3. Inventaire du Vaisseau *Le Saint Pierre de Vannes*, ADM, 9B 208.

4. Robert Durand did not give the details of the ceremony. I have reconstructed it based on descriptions in N****, *Voyages aux côtes de Guinée et en Amérique* (Amsterdam, 1719), pp. 17–22; Jean-Baptiste Labat, *Nouveau voyage aux îles d'Amérique* (Paris, 1722), 1:34–38.

5. Armement, *Le Diligent de Vannes*, May 26, 1731, ADM, Vannes, 9B 208.

6. Merrien, *Vie des marins*, p. 92.

7. Here I am following the watch schedule outlined in Pierre-Marie-Joseph de Bonnefoux and E. Paris, *Dictionnaire de la marine à voile* (Paris, 1987), pp. 612–613. This is a reprint of the second edition.

CHAPTER 14

1. William Dampier, *Dampier's Voyages*, ed. John Masefield (London, 1906), 1:104, 2:358–367; Lista do Bispado de Cabo Verde, May 10, 1731, AHU, Caixa 14, no. 33.

2. Procès verbal de la relâche de St. Jago, July 9, 1731, ADMV, 9 B 208.

3. Alvaro Lereno, *Subsídios para a história da moeda em Cabo Verde, 1460–1940* (Lisbon, 1942), pp. 47–51; statement of the municipal council of Ribeira Grande, 1738, quoted in António Carreira, *The People of the Cape Verde Islands* (London, 1982), p. 13; Dampier, *Dampier's Voyages*, 2:369–370; George Roberts, *The Four Year Voyages of Captain George Roberts* (London, 1726), p. 404; Cabo Verde, April 16, 1731, AHU, Lisbon, Caixa 14, no. 28.

4. Elise Silva Andrade, *Les Iles du Cap-Vert de la "découverte" à l'indépendance nationale* (Paris, 1996), pp. 108–109.

5. T. Bentley Duncan, *Atlantic Islands: Madeira, the Azores, and the Cape Verdes in the Seventeenth Century* (Chicago, 1972), pp. 210, 228–229.

6. António Carreira, *Panaria Cabo-Verdeano-Guineese* (Lisbon, 1983), pp. 62–63.

7. Lista do Bispado de Cabo Verde, May 10, 1731, AHU, Caixa 14, no. 33; Christiano José de Senna, *Subsidios para a historica de Cabo Verde e Guine* (Lisbon, 1899–1913), 1:262.

8. Lista do Bispado de Cabo Verde, May 10, 1731; Cabo verde, April 16, 1731, AHU, Caixa 14, no. 28; Roberts, *Four Year Voyages*, p. 405.

9. Guillaume Delìsle, Carte d'Afrique dressé pour l'usage du roy, 1730, in Map Collection, Sterling Memorial Library, Yale University; D'Anville, Carte de la Côte de Guinée, 1729, BN, Cartes et Plans, Ge D 10630.

10. Jean Mettas, *Répertoire des expéditions négrières françaises au XVIIIe siècle*, ed. Serge Daget (Paris, 1978), 1:91–96.

11. William Snelgrave, *A New Account of Some Parts of Guinea and the Slave Trade* (London, 1734), pp. 193–288; Charles Johnson, *A General History of the Robberies and Murders of the Most Notorious Pyrates* (London, 1724), pp. 194–213; John Atkins, *A Voyage to Guinea, Brasil, and the West-Indies* (London, 1735), pp. 191–194.

12. Mettas, *Répertoire*, 2:609; Pranger to Hertogh, March 18, 1731, in A. Van Dantzig, comp. and trans., *The Dutch and the Guinea Coast, 1674–1742: A Collection of Documents from the General State Archive at the Hague* (Accra, 1978), p. 253.

PART 5 CRUISING THE AFRICAN COAST
CHAPTER 15

1. Part 5 of this book is based on Robert Durand, Journal de bord d'un négrier, 1731–1732, BLY, Gen Mss, vol. 7, pp. 25–51.

2. William Smith, *A New Voyage to Guinea* (London, 1744), pp. 106–109; John Atkins, *Voyage to Guinea, Brasil, and the West-Indies* (London, 1735), pp. 62–68; Paul Roussier, *L'etablissement d'Issiny, 1687–1702* (Paris, 1935), p. viii.

3. Atkins, *Voyage to Guinea*, p. 151.

4. Calculated from figures in David Eltis, "The Volume and Structure of the Transatlantic Slave Trade: A Reassessment," *William and Mary Quarterly*, 3d ser., 58 (2001): 44.

5. Smith, *New Voyage*, pp. 100–101; Atkins, *Voyage to Guinea*, pp. 58–59, 151–152.

6. Jean Mettas, *Répertoire des expéditions négrières Françaises au XVIIIe siècle,* ed. Serge Daget (Paris, 1978), 1:83–84, 102–103.

7. Atkins, *Voyage to Guinea*, pp. 58–59, 151–152.

8. Arent Roggeveen, *Le premier tome de la Tourbe Ardente* (Amsterdam, 1676) is in the New York Public Library. No French copies of volume 2, which covers Africa, are known to have survived. A facsimile of the English edition, entitled *The Burning Fen*, was published by Theatrum Orbis Terrarum in Amsterdam in 1971.

CHAPTER 16

1. This summary of the history of the forts of the Gold Coast is based on Albert Van Dantzig, *Forts and Castles of Ghana* (Accra, 1980), pp. 1–52.

2. This breakdown of the major forts is given in Harvey Feinberg, *Africans and Europeans in West Africa: Elminians and Dutchmen on the Gold Coast during the Eighteenth Century* (Philadelphia, 1989), p. 41. For a complete list of all castles, forts, and lodges on the Gold Coast, see Van Dantzig, *Forts and Castles of Ghana*, unpaginated introduction. For a map of the major forts and castles in 1727, see William Smith, "A New Map of

the Coast of Guinea from Cape Mount to Jacquin," in *Thirty Different Drafts of Guinea* (London, c. 1727), pl. 2.

3. Eltis, "Volume and Structure of the Atlantic Slave Trade," p. 44.

4. D'Anville, "Carte particulière de la partie principale de la Guinée située entre Issini et Ardra, avril, 1729," in Jean-Baptiste Labat, *Voyage du chevalier Des Marchais en Guinée, iles voisines et à Cayenne, fait en 1725, 1726 et 1727* (Paris, 1730, 1731), 2:1.

5. Minutes of the Elmina council, February 16, 1731, in A. Van Dantzig, comp. and trans., *The Dutch and the Guinea Coast, 1674–1742: A Collection of Documents from the General State Archive at the Hague* (Accra, 1978), pp. 257–259.

6. A. W. Lawrence, *Trade Castles and Forts of West Africa* (London, 1963), p. 230.

7. Kwame Daaku, *Trade and Politics on the Gold Coast, 1600–1720* (Oxford, 1970), pp. 137–138; Smith, *New Voyage*, pp. 116–117.

8. Atkins, *Voyage to Guinea*, pp. 75–80; James Houstoun, *Some New and Accurate Observations . . . of the Coast of Guinea* (London, 1725), p. 17.

9. Elmina council minutes, December 28, 1725, in Van Dantzig, *Collection of Documents*, p. 218; Emmanuel Kreike, "Early Asante and the Struggle for Economic and Political Control on the Gold Coast, 1690–1730" (M.A. thesis, University of Amsterdam, 1986), p. 121.

10. Guinée, c. 1724, AOM, col. C 6 10.

CHAPTER 17

1. P. E. H. Hair, "Columbus from Guinea to America," *History in Africa* 17 (1990): 113–129.

2. Johannes Postma and Stuart B. Schwartz, "Brazil and Holland as Commercial Partners on the West African Coast during the Eighteenth Century," *Arquivos do Centro Cultural Calouste Gulbenkian* 34 (1995): 401–407.

3. Ibid., p. 404.

4. John Vogt, *Portuguese Rule on the Gold Coast* (Athens, Georgia, 1979), pp. 57–58; 71–72; Ray Kea, *Settlements, Trade, and Polities in the Seventeenth-Century Gold Coast* (Baltimore, 1982), pp. 197–201.

5. Albert Van Dantzig, *Les Hollandais sur la côte de Guinée à l'époque de l'essor de l'Ashanti et du Dahomey, 1680–1740* (Paris, 1980), pp. 114–115.

6. Calculated on the basis of data in David Eltis, Stephen D. Behrendt, and David Richardson, *The Transatlantic Slave Trade: A New Census* (forthcoming).

7. Short memoir, c. 1729–1730, in Van Dantzig, *Collection of Documents*, p. 240.

8. W. A. Richards, "The Import of Firearms into West Africa in the Eighteenth Century," *Journal of African History* 21 (1980): 45–46.

9. Kreike, "Early Asante," p. 101; Elmina Journal, April 2, 1732, in Van Dantzig, *Collection of Documents*, p. 276.

10. Kreike, "Early Asante," pp. 123–124.

11. Feinberg, *Africans and Europeans in West Africa*, p. 131.

12. Kreike, "Early Asante," p. 115.

13. Minutes of Elmina council, March 26, 1731, in Van Dantzig, *Collection of Documents*, pp. 259–260.

14. Johannes Postma, *The Dutch in the Atlantic Slave Trade, 1600–1815* (Cambridge, 1990), p. 80.

15. Extract from the minutes of the meeting of the Chamber of Zeeland, February 7, 1730, in Van Dantzig, *Collection of Documents*, pp. 237–239.

16. Postma, *Dutch in the Atlantic Slave Trade*, pp. 202–203.

17. Lawrence, *Trade Castles and Forts of West Africa*, pp. 188–189.

18. An estimate of the charges of the Royal African Company of England for the maintenance of the several British forts, February, 1731, PRO, T70 1450, p. 1.

19. P. E. H. Hair, Adam Jones, and Robin Law, eds., *Barbot on Guinea: The Writings of Jean Barbot on West Africa, 1678–1712* (London, 1992), 2:392.

20. Colin Palmer, *Human Cargoes: The British Slave Trade to Spanish America, 1700–1739* (Urbana, Ill., 1981), p. 43.

21. Ibid., pp. 43–44.

22. Francis Moore, *Travels into the Inland Parts of Africa* (London, 1738), p. 49.

23. Calculated on the basis of data in Eltis, Behrendt, and Richardson, *Transatlantic Slave Trade*.

24. *Journal of the Commission for Trade and Plantations from January 1722–3 to December 1728* (London, 1928), pp. 261–263.

25. Smith, *New Voyage*, p. 2. Some of the results of Smith's voyage are reproduced in Smith, *Thirty Different Drafts of Guinea*.

26. A. Shaw, comp., *Calendar of Treasury Books and Papers, 1729–1730* (London, 1897), p. 395.

27. Estimate of the charges of the Royal African Company, p. 14.

28. Gaston Martin, *Nantes au XVIIIe siècle: L'ère des négriers*, new ed. (Paris, 1993), p. 80.

29. Sandra Greene, "The Anlo-Ewe: Their Economy, Society, and External Relations in the Eighteenth Century" (Ph.D. diss. Northwestern University, 1981), p. 123.

CHAPTER 18

1. D'Anville, "Carte de la côte de Guinée, juillet, 1729," in Jean-Baptiste Labat, *Voyage du chevalier Des Marchais en Guinée, isles voisines et à Cayenne, fait en 1725, 1726 et 1727* (Paris, 1730, 1731), 1:1; D'Anville, Carte de la Côte de Guinée par le Sr. D'Anville, July 1729, BN, Cartes et Plans, Ge. D. 10630.

2. William Bosman, *A New and Accurate Description of the Coast of Guinea, Divided into the Gold, Slave, and the Ivory Coasts* (London, 1705); William Smith, *Thirty Different Drafts of Guinea* (London, c. 1727), pl. 2.

3. Greene, "Anlo-Ewe," p. 124.

4. Durand, Journal de bord d'un négrier, p. 49.

5. Compagnie des Indes, May 20, 1728, AOM, col. C 6 25, no. 58, fol. 7r-v.

PART 6 WHYDAH
CHAPTER 19

1. Robert Durand, Journal de bord d'un négrier, 1731–1732, BLY, Gen Mss, vol. 7, pp. 50–51; Jean Mettas, *Répertoire des expéditions négrières françaises au XVIIIe siècle*, ed. Serge Daget (Paris, 1978), 2:702–703.

2. Instructions et orders pour Monsieur Foures commandant le navire *l'Affricain*, 1738, in *Journal de la traite des noirs*, comp. Jehan Mousnier (Paris, 1957), p. 23.

3. Journaliers des officiers-mariniers et matelots (Le Croisic, Batz, Le Poulinguen), 1700–1732, ADLA, 120J 32; *Le More*, January 15, 2728, ADLA, B4583, fols. 48v–49v.

4. Jean Mettas, *Répertoire des expéditions négrières Françaises au XVIIIe siècle,* ed. Serge Daget (Paris, 1978), 1:116–119.

5. The description of the ceremony is based on Chevalier Des Marchais, Journal du voyage de Guinée et Cayenne, 1724–1726, BN, Manuscrits, FF 24223, pp. 79–84; and the unpaginated sketch entitled Couronnement du roy du Juda à la coste de Guinée du mois d'avril 1725. An engraving made from this sketch was printed in Jean-Baptiste Labat, *Voyage du chevalier Des Marchais en Guinée, iles voisines et à Cayenne, fait en 1725, 1726 et 1727* (Paris, 1730), 2: plate between pages 70 and 71.

6. Des Marchais, Journal du voyage, p. 83; Labat, *Voyage du chevalier Des Marchais,* 2: 58–59.

7. Dralsé de Grand Pierre, *Relation de diverses voyages* (Paris, 1718), p. 169; William Smith, *A New Voyage to Guinea* (London, 1744), p. 190; William Snelgrave, *A New Account of Some Parts of Guinea and the Slave Trade* (London 1734), p. 127.

8. Robin Law, "'The Common People Were Divided': Monarchy, Aristocracy, and Political Factionalism in the Kingdom of Whydah, 1671–1727," *International Journal of African Historical Studies* 23 (1990): 225. The problem with the 1717–1718 date is that there is no evidence that Des Marchais was in Whydah at the time. I tend to accept Des Marchais's date of 1725. The standard argument against 1725 is that the kingdom of Allada had been conquered by Dahomey and therefore Allada could not have sent a representative to the coronation. However, King Agaja of Dahomey made it clear to Bulfinch Lambe that Allada in 1725 had a sitting king who paid tribute to Dahomey. The tributary king may have sent a representative to the ceremony in order to strengthen his ties with Whydah. See Robin Law, "Further Light on Bulfinch Lambe and the 'Emperor of Pawpaw': King Agaja of Dahomey's Letter to King George I of England, 1726," *History in Africa* 17 (1990): 218.

9. A peaceful transition is described in Relation du royaume de Judas en Guinée, AOM, DFC Côtes d'Afrique, 75, p. 36; a more violent version is given by Jean Barbot in P. E. H. Hair, Adam Jones, and Robin Law, eds., *Barbot on Guinea: The Writings of Jean Barbot on West Africa, 1678–1712* (London, 1992), 2:644; see also Du Columbier, Copie d'une relation envoyée à la compagnie, August 10, 1714, AOM, col. C 6 25, no. 17, fols. 9v–12v.

10. I. A. Akinjogbin, *Dahomey and Its Neighbors, 1708–1818* (Cambridge, 1967), p. 43.

11. Smith, *New Voyage,* p. 192. Smith arrived in Whydah about a month after the army of Dahomey destroyed its capital city, Savi. He says that his account is based on descriptions from "gentlemen at Whydah." He also took some of his descriptive material on the kingdom of Whydah from William Bosman, *A New and Accurate Description of the Coast of Guinea* (London, 1705).

12. Jean Doublet, *Le Honfleurais aux sept naufrages,* ed. Noël le Coutour (Paris, 1996), p. 239; Relation du royaume de Judas, p. 87; Pierre Verger, *Le Fort St. Jean-Baptiste d'Ajuda* (Dahomey, 1966), p. 11.

13. On the construction of the French fort in 1704, see Doublet, *Honfleurais aux Sept Naufrages,* pp. 239–240.

14. Plan du Fort St. Louis, 1717–1718, AOM, col. C 6 27, no. 175; Simone Berbain, *Le comptoir français de Juda (Ouidah) au XVIIIe siècle* (Paris, 1942), pp. 57–58.

15. William Smith, *Thirty Different Drafts of Guinea* (London, c. 1728), pl. 28–29.

16. Verger, *Fort St. Jean-Baptiste d'Ajuda,* pp. 16–17.

17. Ibid., p. 24; Provisional agreement . . . with the king and grandees of Fida on November 12, 1726, in A. Van Dantzig, comp. and trans., *The Dutch and the Guinea Coast, 1674–1742: A Collection of Documents from the General State Archive at the Hague* (Accra, 1978), p. 220.

18. Labat, *Voyage du chevalier Des Marchais*, 2:241–242.

19. Smith, *New Voyage*, pp. 194–195. These descriptions are very similar to, and perhaps copied from, Bosman, *New and Accurate Description*, pp. 339–343.

20. Smith, *Thirty Different Drafts of Guinea*, pl. 28.

21. Smith, *New Voyage*, pp. 199–200; Des Marchais, Journal du voyage, p. 75.

22. The population estimate comes from Robin Law, *The Slave Coast of West Africa, 1550–1750* (Oxford, 1991), p. 59. Estimates of slave exports come from Des Marchais, Journal du voyage, p. 51; John Atkins, *A Voyage to Guinea, Brasil, and the West-Indies* (London, 1735), pp. 157, 172; James Houston, *Some New and Accurate Observations . . . of the Coast of Guinea* (London, 1725), p. 27. The overall slave exports are calculated on the basis of figures in David Eltis, "The Volume and Structure of the Transatlantic Slave Trade: A Reassessment," *William and Mary Quarterly*, 3d ser., 58 (2001): 44–45.

23. Relation du royaume de Judas, p. 88.

24. Des Marchais, Journal du voyage, pp. 62–64.

25. Labat adds that the Aradas are not to be confused with the people of Allada. Labat, *Voyage du chevalier Des Marchais*, 2:125.

26. Des Marchais, Journal du voyage, pp. 58, 92; Labat, *Voyage du chevalier Des Marchais*, 2:234.

27. Des Marchais, Journal du voyage, pp. 84–87.

28. Ibid., p. 87.

29. Labat, *Voyage du chevalier Des Marchais*, 2:87–89; Atkins, *Voyage to Guinea*, p. 110.

30. Distances are based on map 5, "Dahomey in the Early Eighteenth Century," in Law, *Slave Coast of West Africa*, p. 268.

CHAPTER 20

1. The description of King Agaja comes from Snelgrave, who visited King Agaja in April 1727. Snelgrave, *New Account*, pp. 34–35, 75. See also Dubelay, Lettre de commerce, November 21, 1733, AOM, col. C 6 25, no. 149.

2. Bulfinch Lambe to Jeremiah Tinker, November 27, 1724, reprinted in Smith, *New Voyage*, pp. 171–189.

3. Verger, *Le Fort St. Jean-Baptiste d'Ajuda*, p. 24.

4. King of Dahomey to King George I, January 1726, reprinted in Law, "Further Light on Bulfinch Lambe," pp. 216–217. A similar account was given to Delìsle in 1728, though the number of battles attributed to each king was somewhat different. See Delìsle à Daomé, September 7, 1728, AOM, col. C 6 25, no. 139. For a fuller account of the early history of Dahomey, see Law, *Slave Coast of West Africa*, pp. 261–278.

5. Dubelay, Lettre de commerce.

6. Robin Law, "Warfare on the West African Slave Coast, 1650–1850," in R. Brian Ferguson and Neil L. Whitehead, eds., *War in the Tribal Zone* (Sante Fe, 1992), pp. 103–126; Labat, *Voyage du chevalier Des Marchais*, 2: 235–245.

7. Labat, *Voyage du chevalier Des Marchais*, pp. 236–237; Snelgrave, *New Account*, p. 6.

8. Labat, *Voyage du chevalier Des Marchais*, 1:xii; Snelgrave, *New Account*, p. 78; Smith, *New Voyage*, p. 192.

9. Labat, *Voyage du chevalier Des Marchais*, 1:xii.

10. Snelgrave, *New Account*, pp. 37–39, 106–107; Robin Law, "Human Sacrifice in Pre-Colonial West Africa," *African Affairs* 84 (1985): 53–87.

11. Bulfinch Lambe to Jeremiah Tinker, November 27, 1724, reprinted in Smith, *New Voyage*, p. 173; Robin Law, "'My Head Belongs to the King': On the Political and Ritual Significance of Decapitation in Pre-Colonial Dahomey," *Journal of African History* 30 (1989): 399–415; Edna Bay, *Wives of the Leopard: Gender, Politics, and Culture in the Kingdom of Dahomey* (Charlottesville, 1998), p. 66. On the treatment of heads of slain enemies in Whydah, see Labat, *Voyage du chevalier Des Marchais*, 2:239.

12. Le Herissé, *L'ancien royaume du Dahomey* (Paris, 1911), pp. 39–40; Law, "My Head Belongs to the King," p. 404.

13. Snelgrave, *New Account*, pp. 5–6, 64. There is an ongoing debate among historians about King Agaja's motives for wanting to attack the kingdom of Whydah. For the argument that King Agaja wanted to stop the slave trade, see Atkins, *Voyage to Guinea*, p. 119; I. A. Akinjogbin, *Dahomey and Its Neighbors, 1708–1818* (Cambridge, 1967), pp. 68–109. For the argument that King Agaja wanted to expand his kingdom and gain direct access to the coast, see David Henige and Marion Johnson, "Agaja and the Slave Trade: Another Look at the Evidence," *History in Africa* 3 (1976): 57–67; Robin Law, "Dahomey and the Slave Trade: Reflections on the Historiography of the Rise of Dahomey," *Journal of African History* 27 (1986): 237–267; Law, *The Slave Coast of West Africa, 1550–1750* (Oxford, 1991), pp. 283–287, 300–308. My own reading of the evidence has led me to agree with Henige, Johnson, and Law.

14. Atkins, *Voyage to Guinea*, p. 122; Law, *Slave Coast of West Africa*, pp. 197–198; Albert Van Dantzig, *Les Hollandais sur la côte de Guinée* (Paris, 1980), p. 141.

15. *Journal of the Commissioners for Trade and Plantations* (London, 1928), 6:201.

16. The letter is reprinted in Law, "Further Light on Bulfinch Lambe," pp. 216–220.

17. The German anthropologist Georg Elwert collected this story in Benin in the early 1970s. Elwert's informants claimed that the story dated back to the time of King Agaja's father. See Georg Elwert, "Pouvoir et économie du royaume de Dahomey au 18e siècle" (unpublished manuscript), pp. 98–99. The Benin historian Abiola Félix Iroko collected similar stories in Benin in 1983. See Abiola Félix Iroko, "Cauris et esclaves en Afrique occidentale entre le XVIe et le XIXe siècles," in Serge Daget, ed., *De la traite à l'esclavage* (Paris, 1988), 1:199.

Chapter 21

1. Relation de la guerre de Juda par M. Ringard, 1727, AOM, col. C 6 10. Another copy of this document was published by Robin Law in "A Neglected Account of the Dahomian Conquest of Whydah (1727): The 'Relation de la Guerre de Juda' of the Sieur Ringard of Nantes," *History in Africa* 15 (1988): 321–338.

2. Snelgrave, *New Account*, pp. 9–19.

3. Mendes to viceroy of Brazil, April 4, 1727, in Pierre Verger, *Trade Relations Between the Bight of Benin and Bahia, 17th–19th Century*, trans. Evelyn Crawford (Ibadan, 1976), p. 121.

4. Hertogh, letter of March 18, 1727, in Van Dantzig, *Collection of Documents*, p. 221.

5. Bay, *Wives of the Leopard*, pp. 59–60.

6. Snelgrave, *New Account*, pp. 22–66.

7. Ibid., pp. 60–66.

8. Ibid., p. 125; Robin Law, "Slave-Raiders and Middlemen, Monopolists and Free-Traders: The Supply of Slaves for the Atlantic Trade in Dahomey, c. 1715–1850," *Journal of African History* 30 (1989): 48–51.

9. On the selling price of a slave in British pounds, see Richspence to Commissioners of His Majesty's Treasury, October 7, 1731, PRO, PT I, SP 36/25. For the price of a musket, see Durand, Journal de bord d'un négrier, p. 59.

CHAPTER 22

1. List of debts paid on account of Adomo Tomo, PRO, PT I, SP 36/25. On the fashions of the early eighteenth century, see Iris Brooke and John Laver, *English Costume of the Eighteenth Century* (London, 1931), pp. 10–35.

2. On St. James's Palace in the early eighteenth century, see Christopher Wren, *The Royal Palaces of Winchester, Whitehall, Kensington, and St. James's* (Oxford, 1930), pp. 210–212, pls. XXIX, XXXIII.

3. Richspence to Commissioners of His Majesty's Treasury, October 7, 1731, PRO, PT I, SP 36/25; Richspence to Commissioners for Trade and Plantations, May 27, 1731, PRO, PT I, SP 36/25; *Journal of the Commissioners for Trade and Plantations* (London, 1928), 6:202.

4. Snelgrave, *New Account*, pp. 68–69; List of debts of Adomo Tomo, PRO, PT I, SP 36/25; Inventory of the goods and chattells of Robert Alexander of the City of Annapolis, 1733, MSA.

5. In 1731 the mean inventory price of a prime male slave field hand in Maryland was £31. Allan Kulikoff, "Tobacco and Slaves: Population, Economy, and Society in Eighteenth-Century Prince George's County, Maryland" (Ph.D. diss., Brandeis University, 1976), p. 486.

6. Snelgrave, *New Account*, p. 69.

7. Richspence to Commissioners of His Majesty's Treasury; Richspence to Commissioners for Trade and Plantations; *Journal of the Commissioners for Trade and Plantations* (London, 1928), 6:202.

8. W. H. Pyne, *The History of the Royal Residences of Windsor Castle, St. James's Palace, Carlton House, Kensington Palace, Hampton Court, Buckingham House, and Frogmore* (London, 1819), 3:9–11.

9. *Monthly Intelligencer* 5 (May 1731): 216.

10. Aphra Behn, *Oroonoko, or, the Royal Slave* (1688; reprint, New York, 1973).

11. Arthur Scouten, comp., *The London Stage, 1600–1800: A Calendar of Plays, Entertainments, and Afterpieces* (Carbondale, Ill., 1960–1968), 3:137.

12. Smith, *New Voyage*, p. 189.

13. *Journal of the Commissioners for Trade and Plantations*, 6:198–200.

14. Ibid., 201–203.

15. Richspence to the Lords Commissioners for Trade and Plantations, June 10, 1731, PRO, SP 36/25.

16. The letter is reprinted in Marion Johnson, "Bulfinch Lambe and the Emperor of Pawpaw: A Footnote to Agaja and the Slave Trade," *History in Africa* 5 (1978): 348–349.

17. *Monthly Intelligencer* 9 (September 1731): 401.

18. Richspence to Commissioners of His Majesty's Treasury, October 7, 1731, PRO, PT I, ST 36/25.

19. *Monthly Intelligencer* 12 (December 1731): 542.

20. Snelgrave, *New Account*, p. 71; Scouten, *London Stage*, 3:170–171.

21. Richard Leacroft, *The Development of the English Playhouse* (London, 1973), p. 97.

22. On the use of actors in blackface, see Anthony Barthelemy, *Black Face, Maligned Race* (Baton Rouge, 1987), p. 47.

23. Thomas Southern, *Oroonoko: A Tragedy as It Is Acted at the Theatre-Royal by His Majesty's Servants* (Dublin, 1730).

24. Laura Rosenthal, "Owning Oroonoko: Behn, Southerne, and the Contingincies of Property," in Mary Beth Rose, ed., *Renaissance Drama* (Evanston, 1992), p. 46.

25. John Dodds, *Thomas Southerne: Dramatist* (New Haven, 1933), p. 128.

PART 7 ASSOU
CHAPTER 23

1. Robert Durand, Journal de bord d'un négrier, 1731–1732, BLY, Gen Mss, vol. 7, pp. 52–55.

2. Compagnie des Indes, May 20, 1728, AOM, col. C 6 25, no. 58, fol. 7r-v.

3. Jean Mettas, *Répertoire des expéditions négrières françaises au XVIIIe siècle*, ed. Serge Daget (Paris, 1978), 1:153.

4. René-Josué Valin, *Commentaire sur l'ordonnance de la marine du mois d'août 1681* (Poitiers, 1828), 1:61.

5. Philippe Haudrère, *La compagnie française des Indes au XVIIIe siècle* (Paris, 1989), 2:632–635, 4:1255–1257.

6. Claude Nières et al., *Histoire de Lorient* (Toulouse, 1988), pp. 39–40.

7. Haudrère, *Compagnie française des Indes*, 2:578–579.

8. Marc Perrichet, "L'administration des classes de la marine et ses archives dans les ports bretons," *Revue d'histoire economique et sociale* 37 (1959): 103–104; Haudrère, *Compagnie française des Indes*, 4:1263–1264.

9. Haudrère, *Compagnie française des Indes*, 2:578–585.

10. John Atkins, *A Voyage to Guinea, Brasil, and the West-Indies* (London, 1735), p. 172.

11. Deane, Williams Fort Whydah, 1731, PRO, T70/1450, p. 8; Deane, Williams Fort Whydah, June 26, 1731, PRO, T70/7, fols. 111v–112r; Le Pontchartrain, L'armement, 1731, SHML, 2P 2.

12. Deane, Williams Fort Whydah, June 26, 1731, fol. 112r.

13. Journal de l'Ile, pilote, *Le Pontchartrain*, July 1731, AN, Paris, Marine 4 JJ 70; Le Pontchartrain, L'armement et désarmement, SHML, 1 P 70 and 2 P 24.

14. "Relation du chevalier Damon (1702)," in Paul Roussier, comp., *L'etablissement d'Issiny, 1687–1702* (Paris, 1935), p. 106.

15. Chevalier Des Marchais, Journal du voyage de Guinée et Cayenne, 1724–1726, BN, Manuscrits, FF 24223, p. 59.

16. Dralsé de Grand Pierre, *Relation de divers voyages faits dans l'Afrique, dans l'Amérique et aux Indes Occidentales* (Paris, 1718), p. 168.

17. Des Marchais, Journal du voyage, p. 111; N★★★★, *Voyages aux Côtes de Guinée et en Amerique* (Amsterdam, 1719), pp. 49–51.

18. *Voyages aux Côtes de Guinée,* pp. 54–56.

19. Jean Doublet, *Le Honfleurais aux sept naufrages,* ed. Noël le Coutour (Paris, 1996), pp. 240–241.

20. Relation du royaume de Judas, AOM, DFC Côtes d'Afrique, 75, p. 28.

21. Treaty reprinted in A. Van Dantzig, comp. and trans., *The Dutch and the Guinea Coast, 1674–1742: A Collection of Documents from the General State Archive at the Hague* (Accra, 1978), pp. 115–116; Des Marchais, Journal du voyage, pp. 52–55.

22. Do Coulombier, Mémoire de la suitte des affaires du pays de Juda, February 14, 1715, AOM, col. C 6 25, no. 25; letter of February 4, 1715, in Van Dantzig, *Collection of Documents,* p. 180.

23. I. A. Akinjogbin, *Dahomey and Its Neighbors, 1708–1818* (Cambridge, 1967), p. 98.

CHAPTER 24

1. William Snelgrave, *A New Account of Some Parts of Guinea and the Slave Trade* (London, 1734), p. 65.

2. Mellier to Maurepas, July 12, 1727, AMN, HH 236, no. 15.

3. Compagnie des Indes, May 20, 1728, fol. 4r.

4. Ibid., fol. 5r; Mettas, *Répertoire,* 2:242.

5. Compagnie des Indes, May 20, 1728, fols. 8v–9r; Wilson to Cabo Corso castle, February 24, 1728, in Robin Law, ed., *Correspondence of the Royal African Company's Chief Merchants at Cabo Corso Castle with William's Fort, Whydah, and the Little Popo Factory, 1727–1728* (Madison, Wis., 1991), pp. 19–20; letter from Jaquin, December 15, 1727, in Van Dantzig, *Collection of Documents,* p. 224.

6. Pierre Verger, *Trade Relations Between the Bight of Benin and Bahia, 17th–19th Century,* trans. Evelyn Crawford (Ibadan, 1976), p. 124. There has been a long debate, going back to 1735, about whether or not King Agaja was trying to stop the slave trade. For the arguments of those who thought that King Agaja was against the slave trade, see John Atkins, *A Voyage to Guinea, Brasil, and the West-Indies* (London 1735), pp. 119–132; I. A. Akinjogbin, *Dahomey and Its Neighbors, 1708–1818* (Cambridge, 1967), pp. 68–109. For the arguments of those who believe that Agaja was not trying to shut down the slave trade, see David Henige and Marion Johnson, "Agaja and the Slave Trade: Another Look at the Evidence," *History in Africa* 3 (1976): 57–67; Robin Law, "Dahomey and the Slave Trade: Reflections on the Historiography of the Rise of Dahomey," *Journal of African History* 27 (1986): 237–267; Robin Law, *The Slave Coast of West Africa, 1550–1750* (Oxford, 1991), pp. 301–308.

7. Calculated using data in David Eltis, Stephen D. Behrends, and David Richardson, *The Transatlantic Slave Trade: A New Census* (forthcoming).

8. Compagnie des Indes, May 20, 1728, fol. 11r; Wilson to Cabo Corso castle, April 29, 1728, in Law, *Correspondence,* p. 27; Snelgrave, *New Account,* p. 74.

9. Wilson to Cabo Corso castle, February 24, 1728, in Law, *Correspondence,* p. 20; Compagnie des Indes, May 20, 1728, fol. 3v.

10. Compagnie des Indes, May 20, 1728, fols. 20v–21r.

11. Verger, *Trade Relations*, p. 122.

12. Wilson to Cabo Corso castle, April 29, 1728, in Law, *Correspondence*, pp. 25–26.

13. Ibid.; Compagnie des Indes, May 20, 1728, fols. 11v–13v.

14. Mettas, *Répertoire*, 1:125.

15. Mémoire de la Compagnie des Indes, November 8, 1730, AOM, col. C 6 25, no. 144; Compagnie des Indes, May 20, 1728, fol. 17r-v.

16. Compagnie des Indes, May 20, 1728, fols. 21v–22r; Wilson to Cabo Corso castle, April 29, 1728, and July 12, 1728, in Law, *Correspondence*, pp. 25, 33.

17. Houdoyer Dupetitval, March 17, 1729, AOM, col. C 6 10, pp. 4–8; Snelgrave, *New Account*, pp. 115–120.

18. Compagnie des Indes, May 20, 1728, fol. 1v; Houdoyer Dupetitval, March 17, 1729, p. 12.

19. Mémoire de la Compagnie des Indes, November 8, 1730.

20. Snelgrave, *New Account*, pp. 123–128; Testefolle, Whydah, October 30, 1729, PRO, T70/7, fol. 98v.

21. Snelgrave, *New Account*, pp. 130–133; Mémoire de la Compagnie des Indes, November 8, 1730; Cape Coast castle, December 26, 1729, PRO, T70/7, fols. 99v–100r.

22. Mallis de la Mine, January 8, 1732, ADLA, C 739; Deane, Williams Fort Whydah, June 26, 1731, fols. 111v–112r.

CHAPTER 25

1. Durand, Journal de bord d'un négrier, p. 54.

PART 8 JAKIN
CHAPTER 26

1. Part 8 of this book is based on Robert Durand, Journal de bord d'un négrier, 1731–1732, BLY, Gen Mss, vol. 7, pp. 55–66.

2. Jean Mettas, *Répertoire des expéditions négrières françaises au XVIIIe siècle*, ed. Serge Daget (Paris, 1978), 1:154.

3. David Eltis, Stephen D. Behrendt, David Richardson, and Herbert S. Klein, *The Trans-Atlantic Slave Trade: A Database on CD-ROM* (New York, 1999).

4. Chevalier Des Marchais, Journal du voyage de Guinée et Cayenne, 1724–1726, BN, FF 24223, pp. 124–126.

5. William Smith, *A New Voyage to Guinea* (London, 1744), p. 167.

6. Robin Law, "Further Light on Bulfinch Lambe and the 'Emperor of Pawpaw': King Agaja of Dahomey's Letter to King George I of England, 1726," *History in Africa* 17 (1990): 216; William Snelgrave, *A New Account of Some Parts of Guinea and the Slave Trade* (London, 1734), p. 24.

7. On the construction of tents, see Addition à la déclaration du navire *Le Nestor*, May 28, 1734, ADLA, B 4586, fol. 58v.

8. Thomas Phillips, "A Journal of a Voyage Made in the *Hannibal* of London, 1693–1694," in Awnshawm Churchill, ed., *A Collection of Voyages and Travels* (London, 1732), 6:229.

9. Process described by Alexander Falconbridge, *An Account of the Slave Trade on the Coast of Africa* (London, 1788), p. 2.

10. Procès verbal des pièces de guinée et limancas et indienne, November 27, 1732, ADMV, 9B 208.

11. Each keg contained thirty-two Paris pints. Jean Boudriot, *Traite et navire négrier: L'Aurore, 1784* (Paris, 1984), p. 69.

12. Mettas, *Répertoire*, 1:153.

13. *Le Nestor de Nantes*, March 30, 1733, ADLA, B 4585, fols. 170v–172v; Addition à la déclaration du navire *Le Nestor*, May 28, 1734, ADLA, B 4586, fols. 58r–59r.

CHAPTER 27

1. N****, *Voyages aux côtes de Guinée et en Amérique* (Amsterdam, 1719), p. 124.

2. Ibid., pp. 122–130.

3. Pierre Verger, *Trade Relations Between the Bight of Benin and Bahia, 17th–19th Century*, trans. Evelyn Crawford (Ibadan, 1976), p. 111.

4. Ibid., p. 33.

5. João Basilio, May 20, 1731, in Verger, *Trade Relations*, p. 129.

6. Elmina Journal, May 8, 1727, in A. Van Dantzig, comp. and trans., *The Dutch and the Guinea Coast, 1674–1742: A Collection of Documents from the General State Archive at the Hague* (Accra, 1978), p. 222.

7. Hertogh to Pranger, January 6, 1731; and De la Planque to Hertogh, January 30, 1731, in Van Dantzig, *Collection of Documents*, pp. 251–253.

8. Hertogh to Pranger, March 27, 1731, in Van Dantzig, *Collection of Documents*, p. 253; Verger, *Trade Relations*, p. 58.

CHAPTER 28

1. Duport to Cabo Corso castle, November 12, 1727, in Robin Law, ed., *Correspondence of the Royal African Company's Chief Merchants at Cabo Corso Castle with William's Fort, Whydah, and the Little Popo Factory, 1727–1728* (Madison, Wis., 1991), p. 12.

2. Quoted in C. M. MacInnes, "The Slave Trade," in C. Northcote Parkinson, ed., *The Trade Winds* (London, 1948), p. 261.

3. P. E. H. Hair, Adam Jones, and Robin Law, eds., *Barbot on Guinea: The Writings of Jean Barbot on West Africa, 1678–1712* (London, 1992), 2:634–635; William Bosman, *A New and Accurate Description of the Coast of Guinea* (London, 1705), p. 392; Chevalier des Marchais, Journal du voyage, pp. 71–73.

4. Bosman, *New and Accurate Description*, pp. 214–215; Relation du royaume de Judas en Guinée, AOM, DFC Côtes d'Afrique, 75, pp. 47–48; Jean Merrien, *La vie des marins au grand siècle* (Rennes, 1995), p. 75; John Atkins, *A Voyage to Guinea, Brasil, and the West-Indies* (London, 1735), p. 111.

5. Snelgrave, *New Account*, pp. 125, 130.

6. Ibid., pp. 158–159.

7. Atkins, *Voyage to Guinea*, p. 111.

8. Hertogh, January 9, 1728, in Van Dantzig, *Collection of Documents*, p. 231.

9. Jean-Baptiste Labat, *Voyage du chevalier Des Marchais en Guinée, iles voisines et à Cayenne, fait en 1725, 1726 et 1727* (Paris, 1730), 2:131–132; Savary des Bruslons, *Dictionnaire universel de commerce* (Paris, 1723), 2:860.

10. Des Marchais, Journal du voyage, p. 64; Labat, *Voyage du chevalier Des Marchais*, 2:130; Phillips, "Journal," 6:218; T. Aubrey, *The Sea-Surgeon, or the Guinea Man's Vade Mecum* (London, 1729), pp. 110–126.

11. Hertogh to Elmina, March 21, 1732, in Van Dantzig, *Collection of Documents*, p. 265.

12. Interrogatoire, Durand, February 28, 1733, ADMV, 9B 208.

13. Enquête, September 22, 1732, testimony of Jean Carry, ADMV, 9B 208.

14. Labat, *Voyage du chevalier Des Marchais*, 2:116.

15. Hair, Jones, and Law, *Writings of Jean Barbot*, 2:778.

16. See the description in Snelgrave, *New Account*, p. 190; Atkins, *Voyage to Guinea*, p. 173.

17. On toilets, see Phillips, "Journal," 6:230; Lief Svalesen, *The Slave Ship Fredensborg*, trans. Pat Shaw and Selena Winsnes (Bloomington, Ind., 2000), pp. 92–93.

18. Relation du royaume de Judas, p. 88. On African views of white cannibals, see William D. Pierson, "White Cannibals, Black Martyrs: Fear, Depression, and Religious Faith as Causes of Suicide Among Slaves," *Journal of Negro History* 62 (1977): 147–159; William D. Pierson, *Black Legacy* (Amherst, Mass., 1993), pp. 5–12.

CHAPTER 29

1. Jean Meyer, *L'armement nantais dans la deuxième moitié du XVIIIe siècle* (Paris, 1969), p. 151.

2. Controlle des actes, ADLA, II C 2678, fol. 86v; II C 2679, fols. 29r, 36v, 40v, 46r, 72r; Durand, April 25, 1732, ADLA, 4E 2 1861.

3. Calculated on the basis of prices recorded in Durand, Journal de bord d'un négrier, pp. 3, 59, 93. If a male slave was paid for with brandy, the cost was eighty-eight livres, but if he was paid for with linen cloth, the cost was 220 livres. Slaves were usually purchased with an assortment of goods, placing the average price somewhere in between those two extremes.

4. Testimony of Jean Carry; Instructions et orders pour Monsieur Foures commandant le navire *l'Affricain*, 1738, in *Journal de la traite des noirs*, comp. Jehan Mousnier (Paris, 1957), p. 22.

5. Compagnie des Indes, May 20, 1728, AOM, col. C 6 25, no. 58, fol. 16v.

6. Jean Boudriot, *Compagnie des Indes, 1720–1770* (Paris, 1983), 1:138.

7. Philippe Haudrère, *La Compagnie française des Indes au XVIIIe siècle, 1719–1795* (Paris, 1989), 2:565.

8. Ibid., 2:562–567.

9. Boudriot, *Compagnie des Indes*, 1:138.

10. Compagnie des Indes, May 20, 1728, fol. 16v.

11. Johannes Postma, *The Dutch in the Atlantic Slave Trade, 1600–1815* (Cambridge, 1990), p. 137.

12. Hair, Jones, and Law, *Writings of Jean Barbot*, 2:783.

13. Du Coulombier, Copie d'une lettre écritte de Juda à Mrs. de la Compagnie Royale de l'Asiente, March 22, 1714, AOM, col. C 6 25, no. 17, fol. 2v.

14. Enquête, September 22, 1732, testimony of Leglan, Raillan, and Collimbert, ADMV, 9B 208.

15. Enquête, September 25, 1732, testimony of Robert Durand, ADMV, 9B 208.

16. Inventaire et vente des hardes du deffunt Jean Mahé, décédé le 17 9bre, 1731, ADMV, 9B 208.

17. Phillips, "Journal," 6:229–230.

18. Phillips, "Journal," 6:219; William D. Pierson, "White Cannibals, Black Martyrs: Fear, Depression, and Religious Faith as Causes of Suicide Among Slaves," *Journal of Negro History* 62 (1977): 147–159; Mettas, *Répertoire*, 2:557–558.

19. Phillips, "Journal," 6: 219; Mettas, *Répertoire*, 1:142–143.

20. Phillips, "Journal," 6:219.

21. Calculated from data in David Eltis, Stephen D. Behrendt, David Richardson, and Herbert S. Klein, *The Trans-Atlantic Slave Trade: A Database on CD-ROM* (New York, 1999).

22. On British slave ships in the eighteenth century, the average amount of space per captive was between five and six square feet. H. S. Klein, J. J. Henry, and C. Garland, "The Allotment of Space for African Slaves Aboard Eighteenth-Century Slave Ships," in Serge Daget, ed., *De la traite à l'esclavage* (Paris, 1998), 2:149–158.

PART 9 ATLANTIC ISLANDS
CHAPTER 30

1. Part 9 of this book is based on Robert Durand, Journal de bord d'un négrier, 1731–1732, BLY, Gen Mss, vol. 7, pp. 66–77.

2. Jean Mettas, *Répertoire des expéditions négrières françaises au XVIIIe siècle*, ed. Serge Daget (Paris, 1978), 2:580–581.

3. David Eltis, Stephen D. Behrend, and David Richardson, "The Costs of Coercion: African Agency in the History of the Atlantic World," *Economic History Review* 54 (August 2001).

4. Jean-Baptiste Labat, *Nouveau voyage aux iles d'Amérique* (Paris, 1722), 4: 138–141.

5. For a discussion of informal leadership on slave ships, see Richard Rathbone, "Resistance to Enslavement in West Africa," in Serge Daget, ed., *De la traite à l'esclavage* (Paris, 1988), 1:181–182.

6. Mettas, *Répertoire*, 1:97.

7. Ibid., 1:100, 110; 2:246, 560–561, 580–581.

8. William Snelgrave, *A New Account of Some Parts of Guinea and the Slave Trade* (London, 1734), p. 170.

9. Ibid., pp. 162–163.

10. Chevalier Des Marchais, Journal du voyage de Guinée et Cayenne, 1724–1726, BN, Manuscrits, FF 24223, pp. 68–69.

11. P. E. H. Hair, Adam Jones, and Robin Law, eds., *Barbot on Guinea: The Writings of Jean Barbot on West Africa, 1678–1712* (London, 1992), 2:775.

12. Snelgrave, *New Account,* pp. 182–184.

13. Robert Louis Stein, *The French Slave Trade in the Eighteenth Century* (Madison, Wis., 1979), pp. 95–96; David Eltis, Stephen D. Behrendt, David Richardson, and Herbert S. Klein, *The Trans-Atlantic Slave Trade: A Database on CD-ROM* (New York, 1999).

14. Hair, Jones, and Law, *Writings of Jean Barbot*, 2:770–771; N★★★★, *Voyages aux côtes de Guinée et en Amérique* (Amsterdam, 1719), pp. 116–117.

15. Jean Merrien, *La vie des marins au grand siècle* (Rennes, 1995), p. 195.

16. Jean-Baptiste Labat, *Voyage du chevalier Des Marchais en Guinée, iles voisines et à Cayenne, fait en 1725, 1726 et 1727* (Paris, 1730), 3:57.

17. William D. Piersen, "White Cannibals, Black Martyrs: Fear, Depression, and Religious Faith as Causes of Suicide Among New Slaves," *Journal of Negro History* 62 (1977): 151.

18. Des Marchais, Journal du voyage, pp. 66–67.

19. T. Aubrey, *The Sea-Surgeon, or the Guinea Man's Vade Mecum* (London, 1729), pp. 107–108.

20. Des Marchais, Journal du voyage, p. 70.

CHAPTER 31

1. Mettas, *Répertoire,* 1:150–151.

2. De l'ordre et des usages qui règnent généralement à bord des navires négriers, 1790, AOM, col. F3 61, fols. 87v–88r.

3. Des Marchais, Journal du voyage, p. 70; Jean Boudriot, *Traite et navire négrier: L'Aurore, 1784* (Paris, 1984), p. 35.

4. Durand reported the quantities of food in terms of Portuguese *alqueires*. One *alqueire* equals approximately one English bushel. See Juan Lopes Sierra, *A Governor and His Image in Baroque Brazil: The Funeral Eulogy of Afonso Furtado de Castro do Rio de Mendonça,* ed. Stuart B. Schwartz, trans. Ruth E. Jones (Minneapolis, 1979), p. 182.

5. Des Marchais, Journal du voyage, p. 68.

6. De l'ordre et des usages, fol. 90r; Thomas Phillips, "Journal of a Voyage Made in the Hannibal of London, 1693–1694," in Awnsham Churchill, ed., *A Collection of Voyages and Travels* (London, 1732) 6:229; Observations touchant les soins des nègres dans les voyages de Guinée, n.d., in Gabriel Debien, "Documents sur la traite," *Enquêtes et documents, centre de recherches sur l'histoire de la France atlantique, Nantes* 2 (1972): 199.

7. De l'ordre et des usages, fol. 88r.

8. Phillips, "Journal," 6:232; Barbot's map of the Gulf of Guinea correctly shows the equator running through the southern part of São Tomé, but the inscription insists that the equator runs through the church. See Hair, Jones, and Law, *Writings of Jean Barbot,* 2:739 n. 2.

9. Procès verbal de la relâche de l'Ile St. Thomée, January 11, 1732, ADM, 9B 208.

CHAPTER 32

1. Processus inquisitionis confectus super qualitatibus R.P. patris Joannis Sagum, ASV, Processus Consistorales, vol. 101, fols. 462r–469r; Robert Garfield, *A History of São Tomé Island, 1470–1655* (San Francisco, 1992), p. 149.

2. Pablo Eyzaguirre, "Small Farmers and Estates in São Tomé, West Africa" (Ph.D. diss., Yale University, 1986), pp. 42–43, 137, 148.

3. António Ambrósio, "Manuel do Rosário Pinto: A sua vida e a sua história de S. Tomé," *Studia* 30–31 (1970): 207–210.

4. Manuel do Rosário Pinto, Rellação do descombrimento da Ilha de Sam Thomé, BA, 51-IX–24, fols. 60v–61r.

5. Raimundo José da Cunha Matos, *Compêndio histórico das possessões de Portugal na Africa* (Rio de Janeiro, 1963), p. 143.

6. Garfield, *History of São Tomé,* p. 178.

7. Eyzaguirre, "Small Farmers and Estates in São Tomé," p. 84.

8. Phillips, "Journal," 6:233.

9. Garfield, *History of São Tomé*, pp. 35–36.

10. Eyzaguirre, "Small Farmers and Estates in São Tomé," p. 145.

11. Ibid., p. 137.

12. Charles Johnson, *A General History of the Robberies and Murders of the Most Notorious Pirates*, ed. Arthur L. Hayward (New York, 1927), p. 154. Reprint of 4th ed., 1726.

13. Pinto, Rellação, fol. 63 r-v.

14. Processus Inquisitionen, fols. 462r–469r.

15. Pinto, Rellecão, fols. 63v–64r.

16. Ibid., fols. 64r–65v.

17. Garfield, *History of São Tomé*, p. 55; Eyzaguirre, "Small Farmers and Estates in São Tomé," pp. 42–43; Johnson, *History of the Pirates*, p. 154.

18. Johnson, *History of the Pirates*, p. 155.

19. Pinto, Rellação, 66v–68v.

20. Cunha Mattos, *Compêndio histórico*, p. 188; Eyzaguirre, "Small Farmers and Estates," p. 123.

21. A copy of the original manuscript is in the Biblioteca da Ajuda, Lisbon, 51-IX–24.

22. Quoted in Garfield, *History of São Tomé*, pp. 145–146.

23. Pinto, Relação, 62r-v.

PART 10 THE MIDDLE PASSAGE
CHAPTER 33

1. Melville J. Herskovits, *Dahomey: An Ancient West African Kingdom* (Evanston, 1967), 2:316–317.

2. Thomas Phillips, "A Journal of Voyage Made in the Hannibal of London, 1693–1694," in Awnsham Churchill, ed., *A Collection of Voyages and Travels* (London, 1732), 6:223, 230; De l'ordre et des usages qui règnent généralement à bord des navires négriers, 1790, AOM, col. F 3 61, fol. 93r; Chevalier Des Marchais, "Journal du voyage de Guinée et Cayenne," 1724–1726, BN, Manuscrits, FF 24223, p. 70.

3. Savary des Bruslons, *Dictionnaire universel de commerce* (Paris, 1723), 2:860.

4. Observations touchant les soins des nègres dans les voyages de Guinée, n.d., in Gabriel Debien, "Documents sur la traite," *Enquêtes et documents, Centre de recherches sur l'histoire de la France atlantique, Nantes* 2 (1972): 199.

5. Harvey Oxenhorn, *Tuning the Rig* (New York, 1983), 45.

6. Geneviève Fabre, "The Slave Ship Dance," in Maria Diedrich, Henry Louis Gates Jr., and Carl Pedersen, eds., *Black Imagination and the Middle Passage* (Oxford, 1999), pp. 33–46.

7. P. E. H. Hair, Adam Jones, and Robin Law, eds., *Barbot on Guinea: The Writings of Jean Barbot on West Africa, 1678–1712* (London, 1992), 2:775; Lief Svalesen, *The Slave Ship Fredensborg*, trans. Pat Shaw and Selena Winsnes (Bloomington, Ind., 2000), p. 108; "Evidence with Respect to carrying Slaves to the West Indies," in Sheila Lambert., ed., *House of Commons Sessional Papers for the Eighteenth Century* (Wilmington, Del., 1975), 69:126.

8. Elet Diary, March 23, 1733, in A. Van Dantzig, comp. and trans., *The Dutch and the Guinea Coast, 1674–1742: A Collection of Documents from the General State Archive at the Hague* (Accra, 1978), p. 295.

9. Roger Blanchard, *La Chanson traditionnelle et les naïfs* (Paris, 1975), p. 203.

10. On African views of white cannibals, see William D. Pierson, "White Cannibals, Black Martyrs: Fear, Depression, and Religious Faith as Causes of Suicide Among Slaves," *Journal of Negro History* 62 (1977): 147–159; William D. Pierson, *Black Legacy* (Amherst, Mass., 1993), pp. 5–12; Labat, *Voyage du chevalier Des Marchais*, 2:145.

11. Lecointe-Marsillac, *Le More-lack* (London, 1789), pp. 47–48. Harding's voyage is not listed in David Eltis, Stephen D. Behrendt, David Richardson, and Herbert S. Klein, *The Trans-Atlantic Slave Trade: A Database on CD-ROM* (New York, 1999), but the British records for the 1720s are admittedly incomplete. The database does, however, list slaving voyages of a Captain Jonathan Harding sailing out of Bristol, England, in 1730 and 1732.

12. William Snelgrave, *A New Account of Some Parts of Guinea and the Slave Trade* (London 1734), pp. 52–53; Jean-Baptiste Labat, *Voyage du chevalier Des Marchais en Guinée, iles voisines et à Cayenne, fait en 1725, 1726 et 1727* (Paris, 1730), 2:144.

13. Frank Lestringant, "Le Cannibale et ses paradoxes: Images du cannibalisme au temps des guerres de religion," *Mentalities/Mentalités* 1, no. 2 (1983): 4–19; Bronislaw Baczko, *Ending the Terror: The French Revolution After Robespierre*, trans. Michel Petheram (Cambridge, 1994), p. 211.

14. Testimony of Charles Leglan, September 22, 1732, ADMV, 9B 208.

15. Hair, Jones, and Law, *Writings of Jean Barbot*, 2:780.

16. Jean Mettas, *Répertoire des expéditions négrières françaises au XVIIIe siècle*, ed. Serge Daget (Paris, 1978), 2:564–565; Labat, *Voyage du chevalier Des Marchais*, 3:53.

17. De l'ordre des usages, fol. 91v; Observations touchant le soin des nègres, in Debien, "Documents sur la traite," p. 200.

18. Mettas, *Répertoire*, 1:105.

19. Eltis et al., *Database on CD-ROM*.

20. Hair, Jones, and Law, *Writings of Jean Barbot*, 2:773.

21. Part 10 of this book is based on Robert Durand, Journal de bord d'un négrier, 1731–1732, BLY, Gen Mss, vol. 7, pp. 66–92.

22. Quoted in Daniel Mannix and Malcolm Cowley, *Black Cargoes: A History of the Atlantic Slave Trade* (New York, 1962), p. 145.

23. Eltis et al., *Database on CD-ROM*. For firsthand accounts of the middle passage written by Africans, see Philip Curtin, ed., *Africa Remembered: Narratives by West Africans from the Era of the Slave Trade* (Madison, Wis., 1968).

CHAPTER 34

1. Des Marchais, Journal du voyage, p. 69.

2. Hair, Jones, and Law, *Writings of Jean Barbot*, 2:781.

3. Alexander Falconbridge, *An Account of the Slave Trade on the Coast of Africa* (London, 1788), p. 20.

4. On the creaking of the timbers, see Oxenhorn, *Tuning the Rig*, p. 45.

5. De l'ordre et des usages, fol. 90r; Phillips, "Journal," 6:229. On wooden spoons, see Jean Barbot in Hair, Jones, and Law, *Writings of Jean Barbot*, 2:781; and Svalesen, *Slave Ship Fredensborg*, p. 93.

6. T. Aubrey, *The Sea-Surgeon, or the Guinea Man's Vade Mecum* (London, 1729), pp. 127–128; Des Marchais, Journal du voyage, pp. 67–68.

7. Falconbridge, *Account of the Slave Trade*, p. 22.

8. De l'ordre et des usages, fol. 90r-v; Jean Boudriot, "Le navire négrier au XVIIIe siècle," in Serge Daget, ed., *De la traite à l'esclavage* (Paris, 1988), 2:163; Jean Boudriot, *Traite et navire négrier: L'Aurore, 1784* (Paris, 1984), pp. 35, 86.

9. Quoted in Gaston Martin, *Nantes au XVIIIe siècle: L'ère des négriers, 1714–1774* (Paris, 1993), pp. 110–111.

10. Aubrey, *Sea-Surgeon*, pp. 130–131; David Richardson, "The Costs of Survival: The Treatment of Slaves in the Middle Passage and the Profitability of the Eighteenth-Century British Slave Trade," in *De la traite à l'esclavage*, 2:173; De l'ordre et des usages, fol. 90r-v.

11. Paul Erdman Isert, *Voyages en Guinée et dans les îles Caraïbes en Amérique* (1793; reprint, Paris, 1989), p. 209.

12. Joseph C. Miller, *Way of Death: Merchant Capitalism and the Angolan Slave Trade, 1730–1830,* (Madison, Wis., 1988), p. 422.

13. Snelgrave, *New Account,* pp. 185–190.

14. Colin Palmer, *Human Cargoes: The British Slave Trade to Spanish America, 1700–1739* (Urbana, Ill., 1981), p. 47.

15. Observations touchant le soin des nègres, in Debien, "Documents sur la traite," pp. 197–198; Labat, *Voyage du chevalier Des Marchais,* 3:52; Hair, Jones, and Law, *Writings of Jean Barbot,* 2:779.

16. Hair, Jones, and Law, *Writings of Jean Barbot,* 2:779.

17. William Bosman, *A New and Accurate Description of the Coast of Guinea* (London, 1705), p. 365.

18. Aubrey, *Sea-Surgeon,* 131.

19. Testimony of Jean Leglan, September 22, 1732, ADM, 9B 208; Aubrey, *Sea-Surgeon,* p. 132.

20. John Atkins, *A Voyage to Guinea, Brasil, and the West-Indies* (London, 1735), p. 180.

21. De l'ordre et des usages, fols. 91v–92r.

22. Jean-Michel Deveau, *La traite rochelaise* (Paris, 1990), p. 242; Quoted in Frantz Tardo-Dino, *Le collier de servitude* (Fort-de-France, 1985), p. 47.

23. Quoted in Robert Louis Stein, *The French Slave Trade in the Eighteenth Century* (Madison, Wis., 1979), p. 101.

24. John Newton, "Thoughts upon the African Slave Trade," (London, 1788), reprinted in *The Journal of a Slave Trader (John Newton), 1750–1754,* ed. Bernard Martin and Mark Spurrell (London, 1962), pp. 102–105.

25. Falconbridge, *Account of the Slave Trade,* p. 23.

26. Hair, Jones, and Law, *Writings of Jean Barbot,* 2:783.

27. Laurent de Lucques, *Relations sur le Congo du Père Laurent de Lucques* (1700–1717), trans. J. Cuvelier, Institut Royal Colonial Belge, Mémoires in 8, 32: 1953–1954, p. 283.

28. Atkins, *Voyage to Guinea,* p. 175.

29. David Eltis, Stephen D. Behrend, and David Richardson, "The Costs of Coercion: African Agency in the History of the Atlantic World," *Economic History Review* 54 (August 2001).

30. Snelgrave, *New Account,* p. 163; Phillips, "Journal," 6:229; Hair, Jones, and Law, *Writings of Jean Barbot,* 2:775, 780; "Evidence with Respect to carrying Slaves to the West Indies," in Lambert, *Sessional Papers,* 69:118.

31. De l'ordre et des usages, fol. 88r; "Evidence with Respect to Carrying Slaves," in Lambert, *Sessional Papers,* 69:117, 119.

CHAPTER 35

1. Johannes Postma, "Mortality in the Dutch Slave Trade, 1675–1795," in Henry Gemery and Jan Hogendorn, eds., *The Uncommon Market* (New York: Academic, 1979), 252; Aubrey, *Sea-Surgeon*; Des Marchais, Journal du voyage, p. 70; Labat, *Voyage du chevalier Des Marchais,* 3:53; "Observations touchant le soin des nègres," in Debien, "Documents sur la traite," p. 199.

2. Commerce de Nantes en 1731, January 30, 1732, ADLA, Nantes, C 740. Figures calculated from Eltis et al., *Database on CD-ROM.*

3. Stein, *French Slave Trade*, p. 226 n. 6.

4. Instructions et orders pour Monsieur Foures commandant le navire l'Affricain, 1738, in *Journal de la traite des noirs,* comp. Jehan Mousnier (Paris, 1957), pp. 22, 25.

5. Testimony of Sabatier, Colinbert, Gauguin, Durand, and Laragon, September 22 and 25, 1732, ADMV, 9B 208.

6. Des Marchais, Journal du voyage, p. 70.

CHAPTER 36

1. Hoffmeester, "Jaquin," August 1, 1732, in *The Dutch and the Guinea Coast, 1674–1742: A Collection of Documents from the General State Archive at The Hague,* comp. and trans. A. Van Dantzig (Accra, 1978), pp. 280–283.

2. Pierre Verger, *Trade Relations Between the Bight of Benin and Bahia,* trans. Evelyn Crawford (Ibadan, 1976), pp. 130–131; Snelgrave, *New Account,* pp. 149–151.

3. Hertogh to Pranger, April 16, 1732, September 26, 1732, in Van Dantzig, *Collection of Documents*, pp. 266–269.

4. Atkins, *Voyage to Guinea*, p. 119. Atkins's argument is still being debated by historians. In support of his position, see I. A. Akinjogbin, *Dahomey and Its Neighbors, 1708–1818* (Cambridge, 1967), pp. 68–109. For the arguments against Atkins's position, see David Henige and Marion Johnson, "Agaja and the Slave Trade: Another Look at the Evidence," *History in Africa* 3 (1976): 57–67; Robin Law, "Dahomey and the Slave Trade: Reflections on the Historiography of the Rise of Dahomey," *Journal of African History* 27 (1986): 237–267; Law, *The Slave Coast of West Africa, 1550–1750* (Oxford, 1991), pp. 300–308.

5. Minutes of Elmina Council, June 30, 1733, in Van Dantzig, *Collection of Documents*, pp. 286–287.

6. I. A. Akinjogbin, *Dahomey and Its Neighbors, 1708–1818* (Cambridge, 1967), p. 94.

7. This figure is for the Bight of Benin as a whole. During this period most of the slaves coming out of the Bight of Benin actually came from Whydah. The figures are taken from David Eltis, "The Volume and Structure of the Atlantic Slave Trade: A Reassessment," *William and Mary Quarterly*, 3d ser., 58 (2001): 44.

CHAPTER 37

1. Labat, *Voyage du chevalier Des Marchais,* 3:59–62.

2. Léon Vignols, "La piraterie sur l'Altlantique au XVIIIe siècle: II. Les forbans des Antilles," *Annales de Bretagne* 5 (1889–1890): 337–385; Mettas, *Répertoire*, 1:125.

3. Champigny and D'Orgeville, May 23, 1731, AOM, col. C 8A 42, fols. 39v–41r.

4. Pierre Valteau was a vaunted name in Le Croisic. In 1641 a certain Captain Pierre Valteau became famous in Le Croisic for capturing the Spanish ship *Nuestre Senora del Rosario*. See Stéphane de la Nicollière-Teijeiro, *La Course et les coursaires du port de Nantes* (Paris-Nantes, 1896), pp. 48–53.

5. Vignols, "La piraterie," pp. 373–380; D'Orgeville, November 5, 1729, and March 15, 1732, AOM, col. C 8A 40, fols. 356r–357v; and col. C 8A 43, fols. 191r–192r.

6. Clarissa Thérèse Kimber, *Martinique Revisited: The Changing Plant Geographies of a West Indian Island* (College Station, Tex., 1988), pp. 13–18.

7. Recensement générale de l'isle Martinique, 1732, ADMF, 5 Mi 89.

8. Eltis et al., *Database on CD-ROM*.

9. Mettas, *Répertoire*, 1:152–164.

PART 11 MARTINIQUE
CHAPTER 38

1. Thibault de Chanvalon, *Voyage à la Martinique* (Paris, 1763), pp. 13–16.

2. Recensement générale de l'ile Martinique, 1732, ADMF, 5 Mi 89.

3. Louis-Philippe May, *Histoire économique de la Martinique, 1635–1763* (Paris, 1930), p. 229.

4. P. E. H. Hair, Adam Jones, and Robin Law, eds., *Barbot on Guinea: The Writings of Jean Barbot on West Africa, 1678–1712* (London, 1992), 2:783.

5. Lucien Peytraud, *L'esclavage aux Antilles françaises avant 1798* (Paris, 1973), pp. 127–128.

6. Judge et consuls de Nantes à Maurepas, July 1, 1732, ADLA, C 727.

7. Part 11 of this book is based on Robert Durand, Journal de bord d'un négrier, 1731–1732, BLY, Gen Mss, vol. 7, pp. 92–96.

8. On travel to Fort Royal, see the petition to Blondel and Jouvancourt, July 27, 1725, AOM, col. F3 254, p. 235.

9. Extrait du registre de greffe de l'amirauté du Fort St. Pierre, March 17, 1732, ADMV, 9B 208.

10. For example, Nous Docteur Medecin, July 12, 1715, AOM, col. F3 251, pp. 469–472.

11. D'Orgeville, December 7, 1730, AOM, col. C 8A 41, fols. 94r–98v.

12. Peytraud, *L'esclavage aux Antilles*, p. 118.

13. May, *Histoire économique*, pp. 202–203.

14. Commerce de Nantes en 1731, January 30, 1732, ADLA, C 740, fol. 6.

15. Peytraud, *L'esclavage aux Antilles*, p. 117.

16. Jean Mettas, *Répertoire des expéditions négrières françaises au XVIIIe siècle*, ed. Serge Daget (Paris, 1978), 2:703.

17. D'Orgeville, September 2, 1731, AOM, col. C 8A 42, fol. 250r.

CHAPTER 39

1. Relation de tremblement de terre, November 7, 1727, AOM, col. C 8A 39, fols. 201r–202r.

2. Feuquières et Blondel, November 9, 1727, AOM, col. C 8A 39, fols. 121r–130v.

3. Feuquières et Blondel, November 28, 1727, AOM, col. C 8A 39, fols. 135r–141r; Relation de tremblement de terre, fols. 201v–202r.

4. Feuquières et Blondel, November 28, 1727, fols. 138v–139r.

5. Blondel, January 13, 1728, AOM, col. C 8A 39, fols. 186v–187v.

6. Ibid., fols. 191v–194v.

7. Champigny et Blondel, April 13, 1728, AOM, col. C 8A 39, fols. 51r–56v.

8. Feuquières et Blondel, November 28, 1727, fol. 137r.

9. Jean-Baptiste Labat, *Nouveau voyage aux îles d'Amerique* (Paris, 1722), 3:416–417.

10. Debien, *Les esclaves aux Antilles françaises, XVIIe-XVIIIe siècles* (Fort-de-France, 1974), pp. 343–349.

11. Feuquières et Blondel, November 28, 1727, fol. 138r.

12. Mémoire sur la culture de caffé aux isles du vent, January 28, 1731, AOM, col. C 8B 9.

13. Ibid.

14. May, *Histoire économique,* pp. 96–101.

15. Ibid., pp. 101–103.

16. Champigny et d'Orgeville, November 2, 1732, AOM, col. C 8A 43, fol. 54r.

Chapter 40

1. Quoted in Peytraud, *L'esclavage aux Antilles*, p. 117.

2. G. Debien, "Journal de la traite de *La Licorne* de Bordeaux au Mozambique (1787–1788)," *Caribbean Studies* 19, no. 3–4 (1980): 111–115.

3. George W. Hunter, J. Clyde Swartzwelder, and David F. Clyde, *Tropical Medicine*, 5th ed. (Philadelphia, 1976), 331–332; M. Dazille, *Observations sur les maladies des nègres* (Paris, 1776), pp. 71–72; T. Aubrey, *The Sea-Surgeon, or the Guinea Man's Vade Mecum* (London, 1729), pp. 74–89.

4. Petition to Blondel and Jouvancourt, July 27, 1725, AOM, col. F3 254, pp. 233–240.

5. Debien, *Esclaves aux Antilles,* p. 85.

6. Labat, *Nouveau voyage*, 3:464.

7. Ibid., 4:142–143.

8. Labat, *Nouveau voyage*, 4:380; Recensement générale de l'ile Martinique, 1732; Robert Louis Stein, *The French Sugar Business in the Eighteenth Century* (Baton Rouge, 1988), p. 47.

9. Labat, *Nouveau voyage*, 3:214–216.

10. Recensement générale de l'ile Martinique, 1732.

11. Labat, *Nouveau voyage*, 3:205–206.

12. Ibid., 3:416–417.

13. Recensement générale de l'ile Martinique, 1732.

14. Labat, *Nouveau voyage*, 3:141.

15. Stein, *French Sugar Business*, p. 61.

16. Recensement générale de l'ile Martinique, 1732.

17. Labat, *Nouveau voyage*, 3:457–458.

18. May, *Histoire économique*, p. 84; Recensement générale de l'ile Martinique, 1732.

19. Mémoire sur la nécessité, 1730, BM, ms. 2626.

20. Etat des navires arrivant pendant le mois de février, 1732, AOM, col. C 8A 43, fol. 241r.

21. Labat, *Nouveau voyage*, 3:448.

22. Blondel, August 31, 1725, AOM, col. C 8A 34, fols. 372r-v.

CHAPTER 41

1. November 29, 1729, ADLA, B 4490, fols. 133v–134r; August 7, 1732, ADLA, B 4585, fols. 105r–108v.

2. Mettas, *Répertoire,* 1:74, 111, 194, 235, 259; Mémoire concernant l'affaire du sieur Jean Bonneau, AN, Marine, B3 375, fols. 88r–91r.

CHAPTER 42

1. Enquête, 22, September 25, 1732, ADMV, 9B 208.

2. Jean Meyer, *L'armement nantais dans la deuxième moitié du XVIIIe siècle* (Paris, 1969), p. 244 n. 2.

3. Stein, *French Sugar Business,* pp. 64–67.

4. Christian Schnakenbourg, "Statistiques pour l'histoire de l'économie de planta-tion en Guadeloupe et Martinique (1635–1835)," *Annales des Antilles* 21 (1977): 119.

5. Durand, Journal de bord d'un négrier, p. 94; Décision du Conseil Royal de Commerce portan que les sucres terrés blancs sont cassonadère et ne sont point sucres rafinés, April 12, 1731, ADLA, C731.

6. Stein, *French Sugar Business,* pp. 70–71.

7. Labat, *Nouveau voyage,* 3:405; Schnakenbourg, "Statistiques pour l'histoire," p. 121, reports that a *barrique* contained eight hundred livres of sugar in the 1730s. This corresponds with the figures given for 1742 in Pierre Pluchon, *La route des esclaves* (Paris, 1980), p. 259.

8. Calcul de ce à combien revient à Rouen et Nantes, September 1732, ADLA, C 733; Commerce de Nantes en 1731, January 30, 1732, ADLA, C 740, fol. 9.

9. Direction de Nantes, Entrées 1732, ADLA, C 706.

10. For the weight of a bale of cotton, see Pluchon, *Route des esclaves,* p. 259.

11. Arrest du conseil d'estat du roy portant reglement pour le commerce des cotons, December 20, 1729, ADLA, C 729.

12. Chambon, *Le guide du commerce de l'Amérique* (Avignon, 1777), 1:375–381; Labat, *Nouveau voyage,* 1:252–268.

13. Rocou, July 10, 1720, ADLA, Nantes, C 729.

14. Champigny and D'Orgeville, October 11, 1729, AOM, col. C 8A 40, fols. 104r–105r.

PART 12 THE RETURN
CHAPTER 43

1. Pierre Thomas-Lacroix, *Le vieux Vannes* (Vannes, 1982), pp. 22–25.

2. Le Sieur Robert Billy, July 28, 1700, ADM, 9B 193.

3. The depositions of the crew members are found in Devant nous Charles-Louis Chanu, September 22–25, 1732, ADMV, 9B 208.

4. Ibid.

CHAPTER 44

1. Bounty demanded by the Company of the Indies, January 16, 1734, in Elizabeth Donnan, comp., *Documents Illustrative of the History of the Slave Trade to America* (Wash-ington, D.C., 1930–1935), 2:449–450.

2. Quoted in H. du Halgouet, "Nantes: Ses relations commerciales avec les îles d'Amérique au XVIIIe siècle," *Mémoires de la Société d'Histoire et d'Archéologie de Bretagne* 20 (1939): 159.

3. Evaluation pour la perception des trois et demy pour cent à Nantes, October, 1728, ADLA, C 734, p. 9; Ont comparus les juges et consuls, September 27, 1728, ADLA, C 734, pp. 1–2.

4. Commerce de Nantes en 1731, January 30, 1732, ADLA, C 740, p. 40.

5. Ibid., p. 4; Robert Louis Stein, *The French Sugar Business in the Eighteenth Century* (Baton Rouge, 1988), pp. 99–100; Ernest Labrousse and Fernand Braudel, eds., *Histoire économique et sociale de la France* (Paris, 1970), 2:505.

6. Stein, *French Sugar Business*, pp. 138–142.

7. Ibid., pp. 99–101, 162–164; Sidney Mintz, *Sweetness and Power: The Place of Sugar in Modern History* (New York, 1985), pp. 188–190; Richard Sheridan, *Sugar and Slavery* (Baltimore, 1973), pp. 24–25.

8. Mémoire sur les abus qui se commettent par les négociants de Nantes à l'occasion de la vente et du troc des nègres, 1731, ADLA, C 740, p. 2.

9. Montaudoin Négociant de Nantes, ADLA, C 741.

10. Jean Meyer, *L'armement nantais dans la deuxième moitié du XVIIIe siècle* (Paris, 1969), p. 229.

11. See Appendix A for the estimated balance sheet of the *Diligent*. Accounting practices at the time did not take account of interest losses on delayed returns. Merchants of Nantes were aware of them, however, and estimated them at 6 percent per year. See Jean Meyer, *L'armement nantais*, p. 244.

CHAPTER 45

1. Devant nous Noël Bourgeois, November 22, 1732, ADMV, 9B 208.

2. Devant nous Noël Bourgeois, February 28, 1733, ADMV, 9B 208.

3. Pierre Thomas-Lacroix, *Répertoire numérique de la série B des archivs du Morbihan* (Vannes, 1941), p. 3.

4. The sailing instructions for the ship *l'Affricain* in 1738 prescribed a fine of one thousand livres for each personal slave that the officers carried in excess of their authorization. "Instructions et orders pour Monsieur Foures commandant le navire *l'Affricain*, 1738," in *Journal de la traite des noirs*, comp. Jehan Mousnier (Paris, 1957), p. 22.

5. René Josué Valin, *Commentaire sur l'ordonnance de la marine du mois d'août, 1681* (Poitiers, 1828), 1:48–49.

CHAPTER 46

1. *Le Diligent de Vannes*, Armement, 1733, ADLA, 120J 350; *Le Diligent de Vannes*, Armement, 1733, ADMV, 9B 208; J. Letaconnoux, *Les subsistances et le commerce des grains en Bretagne au XVIIIe siècle* (Rennes, 1909), pp. 178–179. On the grain trade to Marseille, see T. J. A. Le Goff, *Vannes and Its Region: A Study of Town and Country in Eighteenth-Century France* (Oxford, 1981), p. 296.

2. *Le Diligent de Vannes*, May 8, 1734, ADLA, B 4586, fol. 55r.

3. Lettre de capitaine et pilote, October 22, 1736, ADLA, B 4494, 105r.

4. Prestation de serment pour la visite des froments du *Diligent de Vannes*, December 20, 1735; and Ordonnance de siege pour jetter à la mer les froments du *Diligent*, December 28, 1735, ADMV, 9B 208.

5. Lettre de capitaine et pilote, October 22, 1736, ADLA, B 4494, 104v.

6. Jean Mettas, *Répertoire des expéditions négrières françaises au XVIIIe siècle*, ed. Serge Daget (Paris, 1978), 1:222, 269.

7. Gaston Martin, *Nantes au XVIIIe siècle: L'ère des négriers, 1714–1774* (Paris, 1993), pp. 227–228.

8. Mettas, *Répertoire*, 1:293–297.

9. Au sujet de la prise du navire *La Perle de Nantes*, ADLA, B 4590, fol. 29v.

10. John Charnock, *Biographia Navalis* (London, 1794–1798), 5:350; R. Pitcairn-Jones, *Commissioned Sea Officers of the Royal Navy, 1660–1815*, ed. David Syrett and Ralph Di Nardo (London, 1994), p. 340; Isaac Schomberg, *The Naval Chronology* (London, 1815), 4:28.

11. Journal of HMS *Shoreham,* kept by Captain James Osborn, NMM, ADM/L/275; Au sujet de la prise du navire *La Perle de Nantes*, ADLA, B 4590, fol. 29r-v.

CHAPTER 47

1. Etienne Raut and Léon Lallement, "Vannes autrefois: La traite des nègres," *Bulletin de la Société Polymathique du Morbihan*, 1933, pp. 63–65; Patrick André, "La traite des noirs au XVIIIe siècle," in Hubert Poupard and Claudie Herbaut, eds., *2000 ans d'histoire de Vannes* (Vannes, 1993), pp. 212–215.

2. Le Goff, *Vannes and Its Region*, pp. 102, 294–296; David Hackett Fischer, *The Great Wave: Price Revolutions and the Rhythm of History* (New York, 1996), pp. 117–142.

3. P. Thomas-Lacroix, *Le vieux Vannes* (Vannes, 1982), pp. 97–98.

4. René Kerviler, *Répertoire général de bio-bibliographie bretonne* (Rennes, 1886–1908), 2:281–282; *Inventaire sommaire des archives départmentales antérieurs à 1790. Morbihan. Archives civiles, série E, supplément, 2e partie, vol. 5* (Vannes, 1945), pp. 516, 536, 544.

5. Thomas-Lacroix, *Répertoire numérique de la série B*, p. 119.

6. Musée de la Cohue, *Vannes, une ville, un port* (Quimper, 1998), pp. 20–23.

7. Pierre Le Lièvre, *Nantes au XVIIIe siècle: Urbanisme et architecture* (Nantes, 1988), pp. 102–103, 212–213; Association Les Anneaux de la Mémoire, *Les anneaux de la mémoire* (Nantes, 1993), p. 55; Musée Dobrée, *Iconographie de Nantes* (Nantes, 1978), p. 84.

8. Claude Nières et al., *Histoire de Lorient* (Toulouse, 1988), pp. 42–43, 49–52; Gérard Le Bouëdec, *Le port et l'arsenal de Lorient* (Paris, 1994), 2:164.

9. Quoted in Le Goff, *Vannes and Its Region,* p. 24.

10. Letaconnoux, *Les subsistances*, pp. 191–192.

11. Le Goff, *Vannes and Its Region*, pp. 103–106.

12. September 19, 1765, ADMV, B 1270.

AFTERWORD

1. Suite des Baptêmes, Marriages, et Enterrements de la Paroisse de Notre Dame de la Caze Pilote, deuxième registre, 1708, ADM, Fort-de-France, microfilm 5 Mi 53.

2. Mireille Mousnier and Brigitte Caille, *Atlas historique du patrimoine sucrier de la Martinique* (Paris, 1990).

3. Jacques Petitjean-Roget, *La Gaoulé: La révolte de la Martinique en 1717* (Fort de France, 1966), p. 66.

APPENDIX A

1. The amount of sugar in a *barrique* during the 1730s was 800 pounds. Christian Schnakenbourg, "Statistiques pour l'histoire de l'économie de plantation en Guadeloupe et Martinique (1635–1835)," *Annales des Antilles* 21 (1977): 121.

2. Ibid.

3. Direction de Nantes, Entrées, 1732, ADLA, C 706 shows the ratio of common to white sugar at twenty to one.

4. The 15 percent weight loss figure comes from Calcul de ce à combine revient à Roüen et à Nantes un cent de sucre brut Iles qui couste 5 liv. au plus, September 1731, ADLA, C 733, p. 1. Judge et Consuls de Nantes, Commerce de Nantes en 1731, January 30, 1732, ADLA, C 740, fol. 9, uses a figure of 13 percent.

5. Sugar prices at Nantes come from Direction de Nantes, Entrées, 1732.

6. Direction de Nantes, Entrées, 1732.

7. On the weight of a bale of cotton, see Pierre Pluchon, *La route des esclaves* (Paris, 1980), p. 259.

8. For the price of cotton in 1732, see Etat des cottons venant de l'Amerique depuis 1730, 1743, ADLA, C 729.

9. For the weight of a *quart* of rocou, see Rocou, July 10, 1720, ADLA, C 729.

10. Direction de Nantes, Entrées, 1732.

11. Shipping charge taken from Calcul de ce à combien, September 1731, ADLA, C 733.

12. Robert Durand, Journal de bord d'un négrier, 1731–1732, BLY, Gen Mss, vol. 7, p. 3.

13. The costs are taken from Compte de l'armement, missehors, et cargaison du navire *La Concorde de Vannes*, 1731, ADM, Vannes, 11B 52. The *mise-hors* of the *Concorde* included the cost of the ship (26,000 livres), even though the owners had most likely amortized the entire value of the ship on its previous trip to Martinique. Jean Meyer notes that it is was standard practice to amortize the entire value of the ship on each voyage. See Jean Meyer, *L'armement nantais dans la deuxième moitié du XVIIIe siècle* (Paris, 1969), pp. 154–155. For the *Diligent*, I have used the selling price of 18,500 livres. Actes de propriété, 1724–1735, ADMV, 9B 57, fols. 50v–51r.

14. Jacques Ducoin, *Naufrages, conditions de navigation et assurances dans la marine de commerce du XVIIIe siècle* (Paris, 1993), 1:159.

15. Gabare transport from Paimboef to Nantes was 2 sols per quintal of merchandise. See Calcul de ce à combien, September 1731, ADLA, C 733. I am counting triple that amount for transportation from Vannes. 1 livre = 20 sols.

16. Ibid.

17. Calcul de ce à combien, p. 1.

18. Ibid.

19. Armement, *Le Diligent de Vannes*, 1731, ADM, 9B 208.

20. Bounty demanded by the Company of the Indies, January 16, 1734, in Elizabeth Donnan, comp., *Documents Illustrative of the History of the Slave Trade to America* (Washington, D.C., 1930–1935), 2:449–450.

INDEX

acclimatization, of slaves, 352
accordion players, slave ships
   dancing of slaves, 295–296
   salary of, 106
accounting systems, barter, 385–386
Accra, 142–143
Act for the Relief of Insolvent Debtors, 188
Adomo Oroonoko Tomo (Captain Tom), 187–195
   after release from captivity, 187–189
   full liberty of, 194–195
   interpreting for King Agaja, 165, 169
   King Agaja's letter and, 175–177, 190–193
   King Agaja's release of, 176–177
Africa
   canoemen of, 228–229
   geographical knowledge of, 16–17
   independent states of, 127–128
   relations between Europe and, 122–123
   social rank in, 18
Agaja, King, 165–186, 211–224
   army of, 171–172
   Assou/King Huffon attacked by, 214–221
   attacked by Oyo, 213–214, 219
   Bulfinch Lambe as slave of, 165–169
   Bulfinch Lambe released by, 174–177
   court life of, 169–171
   effect on slave trade, 211–213, 245–246, 323–324
   Etienne Gallot and, 216–217
   European forts attacked by, 214–221
   Jakin attacked by, 321–324
   Jakin under authority of, 229–230
   King George I and, 175–177
   physical appearance of, 165
   Portuguese gold and, 212–213
   psychological warfare of, 173–174
   relations with Whydah, 173–174, 177
   Savi attacked by, 179–182
   selling captives as slaves, 183–186, 211–213, 245–246
   wives of, 170–171
agriculture
   French economy and, 36
   Whydah and, 159
Allada, 166, 182
Allançon, Guillaume, 105
Amériquin, 270
ammunition
   Gold Coast warfare and, 135–136
   lessening demand for, 213
   in military of King Agaja, 172
   outfitting *Diligent*, 82–83
   profits of King Agaja, 184–185
Andrade, Jerónimo de
   black priests and, 287–288
   defeat of, 289
   Father Pinto and, 283

Ankober, 131
Annibal, 267, 270
Aqueras, 160
Aradas, 160
army
    Dahomey's, 172–173, 185
    Oyo's, 213–214
    Whydah's, 171–172
Asante
    political power of, 127–128
    trade route wars of, 136–137
assiento contract
    overview of, 34–35
    private enterprise and, 37–38
Assou, 197–224
    European quarrels and, 209–210
    Europeans attacked by, 202–204, 221
    Europeans betrayal of, 221
    King Agaja's attacks on, 214–221
    loyalty to King Huffon, 210, 219–221
    power of, 205–207, 211
    protection of French, 205, 208–209
    religious views of, 207–208
    retreat of, 220–221
    wounding of, 216
Atkins, John
    John Konny and, 130–131
    mutual distrust of
        Europeans/Africans, 122–123
    slave revolts, 314–315
    slave trade and King Agaja, 323
Atlantic Islands, *Diligent* and, 265–292
    currents, 273
    death and burials, 273–274
    Principe Island, 275, 277–280
    São Tomé, 281
    slave revolt, 267–270
Atlantic slave trade. *See* slave trade
Auger, Charles, 103
Aurora, 212
Axim, Fort, 129
Ayois, 160

balance sheet, reconstructing *Diligent's*,
    411–414
Banque Générale
    John Law and, 47–48
    ruination of, 52–54

Baptism of the Tropics ceremony,
    105–106
baptism, slave, 352
Barbados, 188
Barbary pirates, 101
Barbot, Jean
    slave revolt theory of, 272
    treatment of slaves, 300, 314
barter accounting systems, 385–386
Bassa, 123
Batz, 104
Beekesteyn, 317
Beinecke Rare Book and Manuscript
    Library, xi–xiv
Belle Isle, 85–86
Bernard, Pierre
    as captain, 364
    Jean Bonneau and, 362–363, 366–368
    stranded in Cayenne, 367
Bernard, Samuel, 34–35
Billy, François
    background of, 68–69
    calculating profit and losses, 385–387,
        390
    end of slave trade investment, 403
    family and status of, 404–405
    financing *Diligent*, 31–32, 76–77,
        83–84, xviii–xix
    mansion of, 404–405, 407
    purchase of *Concorde*, 76
    suit vs. Captain Pierre Mary, 379
    trade voyages of *Diligent*, 397–399
    wealth of, 70
Billy, Guillame
    background of, 68–70
    calculating profit and losses, 385–387,
        390
    Company of the Indies subcontract,
        79–80
    end of slave trade, 403
    family and status of, 404–405
    financing *Diligent*, 31–32, 76–77, 83,
        xviii–xix
    hiring of slaving crew, 80
    mansion of, 404–405, 407
    obtaining food supplies, 82–83
    purchase of *Concorde*, 76
    selecting trade goods, 80–82

suit against Pierre Mary, 379
trade voyages of *Diligent*, 397–399
wealth of, 70
Billy, Jeanne-Agathe, 404
Billy, Robert, 68–69
bloody flux, 348–349
bocales, defined, 112
Bonet, René, 105
Bonneau, Captain Jean, 361–367
background of, 361
mental disturbances of, 362–363,
366–367
mutiny against, 363–364
re-instated as captain, 365–366
Bosman, Willem, 145
Bouger, Jean
calculation of latitude, 89–91
navigation school of, 95
Bourgeois, Noël, 394
Bourg, Etienne du, 8
Brandenburg Africa Company
Gold Coast habitation of, 126
gold trade and, 129
John Konny and, 130–131
Brandenburg, Fort, 129–130
branding, of slaves, 249–250
brandy
outfitting *Diligent*, 81–82
trading at Jakin with, 233–234
Brazil
gold trade of, 238
tobacco trade of, 237
Britain
Gold Coast slave trade, 138–142
Gold Coast wars against Dutch, 126
private enterprise in, xviii
slave trade of, xv–xvi
sugar use in, 388
trading compound at Savi, 155–157
weak forts at Whydah, 203–204, 214
British Royal African Company. *See*
Royal African Company
Brittany, noblemen in, 70
Brulons, Savary des, 20
Brunet (widow), 76
burials, at sea, 274

cabin boys, 107

cabins, of officers, 104
cambaye loans
defined, 256
interest on, 413–414
Campos, Father, 285
Canary Islands, 101
cannibalism, 252–254, 299–300
canoemen, African, 228–229
Cape Coast castle
British/Dutch warring, 126
description of, 138–139
slave dungeon, 139–140
state of disrepair, 141
Cape Mesurado, 362–363
Cape Verde Islands, 109–112
captains
clothing of, 89
duties of, 101
of large trading company, 201
locating for *Diligent*, 76, 80
salaries of, 106–107
See also officers
Captain Tom. *See* Adomo Oroonoko
Tomo (Captain Tom)
Caribbean
Code Noir and, 21–27
pirates of, 325–328
See also Martinique
Caribs, 344
Carolsburg, Fort, 126
Catholicism, 19
Cayenne, 367
Cézar, 153
chalans, defined, 69
Chateaurenault, 99
China Company, 48
Christiansborg Castle, 126
Clieu, Gabriel de, 345–346
clocks, calculating longitude, 91–92
clothing
Code Noir and, 358
coronation of King Huffon, 153–154
feast day, 104
of officers, 89
wives of King Agaja, 170–171
cocoa plantations, Martinique
coffee growing and, 345–346
earthquake disaster on, 343–345

Code Noir, 19–28
    defending slave trade with, 19, 21–22, 25–28
    plantation slaves and, 357–359
Coedel, Jacques, 398
coffee growing, Martinique, 345–346
Colinbert, Joseph, 369
Commendo, 131
Company of Adventurers of London, 126
Company of the Indies
    coffee monopoly of, 345–346
    Diligent as subcontract of, 79–80
    domination of, 50–52
    formation of, 48
    location of, 48–50
    Lorient compound of, 406
    operations in Whydah, 156–157
    price paid for slaves, 80
    private enterprise vs., 56–60
    private trading and, 60–61, 79–80, 258–259
    ruination of, 52–54
    trading lodge at Jakin, 229
Concorde, 76, 399–400, 403
cooks, salary of, 107
Coote, Theodore, 122–123
Corbun, Alexander, 75
costs, reconstructing balance sheet of
    Diligent, 411–414
cotton
    Cape Verdian, 112
    customs and tariffs on, 387
    discrepancies in *Diligent's,* 233
    Pierre Mary purchases in Martinique, 372, 374
    returns from Martinique, 412, 414
Council of Commerce, 73–74
Council of State, 51–52
cowry shells
    capturing prisoners and, 184
    currency value of, 81
    lives of slaves and, 176
cross staff, latitude, 89–91
customs, 387–389

Dahomey
    attack on Allada, 166–168
    attack on Europeans at Whydah, 214–221
    attack on Jakin, 321–323
    attack on Paon, 179–181
    attack on Savi, 152–153, 181–183
    attack on Whydah, 211–212
    See also Agaja, King
dancing of slaves, 297–298, 310–311
Dangbe, 161–162
D'Anville (geographer), 114
Darquistade, René, 9
Dauphin, 270
death rates, slave ships, 317–318
De Fer, Nicholas, 5–6
Delisle, Guillaume, 16, 114
Delourme, Charles, 75–76
Denis, Captain Jean, 99
Descasaux, Joachim
    Company of the Indies and, 54
    rights of noblemen, 70
    rights of private traders, 33–34
    slaving ship of, 35
Des Marchais, Chevalier
    coronation of King Huffon, 153–154
    health of slaves, 300
    pirate ships, 326
    ship doctors, 275
    slave revolts, 271–272
    slave stereotypes, 160–161
Devigne, Pierre
    Pierre Mary and, 318–319
    private trading of, 256–257
Diligent
    buyers of, 75–76
    crowding of slaves on, 262–263
    death on, 260–261, 273–274, 278
    departure of, 3, 85–86
    fate of slaves from, 350–351
    local events and, xviii–xx
    modifying for slaves, 250–252
    modifying for trade goods, 369–370
    preventing escapes, 261–262
    reconstructing balance sheet of, 411–414
    running aground of, 398–399
    size of, 3
    slave revolt and, 260–261, 267–270

Diligent, outfitting, 76–86
  buyers, 75–76
  Company of the Indies and, 79–80
  costs of, 83–84, 413–414
  departure of, 85–86
  food supplies for, 82–83
  insurance costs, 83–84
  locating captain for, 76
  risks for sailors, 80
  slave irons, 83
  as slave ship, 75–77
  slaving crew, 80
  trade goods, 80–82
Dixcove, Fort, 141
doctors, ship, 274–275
Dominica, 344
Dove, 122–123
draft system, 202
Dubodan, Joseph-Ange
  buyer of *Diligent*, 75
  outfitter of *Concorde*, 403
  status and respect of, 405
Dubourdieu (assistant director), 84
Duc de la Force, 116
Dulaien, Jean-Thomas, 327–328
Dupetitval (director of French fort in
  Whydah)
  attack by Dahomian army, 217–219
  death of, 220
  kidnapping and, 147
  promotion of Etienne Gallot, 216
Duponcel, Captain, 151
Durand, Pierre, 94
Durand, Robert
  attitude towards slaves, 4–5, 303
  calculating ship's latitude, 89–91
  calculating ship's longitude, 91–92
  commanding tent at Jakin, 230–233
  death of, 400–401
  Elmina castle and, 133–134
  fraud of Pierre Mary, 319, 381–382,
    392–394
  illness and departure from Jakin of,
    255–256
  journal entries of, 94
  Martinique and, 373–374
  as officer of *Diligent*, 76, 80
  overview of, xiii

  private trading of, 256–257
  recuperation at Principe Island, 278
  salary of, 106–107
  second voyage of *Diligent*, 397
  slave buying at Jakin, 233, 244–245,
    247–250
  slave trading at Keta, 146–148
  slaving voyages as captain, 399–400
  studies and career of, 94–96
  Whydah and, 223
  wife and children of, 96
du Rocher Sorin, Noël, 199–201
Dutch
  attack on Portuguese fort, 157
  Dahomian attack on Jakin, 323
  de Torres and Hertogh rivalry, 237
  Elmina castle slave trade, 133–137
  Gold Coast wars against Britain,
    125–126
  illegal slave trading of, 57
  involvement in slave trade of, xv
  private enterprise and, xviii
Dutch West India Company
  Hendrik Hertogh and, 236–237
  King Agaja and, 323–324
  private enterprise vs., 32, 137–138,
    259–260
dysentery, 348–349

écus, of silver, 47–48
Elmina castle, 133–137
  conversion to slave trade of, 135–137
  history of, 133
  impressive nature of, 133–134
  Portuguese founding of, 125, 133
  taken over by Dutch, 133–135
England. *See* Britain
equator, 301–302
Espérance, 95
Estaca de Bares, 100
ethnic groups, slaves
  after wars/closing of trade routes,
    247–248
  society of São Tomé, 286–287
  stereotypes, 160–161
Europeans
  1704 peace treaty, 209–210
  Assou blocking trade of, 221

Europeans (continued)
    captives from attack on Jakin,
        321–322
    competition for slaves, 211–212
    Gold Coast wars of, 125–126
    King Agaja's attack on Savi and,
        180–183
    King Agaja's attacks on forts of,
        214–215
    mistrust between Africans and,
        122–123
    modernization of King Agaja's mili-
        tary and, 172
    trading compounds and forts at Savi,
        155–157
    Whydah's succession struggle and,
        155–156
Excellent, 270
Expedition, 327

Falconbridge, Alexander, 313
Feast of St. Peter, 103
Ferdinand, King, xv
financiers, 29–61
    Company of the Indies and, 56–61
    government subsidies and, 40–41
    mercantilism vs. private enterprise,
        35–38
    shift to private enterprise, 31–34,
        38–40
    See also Law, John
Foin, 161
food
    Code Noir and, 357–358
    feast day, 103–104
    in house of Assou, 206–207
    outfitting *Diligent*, 82–83
    slave mealtime, 308–311
    stopover at Principe Island, 279–280
    stopover at Santiago, 109
    typical daily, 108
Fort Axim, 129
Fort Brandenburg, 129–130
Fort Carolsburg, 126
Fort Dixcove, 141
Fort Gross Friedrichsburg, 129
Fort Hollandia, 129
Fort Komenda, 141

Fort Konny, 129–130
Fort Sekondi, 141
Fort St. John the Baptist, 157
Fort St. Louis, 157
Fournier, Catherine, 404
Fournier, Jean Baptiste, 70
France
    Dahomian army and, 215–217
    market towns vs. maritime cities, 36
    operations in Whydah of, 156–157,
        203–204, 214
    private enterprise, xviii
    rights to Gold Coast, 126
    Slave Coast and, 145
    slaves given liberty in, 9–10, xvi
    slave trade of, xix–xx, xvi–xvii
    sugar use of, 388
    vestiges of serfdom in, 23
    war with Britain in 1744, 399–400
French Customs Union, 387–388
French East India Company, 48

Gallot, Etienne
    as director of French fort, 220
    escape from Whydah of, 220–221
    King Agaja and, 216
Gauguin, François, 103–104
Gautier, Augustin, 100
Gauvin, François, 83
Gbe language, King Agaja, 177
George II, King of England, 190
George I, King of England, 175–177
Glewe, 203–204
Gold Coast
    Asante empire and, 136–137
    British forts, 140–142
    Cape Coast castle, 138–139
    comparing Slave Coast with, 135–136
    Elmina castle, 133–137
    European wars for control of,
        125–127
    Fort Axim, 128–129
    fortresses of, 125–127
    history of slave trade on, 127
    John Konny and, 129–131
gold trade
    Brazilian, 238
    Fort Axim and, 128

Fort Gross Friedrichsburg and, 129
Gold Coast wars and, 125–127
Pierre Mary's private trading, 260
Portuguese success in, 212–213
Robert Durand's private trading, 233–234
smuggling of Joseph de Torres, 238
Goos, Pieter, 92–93
grain trade
Billy brothers and, 397–399, 403–404
Vannes and, 71–74, 406–408
Grand Phénix, 364
Grané, Charles, 76
Gross Friedrichsburg, Fort, 129
Grou, Guillame, 406
Guesneau, Jean, 152
Guiamba, 161
Guinea Company
assiento contract, 34–35, 37–38
private enterprise vs., 15, 34–35
supplying slaves, xvi
Guinea, locations of, 114
Gulf of Morbihan
navigating, 65–66
restrictions on grain trade, 73–74
guns
King Agaja's military, 172, 184–185, 213
outfitting *Diligent,* 82–83
warfare among Gold Coast states, 135–136

Happy Deliverance, 221
Harding, Captain John, 299
helmsmen, 107
Henry the Navigator, Prince, xiv
Hermoine, 115
Hertogh, Hendrik
background of, 239–240
Dahomian attack on Jakin, 321–324
promotion of, 241
rivalry between de Torres and, 237, 240–241
wealth and influence of, 236–237
Hirondelle, 151–152
Holland. *See* Dutch
Hollandia, Fort, 129
Hoscouet, Marie Janne, 96

Huffon, King
coronation of, 153–154, 161–162
Dahomian attack on Whydah, 152
efforts to regain country, 219–221
European forts and, 156–158
exile of, 211
loyalty of Assou to, 210, 219–221
relations with Dahomey, 173–174
slave trade revenue of, 161
succession struggle of, 155

Indian cloth, 81
Ingrande, 389
insurance costs, 83–84, 413
Irish beef, 357–358
Isle of May, Cape Verde Islands, 109–110

Jakin, 225–264
authority of King Agaja, 229–230
Dahomian destruction of, 321–324
description of, 229, 235–236
de Torres/Hertogh rivalry, 237, 240–241
European slave ships at, 227–228
getting ashore to, 228–230
King Agaja's effect on slave trade, 323
moving slaves to *Diligent,* 250, 252–254
private trading of Pierre Mary, 256–260
sources of slaves in, 245–247
unhealthiness of, 243
Jakin, Robert Durand at
as commander of tent, 230–233
departure for trading post, 235
illness and departure of, 255–256
slave buying, 233, 244–245, 247–250
Jansenism, 24–28
Jarno, Pierre, 381–383, 392–394
Jason, 202, 204
Jesuits, 24–28
Jolie, 153
Jugan, Louis, 397

Kanelo, Mathieu, 273
Keta, 146–148

kidnapping
  mutual distrust of
    Europeans/Africans, 122–123
  slave trade and, 147–148
King's Edict Concerning Negro Slaves
  arguments to parliament, 26–28
  Jansenists vs. Jesuits, 24–26
  proposal, 23–24
Komenda, Fort, 141
Konny, Fort, 129–130
Konny, John, 129–131

Labat, Father Jean-Baptiste
  life of slaves on plantations,
    351–358
  women on slave ships, 268
La Croix, Michel Buat de
  buyer of *Diligent*, 75
  provider of capital, 77, 83
  status and respect of, 405
ladinas, defined, 112
La Fleur (slave), 74–75
La Massuë, Hubert de, 75, 77
Lambe, Bulfinch, 187–194
  arrival in London of, 187
  authenticity of King Agaja's letter,
    192–193
  Dahomian capture of, 166–168
  debts of, 188
  King Agaja awaiting return of,
    185–186
  as King Agaja's slave, 165–166, 169
  King George II and, 190
  schemes for getting out of captivity,
    174–177
  as slave of King Sozo, 166
  slave selling of, 187–188
  on suffering of captivity, 166
Lamy (slave dealer), 349–350
LaPierre, Mr., 229
La Praya, Cape Verde Islands, 109–113
Laragon, Thomas
  fraud of Pierre Mary, 318–319,
    383–384
  salary of, 106–107
larboard watch, 107–108
latitude, calculating, 89–91
La Tourbe Ardent, 123

law. *See* maritime law
Law, John
  background of, 43–46
  Banque Générale and, 47–48
  Company of the Indies and, 48–50
  domination of slave trade by, 50–52
  France's economy and, 46–48
  power of, 50
  ruination and exile of, 52–54
le Boda, Jacques, 398
Le Croisic, 94–95
Lefur, François, 105
Leglan, John, 152
Le Maistre, Antoine, 27–28
Lemerre the Younger, Pierre, 26–28
Le Palais, Belle Isle, 85–86
Le Pottier, Jean, 35–37
Le Roy, Pierre, 152
Letheris, Pierre Mathieu, 105
linguistics, King Agaja, 169
Liot, Philippe, 312–313
livres, 47–48
log lines, 92
longitude, calculating, 91–92
Lorient
  Company of the Indies location,
    48–50
  headquarters for slave trade, 32
  new growth of, 406
Louis IX, King, 23
Louis of gold, 47–48
Louis XIV, King, 345–346
Lucas, Jean-Baptiste, 75
Lucques, Father Laurent de, 314

Madeira, 188
Magré, Noël
  as accordion player for slave ship,
    296–298
  salary of, 106
Mahe, Jean, 260–261
Mahi, 245, 247–248
malaguetta peppers, 121
Maldive Islands, 81
Mallais, 160
Marie, 99
Marie Anne, 19
Marie-Joseph, 75

maritime law
 duties of captains, 101
 falling asleep on duty, 108
 insurance policies, 83–84
 prostitution, 244
Martinique, 331–376
 coffee growing in, 345–346
 description of, 328–329, 373–374
 earthquake in, 341–346
 government officials and, 334–337
 harbor of St. Pierre, 329, 333–334
 health inspection of ship, 336
 Irish salted beef and, 357–358
 island-wide rebellion threat, 342–343
 life of slaves in, 351–358
 Pierre Mary reports to admiralty,
   335–336
 piracy around, 327
 sale of ship's captives, 336–339
 slave warehouses in, 347–349
 strategy for getting to, 302
 total returns from, 412, 414
Mary, Captain Pierre
 admiralty in Martinique, 335–336
 Barbary pirates, 101–102
 commodities in Martinique, 371–373
 concealing fraud, 318–319
 duties of, 101
 health of slaves, 300
 hiring of, 76
 lack of certification, 99
 missing account books, 391
 outcome of lawsuit, 394–395
 pay increase of, 80
 petty charges against, 386
 private trading of, 256–260
 redistributing weight onboard, 98
 retirement and career of, 98–100
 salary of, 106–107
 small profits made, 338–339, 348–349,
   386
 start of voyage, 100
 testimonies against, 380–384
 treatment of slaves by, 300, 304
matelots, defined, 107
Maurepas, Count of
 background of, 55–56
 Company of the Indies and, 56–60

Mellier, Gérard, 13–20
 background of, 14–15
 court's decision to free slaves, 13–14
 cruelty of slave trade, 18
 defense of slave trade, 19–20
 geographical ignorance of, 16–17
 official recognition of slavery, 21–22
 serfdom in France, 23
 social rank concepts of, 18
Mellon, Paul, xii
mercantilism
 defending slave trade through, 19
 overview of, 35
 private enterprise vs., 35–38
mestiços community, Santiago, 113
Minas Geres, 238
Miranas, 161
mise-hors
 costs of, 413
 defined, 83
missionairies, 112
Mississippi Company, 48
Moll, H., 145
monopoly systems
 defenders of, 35–36
 mercantilism and, 35
 private enterprise vs., 32–34
 See also Company of the Indies;
   Dutch West India Company
Montaudoin, René, 70–71, 99
morality
 anti-slavery sentiment, 28
 fear of slaves getting liberty, 13
 lack of public discussion, 5–6
 Pauline Villeneuve's liberty, 6–11
 See also Mellier, Gérard
More, 152
Morice, Humphrey, 188
mottiers, defined, 23

Na Geze, 182
Nago, 160
Nantes
 birthplace of Pierre Mary, 99
 court decision to free slave, 9–10, 13
 customs and tariffs on trade goods,
   387–388
 description of, 5–6

Nantes (continued)
    embodiment of French slave trade, 6,
        xvii
    freedom of trade, 38–40
    Gérard Mellier and, 14
    mercantilism vs. private enterprise,
        35–38
    new growth of, 406
    slave traders given subsidies, 40–41
négociants
    cowry shells and Indian cloth used
        by, 81
    defined, 33
    inheritable nobility of, 70–71
    John Law, 50–52
    private trade and, 38–40, 61
    subsidy of, 40–41
Négre, Joseph, 256
Nestor, 234, 256
New England, 188
Newton, John, 313
New World, slave trade in
    Dutch ships, xv
    heyday of, xvii
    King Ferdinand of Spain, xv
    sources of, xvi–xvii
Nigritie, 16–17, 19–20
nobility, privileges of, 70–71

Occident Company, 48
officers
    private trading, 257
    salary of, 106–107
    testifying against Pierre Mary, 380–381
    theories on slave revolts, 271–272
    treatment of women on slave ships,
        312–313
    See also captains
Ordonnance de la Marine (1681), 83–84
Oroonoko, production of, 190, 195–196
Our Lady of Calvary convent
    living conditions and ideals of, 7
    Pauline Villeneuve and, 6–10
    status of, 7–8
outfitting, Diligent. See Diligent, outfitting
Oyo
    captives of war sold, 247–248
    horse-mounted army of, 213
    invasion of Dahomey, 213–214

pacotilles
    Diligent's, 263
    illegality of, 258–259
    overview of, 256–257
panyarring, 121–123
Paon, 179–181
Papagaye, 230
Parfait, 270
parlement, 26–28
peasants, of Vannes, 67–68
Perle, 399–401
Philippe le Bel, King, 23
Phillips, Thomas, 314–315
physical examinations, slaves, 248
Pihan, François, 381
Pinto, Domingas, 291
Pinto, Manuel do Rosário
    background of, 283–284
    priesthood of, 284–285
    racial struggle at São Tomé, 281, 285,
        287–288
    victory of, 289
    written history of São Tomé,
        291–292
Piou, Jean, 51
pirates
    Barbary, 101
    Bartholomew Roberts, 115–116
    Caribbean, 325–328
    democracy of, 116–117
Place Louis-le-Grand, 43–44
platilles, 81
Pontchartrain
    attack on tent of, 202–203
    large trading companies and,
        199–202
Popo, 151–152
population density
    defending slave trade, 16–17, 19–20
    Whydah, 159
Porcupine, 115
port permis privileges, 257–258
Portuguese
    domination of slave trade by,
        212–213, xv
    fort at Whydah, 214
    Gold Coast settlement and, 125
    government monopolies and, 32
    operations in Whydah of, 156–157

rivalry between de Torres and Hertogh, 237
Santiago's economy and, 111
slaves chosen by, 247
slave trade of, xiv-xv
Principe Island, 275, 277–280
private enterprise, slave trade and
Britain, 140–141
Company of the Indies, 56–61
Dutch West India Company's demise and, 137–138
economic case for, 38–40
effects of, 200
John Law's domination, 50–52
kidnapping and, 147
limiting slave ships for, 38–39
mercantilism vs., 35–38
subsidies and, 40–41
at time of *Diligent*, xx
prostitution, at Jakin, 244

Renommé, 374
revolts. *See* slave revolts
Ribeira Grande, Santiago, 111–112
Roberts, Bartholomew, 115–117
rocou, 372–374, 412, 414
Roggeveen, Arent, 123
Rollando (master carpenter), 75
Rousseau, Pierre, 406
Royal African Company
Bulfinch Lambe and, 174–175, 187, 190–194
Dahomian attack on, 181
financial problems of, 141–142
operations in Whydah of, 156–157
private enterprise vs., 32
slave trade on Gold Coast, 138–141
Royal Bank of France, 52–53
Royal Council of State, 51–52

Sabatier (pilot), 105, 146–148
Sahagum, Bishop João, 288–289
Sainte Alourzie, 344
Saint René, 115
salaries
aboard *Diligent*, 106–107
expense of, 413–414
in large international trading companies, 201–202

Salé, 101–102
salt, 109
sandglasses
calculating ship's longitude, 91–92
keeping time on watch, 108
Sans Pitié, 328
Santiago, 109–113
cultural mixture of, 112–113
economic depression of, 111–112
stopover at, 109–110
São Jorge da Mina. *See* Elmina castle
São Tomé, 281–292
multiracial society of, 286–287
Portuguese monopoly on slave trade, 290–291
recorded history of, 291–292
slave trade and, 285–286, 289–290
sugar plantations and, 286
Savi
Dahomian attack on, 152
European trading compounds at, 155–156
fall of, 181–182
as home of King Huffon, 163
scurvy, 317
Sekondi, Fort, 141
Senegal, 60
Senegal Company
acquired by John Law, 48
supplying slaves to France's colonies, xvi
serfdom, French, 22–23
Sestos River, stopover, 121–122
shackles. *See* slave irons
Slave Coast
arrival of *Diligent*, 145
defined, 145
Gold Coast vs., 135–136
slave trade at Keta, 146–148
See also Whydah
slave dealers, 337–338
slave irons
high seas and, 315
outfitting *Diligent* with, 83
overview of, 295–296
slave revolts, 272–273
in 1720's on French ships, 270
Aurora, 212
Ayois, 160

slave revolts, 272–273 (continued)
    Captain John Harding and, 299
    Concorde, 403
    less risk at high sea of, 314–315
    maritime insurance policies and, 84
    Martinique and threat of, 342–343
    preventative techniques for, 261
    rebellion on *Diligent*, 267–270
    slave traders' theories on, 271–272
slaves
    acclimatization of, 352
    baptism of, 352
    bargaining over price of, 248–249
    bathing on ships of, 311
    branding of, 249–250
    crowding on *Diligent* of, 262–263
    dancing of, 295–297
    ethnic origins of, 160
    fears of, 252–254
    gender and, 247, 249
    ideal gender ratio of, 247
    inspection of, 247
    life on sugar plantations, 351–358
    living conditions and meals at Jakin
        for, 250
    loss of identity for, 245–246
    physical examination of, 248
    sleeping on slave ships, 305–307
    stereotypes, 160–161
    stopover at Principe Island, 278–279
    suicide choice of, 261–262
slave ships
    accordion players and, 295–297
    accounts of life on, 303
    bathing of slaves on, 311
    cleaning routines on, 310–311,
        313–314
    daily schedule of women on, 311–312
    death toll on, 317–318
    drinking water ration on, 308–310
    issues of shackling on, 315
    mealtimes on, 308–311
    modifying *Diligent* into, 250–252
    outfitting *Diligent* as, 76–77
    quartermasters on, 315–316
    rape on, 312–313
    risks for sailors on, 80
    sleeping on, 305–307

    social organization on, 315–316
    treatment of slaves on, 314
    using toilets on, 306–308
slave trade
    at Asante, 127–128, 136–137
    Billy brothers enter into, 76–77
    Cape Coast castle and, 139–140
    Elmina castle and, 135–137
    Fort Axim and, 129
    Fort Hollandia and, 131
    history of, 127, xiv–xvii
    independent African slave traders, 142
    Keta and, 146–148
    kidnapping and, 147–148
    maritime insurance policies and,
        83–84
    Nantes and, 14–15
    Whydah and, 159
slave traders
    of Asante, 127–128, 136–137
    Assou's attacks on, 202–204, 221
    destinations of European, 227–228
    ensuring health of slaves, 300
    gaining inheritable nobility, 70–71
    illegalities of Pierre Mary, 260
    King Agaja vs., 211–213
    lack of support to French industry
        of, 82
    life on slave ships dependent upon,
        314
    profitability of carrying sugar, 75
    statistics for 1728–29, 213
slave warehouses
    filth of, 347–349
    Pierre Mary takes his slaves to,
        338–339
Smith, William
    description of Whydah, 157–159
    dividing Gold and Slave Coasts, 145
    England's Gold Coast forts, 141–142
    mutual distrust of Europeans/
        Africans, 122
smuggling
    Joseph de Torres and, 238
    tobacco and, 237
Snelgrave, William
    authenticity of King Agaja's letter, 192
    Bulfinch Lambe and, 189

England's Gold Coast forts and, 141
negotiations with King Agaja,
    183–186
pirate ships and, 115
theories on slave revolts, 271–272
Sozo, King, 166
Spain, slave trade of, xv
starboard watch, 107–108
St. Jean Baptiste, 361–368
    buying slaves at Cape Mesurado,
        360
    crew mutinies against mentally
        disturbed captain, 363–364
    fate of, 367–368
    slave purchases of, 365–366
St. Louis, 336
St. Michel, 277
storms, 97–98
St. Pierre, 74–75
St. Pierre
    earthquake damage in, 341–343
    harbor of, 329, 333–334
sugar
    contracts with slave dealers, 370
    customs and tariffs in Nantes on,
        387–388
    Pierre Mary purchases in Martinique,
        371–374
    profitability of, 75
    returns from Martinique, 411–412,
        414
    types of, 370–371
sugar plantations
    earthquake in Martinique and,
        341–343
    São Tomé and, 286
    slaves of Father Labat, 351–358
    slaves on Santiago and, 112
suicide, slave, 261–262
Surinam, 367–368
Swallow, 115
Sweden, Gold Coast and, 126
Swedish Africa Company, 126

Tebou, 161
ten percenters, defined, 140–141
Thaubier, Pierre, 273–274
Tinker, Jeremiah, 187–188, 192

tobacco
    given to slaves, 311
    Pierre Mary's private trading of, 260
    slave trade, 380
    trade of Brazil, 237
Tofo, 183–184
toilets, slave ship
    cleaning, 310
    overview of, 306–308
Tom, Captain. *See* Adomo Oroonoko
        Tomo (Captain Tom)
Torres, Joseph de
    Portuguese fort at Jakin, 239
    rivalry between Hertogh and, 237,
        240–241
    smuggling of, 238
Touchard, Renè, 273
trade goods
    bargaining for slaves with, 248–249
    outfitting *Diligent*, 80–82
trade winds, 301–303
trading companies
    effect of private enterprise on, 200
    working conditions at, 201–202
Trinidade, 284–285
Tropic of Cancer, 105–106

Union, 115

Valeur, 399
Valteau, Pierre
    piracy and, 327
    private trading of, 256–257
    recuperation at Principe Island, 278
    salary of, 106–107
    as second captain of *Diligent*, 80, 101
    slave trading at Keta, 146–148
Vannes
    Diligent returns to, 379
    economic decline of, 71–72
    eighteenth century, 405
    grain trade in, 73–74, 406–408
    high society in, 70
    peasant life of, 67–68
    trade ships departing from, 74–75
Verger, Pierre
    arrest of, 200–201
    as passenger of *Diligent*, 84

Villeneuve, Madame, 6–10
Villeneuve, Pauline
    induction of, 10–11
    Our Lady of Calvary convent and,
        6–10
Vinland Map, xii
Volta River, 145

wages, crew. *See* salaries
watch-team system, 107–108
water
    outfitting *Diligent*, 82–83
    ration for drink on slave ships,
        308–310
    stopover at Principe Island, 279
Whydah, 149–196
    agriculture of, 159
    beauty of, 158–159
    Bulfinch Lambe and, 165–169,
        174–177
    coronation of King Huffon,
        153–154
    dangers for crew at, 199–202
    disaster of Pierre Mary's trips to,
        99–100

European trading compounds at,
        155–158
    fall of Savi, 179–182
    fear of slavery in, 171–172
    military of, 171–172
    population density of, 159
    route from Vannes to, 92–94
    selling of prisoners into slavery,
        183–185
    slave trade at, 159–161, 323
    tense relations with King Agaja,
        171–174, 177
    war-torn conditions at, 152–153
William's Fort, 157
Witten, Laurence C., II, xii
women, on sugar plantations, 355
women, slave ships
    daily schedule, 311–312
    exercising, 297–298
    number on *Diligent* of, 262–263
    rape and, 312–313
    risk of rebellion and, 267–268
    as slaves of officers, 312–313

Yoruba, 248